AMNESIAC SELVES

Amnesiac Selves

NOSTALGIA, FORGETTING, AND BRITISH FICTION, 1810–1870

Nicholas Dames

OXFORD
UNIVERSITY PRESS

2001

OXFORD

UNIVERSITY PRESS

Oxford   New York
Athens   Auckland   Bangkok   Bogotá   Buenos Aires   Calcutta
Cape Town   Chennai   Dar es Salaam   Delhi   Florence   Hong Kong   Istanbul
Karachi   Kuala Lumpur   Madrid   Melbourne   Mexico City   Mumbai
Nairobi   Paris   São Paulo   Shanghai   Singapore   Taipei   Tokyo   Toronto   Warsaw

and associated companies in
Berlin   Ibadan

Copyright © 2001 by Oxford University Press

Published by Oxford University Press, Inc.
198 Madison Avenue, New York, New York 10016

Oxford is a registered trademark of Oxford University Press.

Library of Congress Cataloging-in-Publication Data
Dames, Nicholas, 1970–
Amnesiac selves : nostalgia, forgetting, and British fiction, 1810–1870 / Nicholas Dames.
p. cm.
Includes bibliographical references and index.
ISBN 0-19- 514357-4; ISBN 0-19-517309-0 (PBK)
1. English fiction—19th century—History and criticism.   2. Amnesia in literature.
3. Psychological fiction, English—History and criticism.   4. Autobiographical memory in literature.
5. Nostalgia in literature.   6. Memory in literature.   7. Self in literature.   I. Title.
PR868.A49 D36 2001
823'.809353—dc21   00-050157

First issued as an Oxford University Press paperback, 2003

1 3 5 7 9 8 6 4 2

Printed in the United States of America
on acid-free paper

For Amy Mae

Acknowledgments

Writing a book about the evasion of memory has seemed at times a paradoxical project, given how continually pleasurable it has been for me to recall the people and places involved in this book's gestation. In the spirit of that mnemonic pleasure, then, and in order to be more than nostalgically vague about the deep debts this book has incurred, I gratefully remember the teachers, colleagues, and friends who have made this book possible. Those who know the author of this book will know how much I have enjoyed recalling them.

The idea behind this project came during a conversation with Philip Fisher. The generosity and rigor of his responses, and his unwavering support, have come to form my idea of what an advisor should be. To Elaine Scarry, whose steering of this project past so many obstacles has been sure and unflagging, I owe whatever intellectual imagination this book may possess. David Miller's guidance of my earliest formulations was a resource from the start of my labor, and the acuity of his ear for false notes and grace notes alike helped nurture my own feel for argumentative melody. Robert Kiely and Derek Pearsall made key suggestions at this project's formation. Franco Moretti's eye for the book's deepest allegiances, and his challenge to stay true to them, have been needed goads as I brought the book to its final form. Nancy Armstrong, Catherine Gallagher, and Ann Colley all read parts of this manuscript at various stages of its evolution. The detailed comments of Alison Booth, Dierdre D'Albertis, and Carole Silver, who read the manuscript in its entirety, are palpable throughout the book.

This project's birth was made possible by a Mellon Dissertation Fellowship, while its growth was furthered by the staffs and resources of Widener and Houghton Libraries, Harvard University; Countway Library, Harvard University School of Medicine; Butler Library, Columbia University; the British Library, London; and the New York Public Library. Earlier versions of two chapters of *Amnesiac Selves* have been published previously: a shortened version of chapter 1 has appeared in *Representations* 73 (2001), while an earlier, partial version of chapter 2 has appeared as "The Clinical Novel: Phrenology and *Villette*" in *Novel: A Forum on Fiction* 29, no. 3 (1996), copyright NOVEL Corp. © 1996. My thanks go to both journals for permission to reprint material. At Oxford University Press, Elissa Morris and Karen Leibowitz never forgot to offer the further assistance this project needed.

Many of my fondest recollections of this book's writing involve the colleagues and friends who have been both boon and ballast during the years of its production. To Eric Wilson, Martin Puchner, Amanda Claybaugh, and Lev and Eva Kaye in particular I owe the sense of community that makes nostalgia possible. In recalling this book's genesis I have been continually reminded of my parents, John and Louise Dames, from whom I took my earliest lessons in verbal precision and aesthetic pleasure; their love provided the ground for so many of the nostalgias that they can still recognize as among my most abiding ties.

Five years ago I started work on this book, and that I can only remember those years with more than nostalgic pleasure is the doing of Amy Mae King, my wife, to whom it is dedicated. With her, who has left marks on this book and its writer too profound to be effaced by any amnesias, rests the credit for creating a shared world that is both rich memory and abundant promise.

New York City
December 2000

Contents

AMNESIAC SELVES

INTRODUCTION

Reading Nostalgia

The Novel is a Death; it transforms life into destiny, a memory into a useful act, duration into an orientated and meaningful time.
—*Roland Barthes, "Writing and the Novel"*

Replacing Barthes's hypostatized "Novel" with a historically defined set of "novels," we might say that transforming memories into useful acts—enabling, in fact, the death of memory within it—is preeminently the work of the Victorian novel.[1] A surprising claim, given that we have come to perceive the novel itself, of whatever era, as a form shaped by the impulses and processes of memory; with the modernist novel of Joyce, Woolf, or Proust uppermost in our minds, we have come to understand the novel as an act of remembrance, and as a form with intimate ties to various lived pasts. Thinking of the act of novel writing, we imagine heroic acts of preservation, and as we conceptualize the act of reading novels, we envision a reader engaged in equally difficult acts of thematic and structural remembering.[2] But this template, dependent as it is on later developments in both narrative practice and psychological theory, misrecognizes the earlier Victorian and immediately pre-Victorian novel. Memory, from the social novels of Jane Austen to the sensation novels of Wilkie Collins, is less a valorized theme than a dilemma or a threat, a threat most crucially to the very lessons a novel seeks to impart; the notable absence of explicit remembrance within these texts, as well as the distinct unease surrounding those acts of memory that do occur within them, signals a narrative form struggling to transform the chaos of personal recollection into what is useful, meaningful, able to be applied to the future—into what *works*. The *durée* of the past, its potentially explosive combination of error, lost cathexes, and enigmatic moments, so familiar to us from modernist fiction, is stream-lined by Victorian narrative into a retrospect that remembers only what is pleasant, and only what the self can employ in the present—a form of ret-rospect that goes by the name the nineteenth century itself eventually gave it: nostalgia.

That the novel might have been nineteenth-century European cul-ture's most significant formalization of memory and its processes is a claim few today would dispute.[3] But that the mode of memory formalized by the novel might in fact be a specific kind of forgetting is the paradoxical argu-ment of what follows—that, in the British novel of the early and mid–nineteenth century, we see narratives formalizing and projecting memory by canceling and erasing much of what usually goes under that name. Nos-talgia is an absence; what it lacks is what, after the formidably canonical psychologies and fictions of the late nineteenth and early twentieth cen-tury, has come to be regarded as memory in its purest form. Pure memory, or *mémoire pure*, is in fact one of Henri Bergson's most compelling coinages, and it is matched by William James's "desultory memory," or what Walter Benjamin categorized as "reminiscence" (*Erinnerung*): all are descriptions of the dispersed, diffuse, unpredictable, possibly insignificant moments of everyday memory.[4] Proustian or Joycean analepses are the fictional equivalents to these vast, almost undifferentiated storehouses of memory, and the manner in which they are usually known by the singular detail that underwrites them (a madeleine, a bar of soap) signals both their everydayness and their capacity for unlimited exfoliation. From the Victo-rian novel, however, these immersions in the specificity of the past, rang-ing from the mundane to the hallucinogenic, are largely barred. What re-mains is the opposite of pure, desultory memory: a memory that is enacted only in the light of an end, of death; a memory that is always only the nec-essary prehistory of the present—a mnemonic mode that is termed, in the following pages, "nostalgia." Nostalgia is as much self-definition as mem-ory; it consists of the stories about one's past that explain and consolidate memory rather than dispersing it into a series of vivid, relinquished mo-ments, and it can only survive by eradicating the "pure memory," that enor-mous field of vanished detail, that threatens it.

With this opening premise about nostalgia in mind, it should become clearer why so many retrospective moments in Victorian fiction take the shape of disowning the specific recollections on which they might seem to depend. When in Dickens's *Our Mutual Friend* (1865) we come upon the Boffins deciding to forsake the use of the name "John" for any future adopted orphans, insofar as recollections of the original, now supposedly dead, "John" would then overlap uncomfortably with the present, we see a typical act of nostalgic forgetting and relinquishment that is called, oddly enough, "remembrance." Bella Wilfer hesitantly suggests that any future "John" would be for the Boffins less interesting than the original, but Mrs. Boffin gently corrects her:

> "Well, my dear," returned Mrs. Boffin, giving her a squeeze, "'it's kind of you to find that reason out, and I hope it may have been so, and indeed to a certain extent I believe it was so, but I am afraid not to the whole extent. However, that don't come in question now, because we have done with the name."
>
> "Laid it up as a remembrance," suggested Bella, musingly.
>
> "Much better said, my dear; laid it up as a remembrance."[5]

A remembrance that leaves the past behind, "lays it up," and transforms the trauma of the death of the original "John" into a nostalgic memory because the name itself is now dead: such is the memory of the British classical novel, which in sealing off the past halts its contamination of the present. This is an act primarily of consolidation; if, as Leo Bersani has suggested, "personality is as rigorously structured in the realistic novel as it is in Racinian tragedy," one of the primary tensions keeping this structure aloft is the torsion of nostalgia, which stiffens the self against the weight of mnemonic diffusion that later psychologists and novelists would find so compelling.[6]

example in the most pervasive form—

✓ classic

What results is a peculiarity unique to Victorian narratives: (the equation of remembrance to a pleasurable sort of forgetting) one that is far less strenuous than any dynamic of repression and release might produce. This is a logic often advanced by characters within narratives who are asked to justify the disappearance of one of the narrative's most prized, or haloed, figures — mnemonic apologists who often patiently explain why the reader need not excessively remember the figure whom the novel will not itself bother to recall to our notice. When in Elizabeth Gaskell's *Mary Barton* (1848) the saintly Alice Wilson dies, and her nephew Jem Wilson shows signs of emerging quickly from mourning, the blind Margaret Jennings lodges a complaint about this apparent hardheartedness; but Jem is equipped with the logic of nostalgia:

paradox but further.

> If they've been worthy to be heartily loved while alive, they'll not be forgotten when dead; it's against nature. And we need no more be upbraiding ourselves for letting in God's rays of light upon our sorrow, and no more be fearful of forgetting them, because their memory is not always haunting and taking up our minds, than you need to trouble yourself about remembering your grandfather's face, or what the stars were like, — you can't forget if you would, what it's such a pleasure to think about. Don't fear my forgetting Aunt Alice.[7]

At which point, unsurprisingly, the novel can dispense with mentioning Alice Wilson again, having reassured us that the forgetting of Alice that the novel will actually enact is not to be feared. What this logic hinges on is the notion of pleasure: what is pleasurable to recall will be recalled, while the unworthy or painful will erase itself. The consolidation of personal memory to the pleasurable only, and the assertion that its opposite is just as naturally forgotten, is one aspect of the genteel dialectic of nostalgia; its necessary complement is a folding back again into forgetting, for once the pleasure of remembering Alice Wilson (or, the remembrance of pleasure in Alice Wilson) has been announced, that pleasure is replaced by the fact of her actual erasure in the narrative. No longer necessary for the forward movement of the narrative, her disappearance is explained nostalgically, for nostalgic memory is above all the elision of the unnecessary.

The burden of my argument, then, is the following: acts of memory in the Victorian novel must be *necessary*—must *signify*—and must signify by standing in a directly causal relation, or an obviously symbolic relation, to the present, to the moment of narrating and beyond. "Pure memory," the bursting of an unassimilated and still-powerful past into the present, is forgotten in Victorian novels, forgotten so thoroughly that we forget its absence; although the instances just cited from *Our Mutual Friend* and *Mary Barton* suggest otherwise, it is rare that a Victorian narrative announces its own leavetakings and forgettings with such explicitness. Indeed, the act of reminding a reader of the absence of "pure" or "desultory" memory is, one might say, impolite—it trespasses the boundaries of psychic decorum that the classical novel has so quietly but firmly established. We have Henry James's testimony to remind us of the social interdiction against speaking of the dead in polite society, an interdiction that much of James's fiction flaunts; the mnemonic etiquette that most nineteenth-century fiction adhered to was the very rule that modernist narratives would go to such lengths, literal and figurative, to insult.[8] If we ask what underwrites this decorum, we come continually up against the notion of nostalgia, that secure and sentimentalized relation to irrevocably lost memories. Perhaps some form of "nostalgia" has always been with us, but it is the nineteenth-century novel that lifts it into the light of art and, starting with Austen's fiction, gives it a distinct cultural purpose: the amelioration or cancellation of the past. The nostalgic moment is the sign of a culture freed from its past, freed from consequences and resonances, prepared for the perfections of the future. Seen from this vantage point—the proliferation of texts that define rules for nostalgic remembrance, such as Austen's *Persuasion* or Dickens's *David Copperfield*—it can be said that the nineteenth-century novel invented modern nostalgia: a nostalgia conceived as a cultural habit and as an *askesis*, a method of self-control and regulation.

To call the product of such habitual, ascetic nostalgia an "amnesiac self," as this book does, poses two problems: the identification of nostalgia with forgetting, and the anachronism inherent in the term "amnesia," which, as I will discuss later, does not appear in English usage until later in the century. These difficulties are meant, however, to propose a sustained argument: that the important work of nostalgia can be found in the specific forms of forgetting that it enacts, and that this nostalgic forgetting will lead, as the Victorian novel works out its consequences, to the pathological forgetting we call amnesia. The construction of an "amnesiac self," in other words, a construction that each of the following five chapters will situate in somewhat different but complementary ways, depends on what Hayden White has called, in speaking of historical writing, the "imposition, upon events that are represented as real, of the formal coherency that stories possess," an imposition that will in turn depend on the elision of dispersed memories.[9] Insofar as "pure" or "desultory memory" or what we might as well call *ordinary* memory lacks this narrative coherence, or—as in such overshadowing examples as Joyce's *Ulysses* and Woolf's *Mrs. Dalloway*—ends up demanding a different and experimental kind of narrative coherence, then the Victorian novel must dispense with it. Throughout the following investigations, the psychological imperative to remember only what is "useful" coincides with a narratological imperative to relate only what "signifies." Each of the separate styles of "amnesiac selves" that are mapped here share a nostalgic goal: to eliminate the possibility, in psychological terms, of traumatic fixation, and in narratological terms, of the eruption of desultory, chaotic reminiscences. For Barthes, this excision of the desultory data of memory is a death, but considering the matter from the point of view of Victorian fictional values, we might just as easily say that it promotes a certain kind of life—a life no longer burdened by the past, a life lived as a coherent tale, summarizable, pointed, and finally moralizable.

Victorian Memoryscapes

"All fixed, fast-frozen relations, with their train of ancient and venerable prejudices and opinions are swept away, all new-formed ones become antiquated before they can ossify": thus Marx, in one of the more famous passages of *The Communist Manifesto*, on the revolutionary destructions carried out by bourgeois society. "All that is solid melts into air, all that is holy is profaned, and man is at last compelled to face with sober senses, his real conditions of life, and his relations with his kind."[10] What if, alongside these "sober senses," the techniques of nostalgia were produced by the unstable relations of a mobile society dedicated to a constantly revisionary ethic of newness? To suggest as much is to at least partially connect the formal strategies of nostalgia in nineteenth-century fiction to cultural strategies that rooted an adaptability to social disruption in the fungibility, and revisability, of memory. For however much the ensuing study devotes itself to a taxonomy of nineteenth-century narrative and its technical resources for managing memory, the question of the social use and social meaning of nostalgia will remain paramount. The techniques of nostalgia available to our view in Victorian and pre-Victorian narrative are as well the occasions, and the tactics, of nostalgic memory in a wider cultural frame. The goal of this study, then, is a comprehensive picture of memory in Victorian culture — memory as a cultural fact, necessarily adaptive to social realities — and of the pivotal, even dominant, role of the novel in constructing and propagating the mnemonic strategies of Victorian life. More than any other literary form, certainly more than post-Romantic poetry, which remained attached both to a Wordsworthian suffusion in memory and an eighteenth-century associationism, the novel's representation of memory was indeed new.[11] At the center of the Victorian "memoryscape" is the novel and its presentation of memory; but the novel employed the language and conceptual formulations of other cultural zones in its nostalgic project.

Therefore this book does not consider the novel in isolation. The bridge between a formal study of novelistic practice and a psychosocial narrative about memory in culture is for the most part supplied by examinations of one of the chief parallel practices to the nineteenth-century novel: the nascent field of "psychology." Each chapter that follows situates a specific novelistic genre — the social novel, the Brontëan novel of progress, the fictional autobiography, the sensation novel, the historical novel — alongside a contemporary discourse of science or psychology that not only inflects it but in some sense dictates its form. Each chapter, then, is a historical contextualization that brings into relation a literary fact, such as Austen's social fiction, and a cultural fact, such as the medical commentary that transformed "nostalgia" from a disease into a sentiment. Charlotte Brontë's self-made narrators are discussed through the languages of phrenology and physiognomy; the mid-century fictional autobiographies of Dickens and Thackeray through nineteenth-century associationist psychology; the sensation novel of Collins and the historical novel of Eliot through the new physiologies and pathologies of amnesia. The key intersection between novel and psychology will be the governing postulate throughout, although it must be remembered that the various alignments between fiction and mental theory discussed here differ slightly from each other, and that they need to be considered in isolation as well as in combination. The point to such a method is not merely to push the novel into the category of a "history of psychology," as might seem warranted by a topic such as memory; nor is it to supply a psychologized, much less a psychoanalytic, reading of Victorian narrative. The goal here is, more specifically, to enable *a history of nineteenth-century consciousness* that might be at once broad and specific, broad enough to describe a general cultural phenomenon and specific enough to account for the ways in which the fiction of the period helped determine the shape and eventual outcome of that phenomenon. For if there is one fact about Victorian memory that my study advances most persistently, it is the sharp difference that it maintains, in its emphasis on the generalizable, the vague, the nostalgic, from the epistemes of memory that both preceded and followed it.[12]

The psychological theories studied here are drawn from a wide cultural spectrum, from the popular phenomena of phrenology and physiognomy to the "official," academic doctrine of associationism. However pertinent the differences among these instances, they nonetheless present us with a fairly consistent image in one aspect: the striking, and crucial, *absence of memory* from the mental theories they offer. Nineteenth-century psychology, at least until the advent of Darwinian-inflected psychologies and the birth of psychoanalysis out of hysteria-studies, is better understood as a study of cognition, perception, and sensation — in essence, cognitive philosophy — than an inquiry into the dynamics of remembrance, repression, or genetic memory. Any serious study of nineteenth-century psychological work prior to the 1870s must necessarily concern itself with questions from which memory is absent: how does sensation become perception? How, and why, does the mind move from idea to idea? How are mental tendencies expressed by exterior features of the body?[13] The chapters that follow show in detail how, and why, memory failed to occupy British, and even much of Continental, psychology; but we must initially consider the implications of the fact that "psychology," in the first decades of its institutionalization (and its gradual detachment from "philosophy"), found little to comment on in regard to memory. Whereas memory is central to eighteenth-century associationism, and even more crucial for the psychodynamics of Freud, Breuer, Janet, and others, we are faced with a nineteenth-century interregnum that saw recollection as among the least compelling of mental processes.[14] A psyche not dependent on memory: such is the mental structure offered to us by all manner of psychologies in the nineteenth century. One further from contemporary psychologies cannot easily be imagined.

This absence of memory is not simply an oversight or a naïve omission. We make a mistake if we assume that if Victorian psychology and Victorian narrative evaded such subjects as traumatic memory or detailed, chaotic recollection, then the reason is that such a concept was unavailable to them. As Georges Poulet famously argued, the "great discovery of the eighteenth century is the phenomenon of memory," and the writing of Rousseau, certainly available to nineteenth-century British literary culture, was the most vivid example possible of a powerful, detailed, dispersed faculty of "pure" or "desultory" memory.[15] Moreover, we can find scattered, anomalous instances even within Victorian fiction of persistent, traumatic memory; although it is certainly true that the category of "trauma" belongs to the later nineteenth century, passages such as these from Thackeray's *Memoirs of Barry Lyndon* (1844), in which the narrator describes the system of corporal punishment employed in the Prussian army, should disabuse us of the idea that where traumatic memory was concerned the Victorians were innocents: "Almost all of us yielded to the spell—scarce one could break it. The French officer I have spoken of as taken along with me, was in my company and caned like a dog. I met him at Versailles twenty years afterwards, and he turned quite pale and sick when I spoke to him of old days. 'For God's sake,' said he, 'don't talk of that time; I wake up from my sleep trembling and crying even now.'"[16] That such a scene could be written in the mid–nineteenth century tells us that trauma, fixation, and mnemonic repetition were not impossibilities for Victorian narration; that such a scene is a rarity tells us that the fiction of the time was engaged in constructing a psychic structure that would be utterly different, that would in fact work against what Barry Lyndon gives us in favor of what most nineteenth-century narratives produce instead: a secure, generalizable, willed, genial retrospect that disconnects the present from the past and that operates always with an eye toward the future; a psyche oriented toward perception and sensation—toward the *present*, which emerged as the central topic of psychology—rather than any sundered past. The absence of memory from Victorian psychological thinking must be regarded not as a mistake but as a choice: a choice that should be understood with reference to the social conditions in which it would be lived out as a practical, even strategic, theory.

It is the novel that, as this book will argue, presents us with the fullest account of how this "practical theory" worked, in what situations it would be deployed, and why it might have been so useful as an adaptive strategy among the conditions of displacement, dislocation, and unsettlement that Marx so memorably evoked. The sum of all the various micropractices and psychological theories that discounted an active, detailed memory is, of course, nostalgia: a memory suited to nineteenth-century psychologies in its orientation toward the present and the future, toward perception and cognition, and not backward toward a vanished field of mnemonic data. Nostalgic forgetting, put simply, is the form of memory best suited to the "cognitive philosophy" of the nineteenth century, and most frequently found in the classical novel whose continued nostalgic appeal attests to its power to evoke that form of memory. The fact to keep in mind is *collaboration*: the rigidly antimnemonic psyche of phrenological theory, the tightly relevant nature of memories in associationist psychology, and the stress upon the body's own production, through "sensations," of amnesia in nineteenth-century medical pathology all colluded with the novel in the formation of a subject, an "amnesiac self," that was trained in a mode of forgetting, that forgetting that I call nostalgia.

It is a form of selfhood whose unquestioned dominance is comparatively short, despite the fact that, as I will suggest, its influence has been carried into our own time. The amnesiac self does not represent a *longue durée*, for by the late 1870s a new science of memory has arisen, and new styles of narration, such as Hardy's elaborately memory-scarred narratives, arise with them; from the standpoint of the culture of Freud, Breuer, Janet, Ebbinghaus, Proust, Hardy, and Joyce, it makes a certain sense to describe the Victorian era, in Ian Hacking's recent phrase, as the period "before memory."[17] But to say "before memory" takes for granted the meaning of "memory," a modern meaning based in a psychoanalytic, statistical, neurological contextual field. The "memory" that Victorian fiction evaded — which I have here, after Bergson, called "pure memory" — and the nostalgia it embraced are quite different facts, facts that suggest that memory, and mnemonic consciousness, had a history before psychoanalysis and wartime traumas of 1870 and 1914 configured it differently. The Victorian period lies between the associationism of Locke, Hume, Hartley, and the hysteria-theories of Freud and Breuer, between Rousseauistic reverie and Proustian *mémoire involontaire*, between, that is, two periods well known already for their mnemonic styles; yet it too has its defining features, its deep cultural predilections, and if those predilections were toward a nostalgic *evasion* of both what came before it and what, as yet unforeseen, was to come after it, that fact needs to be as carefully studied and accounted for as anything else about the Victorian period.

Sites and Processes of Nostalgia

Reading nostalgia means, necessarily, reading its discursive manifestations, or what Reinhart Koselleck has called "the linguistic organization of temporal experience."[18] The languages of time deployed by the nineteenth-century novel — retrospects, expectations, ellipses, elisions, reminders — are of course central to any study of nostalgia's workings. No less important, however, will be the spaces in which these languages of time occur: the "sites" or synchronic zones that habitually intersect with nostalgia's diachronic processes. For the purpose of this study, a "site" can be anything from a generic aspect of Victorian narrative, two of which I will define hereafter, to the larger subgenres and spatial indicators that nineteenth-century fiction often used, such the narratives of social, and physical, mobility to which I devote my attention. Bakhtin's very useful term "chronotope" aptly summarizes this methodological point: the need to find the set of interdependent temporal and spatial coordinates that a given genre presents us with, and that are formative for that genre's vision of character, plot, and social reality.[19] The chronotope of narratives of nostalgia might be summarized as the set of sites and temporal processes that reflect, and manage, *dislocation*—experiences of dissonance, disconnection, separation from past spaces and certainties. If anything binds the various novels analyzed in this study, it is their presentation of dislocation; and it might be ventured here, at the outset, that dislocation is the dilemma nostalgia is invented to solve.

Thus most of the narratives discussed here will center on movement, usually enforced movement: running away from home, being forced to leave a home one no longer can afford, being adopted by strangers, taking employment in a new city or country. These familiar genres of nineteenth-century narrative are one sort of "site" for a nostalgic chronotope; the "sites," one might say, of strangeness, foreignness, the "new." It is not co-incidental that recent histories of the discursive formations of emergent nation-states and nationalities concentrate on the nostalgias that buttress these odd new social wholes.[20] To speak more particularly, however, these genres generate smaller "sites" or generic moments that attempt to manage the dislocations and shocks caused by such mobility. One such "site," which will reappear throughout these pages, is what I will term the *life-review*: the attempt by a character, in a situation where dislocation has to be noted, to summarize the events of her life, to summon all the relevant facts into a suddenly coherent, miniature narrative. These moments, so crucial to the novel's moral energies, are one of the Victorian novel's few allowances for memory, but the memory they allow is a nostalgic one only. One such famous life-review, from Thackeray's *Vanity Fair* (1848), will serve to illustrate how this familiar site of Victorian narration offers us a vague yet entirely coherent casting back into the past in the light of an end, be it the death of a character or the end of the narrative itself. Here, Amelia Osborne, reentering the Osborne house in London's Russell Square after a number of years, looks back not only to her previous marriage to George Osborne but to the consequences leading her to what will be her second (and presumptively final) marriage to William Dobbin:

> She went up to one of the open windows (one of those at which she used to gaze with a sick heart when the child was first taken from her), and thence as she looked out she could see, over the trees of Russell Square, the old house in which she herself was born, and where she had passed so many happy days of sacred youth. They all came back to her, the pleasant holidays, the kind faces, the careless, joyful past times; and the long pains and trials that had since cast her down. She

thought of these and of the man who had been her constant protector, her good genius, her sole benefactor, her tender and generous friend.[21]

We should note here what will be true of the life-reviews discussed throughout the chapters that follow: the positing of a complete recall ("they all came back to her"), which is neutralized by the persistently vague language throughout ("the kind faces, the careless, joyful past times"); the transformation of Amelia's scattered recollections into a paradigmatic narrative of happiness, decline, and return to happiness; the refusal of the narrative to linger on Amelia's possibly complex, lost memories — of a dead husband, a temporarily lost child — and its preference for those memories that lead right back to the present and the future, to Dobbin. Thackeray's life-review here, as in so many other places in Victorian narrative, dilutes the facts of the past into a coherent and vague story that points only to what the present would consider "useful" and "meaningful": Dobbin's love. What this "site" shows us, typically, is a nostalgic memory managing the various abysses of dislocation and disconnection that it so genially glides over.

Similarly, many of the readings that follow will concentrate on another key "site" of nostalgia in Victorian narrative: recurrent objects. *Object-reappearance*, the term I employ for the binding of a narrative through continually reemergent objects, signals a similar washing-out and weighing of the past in the service of a hopefully tidier future. Those objects that will come under consideration, from the "souvenirs" of Austen's *Mansfield Park* to the historical relics of George Eliot's *Romola*, enact the condensation of the past into a portable, vague form; like the novels that contain them, they elicit only enough memory to disarm a more complete, detailed recollection of the past. Thus through attention to a character-based narrative site (life-review) and one produced by the narrative voice alone (object-reappearance), my inquiries into the evasion of "pure" memory by Victorian narrative tentatively sketch a formal catalogue of how detailed memory can disappear in fiction: in which synchronic *sites*, and through which diachronic *processes*, diffuse reminiscence can be eliminated in favor of nostalgic remembrance.

For however much nostalgia is lodged in various places, much of this work is devoted to a study of its diachronic tendencies — the alterations that take place, through the actions of nostalgic memory, to a particular datum as it is "remembered" in a narrative. Nostalgia attaches itself to various generic "sites" (life-reviews, object-reappearances) as well as to more literal sites, such as returns home, leavetakings, journeys; but one of its unique characteristics is its ability to act as a narrative, to act in time as well as on time.[22] As a result, we will see memories presented in novels by

Austen, Brontë, and Dickens taking their passage through such nostalgic processes as *dilution*, the gradual elimination of detail; *naming*, the substitution of vague categories for the particularity of recollection; and *disconnection*, the refusal to consider separate memories as related facts. In the sites of nostalgia — the pressure-points, so to speak, that call it forth — and in the processes it enacts we will see a mnemonic mode that not only exists to heal the dislocations of personal and social experience but that in healing these dislocations often insists on the absolute disconnection of past and present.[23] To this end *Persuasion*'s Anne Elliot insists, in a key moment for later nineteenth-century fiction, that "when pain is over, the remembrance of it often becomes a pleasure."[24]

As the fiction of the nineteenth century turns increasingly to a description of the psychic dislocations attendant upon a society for whom mobility and the possibility of rapid change is increasingly likely, nostalgia takes on an ever more central role. The past in its particularity gradually vanishes; the pleasure of recollecting that vague, disconnected past becomes more keen, and more a part of the texture of fiction. The consequentiality of the past dwindles into its capacity to provide pleasure, security, self-definition — above all, utility; the discontinuity of the moment of recollecting and the recollected moment is asserted. For nostalgia there is, literally, no time like the present.

Memory, History, Methodology

More than perhaps any other object of inquiry, memory today seems to offer the hope of a common ground between otherwise distinct disciplines. Studies of remembrance have come out of historical, philosophical, sociological, anthropological, psychological, and neuroscientific fields, not to mention the growing appeal "memory" has had for increasingly interdisciplinary literary studies.[25] It might even be said that, given the rather large overlap between many of these various approaches, memory-studies can be considered a shadow discipline of its own; but unlike the possibly too familiar procedures of the institutional disciplines that give it life, the methodologies involved in a pursuit of human remembrance remain opaque, unsystematized, and persistently (if productively) chaotic. No strong consensus yet exists about the boundaries, forms, and contents of a study of memory, however many different, and compelling, versions of that study may in fact be available to us. As a result, any prolonged discussion of the history and literary manifestations of remembrance must at least partially preoccupy itself with some opening reflections on its own methodological choices.

The key datum for my exploration of the "amnesiac self" is individual, subjective, psychologized experience, the memories and lapses in memory of strongly distinct characters within a form (the nineteenth-century novel) that insists on its ability to convey the normative workings of interiority. As such, Victorian narrative is not far from the goals of nineteenth-century psychology, and in many respects, as I will show, it exerted a determining influence on that psychology. But the datum of individual experience is a notoriously tricky one, and is only part of a larger dynamic between the social forms in which memory can be conceived and the individuals who activate these social forms through particular, discrete acts of remembrance and forgetting. In that sense, the object of this study is a collective, historically defined memory—collective in the sense that Maurice Halbwachs gave it, as a "social framework" that allows memory to exist. "No memory," Halbwachs asserted, "is possible outside frameworks used by people living in society to determine and retrieve their recollections."[26] However much the novels studied here present us with individual nostalgic recollections of individual pasts, that nostalgia is also, and continually, a social fact. That "the individual remembers by placing himself in the perspective of the group," as Halbwachs claims, is matched by the necessary obverse, that "the memory of the group realizes and manifests itself in individual memories."[27] The following paradox will be a central aspect of the Victorian novel's production of nostalgia: that nostalgia is a socially binding form of memory, a memory for society, that nevertheless can only be produced by the spontaneous remembrances of individuals. More familiar collective forms of remembrance, such as rituals, memorials, and historical traumas, yield in importance in Victorian narrative to recollections of a personal past, but those recollections take place through a form of memory—nostalgia—whose origin, justification, and orientation is the collective.

If individual mnemonic experience is often difficult to describe, and collective memory difficult to accurately summarize, nineteenth-century theories of mind have provided me with a useful interpretive model: a pervasive habit of dividing mental processing into distinct parts, and then attaching names, so that an almost spatialized, or diagrammatic, vision of the psyche will emerge. Nostalgia is, as I have claimed, largely a function of disconnecting and naming; and it is no accident that the phrenological diagram, with its diverse, isolated, and taxonomized attributes, is one of this book's recurrent images. That taxonomical urge has proven congenial for this book's own organization. Within each chapter, themselves individual "units" or instances of Victorian nostalgia, there are taxonomies and terms intended to reenact, while analyzing, the epistemological tendencies that coalesce in the "amnesiac self." The first three chapters, in particular, contain prolonged taxonomies of the various styles of nostalgic forgetting they describe, from the depathologized nostalgia of Austen through the embodied amnesias of Brontë to the associationist nostalgias of Dickens and Thackeray. If a specific type of forgetting is this book's topic, it nonetheless seeks to remember, and put to analytic use, the strategies of "detaching" and "naming" that largely constitute nostalgic memory.

These taxonomizations are what one might loosely call structural: a means toward forming a definition of nostalgia as a procedure, a set of tactics, a mnemonic strategy. This approach necessarily leaves open an obvious and pertinent question—what of the content of this supposed nostalgic *askesis* I ascribe to the nineteenth-century novel? What, put more simply, were these nostalgic subjects trying to forget? It is a question not simply about the content of forgetting but about the place of nostalgia in a political, or more broadly ideological, frame of reference. What is the "ideological work" of nostalgic forgetting—how does it both advance, and create, ideologies?[28] The question is particularly urgent for contemporary readers of the classical British novel, who face in our own time the possibility, and possible danger, of forgetting the immense historical traumas that stand between us and the nineteenth century. A formulation of Adorno, on a cultural forgetfulness of Nazism, is tellingly exact: "One wants to break free of the past: rightly, because nothing at all can live in its shadow, and because there will be no end to the terror as long as guilt and violence are repaid with guilt and violence; wrongly, because the past that one would like to evade is still very much alive."[29] What might be the content that is rightly transcended, and wrongly ignored, by Victorian nostalgia, by the "amnesiac self"?

The question becomes even more difficult to answer when the wide range of possible contents is canvassed. On the level of individual experience, this study will explore the class-tactics of forgetting, where the rising protagonist—from *Mansfield Park*'s Fanny Price to *The Woman in White*'s Walter Hartright—escapes a return to lower origins by an elaborate process of psychically erasing those origins; a constant biographical amnesia is just as serviceable when the power relations of gender are primary obstacles, as Brontë's *Villette* demonstrates so vividly. For a reformist age, even the facts of history might be usefully erased, as the data of the Victorian historical novel, here represented through Eliot's *Romola*, suggest. There are as well other constant forgettings of Victorian narrative, which much recent critical practice has sought to examine and bring back into the light of cultural recollection—most notably, of course, the imperial projects that so many Victorian novels cannot entirely forget, projects partially effaced by what has been recently termed "colonial amnesia."[30] Obviously no single content can be asserted to be the focus of a cultural practice of nostalgia, but might there be one of these contents that exerts a determining influence? Might there be a single ideological affiliation that would serve as a heuristic for a definition of nostalgia?

The answer, as reflected in the following pages, is no. My concern here is less with identifying the one or two ideological dynamics that govern nostalgic memory in Victorian fiction than with the possible reliance of ideology as such on the processes of forgetting—with nostalgia as ideological agent per se. Whether we characterize the work of Victorian nostalgia as liberatory, reformist, and progressive or obscurantist, meretricious, and repressive—and as this study will attest, both are possible, even valid, responses—there remains the possibility that forgetting of some form is implicated in any ideology and that the nostalgia so compellingly evoked by nineteenth-century novelists may have been a psychic structure to which combatants from opposite sides of various cultural struggles appealed with equal facility and equal confidence in its "natural" alliance with their positions. Ideology and amnesia have long been linked, particularly in the varieties of Marxist theory that have taken up the subject of belief and class consciousness, from Lukács's analyses of the structural forgetting embedded in reification to Althusser's well-known argument that ideology "has no history."[31] The forgettings that might accompany ideology do, however, have their own discernible historical formations, however varied and even inconsistent their ideological affiliations—and the Victorian "amnesiac self," in its relatively circumscribed but nonetheless vivid life, is one of these particular historical styles of remembrance-through-forgetting. It is necessary to be alive not only to the wide variety of cultural situations into which nostalgia could be inserted but also to the central place nostalgia seems to have held in the production of belief as such—even that belief in its own effectiveness in the world that remains such a salient part of nineteenth-century fiction.

One result of the variety of causes and efforts to which Victorian nostalgia could be recruited—from a progressive "forgetting" of firm class boundaries to an often convenient amnesia about the "forgotten" of society—is a difficulty in forming any one attitude toward it. Our standpoint today is largely formed by a culture for which historical amnesia, and its seemingly constant production by dominant media forms, is a crisis—so much so that it is increasingly obvious that the best cultural work, both within and without the academy, must try to contravene, or at the very least understand, the amnesias of our own time.[32] But it would be incorrect to import back to the nineteenth century and its fiction our own dichotomies and memory-structures, and much of this book is an argument against the applicability of the various binaries—amnesia versus memory, nostalgic recollection versus authentic recollection—that attach themselves so readily to late-twentieth-century and millenial thinking about the subject. "Nostalgia" may be a form, perhaps even the originary form, of what we now call "amnesia," and we may lament the spread of amnesia in our own culture, but it is less easy to take a censorious, or a cel-

ebratory, attitude toward the nostalgias that we find in the Victorian period. What we can do, however, is recognize our own separation from
these nineteenth-century forms of nostalgia and the very different ways in
which they operate, as well as our occasionally uncanny complicity with
them, our continued pleasure in the nostalgic memories they so often
present.

Toward the Nostalgic Reader

We arrive, finally, at the Victorian novel-reader, the person whose subjectivity was most directly the target of these nostalgic evasions and constructions: both the "Victorian reader," the object of historical inquiry, and
the "reader of the Victorian novel," the contemporary phenomenon that
shows a continued, if unexpected, vibrancy. If we say that the age of the
amnesiac self was a circumscribed one brought to an end by a host of late-
nineteenth-century phenomena, how are we to explain the continued
propagation of nostalgia by, and through, the fiction of the nineteenth century? This contradiction, I would suggest, is an illusory one. The cultural
dominance of nostalgic remembrance may have been short, but its presence persists, most obviously through the novels that first shaped nostalgic
memory. Entering a Victorian novel means entering, or reentering, a world
of nostalgic subjects. The nostalgia that pervades our relation to nineteenth-
century fiction is not an accidental effect; it is constitutive of the subjectivities that that fiction depicts, and it is a crucial part of its cultural labor.

But if we say that the novel helped envision and shape a nostalgic subject, how are we to apply that to the reader of these voluminous, vastly
overproductive fictions, which would seem to require the most strenuous
of mnemonic exertions? How is it possible to construct a subject trained
in nostalgic forgetting, in the elision of reminiscential detail, through
texts whose demanding length and crowded texture require, at least on
the surface, attention and frequent recollection? It is toward these questions that this study finally leads, the full answers to which will require
much demonstration and proof. But one large, counterintuitive answer
may be offered here at the outset—that the machinery of Victorian fiction
operates to slowly and gradually erase the field of data, fact, and circumstance with which it starts, and to replace that field with a diluted, stable,
and carefully selected set of details, a set chosen according to the rules of
nostalgic remembrance. Throughout the five studies that constitute this
investigation, I will be suggesting a reader-effect analogous to, in fact produced by, the dilutions of life-review: an effect whereby Victorian fiction
slowly changes our perception of key mnemonic data, so that by the conclusion of a given fiction we too are in a nostalgic relation to it.[33] We

might say that much nineteenth-century narrative, from Austen to Dickens and beyond, sets itself a large problem in its reliance on elaborate detail and unfettered length, but solves this problem through the ingenuities of nostalgic closure, a series of processes whose techniques we, as readers, have absorbed as newly constituted nostalgic subjects or "amnesiac selves." In the recovery, description, and analysis of this amnesiac self, then, my historical contextualizations are also elucidations of the contemporary reader of Victorian texts — a reading of our reading of these novels, and of our failure to register how much the classical novel asks us to forget.

ONE

Austen's Nostalgics

*This morning we have been to see Miss Chamberlayne look hot
on horseback. — Seven years & four months ago we went to the same
Ridinghouse to see Miss Lefroy's performance! — What a different set are
we now moving in! But seven years I suppose are enough to change every
pore of one's skin, & every feeling of one's mind.*
—Jane Austen to Cassandra Austen, April 8, 1805

*Mémoire. — Se plaindre de la sienne, et même se vanter de n'en pas avoir.
Mais rugir si on vous dit que vous n'avez pas de jugement.*
—Flaubert, Dictionnaire des Idées reçues

Protesting against Edward Ferrars's conversational decorum, *Sense and Sensibility*'s Marianne Dashwood proclaims: "I love to be reminded of the past, Edward — whether it be melancholy or gay, I love to recall it — and you will never offend me by talking of former times" (*SS*, 92).[1] Marianne's preference is not, however, reflected in the texts of her creator, which seem more interested in maintaining Edward's tentative avoidance of the past than in cultivating a love of remembrance. Jane Austen's novels do not bask in reminiscence, do not seek out obscure memories, and are not illuminated by sudden bursts of recollection — a tendency amply demonstrated by the fact that, having stated her love of memory, Marianne returns immediately to the topic at hand: how one might dispose of a purely hypothetical fortune. Memory may be invoked, but it does not become a topic in its own right. So prevalent is this avoidance of retrospect in Austen's novels, so silent its interdictions, that we may not even notice the representational parameters whose edges we are only occasionally permitted to see; asking questions that test those edges seems something like an act of incivility. What does Marianne remember of her deceased father, or *Persuasion*'s Anne Elliot of her mother? Why is Fanny Price, in *Mansfield Park*, never seized with vivid memories of her Portsmouth family, her Portsmouth childhood, her Portsmouth pastimes? These questions are naïve only insofar as they blithely pierce interdictions, or absences, that practiced readers of Austen have long learned to take for granted. Posed as challenges to the texts' silences—as illuminations of the boundaries of Austen's art—these questions help us to see how thoroughly Austen's novels condition us to read this absence of vivid retrospect from personality, which is constitutive of what I have termed the "amnesiac self," as normal, as in fact normative. It is with this premise that I begin my investigation of Austen's treatment of memory: the general lack of remembrance from her narratives.

Set alongside texts from one hundred years later, however—indeed, set alongside our own expectations about the workings of the psyche—Austen's silence about the pasts of her characters, as well as their own silence respecting their pasts, can begin to seem like a definite aesthetic fact, a technical choice worthy of comment. It is a choice of which Austen is aware. In *Northanger Abbey*, confronted with the necessity of introducing a new character, she produces this striking statement: "This brief account of the family is intended to supersede the necessity of a long and minute detail from Mrs. Thorpe herself, of her past adventures and sufferings, which might otherwise be expected to occupy the three or four following chapters; in which the worthlessness of lords and attornies might be set forth, and conversations, which had passed twenty years before, be minutely repeated" (*NA*, 34). The overt target of Austen's wit here is the potentially interminable, and highly elastic, ability of eighteenth-century fiction to take retrospective detours; she is also staking out the boundaries of her own novelistic practice, boundaries that are designed to keep out windy analepses or even a sense of character as causally related to past incidents. A series of social and moral terms, which do not depend on detailed past information, are sufficient: "Mrs. Thorpe was a widow," we are told, "and not a very rich one; she was a good-humoured, well-meaning woman, and a very indulgent mother" (*NA*, 34). That the above aesthetic claim centers on a minor character is no real objection to its prevalence; even Austen's protagonists are freed from the necessity of "minutely" relating their "former times." As regards Catherine Morland, after all, we are offered a brief opening sketch of her vivacity, plainness, impatience, and education, with only the firing of her music-master stepping out from the list of imperfect verbs to constitute a distinct memory.

The *technical* choice to avoid remembrance is also a *cultural* choice—as is reflected by Austen's juvenilia, her remarkably accomplished parodies of the most common cultural narratives; throughout these sketches and stories, characters forget their pasts, operating in a perpetually comical state of mnemonic incompetence. Thus in "Henry and Eliza," Lady Harcourt remembers almost twenty years later that the adopted child she and her husband found in a haystack was, in fact, her own, put there by herself a few weeks previously in order to hide the child from her displeased husband. "The Adventures of Mr Harley," one of Austen's briefer tales, presents a similar instance of extreme forgetfulness:

> Mr Harley was one of many Children. Destined by his father for the Church & by his Mother for the Sea, desirous of pleasing both, he prevailed on Sir John to obtain for him a Chaplaincy on board a Man of War. He accordingly, cut his Hair and sailed.
>
> In half a year he returned & set-off in the Stage Coach for Hogsworth Green, the seat of Emma. His fellow travellers were, A man without a Hat, Another with two, An old maid & a young Wife.
>
> This last appeared about 17 with fine dark Eyes & an elegant Shape; inshort Mr Harley soon found out, that she was his Emma & recollected he had married her a few weeks before he left England. (*MW*, 40)

No mere *jeu d'esprit*, Mr. Harley's adventures—like so many of Austen's earliest writings—make tremendous fun out of illuminating a cultural preference for narratives that consign the past to oblivion, and for characters who are not encumbered with overly proficient or active memories.[2] What is blatant comedy in her juvenilia becomes, however, a more discreetly managed choice in her mature works; Austen proceeds, we may say, from anatomizing narratives without memories to producing far subtler versions of them. It is admittedly a large tonal step from Mr. Harley to Fanny Price's reluctance to remember Portsmouth, or even Edward Ferrars's reluctance to bring up the past in conversation; it is a small conceptual step, however, for what these creations have in common, as we will see, is a selfhood not dependent on remembrance.

This is not, it should be made clear, a contemporary conception of personality, indebted as that would be to modernist innovations in the formal structure of narrative and psychoanalytic innovations in the mapping of mental processes. Austen's fiction, that is, presents us with a paradigmatic example of the resistance of early-nineteenth-century fiction to the generic expectations of the novel formed by modernist fiction and its later critics— expectations of a concentration on reminiscence and trauma, childhood formations, and adult recollections.[3] Rather than being characteristic of the novel at large, these later innovations of content are strangers to Austen's work. A list could be compiled of what have come to be considered key indices of real, "rounded" literary characters: the eruption of small-scale, diffuse, possibly insignificant memories; the concentration of these eruptions on the topic of childhood; the problematic effect, both threatening and attractive, that these memories seem to have; and their determining influence on action and choice in the present. What this list shows, when brought into contact with Austen's practices, is how inapplicable it is to her texts. The past, as her *Northanger Abbey* proclamation shows us, tips into a comical irrelevance or a tendentious distraction. Forgetting—both the text's own dispensing with flashback and the general reluctance or inability of her characters to resurrect their pasts—is as constitutive of selfhood in Austen as obsessive remembering is to the novelistic character of the twentieth century.

Perhaps it is imprecise, however, to speak of Austen's novels as lacking memory, for it is my argument in what follows that her texts are involved in the formation of a memory-category that has become a familiar part of our mental landscape: nostalgia. The nostalgia that Austen's narratives increasingly depict and produce is, however, a form of forgetting—a winnowing of the specificity, emotional disturbance, and unpredictability of reminiscence into a diluted, vague, comfortable retrospect, the wistful and sentimental form of longing that we know as nostalgia. Austen's novels do contain traumas; but her artistic task is, in the course of a narrative, to start with a traumatic event and illustrate a subsequent process of nostalgic forgetting of that event. Continually her texts revolve around the past being invoked, summarized or moralized, canceled, and therefore transformed into a nostalgically safe object of contemplation, for the nostalgia that Austen's novels enact is at once a form of memory—it is turned toward a past—and a form of forgetting, for it dispenses with the vividness that the past had previously held. Her texts are engaged, that is, in a project of elision, erasure, and dilution, all in the service of a final nostalgic remembrance: a form of memory that acknowledges the past obliquely, only to register our complete disconnection from it. To explain the unique fact of memory's comparative absence from the conversations, actions, and resolutions of Austen's world, it is necessary to turn to the one form of memory her texts revolve around—the nostalgic—and to understand the "nostalgics," or representational logic based on nostalgia, that her texts create. The first step in such an inquiry is, however, an ironic one, an irony licensed by history itself: to demonstrate how this most nontraumatic of memory styles arose as itself a trauma.

Social Disease, Social Cure

In September 1770, Lieutenant (later Captain) James Cook's vessel the H.M.S. *Endeavor* left the coast of New Guinea in haste, its crew having enjoyed a landing reception of fire darts. On board the *Endeavor* was Sir Joseph Banks, a former pupil of Linnaeus and the ship's resident botanist, who recorded the leavetaking in his journal:

As soon as ever the boat was hoisted in we made sail, and steered away from this land, to the no small satisfaction of, I believe, three-fourths of our company. The sick became well and the melancholy looked gay. The greater part of them were now pretty far gone with the longing for home, which the physicians have gone so far as to esteem a disease under the name of nostalgia. Indeed I can hardly find anybody in the ship clear of its effects but the captain, Dr. Solander, and myself, and we three have ample constant employment for our minds, which I believe to be the best, if not the only remedy for it.[4]

Here "nostalgia" enters the English language—carefully distanced as a medical neologism, one that the physicians have gone "so far as to esteem a disease" in a conceptual leap as large as the geographical journey Cook's crew has gone to contract it. The most immediately curious thing about this taxonomical début is that, as far as a history of nostalgia might go, it seems to represent a dead end. No comfortable sentimentality, the nostalgia of the eighteenth century—elaborately studied in nosologies, tracts, and case studies, particularly in the century's concluding decades—was a danger, a potentially fatal affliction. Banks's journal provides us with a glimpse of nostalgia *in extremis*: a homesickness that was powerful and real, situated first among travelers, among the exotic, far from "home." Indeed, the eighteenth-century study of nostalgia centered on its prevalence in armies and on board ships, in precisely those places where travel, particularly enforced travel, was likely to occur.

This is not quite Jane Austen's nostalgia; nor is the semantic field it encapsulates very similar to contemporary usage. Something has intervened between Banks's illness and the generalized comfort and disembodied quality of current definitions of the word to alter "nostalgia" beyond any real recognition, something more complex and obscure than the fact of European medicine's gradual relinquishment of it as a clinical entity. If during the first few decades of the nineteenth century this medicalized nostalgia begins to disappear from scientific study, and homesickness ceases to be a pathologized concept, something has operated to reclaim nostalgia as a social process and a desirable bit of mental furniture—to depathologize and then propagate a new "nostalgia." If nostalgia is transformed from a wasting illness, one with its own etiology, symptoms, and set of cures, to a regular fact of human memory, the open question is: where might we locate the pivot of this transformation, in time and in cultural space?

The search for this answer takes me away from medicine and overseas travel and toward Austen's novels, a corpus of work that initiates the revision of a pathologized memory linked to the perils of dislocation. In attempting to locate the moment and the site where Banks's nostalgia becomes a contemporary, depathologized nostalgia—where, that is, the idea of a nostalgia that might be *shared* is born — I turn to a set of social novels from the early nineteenth century, at the very moment when the peak of an older nostalgia has passed. In this passage from a pathology to a general cultural category medicine itself is only part of the story; what it is necessary to chart is the passage of nostalgia through literary representation, through the novel, on its path to becoming innocuous, inescapable, normative. It is in Austen's work that we can best detect this conceptual shift taking place. As her career proceeds, we can see the pivot whereby a medicalized nostalgia — where the patient, lost in his or her own particular memories, sickens and possibly dies — becomes a new nostalgia, in which disindividualized, vague, and often communal retrospects are a healthy norm.[5]

Austen's publishing career begins with Marianne Dashwood, who, as we have seen, courts memory, and who suffers through a wasting disease brought on by an excess of regret and reminiscence. The keynote of her character is rung at the novel's outset precisely through her eighteenth-century version of nostalgia: she is the most reluctant of the Dashwood family to leave their former home, Norland Park, and the most consistent in her desire to remain nostalgic; "Elinor," she says to her mother, "in quitting Norland and Edward, cried not as I did" (*SS*, 39). This nostalgia is very real — its referent is a real place, not an inaccessible time — and, of course, highly dangerous, as dramatic in its eventual effects on Marianne's body as any of the case studies discussed by eighteenth-century physicians. The nostalgia of *Sense and Sensibility* is still very much a disease; it is perhaps more a social disease than the traditional medical understanding of nostalgia, insofar as it occurs in a restricted compass of space somewhat unlike the vaster, isolated locales mentioned in eighteenth-century medical texts, but it is a disease nonetheless, a disorder with potentially drastic consequences, and a disease (although undeniably somatic) of excessive remembrance.

Next to this early example of Austenian nostalgia, consider one of the final scenes of *Pride and Prejudice*, in which a newer nostalgia — a mode, as I have said, of forgetting — supplants any sense of nostalgia as a disease; this newer nostalgia is explicitly curative. Elizabeth and Darcy have begun a survey of their fraught, almost accidental courtship, a review potentially laden with unhappy memories and burdensome emotions; in reaction to this possibly dangerous strain of conversation, Elizabeth begins, "Oh! do not repeat what I then said. These recollections will not do at all" (*PP*, 368). When Darcy persists in remembering his earlier, explanatory, often bitter letter to Elizabeth, she responds with customary spirit:

> The letter, perhaps, began in bitterness, but it did not end so. The adieu is charity itself. But think no more of the letter. The feelings of

the person who wrote, and the person who received it, are now so widely different from what they were then, that every unpleasant circumstance attending it, ought to be forgotten. You must learn some of my philosophy. Think only of the past as its remembrance gives you pleasure. (*PP*, 368–369)

What was a troubled memory—and one with a potential to resurrect resentment and ripple the surface of this new pairing—is transformed by Elizabeth's "philosophy" into a nostalgic pleasure.[6] Unlike Marianne's backward-turned pathology, Elizabeth's therapeutic advice asserts the crucial principle of *disconnection*: the past, once gone, is of no further consequence, and because it is of no consequence, it can be forgotten. Of course there is an element of sophistry to this logic, one that Elizabeth's own irony lightly registers—if the past were truly of no consequence, it would hardly be necessary to attempt to forget it; if Darcy's current feelings are indeed "so widely different from what they were," then why is there a lingering unpleasantness that must be forgotten? But however much Elizabeth's claim begs the question of how disconnected their present "really" is from their past, the assertion of discontinuity remains, and it does not depend on any tight logic. Indeed, the nostalgic principle of "pleasure" neatly brushes aside any impertinent queries or lingering doubts; and it is well to remember that fantasy occupies a preeminent place in any theory of nostalgia. Elizabeth's nostalgic fantasy—that all is different in the present, and that the past can be safely, even pleasurably, recalled once that disconnection is asserted—is nothing if not pragmatic. Barring any yearning for the past, or any continued cathexis to memory, her new nostalgia has cured what the older, medicalized nostalgia puts into peril. Darcy will insist on returning to his past, a moment to which I too will return, but Elizabeth's proclamation signals the end of an older style of nostalgia. Her "philosophy" is entirely in the service of the present, and so it is appropriate that this conversation should end by their finding, "on examining their watches, that it was time to be at home" (*PP*, 370), for unlike Marianne's affliction, the new nostalgia increasingly employed in Austen's fiction is turned resolutely forward.

It is possible to take Elizabeth's request, to think only of the past as its remembrance gives us pleasure, as the foundation of Austen's new nostalgia—and as the foundation of the nostalgia we have inherited from the early nineteenth century. Not surprisingly, Austen's critics have registered the importance of nostalgia to her work, but the critical tradition surrounding Austen has understood its importance only obliquely. It is as if nostalgia is an affliction to which Austen's readers are particularly susceptible and for which only the inoculations of a radically denostalgizing criticism are a cure. In her persuasive recent study, Claudia Johnson situates her work and its historicizing methodology as a corrective to old-school readers, and those readers are specifically afflicted with nostalgia: "It is no accident, of course," she writes, "that as modern readers find themselves more nostalgic for the stateliness and stability Austen's world is said to apotheosize, Austen's class gets higher and higher, and she herself is claimed to be more and more conservative."[7] The critic with whom Johnson's study argues most consistently, Marilyn Butler, has in a new introduction to her 1975 book *Jane Austen and the War of Ideas* made a similar move, criticizing the politically neutral tenor of earlier Austen criticism as examples of anything from "simple nostalgia to a more complex and subtle justification for inactivity."[8] Tellingly, both Johnson and Butler affix the unwanted label to the same critic, Lionel Trilling—Johnson claiming that "nostalgia haunts much of Trilling's writing on Austen"[9] and Butler writing of one of Trilling's essays that "the sentence-rhythms and the nostalgia make it sound a little like Burke's eulogy of Marie Antoinette."[10] Both critics can look back to Sandra Gilbert and Susan Gubar, who complain in *The Madwoman in the Attic*—apropos of Rudyard Kipling's 1924 story "The Janeites"—of the transformation of Austen into "a nostalgic symbol of order, culture, England, in an apocalyptic world where all the old gods have failed or disappeared."[11] More recently we have the work of Roger Sales, who in arguing for a Regency rather than a Victorian Jane Austen attempts to undo the work of nostalgizing begun by her nephew, James Edward Austen-Leigh, in his 1870 memoir of his aunt. Austen-Leigh, Sales reminds us, "nostalgically evokes a world that has been lost"—and thus, one presumes, a world that has never existed.[12]

The overall impression gathered by this profusion of nostalgics and nonnostalgics in Austen criticism is the following: that nostalgia is ideologically conservative, softheaded, most likely patriarchal, certainly ahistorical, and a decidedly inappropriate attitude for a serious reader of Austen, all the more inappropriate because of its prevalence. Most of the finest work on Austen in the last two decades—of which Johnson and Butler surely stand as exemplars—is based on the impulse to refute, refine, and unsettle various nostalgic readings. It is as if Austen is uniquely afflicted by such readers, a phenomenon that has been noted since Henry James, who wrote on the commercialized, popular nostalgia for "their 'dear,' our dear, everybody's dear, Jane," and compared Austen to the Brontë sisters, analyzing them as instances of "a case of popularity (that in especial of the Yorkshire sisters), a beguiled infatuation, a sentimentalized vision."[13] One feels here the pressure of the word "nostalgia," a word that had not yet entered common usage by James's time—and one notices the same impulse in James that would later be manifested in such critics as Johnson and Butler: the urge to remove the nostalgic encrustations upon Austen's image, to read nostalgia as an unfortunate fact of reception history, or of popular consumption, that is finally detachable from the fiction itself.[14]

Yet what if the nostalgia so often associated with Austen — and so productively identified and castigated by recent critics — is part of the effect Austen creates? What if readers learn their nostalgia from her texts? What has gone unnoticed in all the recent discussions and corrections of the nostalgic Austen reader is the nostalgia that inhabits her own narratives, the nostalgia that she inherits from eighteenth-century medical diagnoses and begins to transmute into a modern sentimentality and poignant yearning. Forgetfulness of former traumas and contestations, closings of former fissures, a sense of disconnection from the past: these are not usually considered the best equipment with which to explore older texts, but they are conceptual tools that are provided, I would argue, by Austen herself. The very process of becoming a nostalgic reader, as well as the concomitant blind spots and errors, is dramatized in her novels, and there is no better place to understand why the idea of "nostalgia" clings to Austen than her own technical and thematic choices concerning memory. Nostalgic remembrance begins in Austen, with *Sense and Sensibility*, as the object of representation; by the time of *Persuasion* it has become a principle of representation, so thoroughly embedded in her narrative practice that readers learn, perhaps, their nostalgia from these later texts — the very nostalgia that mobilizes the modern Austen critic. In attempting to understand the nostalgia that remains linked to Austen, however, we must return to the earlier "nostalgia" with which Austen begins.

A Brief History of Homesickness

The fact that the medical origins of nostalgia have been largely forgotten is itself a tribute to the success of nostalgia. Hiding or diluting a traumatic past into one safe for contemplation is the basic work of nostalgizing, which has extended to the very concept itself — insofar as current usage forgets nostalgia's original ties to the body and to death, it remains nostalgic, one might say, about nostalgia. Only recently has the denostalgizing work of studying, and recovering, the origins of "nostalgia" been carried on.[15] The word was still in a comparative infancy by Austen's time; it is not listed in Johnson's *Dictionary* and is never used by Austen herself. As an explanation for this fact — the word's presence in Banks's travel journals and its absence from most literary lexicons — one might offer the foreignness of "nostalgia": a term coined by a foreign physician, and still, by the late eighteenth century, very much a medical diagnosis, foreign to other discourses.

Indeed, "nostalgia" begins as an explanation for the often malignant effects of foreignness and distance. Its history begins in Basel in 1688, when the Swiss physician Johannes Hofer published his "Dissertatio medica de nostalgia."[16] Hofer's coinage—combining the Greek *nostos*, or homecoming, and *algos*, or pain—is essentially a translation of preexisting terms, such as the German *heimweh* and the French *maladie du pays*, which Hofer admits.[17] But Hofer's uniqueness consisted in providing the first extended treatment of the perils of what might be more simply called homesickness. Building around homesickness a set of both psychological and physiological symptoms, a specific etiology, and a series of suggested ameliorations and cures, as well as a taxonomic term from the Greek, Hofer gave the malady a new importance and thus prepared the way for its entrance into serious medical research. Indeed, in the scientific literature devoted to nostalgia throughout the eighteenth century, there is very little deviation from the outlines provided by Hofer's thesis.

What was this disease like? One of the best British accounts is from William Falconer's 1788 tract *A Dissertation on the Influence of the Passions upon Disorders of the Body.* Falconer, educated at Edinburgh and Leyden, was a physician at Bath General Hospital from 1784 to 1819—during which time, of course, Austen lived in Bath, suffering through an enforced separation from her Hampshire home. Borrowing from Hofer and succeeding writers, Falconer drew a standard picture of nostalgia's origin and progress:

> This disorder is said to begin with melancholy, sadness, love of solitude, silence, loss of appetite for both solid and liquid food, prostration of strength, and a hectic fever in the evening; which is frequently accompanied with livid or purple spots upon the body. Sometimes a regular intermittent, and sometimes a continued fever attends this disorder; in the management of which, the greatest care is requisite not to exhaust the strength and spirits by evacuations of any kind. Nausea and vomiting are frequent symptoms, but emetics are of no service . . . when the disorder is violent, nothing avails but returning to their own country, which is so powerful an agent in the cure, that the very preparations for the return prove more effectual than anything else, though the patient be debilitated and unable to bear any other motion than that of a litter.[18]

It was, in essence, a disease of yearning—a yearning for home so intense that the most severe pathological effects ensue. Falconer's general description is echoed throughout the medical literature: general listlessness and melancholy—the dangerous first signs—followed by fever and occasionally hallucinatory visions of home; then gastric distress caused by the body's torpor, issuing in severe gastroenteritis; finally, the body succumbs to its weakness, a more severe fever killing the patient.

This was, evidently, not merely a psychological disorder. Hofer's thesis received further theoretical ballast from associationist theories of the mind, particularly from David Hartley's 1748 *Observations on Man*, which claimed that the brain can be physically altered by the overuse of certain mental pathways. This sort of associationist thinking, with its physiological implications, provided nostalgia's eighteenth-century cartographers with a key methodological tool. In 1821 the First Surgeon of Napoleon's Grande Armée, Baron D. J. Larrey, published his extensive research on nostalgia, garnered from his experience during the French westward retreat. Larrey performed a series of autopsies on patients found to have died of nostalgia, and discovered that the sutures and ridges of the brain were often obliterated, and that brain tissue tended to be inflamed. Using an associationist physiology, Larrey claimed that the increased activity of a mind turned obsessively toward home would cause "a sort of expansion in the substance of the brain, engorgement and torpor of the vessels of this organ, and successively, of the membranes which envelope it, and line its cavities."[19] Although Larrey's interest in brain structure is unusual among most writers on nostalgia, his insistence on the physicality of the disorder is not; nostalgia was a somatic fact, a remembrance that threatened to break apart the fabric of health and the normal pathways of the brain.

Who was prone to this disease? Its usual haunt was the military; the "ecological niche," to use Ian Hacking's precise term, for the disease seems to have been army camps and naval vessels, where mobility of an enforced and newly vast sort was common.[20] But throughout eighteenth-century writing on nostalgia a more general clinical profile appears. The nostalgic patient is likely to have an aversion to social intercourse and a preference for solitary meditation, Hofer states, as well as a vivid imagination; that the usual nostalgic sufferer has an excess of "sensibility" is a theme to which most medical writers recur.[21] In addition to the personal characteristics mapped by physicians, there was a more vivid, and more highly contested, range of national characteristics shared by nostalgics. A fascinating linkage is made, starting with Hofer, between liberty and homesickness: the freer the nation, so the reasoning runs, the greater the danger that its citizens will miss their homes and fall into nostalgia. Hofer drew for his evidence on Swiss nationals living in France, and thereafter Switzerland was taken as the preeminent site of nostalgia.[22] The Helvetian origins of nostalgia could be explained as an instance of climatic factors—Larrey, for instance, states that cold regions inspire nostalgia and adds that French troops in Egypt were remarkably free of it—but were more usually adduced as a critique of illiberal governments. Falconer states that nostalgia "is particularly prevalent among the Swiss, and to a certain degree among all nations, those especially where the government is moderate, free, and happy." With a dramatic flourish, Falconer adds that "this is the only endemic disorder, of which we have any knowledge, that can scarcely be called with justice a national misfortune."[23] For George Seymour, an early-nineteenth-century physician and writer on nostalgia, homesickness was virtually identical to a liberal nationalism: in his *Dissertatio medica inauguralis de nostalgia* Seymour cited Wallace, Hampden, and Nelson as early "nostalgics."[24] There are implications here for a consideration of what might be called colonial consciousness, particularly given the fact that by the time nineteenth-century imperial projects reach fruition this disease, with its liberal and *centered* form (a disease that somatically registered distances from national capitals), has disappeared.

Political reflections on nostalgia are given an unexpected inflection in the work of Thomas Arnold, the foremost British expert on insanity at the end of the eighteenth century. Arnold's compendium of mental disorders, the 1782 *Observations on the Nature, Kinds, Causes, and Prevention of Insanity, Lunacy, or Madness*, contained these reflections on the *habitus* of nostalgia: "This unreasonable fondness for the place of our birth, and for whatever is connected with our native soil, is the offspring of an unpolished state of society, and not uncommonly the inhabitant of dreary and inhospitable climates, where the chief, and almost only blessings, are ignorance and liberty."[25] Nostalgia, Arnold claims, is a rural phenomenon only, insofar as the cosmopolitan mixtures of the city break down former partialities and soften obdurate memories. It is also, and for similar reasons, a disease found among the lower orders, thus leading to the following general clinical profile: nostalgia flourishes where social discourse is limited, whether limited by geographical factors (the mountains of Switzerland, England's water barriers), regional characteristics (the comparative isolation of rural areas), social class (the restricted opportunities for travel among lower orders), or personal preferences (the overimaginative, the solitary, the melancholic personality).[26] Homesickness is a disease, therefore, of failed assimilation — of psyches whose geographical, political, social, or constitutional barriers to frequent encounters with new stimuli create an inability to adapt to change. It might also be called a failure to adjust to an increasingly mobile society, or what Richard Terdiman, writing of the nineteenth century, has called "the inadequacy of available memory mechanisms to the needs of a transformed society"— a "memory crisis."[27]

It was, in short, a disease of transplantation, and it is worthwhile to consider how many of Austen's characters fit the profile, how many are forced to leave their home behind, how many of her heroines endure indefinite or permanent removals from home.[28] The Dashwood family in *Sense and Sensibility* must leave Norland Park, the Dashwood seat for several generations, permanently; Fanny Price in *Mansfield Park* leaves Portsmouth, and her family, for her uncle's distant estate, and when the novel's main action begins she has been gone for nine years; and the Elliot family in *Persuasion* is forced by debt to rent their estate with a seven-year lease and move to Bath. With the notable exception of *Emma*, the decisive actions of Austen's plots occur away from home, on prolonged visits, on travels, or during enforced segregations from what constitutes, at the novel's outset, "home." As we have seen from the eighteenth-century creation of the category of the "nostalgic," in situations of transplantation memory becomes a potential danger. How, these medical texts implicitly ask, is memory to be managed in a situation of vastly increased mobility? How does memory function, or malfunction, when those who have never known foreignness suddenly find themselves sundered from the familiar? The clinical profile established in medical writing defines nostalgia as the mind's resistance to adaptation, its refusal to feel at home in a vaster space, a larger world; at the time of Austen's writing, therefore, sending a person from home was a test of mnemonic control, a psychic gamble.[29] The eighteenth-century nostalgic self is unassimilable; confronted with altered circumstances, it begins to malfunction.

Although Hofer begins the discussion of mobility and memory in 1688, the immediate impetus surrounding the European investigation of homesickness is provided by the flurry of nosologies published in the 1760s. The great age of classification, the middle of the eighteenth century found a place for nostalgia in its taxonomic schemes, first in Francisco Boissier de Sauvages de la Croix's *Nosologia Methodica*, published in 1760. Sauvages placed nostalgia among his list of madnesses, alongside such disorders as melancholy, rabies, nymphomania, and hypochondriasis. The great botanical systematizer, Carl von Linnaeus, followed in 1763 with his *Genera Morborum*, which listed nostalgia next to an even greater list of mental aberrations, including hydrophobia, anxiety, and bulimia.[30] Several other nosologies continued to find a place for nostalgia, including Rudolf Vogel's *Definitiones generum morborum* in 1764, and William Cullen's 1769 *Synopsis nosologiae*, which attempted to combine and reconcile Sauvages, Linnaeus, and Vogel.[31] From here nostalgia entered European history at large. The dislocations of the latter two decades of the eighteenth century — preeminently the French Revolution, the mass emigrations that followed it, and the distant movements of armies increasingly based on conscription — led to a rise in diagnoses of homesickness. Two separate "epidemics" of nostalgia swept French armies, the first occurring among the Army of the Rhine from 1793 to 1794, the second afflicting the Army of the Alps starting in 1799; indeed, Didier Jordeuil, the French deputy minister of war in 1793, issued a command intended to reduce desertion by suspending all convalescent leaves *except* those necessitated by a diagnosis of nostalgia.[32] Even American soldiers fighting for independence in the early 1780s were found to be suffering from the disease.[33]

It is not surprising, therefore, that with this combination of medical interest and mass diagnoses, homesickness increasingly inflects the literary representation of personality. One might adduce the 1774 appearance of Goethe's *Das Leiden des jungen Werthers* and its lavishly nostalgic account of Werther's return to his boyhood home, including the retracing of old walks and a glimpse of Werther's old school.[34] One relevant British example is Samuel Rogers's poem *The Pleasure of Memory*, a virtual anthology of nostalgic attitudes that is first published in 1792 but reprinted throughout the next two decades; shortly thereafter the word "homesickness" makes its first appearance in English, in Coleridge's poem "Home-sick," published in 1800:

> Home-sickness is a wasting pang;
> This I feel hourly more and more:
> There's healing only in thy wings,
> Thou breeze that play'st on Albion's shore![35]

The emphasis here is predictably on the virtue of *return* — on the moral and physical benefits of avoiding nostalgia's grip; concomitantly, of course, there is a dramatization of the obstacles to returning home and the "healing" it might provide.

Certainly by Austen's time, literary culture was well aware of medicalized nostalgia, and prepared to incorporate the various strands of that disease — its nationalistic and liberalizing slant, its elucidation of a backward-turned personality, its interest in personality under conditions of transplantation — in its own projects. Nostalgia, that is, provided writers of the late eighteenth and early nineteenth century with a common narrative — the increasing fact of mobility, the necessity of returns — with which to work; but by the second decade of the nineteenth century this narrative would no longer have cultural authority, and the word "nostalgia" itself began its long, slow shift toward its current semantic range.[36] With the strangeness of overlapping facts that is so common in cultural history, Austen's novels stand out among the early-nineteenth-century welter of homesick representations and present a new possibility: the cancellation of a pathology, and the reconfiguration of the unassimilable self, through a set of what might be understood as modern "nostalgic" practices, a modern "nostalgics."

The Plots of Nostalgia

In 1781 an army physician, Robert Hamilton, was stationed with his regiment at Tinmouth, in the north of England, when a recent recruit began to suffer from a mysterious ailment. The young soldier, named Edwards, seemed fit enough, but as Hamilton later recorded, "a melancholy hung over his countenance, and wanness preyed on his cheeks."[37] Frequently dizzy, complaining of a noise in his ears and a general weakness, the soldier was taken into the regimental hospital. Hamilton at first suspected typhus and set about the usual methods to alleviate it, but to no avail—the recruit's appetite had disappeared, and he slept little, spoke less, and sighed frequently. Eventually Edwards's pulse weakened considerably, and a hectic fever set in. After three months in the hospital Edwards seemed to Hamilton to resemble a patient in the final stages of consumption, with hollow eyes and sunken cheeks. "In short," Hamilton relates, "I looked on him as lost" (216).

But at this point Hamilton received some new information:

> On making my morning visit, and inquiring, as usual, of his rest at the nurse, she happened to mention the strong notions he had got in his head, she said, of home, and of his friends. What he was able to speak was constantly on this topic. This I had never heard of before. The reason she gave for not mentioning it, was, that it appeared to her to be the common ravings of sickness and delirium. He had talked in the same style, less or more, ever since he came into the hospital. (216–217)

Aware of nostalgia and its place in the current nosologies, Hamilton responded immediately to the nurse's story. Upon being asked about his home, the young recruit suddenly begged to be returned there, and confided in Hamilton that he was Welsh. Hamilton promised—tactfully neglecting to mention that it was not in his power—that once he regained some strength, he would be granted six weeks convalescent leave in which to return to Wales. "It seems," Hamilton writes, "he had requested leave to visit his native place soon after he joined; but being only a recruit, and but a few months from thence, he was refused. This had hung on his spirits ever since; and from thence I now dated the origin of his illness" (217). Soon after this offer was made, Edwards's illness began to disappear—an appetite returned, along with some strength, although disturbingly enough for Hamilton, he continued to refer to the promise of a furlough. With some trepidation, Hamilton mentioned the offer to his commanding officers, noting that it had gone some way to curing the patient's nostalgia, and the furlough was luckily granted. Edwards, so it seems, was allowed to return to Wales for a time, and the attack of nostalgia was averted.

It is an isolated instance from the medical journals of the time, but it is an ample portrayal of what might be termed the "older" plot of nostalgia. This cultural narrative ran as follows: an initial displacement from home, whether that home be defined nationally, regionally, or even more locally;

a sudden appearance of morbid signs of melancholy, indeed a feminization of the patient through the familiar markers of "sensibility" (sighing, weakness, longing); and then a rapid physical decline, beginning with the onset of fever. From here the nostalgic plot could only envision two possible outcomes: the restoration of home, or death. It is notable that this restoration must be an actual one — although Edwards improves when his fantasies of a return home are authorized with an official promise, Hamilton does not consider the cure final until the furlough has been granted and the trip made. Either an earlier state of being must be returned to — it cannot be merely imagined — or the patient must be consigned to the fatal effects of nostalgia. It is an axiom of eighteenth-century nostalgia that one *can* go home again, and in fact *must* go home again.[38]

Here it is necessary to introduce a set of buried technical choices concerning memory and narrative form that few readers of Austen have acknowledged, a set that revises the exigency of the nostalgic plotting of Hamilton and replaces it with a series of psychic movements that permit the formation of a depathologized, in fact curative, nostalgia. I would list them schematically as follows: (1) pleasure; (2) temporal rather than spatial orientation; (3) disconnection; (4) naming or categorizing; (5) communal dissemination. What this schema does not quite represent, and what a further investigation will have to illustrate, is the interdependency of these five strategies, which — as I will show — almost never exist in isolation in any given moment from Austen's narratives. The simple binary of eighteenth-century nostalgia, repatriation or death, is dispersed and opened up by Austen's novels through this newer nostalgic system, in which each of the five elements exists both as cause, and effect, of the other four. It is imperative to claim this at the start: that the goal of these five processes is as much a readerly memory as the related memories of characters; what they create, I would suggest, is a nostalgic reader far from the nostalgic patients of the eighteenth century.

The first two processes are visible in one of the more obviously "nostalgic" moments of *Mansfield Park*. William Price, Fanny's naval brother, has returned to England with his ship and has obtained leave to visit Fanny at Mansfield; with their conversation during the first few days of his arrival Fanny is entirely pleased. They discuss everything without reserve — William's plans for promotion, Fanny's adjustment to the ways of the Bertrams, the perfidy of Aunt Norris — and it is William "with whom (perhaps the dearest indulgence of the whole) all the evil and good of their earliest years could be gone over again, and every former united pain and pleasure retraced with the fondest recollection" (*MP*, 234). We catch the authentic accents of modern nostalgia in the phrase "fondest recollection," which might bring to mind Elizabeth Bennet's "philosophy" of remembrance — and which constitutes the first, and perhaps the initial, alteration to the older plot of nostalgia. An evident switch has taken place from memory as productive of trauma or sickness to memory as a source of *pleasure*, as a poignant but harmless dip into reminiscence. Fanny and William are both as sundered from their home, Portsmouth, as any of the recruits or travelers mentioned in Hofer's or Larrey's medical texts, but their memory of this inaccessible home does not become malignant. It does not express itself as a yearning for a return or restoration, but instead as a desire for continued occasions to merely recall their childhood home, as if the iteration of memory (we did this, we saw that) was itself enough to supplant any more dangerous desires. Unlike the case of Hamilton's patient, talking is enough.

The shared recollections of Fanny and William are pleasurable despite the deprivations of the past; we hear of "evil" and "pain," but that is all we hear of potential trauma; the lesson of Austen's nostalgia is that very little psychic material is unavailable to the brighter tints of retrospective "fondness." The key to this alchemy of trauma into nostalgia is, perhaps, the fact that for Austen's readers these Price childhood memories are really no memories at all: they refer to nothing we have seen or heard in the text previously, and they do not attain enough of a level of specificity to disturb the sentence's happy conclusion. What "pain" or "evil" the Prices previously suffered remains persistently—one might say *tactically*—enigmatic. Were any of these memories of pain to burst into explicitness (and it is difficult enough to imagine what they might be, so heavy is the curtain hung over childhood in Austen), the sentence's resolution might seem like bad faith or, at best, irony, but insofar as William and Fanny's memories are so persistently vague, the pleasure they yield does not open itself up to suspicion. What we have is the following alignment: particularity of mnemonic detail equals pain, whereas pleasure follows from a determined inexplicitness.

If uncomfortable memories are deflected for the reader through a strategy of vagueness, they are further deflected for Fanny and William through the second pivotal alteration to the older plot of nostalgia: the substitution of an inaccessible *time* for a still-real place.[39] Return is an issue for eighteenth-century nostalgics precisely because it is at every moment conceptually possible, if not physically possible: Hamilton's patient can see Wales again with the help of some official wrangling; Werther needs merely to pause along a journey to bask for a day in his childhood city; Coleridge's "healing" is only as far away as the next ship leaving from Antwerp or Calais. The "nostalgia" of medicine is fixated on a place that does not lose but instead gains power when distant; the nostalgia of Austen, like our nostalgia, desires a time that has already disappeared—and insofar as this nostalgia knows that it desires that which cannot be regained, its desire does not harden into mental disturbance, and it cannot therefore be captured in the return-or-die conflict. When the first part of the older closural system — restoration — is forbidden, the second, fatal sickness is similarly disabled. What evil or pain the Prices endured thankfully cannot be restored, for it is tied to a completed childhood rather than Portsmouth itself — a fact that Fanny's eventual return to Portsmouth, which we will see is an inversion of the older nostalgic "return," demonstrates.

A tour of the newer nostalgic plot's collision with its predecessor might continue with a return to *Pride and Prejudice* and Elizabeth and Darcy, and with the review of the past in which they were engaged. Darcy answers Elizabeth's "think only of the past as its remembrance gives you pleasure" with a renewed allegiance to a putatively painful form of memory:

> Painful recollections will intrude, which cannot, which ought not to be repelled. I have been a selfish being all my life, in practice, though not in principle. As a child I was taught what was *right*, but I was not taught to correct my temper. I was given good principles, but left to follow them in pride and conceit. Unfortunately an only son, (for many years an only *child*) I was spoilt by my parents, who though good themselves, (my father particularly, all that was benevolent and amiable,) allowed, encouraged, almost taught me to be selfish and overbearing, to care for none beyond my own family circle, to think meanly of all the rest of the world, to *wish* at least to think meanly of their sense and worth compared with my own. Such I was, from eight to eight and twenty; and such I might still have been but for you, dearest, loveliest Elizabeth! (*PP*, 369)

Darcy's penitential return to the past constitutes not a refutation of Elizabeth's "philosophy" of remembrance, however, nor even a correction of it, but its fulfillment and amplification. For if, as we have seen, pleasurable retrospect is tied to the inexplicit, Darcy's avoidance here of particular memories — at the very moment when his remorse might be expected to issue in an apology for a specific action or turn of phrase — is a triumphant act of nostalgic remembrance. It is a modern nostalgia in spite of its manifestly regretful tone, for it is not only vague but crucially *disconnected* from the past it relates; much like Fanny and William's musings on their childhood, but in a different emotional key, Darcy's life-review considers his past as passed

The third alteration of the old nostalgic narrative, then, is the switch from a memory that is still very much constitutive of a patient's identity to one that is crucially obsolete, disconnected, and distant from a now-healthy, depathologized subjectivity. Clearly part of the difference consists in the absence, in Austen, of any explicitly national dimension to this subjectivity. Hamilton's patient is still, and continually, a Welshman; Coleridge is still and forever English, however immersed in German culture and acquaintances he may become. Medical nostalgia assumed a psyche that was not capable of periodizing life narratives, of treating development as discontinuous, and yet was highly amenable to the more static identities of nationality. Darcy is here clearly marking a discontinuity in his own sense of himself, a discontinuity that is produced by the delineation of periods, eras, or epochs. What Darcy was from eight to eight and twenty is an identity to itself, not causally related to what follows, for the very definition of what follows—what might be called the Era of Elizabeth—is a rejection of what had constituted, in Darcy's mind, the previous period: pride, conceit, selfishness, solitude. A modern nostalgic consciousness is made up of such revolutions of mind, in which the old is overthrown, barred from further import, and thereby made safe for remembrance; it should be noted that Darcy is in a position to recall his previous life only when he can consider it over, only when a conceptual line can be drawn between it and the present. The newer nostalgia, that is, idealizes not only what cannot be returned to but what is not of any more consequence—not only a *lost* time (as opposed to a still-real place) but a time that is felt to be causally *unrelated* to the present. However phantasmatic such a belief of Darcy may seem—that pride and conceit will not continue to inflect his behavior—the belief is implicit in Austen's own closural processes, which invite us to imagine a contented marriage founded on a revolution of principle. To refuse such a belief, to doubt that an epoch has been made in Darcy's life, is also to refuse the proffered satisfactions of the novel, so that complicity in Austen's narrative logic involves a complicity in the logic of nostalgia as well. We are asked, that is, to see the past as ended: periodized, disconnected, memorable only in the nostalgic registers of Fanny and William's fond recollections or Darcy's relieved regret.[40]

Darcy's remorse, therefore, is not the contrary of Elizabeth's asserted pleasure in remembrance but its corollary, since the pleasure he takes from remembrance consists in finding his memories, in themselves unpleasant, obsolete. Elizabeth's dictum had claimed that the unpleasant should be forgotten, but Darcy's life-review enables us to see that under the conditions of nostalgia the unpleasant can be remembered pleasurably through the lens of disconnection. Darcy's reappraisal, although newly aware of parental failings, is not, as we might expect, incompatible with nostalgia; the suddenly formed consciousness of his flawed past yields more pleasurable relief than discomfort, insofar as his description of that past is felt to put an end to its lingering effects. It ends not in a murmur of regret but a welcome exclamation of release: "such I might still have been but for you, dearest, loveliest Elizabeth!"

What licenses this pleasure of release is not merely the grammar of self-exculpation—the replacement of active constructions ("I have been") with passive ("I was taught . . . I was given . . . I was spoiled")—but a closural device frequent in Austen, in which the particularized memories of the novel's own past, of therefore our past of reading, yield to a more general and nostalgic reappraisal of a past that *we have not seen*. General, and unassailable: protected from our own memories of Darcy's past within the text, of which we have perhaps formed judgments, we instead listen to vague ruminations on a past that we will never know any better. It is the beginning of a nostalgic readerliness, a method in which our textual recollections in all their specificity (and potential for reawakening, given our ability to literally "turn back the pages of the past") are supplanted at the text's end by a new, rather more mystified past.

It is a mystification all the more nebulous for the self-advertising clarity of the terms under which it is brought forth: "I have been a selfish being all my life," "I was spoilt by my parents." What we have here is the fourth alteration to eighteenth-century nostalgia: a replacement of the ineffable particularity of "home" with a process of *naming, categorizing*, or *judging* that binds memory into familiar narrative patterns.[41] The past is contained in Darcy's phrases; it does not burst into any particularity of detail. What Darcy does, in essence, is to provide himself with a series of explanatory terms ("selfish being," "an only son") that situate his past in an understandable narrative pattern: the spoiled but nonetheless principled child brought into contact with, and humbled by, a wider world. Affixing the proper terms, that is, provides the proper narrative context for the past, and helps deflect any specificities that might open up the past to readings other than those provided by the nostalgic narrator. In a similar fashion to the text's tactical silence regarding Fanny and William's childhood pains, the terms provided by Darcy are far more authoritative than a series of examples; were we to know any instances of Darcy's selfish upbringing, we might be inclined to quarrel with his description of his "benevolent" and "amiable" father, but lacking those instances Darcy's own adjectives cannot be supplanted or revised. By shaping the past through a series of stereotypical terms, Darcy can arrive at the sort of judgment—"we were happier then," "I was a badly taught child"— that the newer nostalgia always produces, a sort of insight that is denied to the eighteenth-century nostalgic patient, who cannot judge the past but can only long for its return. So many of Austen's characters are prone to this sort of nostalgic self-review, one that is implicitly pedagogical: an expropriation of an exemplary pattern from the past, a pattern that is at once *disconnected* from the present (insofar as the current moment of retrospect is its culmination, the sign of the past's irrelevance) and *named* (in order to achieve the proper judgment, in order to prevent excessive specificity). If we take trauma, in Cathy Caruth's description, as not simply the reality of past violence but "the reality of the way that its violence has not been fully known," then the function of general, categorical terms in Austen's life-reviews seems to be trauma's opposite: a knowing of the past that would make particularized remembrance obsolete.[42]

And yet why defuse the particularity of memory? What is the purpose of the wrenching of an older notion of homesickness into a new form—the replacements of traumas with pleasures, places with times, constitutive pasts with disconnected pasts, instances with names? I would suggest that the key lies in the vagueness of nostalgia that seems to be apparent in the workings of the four processes listed earlier—that, and in the very social nature of nostalgic remembrance. Susan Stewart has written of the "social disease of nostalgia," and however interesting is the curious persistence of "disease" in reflections on the subject, what is equally important in Stewart's phrase, and perhaps more perspicuous, is her insistence that nostalgia is *social*.[43] In Austen's texts it is inescapably so; and a tentative explanation of the purpose of the four earlier alterations to eighteenth-century nostalgia might be the following: the dilution of the past in the service of making it available to social groups. The fifth and final aspect of modern nostalgia, then, is in fact the summation of all nostalgic processes: a replacement of stubbornly individual pasts with *communal* pasts.

Eighteenth-century homesickness is often a glitch in the act of assimilation. Grouped into armies, explorers' vessels, or urban centers, the homesick individual fails to merge his or her own identity into a new, larger group identity, because his or her memory remains too clear and too pressing. Hamilton's patient is removed into the hospital where "what he was able to speak" is only on the topic "of home, and of his friends" (216); sequestered and ill, he is no longer a functioning part of his new identity, the army, because a preexisting identity (as a "Welshman") maintains its priority. Thomas Arnold understood nostalgia as a failure specifically in urban assimilation, asserting that homesickness "shuns the populous, wealthy, commercial city, where a free intercourse with the rest of mankind, and especially the daily resort and frequent society of foreigners, render the views and connections more extensive, familiarize distant notions with each other, rub off the partiality of private and confined attachments, and while they diminish the warmth, vastly increase the extent of affection."[44] In Austen the emphasis is much the same—the older homesickness is allied with "private and confined attachments," attachments that the newer nostalgia specifically dissolves; with Arnold in mind, we might even see Austen's plots tending toward the creation of more *cosmopolitan* psyches. Claiming a disconnection from the past, naming and judging it, taking a fond pleasure in it rather than taking it as a fount of distress, the Austenian nostalgic makes the individual past available to others.

It is a process most visibly enacted in *Emma*, where the memory of one private and confined attachment—Harriet's former attraction to Mr. Elton—is transmuted, through a literal act of dispensing with the past, into a diluted memory that can be shared. Rather than permitting the memory of Emma's promotion of the affair to harden into a settled resentment or a remembrance that, by virtue of its being unmentionable, would become all the more present to them, Harriet carries to Hartfield a box of souvenirs. The parcel, labeled "Most precious treasures," contains a piece of court plaster and a fragment of a pencil, both once discarded by Elton—highly effective metonymies of the days of Harriet's interest. Harriet begins by asserting a disconnection from this past: "It seems like madness! I can see nothing at all extraordinary in him now" (*E*, 337). Then she proceeds, while wishing the Eltons well, to state her purpose in visiting Emma: "No, let them be ever so happy together, it will not give me another moment's pang: and to convince you that I have been speaking truth, I am now going to destroy—what I ought to have destroyed long ago—what I ought never to have kept—I know that very well (blushing as she spoke).—However, now I will destroy it all—and it is my particular wish to do it in your presence, that you may see how rational I am grown" (*E*, 337–338). The mere destruction of the souvenirs—called later "relicks" and "remembrances"—is not sufficient, for forgetting is not so much the point as is forgetting in the service of a shareable past. Harriet's emphasis is on the burning of the "relicks" taking place before Emma: "I have nothing more to show you, or to say—except that I am now going to throw them both behind the fire, and I wish you to see me do it" (*E*, 340). Of course, before the souvenirs are destroyed and the memory consigned to the fire, Harriet narrates the ambient incidents surrounding the objects, small moments of furtive, imagined intimacy between her and Elton, to Emma; and Emma is therefore able to revise her own memories of those incidents, so that Harriet's "private and confined attachment" is confined to her no longer. By sharing her previously ineffable and appropriately boxed memories with Emma, Harriet enables their disappearance: the destruction of the souvenirs and the sharing of the memories with Emma is a single act, one that in releasing the remembered material from its individual grip annihilates it, bringing nostalgia into contact with the more drastic excisions of absolute forgetting. Should there be any skepticism regarding Harriet's combined act of forgetting, penance, and sharing, the text does not support it—the novel proceeds to its conclusion without any further resurrection of Harriet's memories of Elton. They are common property between Harriet and Emma, and therefore forgotten: "There it goes," Harriet says, "and there is an end, thank Heaven! of Mr. Elton" (*E*, 340).

In sharing the past, Harriet's narration becomes simply interesting, ironic, piquant; it is neither traumatic nor consequential. The nostalgic processes of disconnection, communality, and naming or judgment—Harriet calls her former infatuation "madness" and "nonsense"—lead to a form of memory capable of making former pain, as Elizabeth Bennet had suggested, pleasurable for a social grouping, even those memories that once threatened those social groupings. Of course what Harriet tells us, just as what Darcy tells of his childhood, we have not seen; what is Austen to do with difficulty that we have seen, that must in some sense be resolved and then nostalgized? Here *Emma* is again instructive. Frank Churchill lets slip, during a walk to Hartfield, that he has news of the doctor Mr. Perry's impending use of a carriage, forgetting for the time that the means through which he has acquired this bit of neighborhood gossip is his secret correspondence with Jane Fairfax. The innocuous slip causes Jane some anxious moments, and the others some seconds of suspicion, which are allayed by Frank's claim to have dreamed the information. A series of worried glances pass between Frank and Jane, which are registered by the ever-observant Mr. Knightley, and a small crisis seems to have just passed. With an economy of detail that presages the modern detective novel, Austen does not let this incident pass away; it becomes instead the object of the novel's happy nostalgic close, a microcosmic example of how we are to regard all of the text's earlier crises. Much later, the liaison between Frank and Jane having been brought to light and fully sanctioned, the chance mention of Mr. Perry's name sparks a communalized memory:

> Frank Churchill caught the name.
> "Perry!" said he to Emma, and trying, as he spoke, to catch Miss Fairfax's eye. "My friend Mr. Perry! What are they saying about Mr. Perry? — Has he been here this morning? — And how does he travel now? — Has he set up his carriage?"
> Emma soon recollected, and understood him; and while she joined in the laugh, it was evident from Jane's countenance that she too was really hearing him, though trying to seem deaf.
> "Such an extraordinary dream of mine!" he cried. "I can never think of it without laughing. — She hears us, she hears us, Miss Woodhouse. I see it in her cheek, her smile, her vain attempt to frown. Look at her. Do not you see that, at this instant, the very passage of her own letter, which sent me the report, is passing under her eye — that the whole blunder is spread before her — that she can attend to nothing else, though pretending to listen to the others?" (*E*, 479–480)

What was anxiety is here comedy, safely transformed into a humorous anecdote that Jane and Emma can both understand — a communality that nicely effaces the original confinement of Frank and Jane's mutual secrecy by, in essence, letting Emma in on the joke. The tone is firmly nostalgic: taking pleasure in the recollection of pain when the pain ceases to tell. What had been the transgression of Frank and Jane, their asocial secrecy and longing, is metamorphosed into *the very binding force* of the novel's completed community. The capacity of this community to remember past secrecies as amusing bumps on the road to full revelation is *Emma*'s justification for the alchemies of nostalgia. That is, the text demonstrates the necessity of nostalgia to the formation of new identities, for nostalgia acts as the force whereby previous confinements are pried apart. "How you can bear such recollections," Jane replies, "is astonishing to me!—They *will* sometimes obtrude—but how you can *court* them!" (*E*, 480) The response to Jane is the nostalgic creed: one courts former pains in order to defuse them, to make them pleasures, and particularly to make them social pleasures. Remembrance in Austen, particularly in her closural scenes, is a communal phenomenon, carried out between couples and groups; Elizabeth Bennet's or Anne Elliot's soliloquizing is replaced by a court of mnemonic appeal. The vague, sometimes poignant, often humorous, occasionally earnest retrospects of Austen's texts are social phenomena, enacted in order to cement new alliances and to erase old contentions. Much like Thomas Arnold's cities, Austen's closural retrospects prefer a wide-ranging, forgiving nostalgia to any sickness for home.

The five qualities of modern nostalgia—pleasure, temporal rather than spatial orientation, disconnection, a naming or patterning in the interests of judgment, and communal dissemination—intertwine and interact, working upon each other to insure that the physical potency and danger of eighteenth-century homesickness ceases to afflict the more mobile modern subject.[45] Austen's novels, as I will argue, are crucially involved in the issue of mobility, and the relation of that mobility to memory. They do not, however, merely receive this modern notion of nostalgia—they are instead central texts in the *foundation* of our category of nostalgia. Read sequentially, Austen's work presents us with an instance of the transformation of home-sickness to nostalgia, which I have just depicted in its more synchronic aspects, that is very much still in evolution during her time: Marianne Dashwood's memories are not shaped like Anne Elliot's, and the passage from one to the other is expressive of the creation of an entirely new memory-category, one so new that the very word "nostalgia" had not yet lost its strictly medical connotations. The idea of the unassimilable self yields, as Austen's career proceeded, to the newly nostalgic self, and Marianne Dashwood's disease and reclamation can be considered the first step in the direction of a nostalgia that is no longer sick for home.

Regulating the Nostalgic

"The family of Dashwood had been long settled in Sussex" (*SS*, 3). From this opening statement of a rooted existence *Sense and Sensibility* plots a rapid decline. The novel begins with a dislocation—the death of Henry Dashwood and the subsequent necessity for his second wife and three daughters to leave their ancestral home; what it plots are the resultant psychological and physiological effects of being displaced.[46] Enforced mobility, of the sort suffered by eighteenth-century nostalgics, is the novel's first premise, and all of the novel's initial coordinates are provided only to be revised, its originary settlements cited only to be unsettled. What the novel presents us with at its outset is a language of *summary*, a series of vague yet settled memories that is far from traumatic: "Their estate was large, and their residence was at Norland Park, in the centre of their property, where, for many generations, they had lived in so respectable a manner, as to engage the general good opinion of their surrounding acquaintance" (*SS*, 3). The voice here is expressive of both consistency ("for many generations") and a comfortable abstraction ("general good opinion"): the past can be abstracted or summarized because it has been so consistent, and its consistency—at least in the narrative voice's formulations—is also a function of the abstraction with which it is evoked. The past here might be called one of *settlement*: not yet the traumatic unsettling of early homesickness, nor yet the disconnected vagueness of later nostalgia. Its settlement is insured by the unbrokenness of its consistency, by the comfortable manner in which certain terms—"respectable," "good opinion"—both have applied and still do apply, at least until the point at which the novel's main action is set in motion; even if we choose to read irony into these phrases, the irony itself is consistent across the previous generations. The narrative, unlike many of Austen's later novels, insists on a centeredness of both place and memory—figured by the centrality of the Dashwood house amid their property—and then proceeds to investigate an exile from this center.

In plainer terms, leaving home ignites *Sense and Sensibility*'s plot, much as it does the older plot of nostalgia, which begins only when the centeredness and consistency of home is forsaken. And much as in the older nostalgic plot, memory swiftly metamorphoses from being a solace to being a problem: how does one remember home when it is not accessible? Even after her family has been demoted from proprietors of Norland Park to lodgers, Mrs. Dashwood dislikes the idea of leaving: "A continuance in a place where every thing reminded her of former delight, was exactly what suited her mind" (*SS*, 8). When the former delight is still very much a present delight—when memory is linked to place, and the place is still visible, tangible—memory can be courted; but the effect of transplantation is to sever these more genial ties between the past, the landscape, and the viewer. Indeed the landscape itself is implicated in the unsettling of a settled past: what was rooted will be literally uprooted by John Dashwood, who discloses a plan to cut down Norland's venerable walnut trees in order to construct a greenhouse. The uprooting of a family is, however, the novel's fundamental act of transplantation, and this emphasis on enforced mobility should be contrasted with a popular view of Austen as a writer of the settled gentry. If, as one prominent critic has asserted, "Jane Austen's characters do not have the option of solving their problems by going some place else," it is because their problem is often the very fact of going some place else: the fact of enforced mobility.[47]

Marianne Dashwood is faced, therefore, with the determining conditions of eighteenth-century homesickness, and she can be considered one of the first representations of the nostalgic-as-female. Her symptoms are familiar: a longing for a still-real "home," a reluctance or inability to surrender past cathexes, a difficulty in adjusting or assimilating to new communities, issuing in a debilitating illness. Her perorations are nothing if not "homesick":

> "Dear, dear Norland!" said Marianne, as she wandered alone before the house, on the last evening of their being there; "when shall I cease to regret you! — when learn to feel a home elsewhere! — Oh! happy house, could you know what I suffer in now viewing you from this spot, from whence perhaps I may view you no more! — And you, ye well-known trees! — but you will continue the same. — No leaf will decay because we are removed, nor any branch become motionless although we can observe you no longer! — No; you will continue the same; unconscious of the pleasure or the regret you occasion, and insensible of any change in those who walk under your shade! — But who will remain to enjoy you?" (SS, 27)

The "sensibility" here can be placed in the context of eighteenth-century nostalgia. Marianne cannot perform the mental functions of the modern nostalgic, even if those newer functions make their presence dimly felt as the possibilities that Marianne denies: she cannot, first, envision transforming her recollections into pleasant ones, being unable to put a period on her "regret"; and second, she cannot imagine a successful transplantation— the word "home" will, as she asserts, keep its current referent with undiminished force. Perhaps most crucially, she cannot envision the conceptual switch from place-memory to time-memory. The source of her memories, the trees of Norland, will "continue the same," making the revisions of modern nostalgia inoperative, and making her longing all the more difficult— the return of eighteenth-century nostalgia is both possible (for the trees will not change) and impossible (for, poor and female, she cannot merely will a return journey), a bind of desire that mirrors the binds of Hamilton's conscripted soldier and Banks's sailors. Her ruminations will remain specific and constitutive of her identity, place-based and sorrowful: the etiology of nostalgic diseases.

Matched to these cultural symptoms is solitude, the primary symptom of an unassimilable selfhood, and Marianne's most famous trait; what passes less noticed is the frequency with which her solitary walks and meditations are constructed around acts of remembrance, or indeed motivated by memory: "When breakfast was over she walked out by herself, and wandered about the village of Allenham, indulging the recollection of past enjoyment and crying over the present reverse for the chief of the morning" (*SS*, 83). Thus Marianne after Willoughby's sudden and inexplicable departure from Barton Cottage; although it is true that Marianne courts memory when alone, it is more precise to say that it is *in order to remember* that she shuns society—her nostalgic retrospects work to divide her from any communities. This is the spectacle of the diseased nostalgic: the spectacle of the personality walled in by memories too particular to be summarized, and therefore too particular to be shared; the spectacle of a personality who presents a vivid exemption from a culture's fantasy of a collectively obsolescent past.

Lest we ascribe this bout of remembrance to lovesickness rather than homesickness, however, and draw a sharp diagnostic line between the two, it is useful to turn to the first diagnosticians of nostalgia. Thomas Arnold explicitly linked the disease to "the inconsolable grief of disappointed love, which gradually consumes the vital flame, preys upon it unceasingly till it be extinguished, and is termed by the English a *broken heart*," thus expanding nostalgia beyond the precincts of home, and defining it instead as a disorder in the system of memory.[48] Both lovesickness and homesickness, in Arnold's thinking, instantiate each other, for both are instantiations of the wider mnemonic malfunction on which nostalgia is based. This broader problem, which I have called the "unassimilable self," does not merely surface upon the Dashwoods' leaving Norland Park, although that leavetaking its its first cause; it is elicited several times by the narrative, which continually duplicates the opening trauma of transplantation. Having found it difficult to leave Norland, Marianne will find it difficult to leave any place where she has established herself for any period of time and accumulated any mnemonic capital. Even though London is the scene of her most catastrophic disappointments, the place where Willoughby refuses to see her and refuses to remember their unstated vows, she is unable to leave without a familiar regret: "Marianne, few as had been her hours of comfort in London, and eager as she had long been to quit it, could not, when it came to the point, bid adieu to the house in which she had for the last time enjoyed those hopes, and that confidence, in Willoughby, which were now extinguished for ever, without great pain" (*SS*, 301). The recalcitrance is not shared: "Elinor's satisfaction at the moment of removal, was more positive" (*SS*, 302). Later still, removing the convalescent Marianne from Cleveland back to Barton is another occasion for worry; Elinor must keep a watch to insure that Marianne's "bodily ease" and "calmness of spirits" (*SS*, 341) remain intact. The older nostalgic plot, therefore, is not merely the larger outline of *Sense and Sensibility*, but also a crucial component of its smaller movements, in which the issue of transplantation binds much of the novel's concerns.

The inability to construct modern nostalgic forms of remembrance, the concentration on asocial memories, the anxiety that attends any mobility: these causes coalesce in Marianne's illness, which is not merely allied to a problematic memory, or a simple intensification of it, but is the expected result of such an unassimilable selfhood, a consequence that follows as inevitably as any of the homesicknesses in eighteenth-century medicine. Fond of taking walks through Cleveland's wooded lawn, particularly in those places "where the trees were the oldest" (*SS*, 306) and in which Willoughby's future estate could be seen — walks of solitary memory, of "precious, invaluable misery" (*SS*, 303) — Marianne catches her disease. Its contours are familiar: a general weakness, a consequent fever and delirium, and the patient's inability to focus on topics aside from home.[49] The illness postpones Marianne and Elinor's return to Barton Cottage, and "the idea of what to-morrow would have produced, but for this unlucky illness, made every ailment more severe; for on that day they were to have begun their journey home; and, attended the whole way by a servant of Mrs. Jennings, were to have taken their mother by surprise on the following forenoon. The little that she said, was all in lamentation of this inevitable delay" (*SS*, 308). In her delirium, Marianne asks for her mother, and worries that she will "go round by London" (*SS*, 311) in her path from Barton to Cleveland, a geographic perversity that suggests that Marianne's memory is retracing itself, from Cleveland back to London and then back to Barton: a series of homecomings, of which a return to Norland Park might stand as the final term. Thus the older plot of nostalgia reaches its climax and its crisis-point — and there Austen halts its progress. Marianne will not simply go home and recover; the plot of "return" will not be carried through. An entirely unexpected revision is about to take place, one rooted in the complete reconstruction of the "unassimilable self" into something much closer to the modern nostalgia I have already sketched.

If any generalization can be made about selfhood in the novel, it is how thoroughly inflexible it seems to be, how averse to either changes in locale or revisions of memory, and how highly this inflexibility is esteemed. Of Sir John Middleton and his wife, newly established in London, we are told that "Elinor found, when the evening was over, that disposition is not materially altered by a change of abode" (*SS*, 170) — a lesson most contrary to the operations of modern nostalgia, which bases itself on the disconnections and periodizations of personality shaped by changes of abode and changes of time. Colonel Brandon's felt superiority to Willoughby springs from the opposite principle, that time has made "his character and principles fixed" (*SS*, 338) rather than revisable, that the ideal personality is not open to alteration and certainly not open to forgetting. As for Willoughby, his sudden revisions can only be construed as signs of a morally bankrupt sense of self; Elinor states that "suspicion of something unpleasant is the inevitable consequence of such an alteration as we have just witnessed in him" (*SS*, 79). The proper self, both in society and outside it, does not dislocate itself from the past, and bears instead the traces of an unbroken continuity, the sort of settlement that is described in the novel's opening pages. An abiding or even determining relation to the past is not a sign of trauma but of moral health: Brandon's tenacious memory of the two Elizas, related in a flashback that in its detail and length is almost unique in Austen's novels, is not damaging to his personality but instead taken as a sign of that most prized of traits, consistency. Even Willoughby manages to gain much of his regard through this strategy of inflexibility, particularly when he asks Mrs. Dashwood to avoid any "alteration": "Tell me that not only your house will remain the same, but that I shall ever find you and yours as unchanged as your dwelling; and that you will always consider me with the kindness which has made every thing belonging to you so dear to me" (*SS*, 74). Selfhood, that is, is not yet considered in a *therapeutic* frame, in which consistency becomes fixation and continuity becomes a failure to assimilate or adapt. The self, at the novel's outset, still bears a solely ethical relation to the past, in which a settled remembrance matches settled behavior, and in which forgetting is a lapse of conduct.

Central to this inflexibility of the self is a conception of memory as unrevisable. One of Marianne's most disabling difficulties, in the wake of Willoughby's disappearance and disavowal of her, is her inability to forget the regard he had felt for her — or her inability to reconstruct her memories of that former courtship into a series of memories about a pretended regard:

> He *did* feel the same, Elinor — for weeks and weeks he felt it. I know he did. Whatever may have changed him now, (and nothing but the blackest art employed against me can have done it,) I was once as dear to him as my own soul could wish. This lock of hair, which now he can so readily give up, was begged of me with the most earnest supplication. Had you seen his look, his manner, had you heard his voice at that moment! Have you forgot the last evening of our being together at Barton? The morning that we parted too! When he told me that it might be many weeks before we meet again — his distress — can I ever forget his distress! (*SS*, 188–189)

Convinced that memory is a relation to truth — to what actually happened — Marianne finds it impossible to name her memories of Willougby as "perfidy," as "heartless flirtation," or as any other term that might allow her to relinquish this particular cathexis. This memory is not named; nor is it pleasurable; nor is it communal. All Elinor can share in Marianne's painful retrospect is a fruitless wish ("Had you seen his look . . . !"). Most of all, it is not disconnected—Marianne's own syntax betrays the very present-ness of the scene she relates, as "he told me that it might be many weeks before we *met* [or, *could meet*] again" is bent into the curiously mixed tenses of "he told me that it might be many weeks before we meet again," as if that promised meeting were still impending. Pivotal to this unnostalgic re-membrance is the insistence that Willoughby *as he was experienced* is Willoughby *as he was*, that no interpretive machinery can be brought to bear on these memories of his distress; the sense is that any interpretive ac-tivity, insofar as it is "interpretive," is a falsification, that the memory as it exists encodes the only possible truth. If Willoughby seemed in love, he was, and is still. Only the most mysterious of forces, the "blackest art," can explain the change. The opposite possibility is expressed by the more elas-tic Mrs. Dashwood, who proclaims that there "was always a something,— if you remember,—in Willoughby's eyes at times, which I did not like" (*SS*, 338). This memory, openly revising the past and asking for a confirmation of that revision, is precisely what Marianne cannot yet accomplish.

Parallel to this inflexible mode of memory are the various objects that persist throughout the novel: a lock of hair, a piano, drawings, the sheet music of an opera bearing Marianne's name in Willoughby's handwriting. The objects cannot receive new mnemonic frames; although the circum-stances surrounding them may change — they may be moved to new houses, the relationships that created them may have ceased — they continue to bear their original traces and keep their original impacts. Gazing at the tell-tale opera, Marianne can only hide it. Producing the evidentiary lock of hair, Marianne feels that it can only tell one story: the story of Wil-loughby's undoubted former regard. These are not what I will later define as "souvenirs"; they are loci of memory that retain everything of the scene of their birth.

What, then, happens when this inflexible style of psyche — the unas-similable self, the eighteenth-century nostalgic — meets with a real trauma? What happens when the consistency of memory leads to a nearly fatal ill-ness? The answer is a conceptual shift as dramatic, and as painful, as any in Austen's fiction: the shift away from this "unassimilable" model to a pro-totype of the modern nostalgic. The shock of Marianne's illness permits the older model of selfhood to pass away because it permits treating the older model *therapeutically*; suddenly what had been taken as ethically com-mendable, an unbroken relation to the past, can be approached as a disease. At the very moment when nostalgia as a disease enters the text most vividly, when it blossoms into a full set of pathological symptoms, a new nostalgia is brought to bear as its cure, as the only proper method of treatment.[50] And Elinor—who had earlier been the foremost exponent of the unassimilable self—metamorphoses into the analyst whose duty it is to create, and inculcate, a personality that is able to absorb change and assimilate new wholes. *Sense and Sensibility* begins as a leavetaking of home, and concludes as a complete course of treatment of the complications arising out of that leavetaking.

That treatment is, primarily, narratological: it focuses on how Marianne will relate her past, and it attempts to shortcircuit the style of narration exemplified in her speech to Elinor refusing to "forget" Willoughby's "distress." The first therapeutic criterion is *regularity*. Having broken the news of Edward Ferrars's secret engagement to Marianne, Elinor is disturbed in the course of her neat narration: "Marianne's feelings had then broken in, and put an end to all regularity of detail" (*SS*, 262). The retelling of the past must, that is, be *regulated*—evenly paced, told in generalities, without any disruptive regressions into extreme particularity. Another useful narratological term provided by the text, and crucially bound up with the notion of remembered stories, is *concision*; Colonel Brandon, while clearly unsettled by his relation of the story of the Elizas, is explicitly aiming at such a goal: "Ah! Miss Dashwood—a subject such as this—untouched for fourteen years—it is dangerous to handle it at all! I *will* be more collected—more concise" (*SS*, 208). Both concision and regularity act in the manner of the novel's opening sentences, as summaries, as careful dilutions of a complex past into something manageable, something "collected." An ethic of narratological health governs the text's moments of remembrance, and it is explicitly—through Marianne's illness—linked to physical health. The regulation of retrospective narratives helps them become disconnected, named and judged, and finally communalized; with the proper regulation, a traumatic narrative becomes something like a nostalgic narrative.

Such is the goal, at any rate, of Marianne's therapy. How does the process of transforming Marianne from an eighteenth-century nostalgic into a more or less modern nostalgic begin? Upon her return to Barton Cottage—a return that calls to mind the repatriations of eighteenth-century sufferers—a radically new therapy begins, with acts of physical self-censorship:

> After dinner she would try her piano-forté. She went to it; but the music on which her eye first rested was an opera, procured for her by Willoughby, containing some of their favourite duets, and bearing on its outward leaf her own name in his hand writing.—That would not do.—She shook her head, put the music aside, and after running over the keys for a minute complained of feebleness in her fingers, and

closed the instrument again; declaring however with firmness as she did so, that she should in future practice much. (*SS*, 342)

The persistent object is moved aside, the memory rejected; in its stead is a promise for future conduct, and future work.[51] Memorabilia must be hidden, no longer courted, and the narratological concision and regulation espoused by Elinor and Brandon becomes a syntactical concision, as Marianne's sentences become clipped, almost remedial: "I know we shall be happy. I know the summer will pass happily away. I mean never to be later in rising than six, and from that time till dinner I shall divide every moment between music and reading. I have formed my plan, and am determined to enter on a serious course of study" (*SS*, 343). The past is so thoroughly, almost violently, disconnected from the present that even the past tense becomes illicit, suspicious. Clearly, of the five processes that shift "homesickness" into a newer nostalgia, disconnection is the first step in Marianne's progress. Lest we think that we are importing an anachronistic narrative of therapy into Austen's text, we have the text's own foreshadowings of that very narrative to assuage us: we have Elinor's cautious observing eye and correcting hints; we have Marianne's backslidings and adjustments, for "though a sigh sometimes escaped her, it never passed away without the atonement of a smile" (*SS*, 342); we have the medical language of Marianne's "happy symptoms" (*SS*, 343); and we have a similar mixture of chastening and education, of pointing out the patient's errors and desiring the patient's remorse for those errors.[52] Marianne's most pervasive error, evidently, has been to keep a tenacious hold on a still-vivid past, her past courtship with Willoughby; and the goal of her therapy is to induce a self-motivated confession of that past's obsolescence.

The confession must be public — it must assert the newly discovered communality of the past — and it must reassert the pastness of the past; it must speak only in the frame of the present moment. Encountering with Elinor the scene of her first meeting with Willoughby, the spot of her fall and rescue, Marianne begins to speak as a modern nostalgic:

> "I am thankful to find that I can look with so little pain on the spot! — shall we ever talk on that subject, Elinor?" — hesitatingly it was said. — "Or will it be wrong? — I *can* talk of it now, I hope, as I ought to do." —
> Elinor tenderly invited her to be open.
> "As for regret," said Marianne, "I have done with that, as far as *he* is concerned. I do not mean to talk to you of what my feelings have been for him, but what they are *now*." (*SS*, 344)

The double valence of Marianne's "ought" — as both that which she *must* do (she "ought" to speak of the past) and that which she must do *correctly* (she should speak as she "ought" to) — catches her in the bind of the con-valescent nostalgic, compelled to retell the past only if the past is retold in the right manner. The right manner begins with an assertion of disconnec-tion — "what they are *now*" — and proceeds to attach names to the past, names that Marianne's previous memories kept at bay through their insis-tent particularity. Now, having relinquished that vividness, she judges her conduct as "a series of imprudence," a "want of kindness to others," and a "want of fortitude" (*SS*, 345). Her memories are condensed into a nicely summarized form: "Whenever I looked towards the past, I saw some duty neglected, or some failing indulged" (*SS*, 346). And as a pledge of her newly won status of health, Marianne adds: "The future must be my proof" (*SS*, 347). A forward-looking psyche, determinedly refusing to look backward now that the past has been safely summarized, has supplanted the eighteenth-century nostalgic; the past exists now only to provide a se-ries of educative examples for the future.

The process is not limited to Marianne alone; Elinor's retellings of Willoughby's penitential visit to Cleveland offer further examples of the regulations and dilutions of modern nostalgia.[53] To Marianne, Elinor "re-lated simply and honestly the chief points on which Willoughby grounded his apology" (*SS*, 347), translating his language, summarizing his position, and avoiding unnecessary detail, as if presenting an abstract of a longer and somewhat diffuse work; Elinor "softened only his protestations of present regard" (*SS*, 347), since those protestations maintain a continuity between past and present, a continuity that must be broken for Marianne to be cured of her eighteenth-century nostalgia. Present applicability or conse-quence is surgically removed from the available corpus of Willoughby's apology. Before Mrs. Dashwood, Elinor's narration is even further cur-tailed; she decides to "declare only the simple truth, and lay open such facts as were really due to his character, without any embellishment of tender-ness to lead the fancy astray" (*SS*, 349). The business of Elinor's narrations is handled with much ado by Austen, although the narrations themselves are not cited, as if we too are nostalgic patients, unable to hear again what we have already heard of Willoughby, unable to withstand another intru-sion of this most problematic memory into the text; instead, Elinor's *nar-rative choices* are presented with much detail, and along with Elinor we be-come theorists of retrospect, deciding with her which aspects of the past can survive a new nostalgic regime and which cannot. Elinor's choices rep-resent a miniaturized version of the therapy Marianne has just undergone, and they condense the attitude toward the past that *Sense and Sensibility* eventually settles on: a disconnected, communal, moralized, and summa-rized vagueness for a lost time.

Yet what of the missing term, Elizabeth Bennet's "pleasure" in re-membrance? Why do Marianne's flat phrases of disavowal and planning seem still very far from a modern nostalgia? Perhaps a clue can be found in one of Marianne's final pronouncements: "As for Willoughby — to say that I shall soon or that I shall ever forget him, would be idle. His remembrance can be overcome by no change of circumstances or opinions. But it shall be regulated, it shall be checked by religion, by reason, by constant employment" (*SS*, 347). In choosing to focus a novel on a nostalgic character, Austen has exposed, perhaps uncomfortably, the suffering of eighteenth-century nostalgia and the *askesis* of modern nostalgia; we are permitted to see the separations, censorings, and interdictions of this newer form of remembrance growing out of an old trauma. By seeing too much of the process of nostalgia in construction, the final product seems marred by effort. If nostalgia is to truly have the aura of the "nostalgic," it must be effortless, spontaneous; the act of cutting off the past from the present in order to celebrate its disconnection — the act of finding in past pains the "fond recollection" of Fanny and William Price — must be immediate, or else the relinquished past maintains a shadow presence. In Marianne's frank assessment, only strenuous and constantly renewed efforts at self-control prevent a regression into a deeply troubled retrospect, and in the face of all this foretold mental labor very little pleasure can be detected. By being privy to so much of both the tactical amputations of nostalgic therapy and their larger strategic justifications, we are barred ourselves from becoming nostalgic readers; the disturbing impact of Willoughby remains, if only because so much discussion and textual cogitation has gone into eliminating his presence. The eighteenth-century nostalgic — the lineage of Banks, Hamilton, Arnold, Goethe, and others — disappears from Austen's fiction, and so does the work that went into effecting that disappearance. What we will increasingly find in Austen's novels is nostalgia presented as a finished product, a nostalgia that is no longer the topic of representation but the very technique of representation, a nostalgia masked for us by its very prevalence and familiarity.

The Harmonies of Distance

Pausing to inspect a row of shrubbery, *Mansfield Park*'s Fanny Price is moved to uncharacteristic volubility:

> "If any one faculty of our nature may be called *more* wonderful than the rest, I do think it is memory. There seems something more speakingly incomprehensible in the powers, the failures, the inequalities of memory, than in any other of our intelligences. The memory is sometimes so retentive, so serviceable, so obedient — at others, so bewildered and so weak — and at others again, so tyrannic, so beyond con-

troul!—We are to be sure a miracle every way—but our powers of recollecting and of forgetting, do seem peculiarly past finding out." (*MP*, 208–209)

To this outburst Fanny's interlocutor, Mary Crawford, says nothing—it seems she has not heard. Fanny's speech is not merely, however, a foil to Mary's worldliness and lack of reverence; what she expresses is a key to the novel's conversion of "memory," that vast category, into something more narrowly conceivable as a modern nostalgia. To understand what Fanny might be doing with memory, it is necessary to look not after her speech—to Mary's bored inattention, to the moment's satiric purpose as a device of contrast—but to the observations that lead Fanny to memory, to the moment's conceptual purpose.

Fanny begins with a meditation on use and obsolescence:

> "This is pretty—very pretty," said Fanny, looking around her as they were thus sitting together one day: "Every time I come into this shrubbery I am more struck with its growth and beauty. Three years ago, this was nothing but a rough hedgerow along the upper side of the field, never thought of as any thing, or capable of becoming any thing; and now it is converted into a walk, and it would be difficult to say whether most valuable as a convenience or an ornament; and perhaps in another three years we may be forgetting—almost forgetting what it was before. How wonderful, how very wonderful the operations of time, and the changes of the human mind!" (*MP*, 208)

Fanny's vision is of a succession of object-incarnations, a passage from one life to another for objects, a passage that almost but not quite manages to efface the previous incarnation. The change from one state to another is motivated by an increasing utility: the original hedgerow, "never thought of as any thing," is "converted" into a walk whose use is the occasion of Fanny's remarks. The alterations undergone by this row of shrubbery are, importantly, not finite, as Fanny can envision a time when the convenience of the walk may become the increased convenience of some other incarnation. What Fanny produces here is, of course, a disguised autobiography, a version of her own progress from inconsequence to useful ornamentality. What she also describes is the novel's imagination of memory, as a power that records the journey of objects (or of people) into increasing utility and beauty, and that thus records the past as the unhappy prologue to the clearer present. Thus it is that Fanny's speech is peppered with curtailings of the scope of memory, with its "failures" and "inequalities" and weaknesses, with its "almost forgetting"—because in *Mansfield Park* the power of memory lies in its ability to selectively eliminate the past, to refine it into the vision of progress that governs Fanny's account of the parsonage shrubbery.

How does a past potentially riven with loss and alteration become a narrative of discrete, increasingly beneficial incarnations? How does a memory cope with such sweeping change? Precisely by becoming an "almost forgetting"—a nostalgia that sees the past as a growth into the present's more complete perfection. *Mansfield Park*, after all, begins with the most traumatic of all the dislocations that inaugurate Austen's novels, Fanny's move to the frighteningly unfamiliar precincts of Mansfield; it is a testament to the effectiveness of the novel's deployed nostalgia that that originary homelessness is transmuted into a narrative about Fanny's growth into use and beauty. One of the novel's fundamental processes is, then, a pairing of an "obedient" and "retentive" memory with a "bewildered" and "weak" one, coalescing into a form of remembrance that obediently retains only a story of beneficial alterations. The novel will present us with modern nostalgia in its severest form: rather than pining for a lost home, Fanny will learn to embrace an entirely new home—thus disabling the eighteenth-century plot of nostalgia—and, furthermore, will learn to efface even the imperfections of that new home through a highly selective nostalgizing retrospect.

Where we can see this modern nostalgia clearest is in the new category of objects introduced by *Mansfield Park* into Austen's fiction: the souvenir. Of all Austen's novels, perhaps, *Mansfield Park* is the most riddled with objects that persist through time, and any reader of the novel can recall at least a few of these famous nodes of energy, such as William Price's cross, Edmund's simple chain, or "little Mary's" knife bequeathed to Fanny's sister Susan. Although not all of the text's objects are unequivocal souvenirs, few of them function in the manner of Willoughby's song-books carefully avoided by Marianne; few of them retain unaltered the feelings of the past. They are more commonly indices of the past's disconnection from the present, tangible condensations of what can still be safely remembered and tangible dilutions of what can no longer be remembered. The souvenir periodizes the past, proclaiming that its experience is over, that its past is recoverable only by the ritualistic retrospects called forth by contemplating it. No traumas are evoked by the souvenir, no fresh recollections spurred by its presence; its comfortable persistence changes the unpredictability of reminiscence into the habitual observations of nostalgia.

In its purest form, the souvenir produces distance; it is the dead end of the past. "We do not need or desire souvenirs of events that are repeatable," Susan Stewart has written. "Rather we need and desire souvenirs of events that are reportable, events whose materiality has escaped us, events that thereby exist only through the invention of narrative."[54] To carry Stewart's logic one step further, it might be said that we need and desire souvenirs *in order to* place the past beyond us, *in order to* make the past not repeatable. Such, at least, is the logic of *Mansfield Park*'s objects. As Stewart illustrates in her study of longing, the souvenir does not maintain an unbroken link to the past it encapsulates; its referent is not precisely the past but the gap that separates us from the past. It is therefore, as Stewart admits, the perfect vehicle for the nostalgic. "The nostalgic is enamored of distance," she writes, "not of the referent itself."[55] That word, "distance," will echo across the novel's pages, and one of *Mansfield Park*'s secrets is that the physical distance of eighteenth-century nostalgia becomes the temporal, and irremediable, distance of modern nostalgia. Fanny, like any modern nostalgic, is enamored of souvenirs because she is enamored of distance; to place the past out of reach is her goal, and one of the surest paths to that goal is to place the past within easy reach, as a series of souvenirs.

Not all souvenirs, perhaps, are preferable in the novel's ethical balance sheet, but all do in some fashion represent the past's cancellation. As Mansfield's inhabitants tour Sotherton, they encounter the "family portraits, no longer any thing to any body but Mrs. Rushworth, who had been at great pains to learn all that the housekeeper could teach, and was now almost equally well qualified to shew the house" (*MP*, 85). Percipient as she is in depicting — and, we cannot help but feel, lamenting — the decline of the past into an amateurish antiquarianism, Austen is as deft in describing the nostalgia-effect such souvenirs of the past create. Fanny is entranced by Mrs. Rushworth's stories; she "attended with unaffected earnestness to all that Mrs. Rushworth could relate of the family in former times, its rise and grandeur, regal visits and loyal efforts, delighted to connect any thing with history already known, or warm her imagination with scenes of the past" (*MP*, 85). Fanny's pleasure is not a contrast to the disconnected nostalgia of Mrs. Rushworth, who relies on her housekeeper for facts about the family history; it is its natural complement. One might note that Fanny's pleasure is elicited not by the Sotherton housekeeper, whose oral histories might be a link back to an older mnemonic culture, but by the redactions of Mrs. Rushworth. Simply because the Sotherton past is so comically separate from its prosaic present, Fanny's imagination can come into play. Her pleasure would be negated by a Sotherton as august as its past is reputed to be, but before these disconnected souvenirs, Fanny is as distant from the Rushworth past as her tour guide, and her delight is therefore the more unfettered. The touristic meditations of Fanny are licensed by the historical amnesias of Sotherton's owners, and however much satire we might find in the Sotherton paintings, a nostalgic pleasure is yielded by them.

Those objects that are not so well sundered from their origins are more dangerous. The elaborate gold chain given to Fanny by Mary — a not-so-veiled gift from Henry Crawford — is, as Mary claims, a "family remembrancer," and to Fanny falls "the duty of remembering the original giver" (*MP*, 259). It is all the more a source of anxiety, then, since it is felt to compel a certain remembrance; it is not a souvenir, and Fanny cannot easily keep it. Objects from the disastrous theatrical remain about the house once Sir Thomas has arrived to halt the début, but as these are not souvenirs — an unacceptable taint of Mr. Yates and Mrs. Inchbald still covers them — they can only be collected and expelled. Sir Thomas "meant to try to lose the disagreeable impression, and forget how much he had been forgotten himself as soon as he could, after the house had been cleared of every object enforcing the remembrance, and restored to its proper state" (*MP*, 187). In expelling Mr. Yates, Sir Thomas hopes, we are told, "to be rid of the worst object connected with the scheme, and the last that must be inevitably reminding him of its existence" (*MP*, 194–195).[56] "Enforcing the remembrance," "inevitably reminding": these are not the offices of the souvenir. Much like Willoughby's song-books, these objects have not lost their almost totemic power, and so all the text can do with them is remove them. Like the therapy facing a recovering homesick patient, Sir Thomas's clearances turn the past into a potential threat — why clear the house of such objects if there is no threat of a return to the past? For the past to be a truly nostalgic past — poignant, wistful, vague — the souvenir is needed. The inset parable of "little sister Mary" and her knife is instructive. The knife, bequeathed to Susan Price, is taken instead by the younger daughter Betsey, on whom Mrs. Price dotes; Fanny is shocked by this disregard of her dead sister's wishes, having just been musing on Mary and her amiability. Forgetfulness of sister Mary's will is not possible, and Fanny applies the only possible remedy, buying Betsey a newer knife to replace the relic. The lesson of this most nonnostalgic of objects, an object of vexed provenance, undiminished emotional power, and deep regret, is simple: the past cuts.

The souvenir, productive of so much nostalgic distance, is instead a solace. Having been nearly bullied into performing in the theatricals, and rebuked for her persistent abstention, Fanny retreats to the "East room," her own theater of the past, full of her collections and mementos.

> She could go there after any thing unpleasant below, and find immediate consolation in some pursuit, or some train of thought at hand. — Her plants, her books — of which she had been a collector, from the first hour of her commanding a shilling — her writing desk, and her works of charity and ingenuity, were all within her reach; — or if indisposed for employment, if nothing but musing would do, she could scarcely see an object in that room which had not an interesting remembrance connected with it. (*MP*, 151–152)

Here are kept old drawings of Maria and Julia Bertram's, a sketch of William Price made in the Mediterranean, workboxes given her by family members: a short lifetime's worth of "memorials," all stored with assiduous care. The history encoded by these souvenirs is not one of loss; it is one of loss ameliorated and overcome:

> Every thing was a friend, or bore her thoughts to a friend; and though there had been sometimes much of suffering to her—though her motives had been often misunderstood, her feelings disregarded, and her comprehension under-valued; though she had known the pains of tyranny, of ridicule, and neglect, yet almost every recurrence of either had led to something consolatory; her aunt Bertram had spoken for her, or Miss Lee had been encouraging, or what was yet more frequent or more dear—Edmund had been her champion and her friend;—he had supported her cause, or explained her meaning, he had told her not to cry, or had given her some proof of affection which made her tears delightful—and the whole was now so blended together, so harmonized by distance, that every former affliction had its charm. (*MP*, 152)

The "East room" objects do not tell a detailed narrative. Like any nostalgic retrospect, the past is "blended" and "harmonized by distance" into a sealed "whole," a completed period whose particular pains and disappointments are united into something more pleasant than distressing. We are offered a catalogue of what Fanny might choose to remember—from "tyranny" to "neglect"—so that the cancellations performed by the "East room" souvenirs might seem more striking by contrast. The specifically nostalgic function of disconnection carried out by the room's objects is mirrored by their context-free juxtapositions: three souvenir transparencies fill the lower panes of one window, "where Tintern Abbey held its station between a cave in Italy, and a moonlight lake in Cumberland" (*MP*, 152). Furthermore, these souvenirs are literally contained, held in one room, not permitted to spill over into the house at large—like souvenirs in a drawer, they exist to be consulted occasionally, but not to interfere with work or plans made elsewhere, not to become, that is, living objects again. What Fanny celebrates here, what these souvenirs provide her with, is not past events but the conclusion of those events. She is enjoying, in the company of the Bertram sisters' childhood accomplishments and old gifts, the spectacle of the past's condensation and conclusion. Threatened with a resurrection of old tyrannies, specifically Aunt Norris's reminder that Fanny is not in a social position to refuse to act in the theatricals, Fanny has at least the "East room" and its souvenirs, where all the old tyrannies are over.

Pruning and cutting back her retrospects, then, permitting the flowering of only the most vague and contented memories, Fanny embodies the modern nostalgic despite the fact that her situation is characteristic of the eighteenth-century nostalgic. *Mansfield Park* is, after all, a narrative of homelessness, a novel that begins with enforced mobility; we hear of Fanny's "transplantation to Mansfield" (*MP*, 276), but suddenly, in the midst of Austen's career, the idea of transplantation becomes analogous to the idea of a cure. In a complete reversal of the older plot of nostalgia, movement is equated with health. Mrs. Grant tells Mary Crawford that "Mansfield shall cure you both" (*MP*, 47), while Fanny, dismayed by Henry Crawford's sudden affection for her, decides that "London would soon bring its cure" (*MP*, 324). What are these offered cures but the cure of *being somewhere else*? The transparencies of Tintern Abbey and Italy in the "East room" speak to this same characteristic of the novel: the mobile psyche, able to travel away from its past as well as away from its physical "home," is far sturdier than the unassimilable self of the eighteenth-century nostalgic plot.[57] The "cure" that Mary Crawford's move to Mansfield or Henry Crawford's move to London will bring is, in each case, forgetfulness—a forgetfulness, respectively, of a cynical upbringing and of Fanny; the following equation is therefore set up: movement equals cures equals forgetting. This firm linkage welds together what eighteenth-century medicine had thought irreconcilable, for nowhere in the case studies and tracts of the decades of Austen's youth was travel thought of as curative, and nowhere in those narratives was travel thought of as conducive to forgetfulness. For Fanny, the reader of Lord Macartney's Chinese travel journals, movement is a curative reality, and distance from the past, from its traumas as well as from its physical places, is to be prized.

Stressing Fanny's strategic forgetfulness admittedly flies in the face of her role as a guardian of traditions, both personal and cultural. It is Fanny who elegizes the doomed avenue of trees at Sotherton, and who is dismayed at Mary Crawford's wittily sarcastic account of the generations of bored worshipers in the now-defunct Sotherton chapel; it is Fanny who, as Edmund Bertram reminds us, is surrounded by many "holds upon things animate and inanimate, which so many years growth have confirmed, and which are considerably tightened for the moment by the very idea of separation" (*MP*, 348). This would seem to invalidate Fanny's status as a nostalgic who bars the past from further import; it would seem to make Fanny a muted version of Marianne Dashwood, less violently but all the more firmly rooted in the world of memory. What this conception of Fanny elides, however, is the content of her remembrances. Fanny may be the carrier of memory in the novel, more attuned to pastness than her companions, but the pastness that she cherishes is precisely a nostalgic one: disconnected, vague, phantasmatic, unalterably pleasant. Edmund, for his part, admits that Mary's debunking of Sotherton's former religious habits is accurate, conceding that "human nature cannot say it was not so" (*MP*, 87), but accuracy is not Fanny's complaint. The past, for Fanny, must be qualitatively different from the present: another time, other habits, ineffably superior ways; and this past is necessarily imprecise. "There is something in a chapel and chaplain so much in character with a great house, with one's ideas of what such a household should be!" (*MP*, 86), Fanny exclaims, leaving the "something" undefined and rather tautological. Mary's imagined past, by way of contrast, is all too particular, down to the unattractive chaplain, the sleepy congregation, and the unwilling belles, "young Mrs. Eleanor and Mrs. Bridgets" (*MP*, 87). Fanny's hold on remembrance is always on the lost or almost lost, such as the Sotherton trees, or on an idealized past that cannot recur. It is this characteristic of the modern nostalgic — the gentle yearning and lament for what cannot return — that Fanny exemplifies, and in this yearning's gentleness and very impossibility Fanny stands apart from *Sense and Sensibility*'s harsher mnemonic universe. Insofar as Fanny's ruminations are so persistently elegiac, they avoid the more traumatic narratives of eighteenth-century homesickness.

The constant disapprobation of the "new" that the novel evinces, from the Crawford's updated ethics to the planned improvements at Sotherton, masks the obsolescence of the "old." This obsolescence is a cultural one, of course — nowhere does the novel hold out the hope that the ancient forms of worship at Sotherton can be revived — but is more crucially a personal one. The pains and defeats of the past will not matter any longer if they are not remembered, and Fanny's nostalgic retrospects, by censoring the past's negative content, make her past of transplantation and maltreatment as obsolescent as Sotherton's vestigial chapel. For her cousins Maria and Julia, whose treatment of Fanny traversed the territory between neglect and abuse, Fanny has only the fondest of memories, and the fondness clearly bursts the bounds of psychic realism. Such is the case upon their being exiled from Mansfield following the aborted theatricals: "Even their mother missed them — and how much the more their tender-hearted cousin, who wandered about the house, and thought of them, and felt for them, with a degree of affectionate regret which they had never done much to deserve!" (*MP*, 204). When their absence allows Fanny to lead the Mansfield ball, her nostalgic regret is explicitly matched with a sense of the past's utter separation from the present:

And her thoughts flew to those absent cousins with most unfeigned and truly tender regret, that they were not at home to take their own place in the room, and have their share of a pleasure which would have been so very delightful to them. So often as she had heard them wish for a ball at home as the greatest of felicities! And to have them away when it was given — and for *her* to be opening the ball — and with Mr. Crawford too! She hoped they would not envy her that distinction *now*; but when she looked back to the state of things in the autumn, to what they had all been to each other when once dancing in that house before, the present arrangement was almost more than she could understand herself. (*MP*, 275–276)

The processes of modern nostalgia intertwine delicately in this moment of assessment. Fanny's memories of former disharmony, nicely euphemized as "what they had all been to each other," are now *pleasant* because they are over, *disconnected*—"the present arrangement" has, through its improved prospects, canceled the disruptions of the past; and despite the identical place of the former discomfort and present triumph—Mansfield itself, "that house"—by placing the pains in an inaccessible *time*, "the autumn," Fanny pushes them beyond further consequence. They continue to matter only as an effective and piquant contrast to the current ball's incipient satisfactions. We might extend the roster of modern nostalgic processes by stating that this retrospect is suddenly *communalized*, as it contains no resentment, vengeful glee, or continued hurt that could not be voiced; Fanny's resolutely nostalgic narrative is a story of progress amply atoning for, and indeed concealing, the defects of her earlier life.[58] Like the shrubbery remembered for its metamorphosis from a hedgerow "never thought of as any thing" into a valued piece of property, Fanny's autobiographical memory records only the beneficent alterations of the past. The once traumatic alterations, including the "separation from every body and every thing she had been used to" (*MP*, 14), are no longer acutely felt.

Understanding Fanny's mnemonic elisions means understanding that the harmonies of distance, the disconnected nostalgia under construction in Austen's work, entails a removal of the past's component "parts" in favor of a closed-off "whole." Lecturing Fanny on the respect due Mrs. Norris—despite her refusal to grant Fanny a fire—Sir Thomas touches on the central aspect of Fanny's nostalgia:

> "You have an understanding, which will prevent you from receiving things only in part, and judging partially by the event.—You will take in the whole of the past, you will consider times, persons, and probabilities, and you will feel that *they* were not least your friends who were educating and preparing you for that mediocrity of condition which *seemed* to be your lot." (*MP*, 313)

The application of the general principle seems undeniably misguided in this instance—surely the "whole of the past" of Mrs. Norris would consist of her venom above all—but, as we shall see, that is not the case, at least not for Fanny. She does indeed judge by the "whole" of the past, reducing the many particular instances of mistreatment, many of which have been presented to the reader, to a "whole" that is not only greater than the sum of its parts but entirely different. The "whole" by which Fanny judges is a general progress, a general habit of considering previous difficulties as overcome, previous misunderstandings as resolved, previous disadvantages as rectified. Henry and Mary Crawford's memories, by contrast, are far more particularized. Mary, entering the "East room" for the first time since the theatricals, remembers her last appearance there: "I came to rehearse. Your cousin came too; and we had a rehearsal. You were our audience and prompter. A delightful rehearsal. I shall never forget it. Here we were, just in this part of the room; here was your cousin, here was I, here were the chairs. — Oh! why will such things ever pass away?" (*MP*, 358). These, certainly, are not retrospects in the modern nostalgic mode; insistent in their particularity, explicit in their linkage of present and past times ("here was I, here were the chairs"), and carefully implicit in their hope for a return of the past — Mary is deftly announcing her hopes of capturing Edmund at last — they stand directly against the vaguer memories of Fanny, for whom these specific recollections are not at all pleasant. Perhaps most important, this surrender of Mary's to a mnemonic influence is firmly asocial: "Happily for her companion, she wanted no answer. Her mind was in a reverie of sweet remembrances" (*MP*, 358). Fanny's "whole of the past" does not include such vivid returns of the theatricals; her "whole" is usefully limited to instances of general progress.

These isolated textual moments help to elucidate the novel's alteration of Marianne's eighteenth-century homesickness into Fanny's nineteenth-century nostalgia, but *Mansfield Park* does more than adjust the possibilities of personal memory on a local level. Its most drastic revision of eighteenth-century nostalgia is on the level of plot: it provides us with the expected "return home," only to utterly alter the meaning and consequences of that return. It deals a final blow to the older plot of nostalgia, which I have called the plot of repatriation or death, by bringing Fanny back home to Portsmouth in order to negate the curative connotations of returning — in order to remove, one might say, the very *possibility* of return. The nostalgic patient of Hamilton can go home again, and does. Fanny, the modern nostalgic, cannot go home again, because the very act of returning proves the word "home" to have no stable referent. Place and "home" are dissevered, and "home" can be called such simply because one has chosen to call it that. The unassimilable self, the figure that haunts *Sense and Sensibility* and most eighteenth-century medical writing on mobility and memory, is replaced by the nostalgic self, the figure burdened by no irremovable past — and all this is accomplished by Fanny's startlingly revisionary return to Portsmouth.

The Portsmouth sequence has been seen as many things: as a social contrast to Mansfield's Tory values, as a testing of Fanny's budding Evangelicalism, or even as an inset travelogue, catering to Regency readers eager to explore the kingdom's newest center of technological advance.[59] I would like instead to place it against the background of the plot of nostalgia as it was transmitted by eighteenth-century travelers, doctors, and writers, and therefore to consider it as the reversal of medicalized nostalgia. It is a parody of the homesick patient's return home, and yet more than a parody, for it suggests a powerful alternative: a selfhood that can choose alliances, sympathies, and identities through a selectively vague mode of memory. The parodic and reconstructive instincts of the Portsmouth return converge in a single, fascinating narratological tendency: that Fanny's return home evokes few memories of her childhood but many memories of Mansfield. Perhaps the most stunning of these reversals of expectation is Fanny's thought upon being reunited with her mother, "who met her there with looks of true kindness, and with features which Fanny loved the more, because they brought her aunt Bertram's before her" (*MP*, 377). The return home has become mnemonically empty, productive of nothing but dissonance, to the point that the maternal visage dissolves before an image of Lady Bertram, who has scarcely filled the role of mother to Fanny. Either Fanny entirely lacks the memories requisite to a real repatriation, or those memories she does possess are shattered in a collision with the realities of Portsmouth life:

> Tom she wanted to keep by her, to try to trace the features of the baby she had loved, and talk to him of his infant preference of herself. Tom, however, had no mind for such treatment: he came home, not to stand and be talked to, but to run about and make a noise; and both boys had soon burst away from her, and slammed the parlour door till her temples ached. (*MP*, 381)

But it is not simply that Fanny's memories, because of her length of stay at Mansfield, are entirely composed of its inhabitants and ways; it is not simply that "home" has become Mansfield because of a prolonged separation from Portsmouth. The emptiness of retrospect that pervades the Portsmouth visit is mirrored by the *comparative emptiness* of her memories, when there, of Mansfield — an emptiness that has been noticed by many wondering critics. What to make of her pining for her Mansfield relatives, for "the friends who had done so much — the dear, dear friends" (*MP*, 382)? What to do with the sudden forgetfulness of Mansfield realities — of the transmutation of the disorder of the theatricals into "elegance, propriety, regularity, harmony," of its contentious inhabitants into its "beloved inmates, its happy ways" (*MP*, 391)? How to resolve the alteration of Mrs. Norris's bruising mental assaults into her "little irritations" (*MP*, 392)? The answer does not rest in Portsmouth's palliation of any earlier traumas; as Claudia Johnson has been the most recent critic to notice, the trip to Portsmouth "sustains rather than settles the problems the foregoing material has uncovered."[60] A more physically uncomfortable place than Mansfield, Portsmouth throws into relief the peculiarly mental forms of injury Fanny had suffered during her Mansfield upbringing; but these injuries Fanny is firm in not remembering. The key to the dilemma — the key to understanding how Mansfield could be, in retrospect, so idealized — lies with Fanny's empty memories of Portsmouth, in the vague, disconnected nostalgia of Fanny, which protects her both from eighteenth-century homesickness for Portsmouth and from resentment at her marginalization at Mansfield. This disconnection of memory is the central feature of the easily assimilable self, the flexible self, the nostalgic self — and it licenses the blotting out of the old plot of nostalgia. Fanny does not go home, because that home has disappeared; and she does not die. What she does, of course, is to reconstitute "home" as Mansfield, and to feel herself free to long for a home of her own choosing — a home, we might even say, of her own nostalgic invention.

Hence Fanny is free to perform what Hamilton's patient, and Banks's sailors, could not envision: a real transplantation. "When she had been coming to Portsmouth, she had loved to call it her home, had been fond of saying that she was going home; the word had been very dear to her; and so it still was, but it must be applied to Mansfield. *That* was now the home. Portsmouth was Portsmouth; Mansfield was home" (*MP*, 431). When the individual is freed by a vague memory to recreate "home," homesickness is no longer a worry, and thus *Mansfield Park* has announced the end of Hofer's disease. The word "home" is affixed with a precision, and, more important, with a freedom, that no eighteenth-century nostalgic could possess. Fanny Price, as Austen's first fully fleshed modern nostalgic, fulfills the request of Elizabeth Bennet to "think only of the past as its remembrance gives you pleasure" — and by inverting the older cultural plot of the return home, she begins to adumbrate a newer plot of nostalgia, a plot of physical and mental mobility, inhabited by a psyche that is rooted nowhere but in a capacity for accurate judgment. But, of course, Fanny Price's own mobility has a limit. Having chosen Mansfield, the process of separation and nostalgic disconnection comes to an end; Fanny's mobile memory finds itself at rest. *Mansfield Park* may have signaled the end of the older nostalgic plot, and it may have offered the possibility of true transplantations, but for a narrative entirely structured by modern nostalgia — a narrative that would envision the potential for an always renewable mobility — we must turn to the end of Austen's career.

Naval Memories

As the family move from Steventon to Bath approached in the winter of 1801, Austen wrote of the impending transplantation to her sister Cassandra. The letter, one of the very few to have survived that mention the move, mediates between resignation and humor:

> I get more & more reconciled to the idea of our removal. We have lived long enough in this Neighborhood, the Basingstoke Balls are certainly on the decline, there is something interesting in the bustle of going away, & the prospect of spending future summers by the Sea or in Wales is very delightful. — For a time we shall possess many of the advantages which I have often thought of with Envy in the wives of Sailors or Soldiers.[61]

Although it is certainly possible to find irony in the final line, with the figure of Anne Elliot in mind we may detect in Austen's invocation of "Sailors or Soldiers," the professionally mobile, more than just a joke. Austen's last heroine is a vivid demonstration of precisely what the "advantages" of being allied with the army or navy might be: the advantages of an unmoored memory.[62] However ironic Austen's letter is — considering the reports of her reaction to the move to Bath, it is most likely deeply so — it is also proleptically earnest, for in *Persuasion* we encounter Anne Elliot, the eventual wife of a sailor, who possesses by the end of the novel a most mobile nostalgia, a memory no longer tied to a particular place or even a particular time. Mobility and a blessed elision of the past are strongly linked in Austen's last narrative, and through this most homeless of Austen's heroines we see how the capacity to judge the past replaces the capacity to vividly remember it. Banks's mid-eighteenth-century sailors may have been afflicted by a severely medical nostalgia, but by 1818 the navy has become, in Austen, a figure for a new nostalgia that can condense and detach even the most fraught of pasts.

The contention that mobility is central to Austen, and to Austen's conception of remembrance, conflicts with the prevalent view of her narratives as tending toward settlement, toward the "always home" of Novalis's aphorism. The gap between Austen and the mobile is often voiced as a commonplace; "we know that Jane Austen is no novelist of the pícaro, the unhoused and unhomed," Tony Tanner informs us.[63] The wanderings of Anne Elliot — removed from Kellynch Hall to Uppercross, from Uppercross to Bath, the pawn of a family whose debt has resulted in a strategy of rental and travel — suggests otherwise: Anne may not be destitute, but she is certainly unhomed. So strongly does Anne feel these uprootings that at the novel's beginning we may feel that we have reentered the mnemonic world of *Sense and Sensibility*, as Anne, "transplanted into" (*P*, 43) her sister's residence at Uppercross, sorrows for the loss of her home; although she understands the urgency of quitting Kellynch Hall and financially retrenching, she desires a local transplantation, where she might at least be able to see the grounds of Kellynch from time to time. Lady Russell, for one, feels that Anne "had been too little from home" (*P*, 15). As in *Sense and Sensibility*, the problem with enforced mobility is primarily a problem of memory. Anne laments leaving Kellynch, the scene of her most pressing memories, and when at Uppercross resigns herself to the necessity of re-making her sense of the past: "With the prospect of spending at least two months at Uppercross, it was highly incumbent on her to clothe her imag-ination, her memory, and all her ideas in as much of Uppercross as possi-ble" (*P*, 43).

Furthermore, as with Marianne Dashwood, Anne's reluctance to leave her original home is matched to a series of vivid personal retrospects that she cannot easily relinquish. The past is omnipresent at the novel's outset, to a degree unparalleled in Austen's fiction. Hearing that Captain Went-worth's sister was likely to inhabit Kellynch brings on "a revival of former pain" (*P*, 30); seeing Wentworth again is little short of a complete regres-sion into the past, as "former times must undoubtedly be brought to the recollection of each; they could not but be reverted to; the year of their en-gagement could not but be named by him, in the little narratives or de-scriptions which conversation called forth" (*P*, 63). The specificity of these memories — the precision with which they are dated, the minute detail of the "little narratives," the constancy of their occurrence — is more akin to eighteenth-century nostalgia than its modern successor, and like the men-tal construct of Hofer's homesickness, these memories are inexorably tied to specific places; Anne cannot bear seeing Wentworth in Kellynch itself, feeling that "those rooms had witnessed former meetings which would be brought too painfully before her" (*P*, 93). The passing of time since "the year six" does not alleviate the pressure of remembrance, and although Anne does not court a retrospective melancholy in the self-defeating man-ner of Marianne Dashwood, the melancholy is no more avoidable:

> What might not eight years do? Events of every description, changes, alienations, removals, — all, all must be comprised in it; and oblivion of the past — how natural, how certain too! It included nearly a third part of her own life.
> Alas! with all her reasonings, she found, that to retentive feelings eight years may be little more than nothing. (60)

The modern nostalgic gap between a qualitatively different past and the present is closed, the disconnection voided. As for any of Elizabeth Ben-net's mnemonic pleasure, Anne's retrospects are instead difficult to bear. And the communality of nostalgic memories is here confined to an indi-vidual silence; "the subject," we are told of Anne and Lady Russell, "was never alluded to" (*P*, 29). In essence, it seems as if at the outset of *Persua-*

sion that we have taken a step backward — back to the older plot of nostalgia, a plot of restorations or defeats, a plot of yearning and of continually active reminiscences.

Matched to Anne's active retrospect, which cannot achieve an "oblivion of the past," are other characters satirized on the basis of their forgetfulness: Sir Walter Elliot, who can forget the existence of Mary when convenience dictates, introducing Anne as his youngest daughter; Captain Benwick, whose conversion from a seemingly irreparable loss to becoming Louisa Musgrove's husband is comically rapid; and the Elliot family as a whole, whose "general air of oblivion" (*P*, 30) concerning Wentworth and Anne's former affair is welcomed by Anne as a balm at the same time as it is deplored as a lack of sympathy. It would seem, then, that an active and accurate memory is what functions as the novel's ethical litmus test. When Mrs. Musgrove's remembrances of a dead son, the "thick-headed, unfeeling, unprofitable Dick Musgrove" (*P*, 51), are so thoroughly castigated by the narrator on the basis of their implausibility — and so bluntly corrected — it would seem that these suspicions of the novel's high estimate of memory are confirmed.[64] But a closer look at the narrator's famous debunking of Mrs. Musgrove's maternal laments demonstrates that, at this point in the novel, something else is transpiring: the sloppiness of unregulated, unjudged memories is being declared illicit. Mrs. Musgrove's memory is not too nostalgic; it is, in the terms Austen has provided throughout her career, *not nostalgic enough*, neither pleasurable, nor communal, nor, most crucially, named and judged. The *feeling* that flows through Mrs. Musgrove's retrospect is precisely what is being deemed worthy of correction — hence the outrage against tact that the passage is often felt to be, for what is more tactless than to rail at maternal loss? Her feeling prevents her from a nostalgic dissolution of the links between present and past, and her feeling disrupts the social intercourse of an evening.

The history of Dick Musgrove is inaugurated by his sisters, who come to Uppercross cottage to explain the temporary indisposition of their mother, who — through "one of those extraordinary bursts of mind which do sometimes occur" (*P*, 51) — has recalled that Wentworth had been Dick's captain on board the frigate *Laconia*. The burst of reminiscence has called his death to mind and has ruined Mrs. Musgrove's normally irrepressible spirits. At this point the narrator intervenes:

> The real circumstances of this pathetic piece of family history were, that the Musgroves had had the ill fortune of a very troublesome, hopeless son; and the good fortune to lose him before he reached his twentieth year; that he had been sent to sea, because he was stupid and unmanageable on shore; that he had been very little cared for at

any time by his family, though quite as much as he deserved; seldom heard of, and scarcely at all regretted, when the intelligence of his death abroad had worked its way to Uppercross, two years before. (*P*, 50–51)

Two years later, Mrs. Musgrove's memory has turned him into a "steady" boy, an "excellent correspondent" (*P*, 67). Why the forcefulness of the correction? Why, when the nostalgia exhibited by Austen's texts is so thoroughly vague, so often phantasmatic, the sudden emphasis on the "real circumstances" of the story? Why the need to reduce Dick Musgrove, to expose his mother's memories as fraudulent? The answer lies in Mrs. Musgrove's opening of an *elegiac* mode into the novel. With Dick Musgrove's loss we see a mode of memory that privileges a lost past, not as the faulty preparation for the present but as the fuller, happier predecessor to the present. We see a retrospect that does not harmonize pain and pleasure into "fond recollection" through "distance," but a retrospect that insists on continual pain. We see, in other words, the possibility open to Anne: to consider the past eight years as a loss and a waste, to consider her youthful self as superior in freshness and hope to her current situation, to consider the peregrinations of the Elliot family as a fall from their previous grandeur. Thus the tremendous interest the novel takes in revising Mrs. Musgrove's memory, in insisting that the past was not, in other words, as good as it seems. What does the work of inoculating the novel against the elegiac mode is a harsh language of *judgment*. Dick Musgrove was "a son, whom alive nobody had cared for" (*P*, 68), a son who does not deserve even his sister's apostrophes to "poor Richard," as he "had never done any thing to entitle himself to more than the abbreviation of his name, living or dead" (*P*, 51). Named in the firmest possible manner (as "Dick" rather than "Richard"), judged with a severity little short of absolute, Dick Musgrove is found unworthy of elegy, and elegy is found unacceptable to the world of *Persuasion*.

Consider the fate of Benwick's continual elegies for Fanny Harville, his memorizations of poetry, his insistence on an irretrievable loss, all of which issues in a swift reversal, as if the mental stamina needed to sustain the elegiac is exhausted by the superior interest of real-life attractions.[65] Consider as well the inability of Anne to elegize the Elliot family:

In such moments Anne had no power of saying to herself, "These rooms ought to belong only to us. Oh, how fallen in their destination! How unworthily occupied! An ancient family to be so driven away! Strangers filling their place!" No, except where she thought of her mother, and remembered where she had been used to sit and preside, she had no sigh of that description to heave. (*P*, 126)

Despite the pressure of memory that opens the novel, the past is so persistently deidealized and judged that the effort to remember it increasingly comes to seem a wasted effort. Thus the lesson of Mrs. Musgrove's retrospective affection: the past is always less valuable than it seems. This is not, it must be insisted, an antinostalgic posture. Instead, it is the very *foundation* of modern nostalgia — for to consider the present as the essentially improved goal of the past allows one to recollect genially and without pain, to remember the past fondly and poignantly but not sorrowfully. The judging of the past and the barring of the elegiac mode performs in *Persuasion* what the figure of the souvenir performs in *Mansfield Park*: the preparatory condensation and disconnection of the past that is necessary if a modern nostalgia is to flourish. Since loss hovers everywhere in the corners of Austen's last novel, from the loss of an unloved son to the loss of a former lover to the loss of a family's social position, all this loss must be negated *through judgment* before a fully nostalgic memory can flourish. The unhappy alternative is a memory continually racked with missed opportunities and missed happiness, forever linked to old identities (and, as in eighteenth-century homesickness, old places). By eliminating the elegiac with such fervor, Austen insures that nostalgia remains the keynote of *Persuasion*'s harmonies of distance.

The new note of judgment, which replaces vivid remembrances, is rung at the novel's end by Anne herself, thus bringing to fruition the process of reassessment so noisily begun with the castigation of Mrs. Musgrove: "I have been thinking over the past," she announces to Wentworth, "and trying impartially to judge of the right and wrong, I mean with regard to myself; and I must believe that I was right, much as I suffered from it, that I was perfectly right in being guided by the friend whom you will love better than you do now" (*P*, 246). "Recollecting" the past yields to "thinking over" and "judging" the past; the series of retrospective narratives that had previously pervaded conversation between Anne and Wentworth is whittled down to a right-or-wrong dilemma, one that is easily solved:

> "It was, perhaps, one of those cases in which advice is good or bad only as the event decides; and for myself, I certainly never should, in any circumstance of tolerable similarity, give such advice. But I mean, that I was right in submitting to her, and that if I had done otherwise, I should have suffered more in continuing the engagement than I did even in giving it up, because I should have suffered in my conscience." (*P*, 246)

It is a strong nostalgia that Anne here voices. The past is barred from further consequence through Anne's paradoxical declaration that the mistake will not be repeated, and that the mistake was not, at the time, a mistake at all: the first claim defeating the possibility of the past's recurrence, the second claim defeating the possibility of remorse over the past. The present is, one feels, so thoroughly different from the past that what would be wrong now was right then; a deft bit of reasoning that accomplishes the aims of nostalgia with amazing economy. The even syntax, the equanimity with which the past is suddenly being described, the open manner in which it can be shared: nostalgic characteristics all, arrived at through the triumph of judgment over reminiscence.

What makes these judgments possible? The answer is the novel's multiplication of departures. Although the novel's largest possible motion is a return—Anne and Wentworth's return to each other—the return is achieved through a series of leavetakings and exits, and even that largest return is figured as the most dramatic departure possible, the departures implied in the "tax of quick alarm" (*P*, 252) Anne must pay for being a soldier's wife. Real restorations are not possible, in the fullest nostalgic sense. Anne is offered the possibility of a "restoration" in the person of Mr. Elliot, and is not at first entirely disinclined: "The idea of becoming what her mother had been; of having the precious name of 'Lady Elliot' first revived in herself; of being restored to Kellynch, calling it her home again, her home for ever, was a charm which she could not immediately resist" (*P*, 160). But resist it she does, of course; the return home flashed before her consciousness is rejected fairly quickly, far sooner than in *Mansfield Park*, where the return home to Portsmouth has to transpire before its importance can be negated. *Persuasion* instead leaves the plot of restoration behind, departs from its consequences before they can become dangerous, and chooses instead a constant mobility that leaves its traces on the memories of its characters.[66] Anne's modern nostalgia is most evident upon leaving a place or scene, upon considering a period of time to have concluded; thus her second departure, from Uppercross to Bath, is far less difficult than her departure from Kellynch, for this time she feels the departure to coincide with the closing of an era, with a nostalgic disconnection: "Scenes had passed in Uppercross, which made it precious. It stood the record of many sensations of pain, once severe, but now softened; and of some instances of relenting feeling, some breathings of friendship and reconciliation, which could never be looked for again, and which could never cease to be dear. She left it all behind her; all but the recollection that such things had been" (*P*, 123). A softening of pain, a distancing: it is a description of Elizabeth Bennet's philosophy *in progress*, moving from remembrance of pain to remembrance of what gives pleasure.

It should be no surprise, then, that discussions of memory in *Persuasion* occur in the context of discussions of travel. Arguing with Captain Harville about gendered memory during the novel's climactic scene, Anne insists that the mobility of men enables their forgetfulness — women "live at home, quiet, confined, and our feelings prey upon us," while men "have always a profession, pursuits, business of some sort or other, to take you back into the world immediately, and continual occupation and change soon weaken impressions" (*P*, 232). When Harville replies by depicting the homesickness of departed sailors, Anne counters by claiming for the immobile woman the power "of loving longest, when existence or when hope is gone" (*P*, 235). What is at stake in this pivotal argument is the shift from one form of selfhood — the naval memory of Banks's homesick sailors, the unassimilable self — to another form, which finds in mobility a rescue from the confinements of remembrance. The terms of the argument are significantly naval, and the theme of the argument is the shift, coming to its end in Austen's fiction, from an older medical nostalgia to the newer nostalgia that will be its cure. The lesson is voiced early in the novel: leaving Kellynch for Uppercross, we learn that "a removal from one set of people to another, though at a distance of only three miles, will often include a total change of conversation, opinion, and idea" (*P*, 42). It is only later in the novel that the lesson is implemented. Concluding her narrative as a wife prepared for sudden alarms and movements, as a wife unmoored from family locales and family examples, Anne has, one assumes, undergone a "total change" — a sea change, perhaps — and has left behind the yearnings with which she began.

This, then, is the new horizon of nostalgia, more thoroughly delineated by Austen's last fiction than any of her previous narratives of dislocation. A leavetaking of home spurs a series of further leavetakings; a trauma rooted in the memory is ameliorated, judged, and left behind; former mistakes are canceled, former times periodized and then ended, stopped with a mental period; and what is left is a capacity for communalized retrospect, for what, during a conversation between Anne and Mrs. Smith, is called "the interesting charm of remembering former partialities and talking over old times" (*P*, 153).[67] Having arrived at this nostalgia, the novel's earlier, truculent insistence on the "real circumstances" of the past begins to fade. Wentworth can claim that "to my eye you could never alter" (*P*, 243), which is, of course, directly contradicted by his earlier statement that Anne was "so altered he should not have known you again" (*P*, 60). Anne lets the discrepancy pass, however: "It was too pleasing a blunder for a reproach. It is something for a woman to be assured, in her eight-and-twentieth year, that she has not lost one charm of her earlier youth: but the value of such homage was inexpressibly increased to Anne, by comparing it with former words, and feeling it to be the result, not the cause of a revival of his warm attachment" (*P*, 243). Her memory, that is, acts only as a vehicle of contrast, and one that will throw a warm glow upon the progress of the present; within such a structure of remembrance, factual inaccuracy is meaningless—it simply does not signify, insofar as the past itself ceases to signify except as the present's ironic prologue. Whereas Marianne Dashwood had concerned herself with the truth of the past—and interpreted that truth as identical to what it had seemed to be at the time—Anne's revisionary memory can interpret even dissonances of fact and assertion. What has been achieved is not only a disconnection from former facts, however, but a disconnection from the past feelings those facts had evoked.

As the accuracy of past particulars recedes as a concern, a vista of travel—movement, new scenes, new places—opens up and is matched to this new nostalgia. When Anne voices her *ars memorativa*, she appends to it a subtle announcement of intentions: that her formerly unassimilable self will open up to a new mobility. Asked by Wentworth if "disgust" permeates her remembrance of Lyme, if memories of Louisa Musgrove's injury efface all else, Anne responds with a formula for a new nostalgia:

> "The last few hours were certainly very painful," replied Anne: "but when pain is over, the remembrance of it often becomes a pleasure. One does not love a place the less for having suffered in it, unless it has been all suffering, nothing but suffering—which was by no means the case at Lyme. We were only in anxiety and distress during the last two hours; and, previously, there had been a great deal of enjoyment. So much novelty and beauty! I have travelled so little, that every fresh place would be interesting to me—but there is real beauty at Lyme: and in short" (with a faint blush at some recollections) "altogether my impressions of the place are very agreeable." (*P*, 183–184)

"Novelty" over trauma, "every fresh place" over regret: a vision of a mobile consciousness fulfills the preference for pleasure over pain that Elizabeth Bennet had previously advised. Furthermore, what is a "philosophy" in *Pride and Prejudice*—a piece of advice, an effort that must be undertaken—becomes a natural process in *Persuasion*, a usual occurrence, a psychological metamorphosis that occurs in spite of the most vivid traumas. Pain is foreshortened into a "few hours," and pleasure is widened to fill the vacuum, all with an effortlessness, an ease, that was missing from the wrenching transmutations of *Sense and Sensibility*. It is the new semantic range of "nostalgia" that Anne defines here, and she does so by naturalizing it and by invoking a renewable mobility alongside it.

There is, famously, no settlement awaiting Anne at the novel's conclusion, "no Uppercross-hall before her, no landed estate, no headship of a family" (*P*, 250)—what has been accomplished instead is the judgment, dilution, and cancellation of a difficult past, nowhere better exemplified than in the small-scale cancellation of Louisa Musgrove's crisis at Lyme. Nostalgia is a closural process in Austen, a way of halting the reverberations of narrative—for how can a narrative end unless a finality of consequence is asserted? It is a method whereby the traumatic dislocations and injuries of Austen's openings do not obscure the happier dispositions of her plots, and whereby the reformations and assimilations that complete her narratives are not shadowed by earlier fractures and fissures. Yet nostalgia is more than a narratological principle; in Austen's final novel, it is a narratological principle naturalized as a psychological process, since the principle exhibited by the texts—the elision of Fanny Price's Portsmouth upbringing, of Anne and Wentworth's eight missed years, of Elizabeth and Darcy's mutual woundings—must be learned by Austen's characters themselves *as a mnemonic habit*. Austen's novels, that is, instruct her characters in the form of memory that will help close her fictions. Uncovering the "nostalgics" of these texts—their nostalgic logic—is not simply elucidating a technical choice, then, but is also arriving at a sense of where a more contemporary "nostalgia," to use the word so often employed by Austen's later critics, begins: where it is first taught, out of what situations it arises, against what it first reacted. In *Persuasion*, nostalgia is taught as a reaction to the naval homesickness of Banks's sailors; we are taken from "home" to "every fresh place," to a naval memory that celebrates departures and not returns.

The Last Exception

"*That* is all to be forgot," Elizabeth Bennet tells her sister Jane of her former abuse of Darcy. "Perhaps I did not always love him so well as I do now. But in such cases as these, a good memory is unpardonable. This is the last time I shall ever remember it myself" (PP, 373). Perhaps it is necessary to pause at this sentiment and to recognize it as a most striking *anachronism*. Who, coming upon these sentences today, particularly were they to be unattributed, would believe the speaker? Who would lend credence to such a sweeping and confident revision of the past—who would not believe instead that the "repressed" of Elizabeth and Darcy's courtship will "return," that her proclamation of forgetfulness is an exercise in either self-parody or false consciousness? In part, our inability to read Elizabeth's frank nostalgia—the remembrance of the past only as it brings pleasure—is a result of its nearly two-centuries-old scientific disappearing act. Beginning in Austen's time "nostalgia" gradually fades from psychological investigation: the eighteenth-century tracts cease to appear, the interest in military illnesses of the kind described by Hamilton stops, and newer psychologies take the field, from Gall's phrenology to the invasive procedures of French clinicians, which find nothing credible in notions of "homesickness."[68] Debunked as a disease, nostalgia gradually loses its dignity as a mode of memory, and although twentieth-century writers on memory know of its existence—the existence of the concept, at least—they do not grant it the strength of other styles of remembrance. If we doubt Elizabeth's sudden nostalgic forgetting, it is because we doubt that nostalgia like hers is *possible*; we doubt that it can effectively elude the reach of past pain. We accept, perhaps, the existence of nostalgia, but we nonetheless place the greatest power in the "real circumstances."

What has edged nostalgia out of serious consideration, what has made it the subject of attack and disdain, is a current conception of memory based solely on the processes and characteristics of trauma. It is as if the troubled memories of eighteenth-century nostalgics have returned to us, although severed from their links to origin and nationality. Repression, obsession, "recovered" memory, memorialization, involuntary memory, amnesia: these categories are all modes of, or evasions of, trauma—they signal the presence of past woundings, and even when attempting to escape those pains they still reflect the power and consequence of earlier traumas. They are our mnemonic categories, some studied by clinical neuroscientists, some by psychologists, some by social historians, but all firmly implanted in our culture; they inflect our own ways of speaking about memory. Of nostalgia, there is little said; what is said is uniformly hostile, as if it were, like Elizabeth's pledge to forget the unpleasant history of her courtship, both dishonest and impossible, dishonest precisely because of its impossibility. Nostalgia is, in the words of Susan Stewart, "a longing that of necessity is inauthentic because it does not take part in lived experience"; for Frederic Jameson it is "an elaborated symptom of the waning of our historicity, of our lived possibility of experiencing history in some active way."[69] What might authentic memory be? Exactly what is nonnostalgic: the traumatic, the particular, the accurate, the connected, the unwilled, the unpleasant. A mode of memory that wills a disconnection from the past, that shapes it anew into a vague poignancy and pleasure, that effaces traumas in favor of a vision of progress, is denied to be a form of memory at all, and is instead considered a mode of imagination. It is significant that the last time "nostalgia" found cultural and scientific respect, it was an illness.

Yet the nostalgia that arises in the early nineteenth century persists, continually expressed and invoked by Austen's novels, a familiar if denigrated mode of cultural and personal memory. Nostalgia is, I would argue, the last form of memory available to us that is not, at its base, a form of trauma, and to understand its significance—both in Austen's texts and in later historical development—it is necessary to imagine a retrospect that is not merely an evasion of trauma but its cancellation, its willed conclusion. To say with Elizabeth that "this is the last time I shall ever remember it myself" is to say, in effect, that "this is the last time the past shall be remembered *in this way*": to put an end to one sort of past and to replace it with another, to assume, that is, the fungibility of memory. The shaping power of the will in Austen extends to the material of memory as well, and it is this startling fact—the existence of a psyche that can alter, or improve, the landscape of the past—that explains the absence of vivid, particular reminiscences from Austen's novels. If our prevalent conceptions of memory are largely based on trauma, then Austen's work demonstrates the initiation of an exception: a genial but firm forgetting, a halting of the past's resonances, a leavetaking.

TWO

Amnesiac Bodies

PHRENOLOGY, PHYSIOGNOMY, AND MEMORY IN CHARLOTTE BRONTË

While keeping as close as possible to facts, we must attempt
to discover where, in the processes of memory, the function of the
body begins and where it ends.
—*Henri Bergson,* Matière et mémoire

In the summer of 1851 Charlotte Brontë and her publisher George Smith visited a London phrenologist of some fame, a Dr. J. P. Browne, to have their faces and skulls "read" in the popular manner of the day.[1] Into this encounter both Brontë and Smith went metaphorically masked, preferring the pseudonyms "Mr. and Miss Fraser" to their everyday identities. Remaining silent before Browne's trained gaze, with the ambiguous, tangled, and often painful facts of their respective pasts temporarily irrelevant, and with only the immutable signs of their heads offered for inspection, both author and publisher were clinically examined; within days Browne issued two written reports of his findings, and soon thereafter Brontë, back in the haven of Haworth, received the reports from Smith. It did not take long for Brontë to register her enthusiasm about the success of the readings. "I wanted a portrait, and have now got one very much to my mind," she wrote to Smith on July 2; "it is a sort of miracle—*like*—*like*—*like* as the very life itself."[2] Superior to any image, for Brontë, is this strange textual form, a "sketch" that is validated by the clinical technologies—both verbal and physical; Browne may have used calipers in his examination—that went into its making. Evidently exhilarated by the potential of *seeing* so accurately, so completely, and so quickly, Brontë considered herself amply represented by Browne's eye and pen.[3] We may wonder at how a brief scanning of a skull could result in such a powerfully effective character sketch; we may doubt the effectiveness of any psychological evaluation that ignores the facts of birth, development, prior trauma, indeed of all history, in favor of the merely visible. But it is in this elision of psychological "history" that we can locate the lure of Browne's method.

What, precisely, did Dr. Browne read in Brontë's skull? The language of the report—entitled "A Phrenological Estimate of the Talents and Dispositions of a Lady"—provides us with an excellent glimpse of the phrenological mindset at work:

> Temperament for the most part nervous. Brain large, the anterior and superior parts remarkably salient. In her domestic relations this lady will be warm and affectionate. In the care of children she will evince judicious kindness, but she is not pleased at seeing them spoiled by over-indulgence. . . . Her attachments are strong and enduring— indeed, this is a leading element of her character; she is rather circumspect, however, in the choice of her friends, and it is well that she is so, for she will seldom meet with persons whose dispositions approach the standard of excellence with which she can entirely sympathise.[4]

In such a vein the report continues for several hundred more words, describing the subject's attitudes toward money, color, symmetry, and language. The abrupt leap from the size of the "lady's" brain to her domestic habits is characteristic of phrenological discourse, which rarely strays from the middle-class in either its descriptions or its aspirations; what might also be pointed out is the mystification of this clinical gaze, for it is not explained why, or how, the salient anterior and superior parts of the brain contribute to an understanding of the subject's attitudes toward children or friends. But the most symptomatic facet of Browne's prose is its sedulous avoidance of the past tense. Brontë's "character" and "temperament" are entirely thrown into the future by this phrenological gaze: she "will be warm and affectionate," and "will evince judicious kindness," but there exists no clue as to her past dealings, and no such clue is necessary. This temporal outlook, which combines present and future tenses to create a static and therefore *summarizable* personality, does not allow for a developmental psychology; Brontë's self, as constructed by this phrenological text, does not depend upon a series of traumas, or merely contingent events, that have altered her mental vision and impinged upon her psyche. Instead, selfhood is flattened out, leveled in order to achieve a maximum legibility—and this flattening depends crucially upon the absence of memory. A historical causality—selfhood constructed out of a chain of previous events—yields to a biological causality. The past disappears, to be replaced by skull formation.

Browne's reading of Brontë is not significantly different from normal phrenological practice.[5] Perhaps the most stunning, and most overlooked, fact of the phrenological diagram is that it does not contain a faculty of memory (see figure 2.1). However much it is altered by various nineteenth-century phrenologists, this Victorian map of the mind continued to lack a faculty of remembrance. It has room in it for many things—it is spacious enough to accommodate a hodgepodge of instincts, propensities, and intellectual powers, such as a faculty for hunger and a faculty for child-rearing, and it could be continually expanded and revised; memory, however, remained absent. This fact, I want to suggest, should surprise us, and should give us pause. It should indicate that important Victorian conceptions of mind could comfortably excise memory, and that this excision worked its way into discourses that were other than the strictly phrenological, such as Charlotte Brontë's fiction. However ridiculous or partial Browne's reading of Brontë's head may seem to twentieth-century readers, it points us to a significant insight, and therefore to new ways of reading Brontë's texts.

In particular, it points us to the process in which the body, synecdochically reduced to the face and skull, becomes a substitute for memory. The absence of memory from much of Brontë's fiction has been thoroughly noted by various critics; *Villette*, most famously, is often noted as an instance of narrative repression, for we are aware throughout Lucy Snowe's narration of what is being withheld.[6] We do not know anything about Lucy Snowe's childhood or parents; in *The Professor*, Brontë's other Belgian narrative, William Crimsworth's past is similarly occluded. These examples demonstrate a familiar fact—that memories are avoided in Brontë's texts, that her narrators are notably laconic when facts of personal history are at issue. My aim is somewhat different: to elucidate how memory, as a faculty, a component of mental functioning, and as an organizing principle of narrative, is similarly absent. That is, the removal of remembrance from these texts exists not only on the large scale but infiltrates every aspect of Brontë's novels; we can see its absence in ordinary encounters, in dialogue, in the processes of speaking and gazing that she anatomizes. The empty spaces in these texts—the spaces where we expect memory to be—mirror the empty spaces of the phrenological diagram, and each of these two complementary images of the early Victorian psyche helps explain the other. In essence, Brontë's fiction and phrenological theory can be considered parallel discourses illustrating a general early to mid-Victorian tendency: the elision of memory that contributes to the "amnesiac self" and the replacement of memory by the legible body.

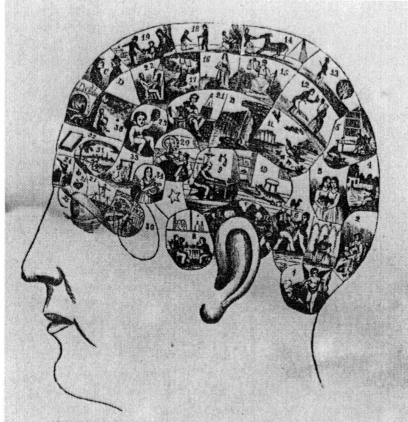

NUMBERING AND DEFINITION OF THE ORGANS.

1. AMATIVENESS, Sexual and connubial love.
2. PHILOPROGENITIVENESS, Parental love.
3. ADHESIVENESS, Friendship—sociability.
A. UNION FOR LIFE, Love of one only.
4. INHABITIVENESS, Love of home.
5. CONTINUITY, One thing at a time.
6. COMBATIVENESS, Resistance—defence.
7. DESTRUCTIVENESS, Executiveness-force.
8. ALIMENTIVENESS, Appetite, hunger.
9. ACQUISITIVENESS, Accumulation.
10. SECRETIVENESS, Policy—management.
11. CAUTIOUSNESS, Prudence, provision.
12. APPROBATIVENESS, Ambition—display.
13. SELF-ESTEEM, Self-respect—dignity.
14. FIRMNESS, Decision—perseverance.
15. CONSCIENTIOUSNESS, Justice—equity.
16. HOPE, Expectation—enterprise.
17. SPIRITUALITY, Intuition-spiritual revery.
18. VENERATION, Devotion—respect.
19. BENEVOLENCE, Kindness—goodness.
20. CONSTRUCTIVNESS Mechanical ingenuity.

21. IDEALITY, Refinement—taste—purity.
B. SUBLIMITY, Love of grandeur.
22. IMITATION, Copying—patterning.
23. MIRTHFULNESS, Jocoseness—wit—fun.
24. INDIVIDUALITY, Observation.
25. FORM, Recollection of shape.
26. SIZE, Measuring by the eye.
27. WEIGHT, Balancing—climbing.
28. COLOR, Judgment of colors.
29. ORDER, Method—system—arrangement
30. CALCULATION, Mental arithmetic.
31. LOCALITY, Recollection of places.
32. EVENTUALITY, Memory of facts.
33. TIME, Cognizance of duration.
34. TUNE, MUSIC—melody by ear.
35. LANGUAGE, Expression of ideas.
36. CAUSALITY, Applying causes to effects.
37. COMPARISON, inductive reasoning.
C. HUMAN NATURE, perception of motives.
D. AGREEABLENESS, Pleasantness—suavity

2.1 Phrenological diagram from O. S. Fowler, *Education and Self-Improvement, Founded on Physiology and Phrenology* (New York: 1844), 2.

The Unveiled Self

The science that Browne practiced on Charlotte Brontë and George Smith was, by 1851, thoroughly interwoven with Victorian cultural thought. Farces poking fun at the world of skull diagrams and calipers played at Covent Garden in the 1830s; mock poems, with titles such as "The Craniad" or "Travels in Phrenologasto," emerged from the presses starting in 1816.[7] Between 1810 and 1819 the founder of phrenology, the Austrian Franz Josef Gall, issued the crux of his pioneering work in the localization of brain function, and in this period his foremost student, Johann Gaspar Spurzheim, traveled to Britain to deliver a celebrated series of lectures which insured that phrenology would become, and long remain, a property of English-speaking nations. The excitement surrounding Spurzheim's medical ministry was ruefully acknowledged by the scientific establishment; a *Blackwood's* writer noted the stir in 1817: "At Clifton, he [Spurzheim] had gained many proselytes; and so occupied were the ladies there in settling the bumps on each other's skulls, that carefully to braid the hair, in order to conceal wrong propensities, became a matter of very serious attention."[8] That enthusiasm for phrenology was not merely a phenomenon of large cities seems clear from the rural path of Spurzheim's travels, and we have Brontë's own ease with phrenological vocabulary to attest to the fact that it had spread to the comparatively far-flung world of Lancashire and Yorkshire. As Sally Shuttleworth has recently proven, it is not at all unusual for a young woman in Haworth to have learned to speak of cranial organs: in 1836 the nearby Keighley Mechanics's Institute, where the young Brontës acquired much of their reading, sponsored a phrenological lecture and purchased both a *Manual of Phrenology* and a phrenological bust.[9]

What must be grasped is that when Brontë speaks of "organs of philo-progenitiveness"—or when she lauds Browne's clinical readings—she is not indulging a private, and somewhat embarrassing, taste; she is participating in a cultural endeavor whose consequences are significant and far-reaching. Never entirely accepted by the medical establishment, and never entirely discredited either, phrenology existed in a space between outright quackery and official clinical opinion—the space, that is, where early Victorian cultural structures were formed, a space of serious contention. Its equal distance from the seats of medical power and the garbage heap of discarded medical theory made it an ideal site for rehearsing various key social battles, among them the continued rise of the middle class and the growing insistence on individualistic psychologies. The story of George Combe, Britain's most respected and prolific phrenological theorist, illustrates the insecure yet pervasive place of phrenology in the first half of the nineteenth century. Combe's 1828 magnum opus, *The Constitution of Man*, was a tremendous publishing success; one source claims that, in the middle decades of the century, only the Bible, *Pilgrim's Progress*, and *Robinson Crusoe*, icons all of middle-class literacy, outsold Combe's treatise.[10] Yet Combe's 1836 candidacy for a chair in logic at the University of Edinburgh was rejected in favor of the noted antiphrenologist Sir William Hamilton, and the bulk of British medical opinion never accepted phrenological ideas, for reasons that were at once theological, metaphysical, and clinical.[11] Combe's celebrity was not damaged by these setbacks, however, and he remained an influence on mid-century intellectual life; well-connected converts such as Charles Bray, the first of George Eliot's mentors, continued to attach themselves to him. Phrenology was neither an "official" discourse nor a revolutionary one, though it borrowed from both registers — it was a distillation of much middle-class Victorian anxiety and ambition. The phrenological diagram, with its well-apportioned spaces, its implicit hierarchy — the "baser" instincts or appetites lodged near the base of the skull, the loftier sentiments such as "Reverence" placed at its apex — and its emphasis on specialization and division of function, is one very provocative image of the culture out of which it arose.[12] Brontë's interest in this diagram is not at all unusual; what is unusual in her writing is her *unembarrassed* application of phrenological vocabulary and assumptions. She therefore provides us with a particularly clear example of a significant Victorian psychological theory at work — a theory that was wedded to sight, and the triumph of sight over the invisible.

Attention to the visual becomes, in phrenological practice, a duty, and akin to an obsession. As described by O. S. Fowler, the premier American popularizer of the science and, after Combe, one of the movement's most important figures, the visual supersedes all other forms of interest:

> Even in church, when you would fain exercise your religious feelings, before you were aware, you found yourselves intently inspecting this head and that, and the other; nor were you satisfied without closely scrutinizing the developments of all you saw. It is not probably too much to say, that of all other promotives of observation, Phrenology is altogether the most effectual. Its observations so thoroughly interest as to create a SEEING MANIA which scrutinizes everybody and every thing.[13]

Whether phrenology creates the urge to observe, or merely feeds on a prior tendency, is a question obscured by Fowler's breathless prose, but the central point is clear: in a phrenological world, everything is visible, and therefore visibility is everything.[14] If, as the phrenologists insisted, mental capacity is perfectly indexed by the size of various bumps and protrusions of the skull, and if the location of various mental "faculties" can be arrived at through inductive reasoning, then nothing in mental life is truly hidden from view, and to be without the necessary theoretical armature for decoding the skull is to be literally defenseless. Combe makes this point at the start of *The Constitution of Man*: "In such a state of things, knowledge is truly power; and it is highly important to human beings to become acquainted with the constitution and relations of every object around them, that they may discover its capabilities of ministering to their own advantages."[15] This technique of seeing — the superimposition of a static diagram on a living head — is a technique that promises mastery, and it promises mastery because it forcefully places limits on the psyche. By dispensing with certain mental functions, most notably those functions that cannot be *visualized* by an observer, phrenology lends an almost untrammeled power to sight. In Brontë's novels we see this cultural emphasis on sight vividly dramatized, and we see as well what is missing when the body speaks amply for the mind.

Perhaps the most famous instance of body-reading in the English novel occurs in *Villette*, when Lucy Snowe, newly arrived in her adopted city, bereft of her native language as well as her possessions, which have been waylaid at the port, begs for a job at the pensionnat of Madame Beck. Paul Emanuel, described to us as "a small, dark and spare man, in spectacles," arrives at the behest of Madame Beck to provide his expert assessment of Lucy's character:

> "Mon cousin," began madame, "I want your opinion. We know your skill in physiognomy; use it now. Read that countenance."
> The little man fixed on me his spectacles. A resolute compression of the lips, and gathering of the brow, seemed to say that he meant to see through me, and that a veil would be no veil for him.
> "I read it," he pronounced.
> "Et qu'en dites vous?"
> "Mais — bien des choses," was the oracular answer. (*V*, 128–129)[16]

On the basis of this swift act of reading, Lucy is hired by Madame Beck. What we are witnessing in this scene is the triumph of a specific, clinical technology of sight over a line of investigation that would probe Lucy's past. Her memory — her previous training, the steps that led her to Villette and to Madame Beck's door, her reasons for desiring this particular occupation in this particular place — can be dispensed with, for her capabilities are clearly legible. To M. Paul, Madame Beck, and, as we will see, Lucy herself, the psyche can be usefully condensed into one question: what can, or will, this person do? Furthermore, this condensation is signified on the body, on the "countenance." Lucy is literally transparent, completely *unveiled*, by M. Paul's gaze, and the reading he produces is validated by the narrative itself, as it is in almost every case; when he suspects here that Lucy would make an effective employee, he is correct, and when later he decides that she would perform well in the school theatricals, he is again borne out by the event. Brontë does not cloak this "skill in physiognomy" in any oblique irony—these "readings," with their air of the occult to a twentieth-century reader, are unerring.[17] This signifying psyche, as well as the readings that call it forth, is resolutely proleptic; like Browne's reading of Brontë, it will only consider personality in a present or future tense. Madame Beck tells M. Paul that Lucy "tells a tale full of integrity, but gives no reference" (*V*, 129), and that is literally true—we as readers are bereft of the referentiality the past might give us, the shadows its light might throw upon Lucy. But those "references," both in the sense of a verbal résumé and a collection of analepses, are irrelevant, for the body speaks amply, and it speaks to the one important question: the future.

The very process of conversation has, therefore, been radically altered in Brontë's text, from one of excavation—what has this person done?—to a power struggle, a swift and decisive combat of methodologies. Lucy reads M. Paul reading her: she gleans from "the resolute compression of his lips, and gathering of the brow" that "he meant to see through me, and that a veil would be no veil for him"—the paths of the phrenological gaze move in both directions. The result, in Brontë, is the notably laconic, harsh, and blunt texture to her moments of dialogue, for the modes of excavation (insinuation, probing, innuendo) are supplanted by modes of confrontation. The field of personal encounter becomes a clash of mutually visible bodies. One sort of language, which is guarded, somewhat obscure, and full of various rhetorical strategies for concealment, such as irony, sarcasm, or euphemism, yields in Brontë to a language full of imperatives ("Read that countenance"), declarative sentences ("I read it"), simple queries ("Et qu'en dites vous?"), and the silence of the visible, unveiled subject. It is the removal of mnemonic material from the realm of conversation, and its replacement by visible propensities and faculties, that motivates Brontë's uniquely terse style.

Madame Beck's use of the term "physiognomy" should not obscure the specifically phrenological technique that M. Paul is employing; while trying later to convince Lucy to perform in the school theatricals, he says: "I read your skull, that night you came; I see your moyens; play you can; play you must" (*V*, 202). That it is the skull at issue here, rather than the fleshier, more mobile aspects of the face, points us to phrenology, which was known under a series of names in the nineteenth century: *craniology, cranioscopy, organology*, and even the umbrella term *physiognomy*.[18] The word "moyens" amply expresses, along with a host of other terms—faculties, propensities, aptitudes—the future-oriented emphasis of the phrenological gaze, an emphasis that could also produce mysterious judgments and vast ambitions. The vagueness of M. Paul's verdict ("bien des choses") should not invalidate his process of reading, for it mirrors the deliberately unlimited scope of phrenology's reformist aims. Promising a better future, it yet provided room for all sorts of better futures, some of them contradictory. George Combe could hint, in *The Constitution of Man*, that even pain in childbirth could be corrected with an application of phrenological wisdom, while maintaining a stern social Calvinism in his *Lectures on Moral Philosophy*: "Gradations of rank being thus institutions of God, those men are wild, enthusiastic dreamers, and not philosophers, who contemplate their abolition."[19] M. Paul's indefiniteness, his refusal to make explicit his clinically informed vision of Lucy's future actions, is at once a pose of *mastery*—an obfuscation designed to discomfit Lucy—and a sign of the indefiniteness at the heart of the phrenological enterprise, which was neither radically reformist nor conservative, although it could be both. Freed from the past, and freed from an obligation to excavate the memory of its objects of reading, the phrenological gaze could be freely inexplicit.[20]

When the phrenological gaze does confront the past, it does so only according to the category of habit: the past as the continually undifferentiated rehearsal of what is visible on the body in the present. Lucy, as much an amateur body-reader as M. Paul, brings phrenological language to the foreground when she explains why she did not rebuke a servant, Rosine, for her use of vulgar language: "I had no pacifying answer to give. The terms were precisely such as Rosine—a young lady in whose skull the organs of reverence and reserve were not largely developed—was in the constant habit of using" (*V*, 441). Another unveiled body, Rosine is here defenseless before Lucy's trained methodology; she is as legible as a page of printed text. Lucy's evaluation, which is even more overtly "phrenological" than Browne's assessment of Brontë in its use of the clinical terms "skull" and "organs," adopts the imperfect tense of the trained psychologist: Rosine is "in the constant habit" of using inappropriate language because the contours of her skull, which are of course beyond her power to change, dictate her behavior. The phrenological signs Lucy reads are, therefore, temporal constants; completely externalized and not at all susceptible to any repression, they elide the facts of Rosine's past, such as her training, her class background, or her exposure to others from whom she may have learned her vulgar language. A fact of behavior—the use of a specific, class-based discourse—is removed from the contingencies of social life, from individual memory or development, and mapped onto the bony structures of the head. Rosine's lexicon (her "terms") is perfectly equivalent to her body (her "organs"). It is a small but nonetheless apt example of how the body, and its immediately legible signs, supplants the past through the phrenological gaze. That contingency of any kind could be replaced by a brute biological determinism was one of the aspects of phrenology most often attacked by its critics and parodists; *Blackwood's*, as always, was quick to seize on this implication of the science, and in 1821 the pseudonymous "Sir Toby Tickletoby" submitted a Modest Proposal to have all infants submit their heads to phrenological examination, so that the "infant murderer, or the confirmed thief, might pay the forfeit of their intended crimes long before their little arms were able to wield a rush, or their eyes distinguish one species of property from another."[21] As the *Blackwood's* critic understood, to a phrenologist all phenomena of mental life are only singular instances of long, ineradicable habits, and the past is irrelevant insofar as it is only the previous repetition of occurences amply visible in the present.

What motivates Lucy's reading of Rosine is, in fact, Rosine's overly intimate *reference* to the past. Rosine had, it is worth noting, been describing "Dr. John" in appreciative terms: "Qu'il est vraiment beau, mademoiselle, ce jeune docteur! Quels yeux — quels regard! Tenez!" (*V*, 441). It is not Rosine's vulgar bluntness that flusters Lucy so much as her resurrection of a past desire — Rosine has dared restore to Lucy an uncomfortable memory of a previous cathexis. In response, Lucy employs a phrenological gaze, one that not only elides Rosine's past but also shrouds her own past by displacing her reaction from regret, a mode of memory, to clinical evaluation. Rosine is diagnosed, labeled, and dismissed, with one swift application of phrenological terms. Rosine has been leveled by Graham Bretton's glance ("Quels yeux — quel regard!"), but Lucy will not be similarly affected by this summoning up of the past, for she has recourse to a clinical gaze.[22]

The strangeness of this gaze, a gaze that avoids the "interior" of memory in preference for the "exterior" of visible behavior and legible bodies, is usually ignored in studies of Brontë's work. Everywhere in criticism of the classical novel, particularly in criticism of Brontë's texts, is the assumption that meaning and human significance reside in a deep interior, which is masked by duplicitous surfaces; the keynote of this motif is struck by Sandra Gilbert and Susan Gubar, who argue that Brontë, among other women writers, produces "works whose surface designs conceal or obscure deeper, less accessible (and less socially acceptable) levels of meaning."[23] Ultimately this privileging of depth — the interiors of texts, and the interiors of characters within texts — can be traced back to an investigation of the gaze, of that process of (usually male) seeing that, by concentrating on surfaces, is blind to true value. Critical opinion on Brontë centers around a strong consensus: that the secret, the deep, the nonvisual is where value rests for Brontë and her narrators. This consensus borrows much of its force from Laura Mulvey's reading of Lacan and film, for it is here, with the combined influences of psychoanalysis and Hollywood, that visuality becomes linked to, as Mulvey phrases it, "taking other people as objects, subjecting them to a controlling and curious gaze," a gaze that oppresses and denies latent interiority.[24] Yet against this paradigm stands the strange, phrenologically inflected nature of so many moments in Brontë's work — moments in which, as with the analysis of Rosine, definite sorts of labeling and classifying occur; moments in which, as in M. Paul's first reading, Lucy does indeed become a spectacle, and is not harmed by the experience; moments, that is, in which the interiority guaranteed by memory is elided in favor of an objectifying, indeed a reifying, gaze. Lucy is comfortably summarized, by M. Paul, as a collection of "choses," and as a result of this gaze Lucy gains employment, a friend, and eventually a romance.[25]

The paradigms of visuality, and therefore of personality, stemming from a critique of objectification are, I want to argue, anachronistic — they ignore the specific implications of a science of seeing that Brontë, among others in her society, took seriously and that she employed consistently. As Jonathan Crary suggests, any study of the seeing subject should be based not on the "spectator," the transcendental subject, but the "observer," the figure who "sees within a prescribed set of possibilities, one who is embedded in a system of conventions and limitations."[26] I will suggest that attention to a different model of visuality — the clinical project of phrenology and physiognomy — compels us to revise, or nuance, our more usual privileging of depth over surface, and that it compels this revision by signaling to us its effacement of memory from psychological functioning. The disappearance of memory from clinical consideration is highlighted by phrenology, and by what I have called the "empty space" in the phrenological diagram, but it is a disappearance with some pedigree; even the founder of physiognomy, J. C. Lavater, whose *Physiognomische Fragmente* began appearing in the 1770s, refused to consider memory a key mental faculty. "To know, to desire, to act, or accurately to observe and meditate, to perceive and to wish, to possess the power of motion and resistance — these combined constitute man an animal, intellectual, and moral being," he writes, nicely summarizing a model of personality from which remembrance is absent.[27] It seems, therefore, that implicit in the body-reading theories and practices of the late eighteenth and early nineteenth centuries is an ethic of progressiveness, of future-oriented activity, that excludes memory altogether — as if in the act of *surfacing* the personality, of making it completely legible, what we as twentieth-century readers habitually associate with interiority, namely memory, is obscured and demoted. "Man," Combe wrote in his *Constitution*, "is evidently a progressive being."[28] If Brontë's investment in the phrenological enterprise is taken seriously, and if her phrenologically influenced elision of remembrance is noted, then our habitual (and ritually asserted) claims for the "interiority of the Other" must seem less secure. We might in fact say that Brontë's work is less a critique of repression than an instance of a psychological model that prefers the progressive, the active, the forward-looking to the backward-turned visages of retrospect. Like Brontë's plots, the phrenological mind is dynamic, an entity that performs tasks, satisfies or fails to satisfy needs, makes plans, and advances into the future. It does not linger over remembrance; within phrenological precincts, the past (as exemplified by the attic of *Jane Eyre*'s Thornfield Hall or the nun's burial ground in *Villette*) is stasis and danger. Combe goes on to be more explicit: "If, then, wisdom and benevolence have been employed in constituting man, we may expect the arrangements of creation, in regard to him, to be calculated, *as a leading object, to excite* his various powers, corporeal and mental, to *activity*."[29] When the self is unveiled as it is in Brontë's work, we can see that it faces resolutely forward.

What is unveiled is not, therefore, a symptom in the psychoanalytic sense—not a clue to prior trauma; what is unveiled are "faculties," and a faculty is a tool for the progressive personality.[30] One more of Brontë's explicit uses of phrenology, this from *The Professor*, makes the distinction between "symptom" and "faculty" clear. The novel's narrator, William Crimsworth, is being interrogated brusquely—much in the manner of M. Paul —by the wealthier, eccentric Hunsden Yorke Hunsden:

> "Is it your intention to become a tradesman?" he inquired presently.
> "It was my serious intention three months ago."
> "Humph! the more fool you—you look like a tradesman! What a practical business-like face you have!"
> "My face is as the Lord made it, Mr. Hunsden."
> "The Lord never made either your face or head for X—. What good can your bumps of ideality, comparison, self-esteem, conscientiousness, do you here?" (*P*, 60)

Of a faculty, one never asks questions of derivation, such as: where is it from? where did it begin? That question is occluded by Crimsworth's quasi-biological, quasi-theological formula, "my face is as the Lord made it," which means in essence that because the origins of phrenological signs (skull bumps) are mysterious, they are out of the realm of human agency. A symptom is as the owner of that symptom has made it—it is a sign traceable in time, a displacement of memory. A faculty, however, replaces derivation with predication: what is it for? What, as Hunsden asks of Crimsworth, will it do? That faculties require to be tied to actions should remind us of Jane Eyre's impassioned comment that women "need exercise for their faculties, and a field for their efforts as much as their brothers do" (*JE*, 141); effort, striving, will is implied by this use of phrenological language, rather than past accomplishment or failure. A faculty is not a sign of the repression of remembrance, as is the symptom, but is instead a sign of the irrelevance of memory. Brontë's women, no less than Combe's "man," are constitutionally progressive beings, and they continually seek in new places and, more crucially, new faces salvation from the perils of retrospection. The absence of memory from the phrenological diagram — that absence that I have already detected in Dr. Browne's "report," in phrenological theorizing, and in Brontë's work — is not merely a sign of repression. It is an index to an entirely new conception of character, one that does not owe much to our notions of a largely mnemonic "interior" but refers instead to a visible, unveiled, assertive set of surface signs. It is, most fundamentally, an enabling absence, for it permits the sudden changes of scene that keep Brontë's narratives vital, and it permits Lucy Snowe to utter what can be taken as the motto for the phrenological psyche: "It was better to go forward than backward" (V, 107).

The Memory Debate

As a boy, Franz Josef Gall noticed that a schoolmate with protruding eyes was remarkably quick to memorize passages from books. As a young man, he returned to this observation continually, noticing a similar pairing of bulging eyes and retentive memories in many of his colleagues; the persistence of this linkage led Gall to formulate his first theories of cerebral localization. Here phrenology begins: with the assertion that if a facility for memorization is accompanied by the protrusion of the eyes, then the faculty for verbal memory must be on the orbital surface of the frontal lobes of the brain; and if this "organ" is enlarged, then a resulting pressure on the orbital plate would push the eyeballs outward.[31] The concept now known as "functional localization," then, begins with a theory about memory. Although Gall would replace this faculty for verbal memory, located behind the eyes, with a faculty for language, he would not forget the role memory had played in his earliest psychological researches; of the twenty-seven original faculties mapped by Gall, four would be devoted to kinds of memory.[32]

And yet this science, which begins with seeing memory, evolved into the phrenology of Spurzheim — the phrenology first carried to Britain — which can see no memory at all. Spurzheim took Gall's twenty-seven "organs," and added eight more, but drained from Gall's four mnemonic faculties their function of remembrance. In *A View of the Philosophical Principles of Phrenology*, first published in 1825, Spurzheim makes his case for the demotion of memory from its place as a fundamental part of the psyche. Memory, he claims in a concluding glossary, is "an internal repetition of its function by every intellectual faculty."[33] That is, only the intellectual faculties — those clustered on the forehead, as opposed to the "affective faculties" or "propensities," such as Destructiveness or Benevolence, which are found on the back, top, and sides of the skull—have any memory whatsoever; and this "memory" is only a repetition, only, as we have seen with Lucy's reading of Rosine's head, a habit. Forgetting for the time being his teacher's espousal of some mnemonic faculties, Spurzheim presses the following argument:

> Is memory, then, a fundamental power of the mind? Dr. Gall thinks not; he considers it as the second degree of activity of every organ and faculty; and therefore admits as many memories as fundamental faculties. . . . My opinion also is, that memory is not a fundamental faculty, but the repetition of some previous perception, and a *quantitive* [*sic*] mode of action. However, as I think the affective powers are blind, and without clear consciousness, I do not believe they have any memory. I, consequently, confine the mode of action under discussion to the intellectual faculties.[34]

Two points are intended to be clear in this passage. First, memory is to be dispersed among all thirty-five faculties, rather than receiving the dignity of its own localized "organ"; and as Spurzheim is firm in stating, this dispersal is a demotion, from a "fundamental power of the mind" to a "second degree of activity." In addition, this dispersed memory is denied to all but a fraction of the brain's powers. Only "intellectual faculties" can remember, and these faculties—called by Spurzheim and, later, Combe by the names Individuality, Form, Size, Weight, Coloring, Locality, Number, Order, Eventuality, Time, Tune, Language, Comparison, and Causality— are cut off from their "affective" brethren, that is, from emotion.[35] Remembrance of affect (be the affect Hope, Wonder, Wit, or Amativeness) is explicitly discarded. What remains of memory is an affectless, merely repetitive function.

Why refuse memory its own place on the diagram? One answer is provided by O. S. Fowler in 1847: "Memory recalls past ocurrences [*sic*], doings, acquisitions of knowledge, etc. It is not however a single faculty, else all could remember every thing equally well; which is not the case; but every intellectual faculty recollects its own past functions. . . . This diversity in the memories of men, entirely precludes the idea that memory is a single faculty."[36] In a move remarkably prescient of modern neuroscience, Fowler asserts that memory is not one function but many functions loosely classified under one rubric. Insofar as part of the rigor demanded by phrenology was the purity of its "organs," so demonstrably impure a mental function as memory, which can remember words and images with widely different efficacy, must not be dignified with its own space. There is, however, a further reason for the demotion of memory that Spurzheim proclaimed—one that deals less with the inner consistency of phrenological theory and more with the sort of personality envisioned by phrenologists. Here, as always,

Combe in *The Constitution of Man* is most clear, and most clearly self-conscious, about the phrenological psyche:

> Every faculty stands in a definite relation to certain external objects: when it is internally active it desires those objects; when they are presented to it they excite it to activity, and delight it with agreeable sensations. Human happiness and misery are resolvable into the gratification, and denial of gratification, of one or more of our mental faculties, or of the feelings connected with our bodily frame. The faculties, in themselves, are mere instincts; the moral sentiments and intellect being higher instincts than the animal propensities.[37]

The linkage of "faculty" to "instinct" is itself fascinating, but what is most notable about Combe's explanation is the insistence on the external orientation of the mind. If every faculty is a way of relating to external objects, then no faculty can be a way of relating to internal objects—that is, to memory, to the inner images created by remembrance.[38] There is no "instinct to remember" in Combe's theory, because if the urge to activity and striving that we have seen elsewhere in Combe (and that is so visible in Brontë) is to triumph, the mind must be fully outer-directed. When a "faculty" is defined in these terms, memory cannot become a faculty. Perhaps in this externally driven psyche we can see Combe's retort to the older, firmly entrenched associationist theories of Stewart and Reid, which are based on the movements of inner images; living in Edinburgh, Combe could hardly have failed to be in competition with the Scottish psychological tradition. With the rejection of memory phrenology makes perhaps its most startling, and underappreciated, attempt to sever its ties with previous scientific tradition—a new psyche is being formed. Fowler's common-sense reason for the removal of remembrance from the phrenological diagram and Combe's metapsychological justification for the demotion of memory together provide a good backdrop for the absence of the mnemonic that I have begun to trace in Brontë.

Nevertheless, the consensus about memory that obtained between Spurzheim, Fowler, and Combe, which was dominant from 1820 to the 1840s, began to break apart as the century neared its midpoint. By 1855, the year of Brontë's death, phrenologists themselves were giving slightly wider scope to memory, and critics of the phrenological system had finally selected memory as the ram with which to batter the long-besieged theory. Much of the discussion focused on the intellectual faculty called Eventuality, which Spurzheim and Combe located, significantly enough, in the center of the forehead—its orientation was directly forward. Combe described the faculty simply: "Takes cognizance of occurrences or events."[39] Spurzheim complicated the picture somewhat by asserting that although every intellectual faculty has its own memory, the memory of Eventuality (itself an oxymoronic concept) is to be specially termed Reminiscence: "We have reminiscence, if we remember how certain perceptions have been acquired, while memory consists in their perfect reproduction. . . I neither consider reminiscence as a fundamental faculty, nor as a modification of memory, but as the peculiar memory or repetition of the functions of *Eventuality*, that faculty which takes cognizance of the functions of all the others."[40] In Spurzheim's work, Reminiscence, a second-order mental function, serves to introduce a slight element of self-conscious remembering into the mind; unlike the rest of phrenological memory, which as we have seen is merely repetition of an instinct, Reminiscence is a repetition that recognizes itself to be a repetition. This comes far nearer to modern notions of memory than is usual for phrenology, and it means that Eventuality can with some justice be said to be the protomnemonic phrenological faculty, the place where memory gained a foothold, however slight, on the phrenological diagram. Finally, by 1855, Spurzheim's notion of Reminiscence had been digested by phrenological theorists, and in that year O. S. and L. N. Fowler's *Illustrated Self-Instructor in Phrenology and Physiology* offered an expanded account of what Eventuality does: "Memory of FACTS; recollection of CIRCUMSTANCES, NEWS, OCCURRENCES, and historical, scientific, and passing EVENTS; what has been SAID, SEEN, HEARD, and once KNOWN. Adapted to ACTION, or those changes constantly occurring around or within us."[41] While Spurzheim's Reminiscence threatened to break apart the externally oriented, instinct-driven model of personality native to phrenology, the Fowler brothers have here safely contained it. The work of Eventuality in this account is far less inner-directed, and far more externally based, than Spurzheim's; much like a newspaper, the Fowlers' "reminiscences" are records of external events that are noted and stored — Eventuality becomes, as it were, the faculty of record. The eruption of a vivid personal past is not imagined in their version. The debate over memory within the phrenological world was largely decided by the moves exemplified by the Fowlers: memory may have a liminal place within Eventuality, but that memory is by no means an internalized mode of existence. The individual with a large organ of Eventuality will, so the Fowlers state, have "a clear and retentive memory of historical facts, general knowledge, what has been seen, heard, read, done, etc., even to detail; considering advantages, is well informed and knowing; desires to witness and institute experiments."[42] The path that might have led to self-attention has been diverted back to the outside world.

A clear example of how vivid personal memories are cast out of phrenological considerations is offered by Hewett Watson, the editor of Edinburgh's *Phrenological Journal* in the 1830s and a well-known lecturer on phrenology and botany. In an 1831 article entitled "Remarks on the Peculiarities of Memory," Watson is at pains to describe various forms of memory, and to which faculties they are attached; a good botanist, he explains, will have a large faculty of Language, enabling him to remember names of plants, and a large faculty of Form, which will insure remembrance of the plants themselves. In the midst of his article Watson turns to "men who are capable of remembering what they see, hear, or do, during a very long period; their mental impressions appear to bid defiance to time, and to bear its daily attritions almost without change." This, as Watson makes clear, is personal, emotive memory: "Whether the subjects remembered be few or many, and of whatever kind or nature, still mental images of them once formed remain deep and distinct. Individuals endowed with this variety of memory in its highest degree, will often converse nearly as easily and correctly of occurrences years gone by, as others do of those which happened but a week before." A psyche such as this—one that remains tethered to a deeply impressed set of remembrances that have not lost their affect—is not accounted for in phrenological theory. Watson is frank in admitting that phrenology cannot literally locate this mode of memory: "It seems yet an unsolved problem on what organic peculiarity this depends. That it is not attributable to size, or at least to size alone, every day's experience must assure us."[43] Watson is one of the first phrenologists to admit such an absence, and perhaps the sole example of a phrenologist admitting the absence as an unresolved dilemma; on the whole, phrenological writing on memory preferred to ignore the sort of personal remembrance Watson discusses and to claim for the phrenological diagram a second-order memory of facts, "general knowledge," and "information."

Despite the work performed by the Fowlers in containing the memory of Eventuality, and despite admissions such as Watson's, the debate over the validity of phrenology as a whole began to hinge more and more on the absence of memory, and less could be done by the phrenologists to combat these criticisms. Increasingly, the phrenological dismissal of memory was seen as its chief defect. When in 1855 a *Blackwood's* writer used a review of Sir Benjamin Brodie's *Psychological Inquiries* as an occasion to debunk phrenology, the reviewer did it through a discussion of memory. In the book under review, Brodie considers memory the center of consciousness, but although he condemns phrenology, he does not do so through its lack of a faculty of memory; it is the anonymous reviewer's innovation to combine Brodie's two opinions, the paramount importance of memory and the fallacious nature of phrenology, into one line of argument. The argument advanced runs as follows: there are only two modes of consciousness, thought and sensation, and memory is the fount of all thought. "We are unable to regard the brain with any distinctness," the reviewer asserts, "except under two aspects: 1. As the organ of memory, or that association of ideas which may be described as a development of memory. 2. As the center of the whole nervous system."[44] Following Brodie's lead, the reviewer places memory at the center of all mental functioning except the senses, and this emphasis on memory helps to explain the review's sudden turn toward a critique of phrenology — the reviewer finds it necessary to discuss the one, familiar, popular psychological theory that demotes memory from the position of prominence to which it should be raised. Having asserted that the brain is the "organ of memory," the reviewer turns to the dispersal I have been sketching: "The system of Gall and Spurzheim gives to each organ its own memory; but when you have once introduced this great organ of memory, you have swallowed up in it a number of minor organs. Amongst others, an organ of speech or language becomes a manifest redundancy."[45] The point here — an absolutely critical one — is that if, as Brodie and the reviewer do, memory is made the fount of consciousness, then all phrenological organs are useless, insofar as they are subject to the rule of memory. It can also be said, from the opposite direction, that if the phrenological organs are taken seriously, as in the work of Spurzheim, Combe, or Fowler, then it is memory that is useless. An all-or-nothing dilemma has been sketched, implicitly, in the reviewer's contentious argument: either a psychological theory depends wholly on memory, or it dispenses with it altogether; memory either rules consciousness, or is outcast from consciousness. The reviewer's preference is plain: "It is in memory alone that the brain becomes a distinct and special instrument."[46] We shall see later how this dualistic argumentative structure (memory over all, or all over memory) informs Brontë's texts, in which succumbing to memory can only be an all-consuming act, and in which memory is never comfortably integrated into a larger consciousness. For the time being, however, what must be noted is that by the date of Brontë's death, and only two years after the publication of *Villette*, arguments about phrenology from without and within the science were beginning to center on remembrance.

The infiltration of these debates, carried on within medical and popular journals and between psychologists and doctors, into the underpopulated world of Brontë's fiction should not be a matter for great surprise. We have the recent work of Lawrence Rothfield to remind us that the invocation of the nineteenth century's still-emerging sciences — be that science surgical medicine, economics, or phrenology — in fiction created new structures of character, of plotting, and of reading; in short, that even the most putatively nonscientific fictional texts borrowed some of their "truth-effects" from scientific discourses.[47] More crucially, perhaps, we must recognize that phrenology itself was a school of fiction, a way of constructing "characters" that share the key novelistic virtues of consistency and vividness. Combe, in his *System of Phrenology*, makes it clear that phrenological judgments and "natural" judgments share the same territory: "In regard to the feelings, men practiced in the business of life have observed, that one individual is strongly addicted to covetousness,—another to cruelty, —another to benevolence,—another to pride,—another to vanity; and they are accustomed to regard these dispositions as natural, uniform, and permanent."[48] Phrenology will do nothing to shake these businesslike observations. Spurzheim was blunter: "Characters," he advises his reader, "are commonly divided into good and bad," and thus will he consider the subjects of his analysis.[49] Phrenological thinking, therefore, was if anything helpful to the novelist, insofar as it provided a scientific justification for the presentation of "natural," "uniform," and visible characters. Visibility is the key: it is the emphasis that, in phrenological thinking, replaces the reliance on memory that Brodie and his reviewer preferred, and it is a powerful enough idea that Hegel, early in the career of phrenology, subjected its brand of visibility to a lengthy critique in his *Phänomenologie des Geistes*.[50] It is what made phrenology so persuasive a method for novelists, and what made the entrance of phrenology into the novel so easy; it is, above all, what made the excision of memory from personality and narrative possible. Around visibility, in fact, the debate over memory continually hovered, so that the debaters themselves seem continually to be asking one question: can everything in and of the self be seen? Is it indeed possible to study a face and skull and to say, with M. Paul, "I read it"?

The Work of Phrenology

To excise memory through a certain technique of sight is a task, and a task with definite steps that can, with patience, be elucidated. It will be more possible to consider phrenological gazing as a technique with its own set of tasks if we understand it as part of what Michel Foucault has called the "clinical gaze," a gaze that is justified by an institutional lexicon, that is always aware of deviancies and the exceptional, and that is continually calculating propensities—a gaze, as Foucault stresses, that performed a crucial role in clinical medicine near the end of the eighteenth century. By the nineteenth century, this technique—which originated in the clinic—has been disseminated popularly and has become a common possession, as available (through the filters of phrenology and physiognomy) to the lay student such as Brontë as to the professional such as Dr. Browne. Foucault's description of the clinical gaze is a more than adequate summary of phrenological sight as well. By lifting inchoate inner emotions into the ordered clarity of a scientific language, the clinical gaze, Foucault asserts, posits "the possibility of an exhaustive, clear, and complete reading" of the object of study.[51] No residue of subjectivity eludes the clinical signifier, and the signifier itself never exceeds the signified of the clinical body. Before the need to "open up a few corpses" arrived, before the depth of the body began to be considered, Foucault argues, there was the clinical gaze in its purity, a gaze of surfaces for which nothing is hidden. The clinical gaze is, as we can see from Foucault's analysis, a tool—and insofar as phrenology is a popular, later manifestation of this structure of sight, it is a tool as well, one that with certain discrete functions pries apart memory from the psyche. A brief explanation of these functions, then, will help give depth to my later examination of Brontë's texts and will help explain how, precisely, a gaze can triumph over remembrance. As will be evident, the five functions of the phrenological or clinical gaze that I outline hereafter bear a pertinent resemblance to the list of nostalgic transmutations of the past that I have mapped in relation to Austen. The central difference is that here a dependence on the body, particularly the visual body, underwrites these more scientized functions.

During one of Jane Eyre's first conversations with Mr. Rochester, explicit phrenological assessment makes a vivid appearance when Rochester demands Jane's opinion of his visible self:

> He lifted up the sable waves of hair which lay horizontally over his brow, and showed a solid enough mass of intellectual organs; but an abrupt deficiency where the suave sign of benevolence should have risen.
>
> "Now, ma'am, am I a fool?"
>
> "Far from it, sir. You would perhaps think me rude if I inquired in return whether you are a philanthropist?"
>
> "There again! Another stick of the penknife, when she pretended to pat my head: and that is because I said I did not like the society of children and old women (low be it spoken!). No, young lady, I am not a general philanthropist; but I bear a conscience;" and he pointed to the prominences which are said to indicate that faculty—and which, fortunately for him, were sufficiently conspicuous; giving, indeed, a marked breadth to the upper part of his head. (*JE*, 163)

When one remembers that Jane and Rochester have just met, what is most remarkable about this exchange is how visible personality becomes. This is the first, and perhaps primary, task of phrenological sight: to *surface* character. A depth psychology this is not; character traits are raised from hidden propensities to visible faculties, and inscribed upon the skull in such a way that even viewers in dependent and awkward positions such as Jane are capable of deciphering them.[52] The judgments that result from such readings are not entirely clumsy or simple—Jane and Rochester are capable of detecting a subtle balance between a lack of benevolence and a wealth of conscience that can be, even for the modern reader, an adequate guide to Rochester's conduct; those judgments must, however, dispense with a developmental model. "Surfaced" character does not possess the three-dimensionality or temporal regression of mnemonic character. Jane as yet knows nothing of Rochester's past, but—a point too important to be ignored—her phrenological assessment is neither faulty nor lacking, and it gives her a measure of conversational power that would otherwise be denied her. Equipped with phrenological skill, Jane finds herself in the position of the clinical reader, able to use a knowing sarcasm ("you are a philanthropist?"), able to reach a footing of conversational equality with her employer. It is the past, in *Jane Eyre*, that will remove these footholds and create various vertiginous perils; on the contrary, "surfaced" character, which exists in a constant present—the present of propensity, not the past of symptom—insures some safety and reciprocity.[53] As much as Lucy Snowe's self is unveiled to M. Paul, Rochester is here, with only the lifting of hair a prerequisite, unveiled to Jane, because his psyche has been inscribed on the now-visible surfaces of his skull.

This tangibility was the most frequently trumpeted aspect of the science. The Fowler brothers proudly announced that phrenology "reduces mental study to that same *tangible* basis of *proportion* in which all science consists; leaving nothing dark or doubtful, but developing the true SCIENCE OF MIND, and the laws of its action."[54] Combe, with more restraint, also saw the surfacing of character to be the virtue that set phrenology most firmly aside from its competitors, for

> the organs of the mind can be seen and felt, and their size estimated,—and the mental manifestations also that accompany them can be observed, in an unlimited number of instances,—so that, assuming the existence of organs, it is clear that a far higher degree of certainty in regard to the natural endowments of the mind may be attained by these means, than by any other previously applied.[55]

There is no question of being trapped in one's own consciousness—to both Combe and Fowler the true stumbling-block of mental inquiry; through the alleviating power of sight, and through this sight's clinical ability to externalize or "surface" mental capacity, psychological (and indeed epistemological) research becomes entirely empirical. Cartesian meditations are, as it were, replaced by diagrams and calipers, signs of a science wedded to surfaces. And insofar as only capacity can be surfaced—the past cannot be surfaced, for the discovery and conceptualization of the "symptom" awaits Charcot and Freud—memory remains outcast.

If the self can be surfaced, then it can also be named. The second of the key phrenological tasks is to attach names to mental phenomena—to *taxonomize* the object(s) of the clinical gaze. Once the disparate phenomena of mental life have been raised to visibility, they can be translated into language; in such a way the phrenological diagram functions, for it not only claims to surface the psyche but also organizes and compartmentalizes it, covering it with words. What Barbara Stafford has called a neoclassical urge—a "draining of substance through schematization" and a "wholesale, and often inappropriate, application of rigid and calculable norms"—is at the heart of the phrenological or clinical gaze.[56] Like so many other Enlightenment classification schemes, from Linnaean botany to Diderot's encyclopedia, the phrenological system is at once democratically open and firmly controlled by a linguistic imperative: everything must have names. The path of increasing regularization is visible in the phrenological diagram itself; whereas Gall's early depictions of surface organs were as literal bumps on a realistically rendered countenance and head, the diagrams of the 1820s displayed stylized, asexual heads with smooth, geometrical surface divisions—an almost mathematical quantification had taken over a putatively empirical clinical theory.[57] This classificatory precision enabled, indeed required, a process of naming in all phrenological judgment: one looks at and reads the head and face, then applies a name.

The names applied, as can be seen in Brontë's fiction, need not be explicitly "clinical." While they often are—witness the references to Rochester's "sign of benevolence"—they are perhaps more often "everyday" judgments that are nonetheless phrenological because they borrow their authority from a practiced study of the face and skull. That is, clinical gazes often taxonomized and named human behavior with quite common terms; once the clinical gaze escaped the confines of actual clinics, it was free to employ less obviously scientific or medical terminology, however identical the actual practice of gazing remained. Such a process of everyday taxonomizing occurs in *The Professor*, when Crimsworth, standing before a portrait of his mother, elicits Hunsden's clinical judgment:

> "Do you consider the face pretty?" I asked.
> "Pretty! no—but how can it be pretty, with sunk eyes and hollow cheeks? but it is peculiar; it seems to think. You could have a talk with that woman, if she were alive, on other subjects than dress, visiting, and compliments."
> I agreed with him, but did not say so. He went on.
> "Not that I admire a head of that sort; it wants character and force; there's too much of the sen-si-tive (so he articulated it, curling his lip at the same time) in that mouth; besides, there is Aristocrat written on the brow and defined in the figure; I hate your aristocrats." (*P*, 58)

Hunsden's reading is explicitly "clinical," insofar as it bases itself on a visual investigation of the face and skull (concentrated here in the brow); yet it issues in an everyday term: Aristocrat. The offered diagnosis is, therefore, both inspired by phrenology and couched in lay terms, and Crimsworth's mother has been placed—she fits, now, in an impromptu taxonomical scheme of "Aristocrats" and nonaristocrats. The process loosely runs as follows: a phrenologically inspired visual assessment; a naming; the imposition of an organizational or classificatory scheme. Such is taxonomy, moved outside the clinic and into the home.

For my purposes, what is crucial about taxonomizing as a phrenological task is that it enables personality to be discussed without reference to memory; the schemes imposed by phrenological or clinical gazes are explicitly antimnemonic, as the continuation of Hunsden's "reading" shows: "'You think, then, Mr Hunsden, that patrician descent may be read in a distinctive cast of form and features?' 'Patrician descent be hanged! Who doubts that your lordlings may have their "distinctive cast of form and features" as much as we — shire tradesmen have ours?'" (P, 59) In one of the most revealing phrenological moments in Brontë's fiction, Hunsden demonstrates how the taxonomical schemes produced by phrenology owe nothing to the past. A term that seemingly exists only with reference to heredity and cultural memory ("Aristocrat") is here employed with reference solely to a sort of biological present; the historical causality of aristocracy ("patrician descent") is explicitly rejected by Hunsden and replaced by a biological causality: the features make the aristocrat. "It is you, William," Hunsden tells Brontë's narrator, "who are the aristocrat of your family" (P, 59) — every family and every class has its own aristocrats. The implied classificatory scheme set up here, aristocrat/commoner, exists without reference to any past that might determine it, much like the larger taxonomical scheme of the psyche promulgated by Spurzheim and Combe.

The way *taxonomizing* implies a severance from the past, or "descent," leads us to the third of the phrenological tasks: the work of *decontextualizing*. A good way to understand this task is to consider, briefly, the phrenological diagram. Its head abstracted from the body, its facial features betraying no discernible gender or age, its expression bearing no reference to emotion, it is a testament to a decontextualized gaze, one that takes into account only those biological features that directly signify the psyche. Such a practice of gazing began before Gall's first researches; Lavaterian physiognomy often employed the silhouette as its method of investigation, since the outline of a face performed the necessary work of draining the object of study of any encumbering factors. Indeed, these decontextualized silhouette images lent themselves to a neat typographical taxonomy; in Lavaterian texts they were often grouped six or eight to a page, reduced to identical sizes and placed in neat boxes.[58] In phrenological texts this visual decontextualization finds its counterpart—analyses of skulls and heads, much like Dr. Browne's reading of Brontë, are performed without reference to social position or past history; and in Brontë's own fiction this clinical process of gazing and analyzing is often exactly reproduced, as in William Crimsworth's reading of one of his female students, Juanna Trista:

> I wonder that anyone, looking at the girl's head and countenance, would have received her under their roof. She had precisely the same shape of skull as Pope Alexander the Sixth; her organs of benevolence, veneration, conscientiousness, adhesiveness, were singularly small, those of self-esteem, firmness, destructiveness, combativeness, pre-posterously large; her head sloped up in the penthouse shape, was contracted about the forehead, and prominent behind; she had a rather good, though large and marked features; her temperament was fibrous and bilious, her complexion pale and dark, hair and eyes black, form angular and rigid but proportionate, age fifteen. (*P*, 129–130)[59]

This extraordinary moment, notable for its comfort with clinical syntax and terminology as well as its venom, encapsulates the many elisions that are motivated by phrenological decontextualization. We know of Juanna that her ancestry is mixed Belgian and Spanish and that her Catalonian father is a colonial merchant, but that information is oddly irrelevant compared to the wealth of biological information we possess — it cannot account for her insurrectionary behavior in the classroom or for the fact that, as Crimsworth notes, she "remained in Europe long enough to repay, by malevolence and ingratitude, all who had ever done her a good turn" (*P*, 130). Only her clinical profile, her organs (listed with a unique exhaustiveness), can explain Juanna. Although we can detect some elements of "personal history" in this phrenological analysis — the reference to Pope Alexander VI alludes to her Catholicism, her age is mentioned, and there are hints of a racialized assessment — Juanna's person is severed from these mnemonic, or developmental, facts. We can formulate this severance in the following way: Juanna's visible, phrenological organs are directly explanatory of her behavior, while her upbringing and parentage are more epiphenomenal than matters of real consequence. When Crimsworth seeks an explanation for his student's actions, he turns to a simple (and somewhat brutal) reading of her organs and not to any developmental account. A clinical resemblance to a long-dead pope is of more use than an elucidation of Juanna's past. The decontextualizing work of phrenology is, therefore, usually a separation from the contexts of personal memory.

Decontextualization as a function is not possible without the fourth of the phrenological tasks: the *detaching* of mental faculties from one another, as well as the detaching of faculties from surrounding contexts. If we recall Lucy Snowe's evaluation of the servant Rosine, we will remember that her behavior is explained on the basis of the fact that her "organs of reverence and reserve were not largely developed"; only two of the thirty-five faculties are in play, it seems, while the others remain unimportant. That is, phrenology envisioned a world of detachings and separations: a world in which mental faculties could operate without reference to each other, or in which the personality could operate without reference to its surroundings — what Barbara Stafford has aptly termed the "tendency to simplify, abstract, isolate, and detach segments of the body" in phrenological theory and practice.[60] Like the groupings of detached noses and eyes that Brontë produced when studying drawing, phrenological sight required of its advocates a concentration on the individual unit, detached from its neighbors.[61] Crimsworth's analysis of Juanna is a list — the form clinical assessment must take, for there is no real binding force between the various members of the list, no way to incorporate them into a larger narrative; Dr. Browne's reading of Brontë is formed in much the same manner, for it is an expanded list of attributes, not a developmental narrative or cohesive account. Phrenological readings are necessarily and constitutively paratactic.

How does this function of detaching erase memory? Quite simply by refusing to lend to its objects the possibility of an explanatory, consequential narrative — by refusing to make the psyche hypotactic. The readings of Rosine in *Villette* and of Juanna in *The Professor* are amply illustrative of this fact. In both, certain physical details — explicitly phrenological organs, although this explicitness is not necessary in every case — are detached from the bodies of the viewed women, and then subjected to study; as a result, their actions are detached from any explanatory narrative. Juanna's malevolence cannot be the result of psychic development because it has already been explained as the result of her immutable, detachable skull organs. And lest we think that this sort of logic is extended only to Brontë's minor characters, we have the evidence of William Crimsworth himself, and how his "bumps of ideality, comparison, self-esteem, conscientiousness" (*P*, 60) lead him out of his industrial clerkship and into a career in education. The logic of hypotaxis (had such an event not occurred, my current situation might have been different) is denied Brontë's characters, whose actions are always compelled by certain ineradicable desires, instincts, and propensities, mental properties that are also visible. Here it is useful to recall Jane Eyre's requirement for "exercise" for her "faculties," and how that requirement sends her, suddenly and with an admixture of randomness, away from Lowood School and to Thornfield Hall. The parataxis I have been sketching — borne out of this function of detaching — operates, therefore, at the level of Brontë's plots as well as in the syntax of her phrenologically inspired descriptive moments; parataxis is the syntax of action and personality in Brontë's world.

The denial of explanatory narrative to Brontë's characters (indeed to all phrenological subjects) is not solely the act of detaching. It derives equally from the fifth and final of the tasks of the phrenological gaze: the act of *fixing* character, rendering it static and incapable of much development. When Lucy Snowe reads the character of the king of Labassecour from across a concert hall, we are presented with an example of how clinical gazes fix character and elide memory:

> I had never read, never been told anything of his nature or his habits; and at first the strong hieroglyphics graven as with iron stylet on his brow, round his eyes, beside his mouth, puzzled and baffled instinct. Ere long, however, if I did not *know*, at least I *felt*, the meaning of those characters written without hand. There sat a silent sufferer—a nervous, melancholy man. Those eyes had looked on the visits of a certain ghost—had long waited the comings and goings of that strangest spectre, Hypochondria. (*V*, 290)

This passage enacts several of the earlier "tasks" I have been elucidating; the king's personality is surfaced into visible "characters written without hand," and these "characters" are decontextualized from his kingship, his nation, or his age; furthermore, the passage issues in a familiarly taxonomic moment, as we are offered the term "Hypochondria" as an adequate and full description of the king's psyche. Above all, however, Lucy's reading insures that the king's personality is fixed. Lucy's phrenological system (searching the signs of face and brow) expects to find a constant and transhistorical referent for the series of signs presented to it; thus it is not surprising that Lucy, in a later diagnostic discussion, decides that the king's mysterious "Hypochondria" arises not from any event traceable in time, such as his "foreign crown" or possible "early bereavement," but instead from "that darkest foe of all humanity—constitutional melancholy" (*V*, 290). The transient facts of personality, contingent on so many twists of historical fate—what I have called the hypotactic model of the psyche—are here appreciably simplified.[62] This king did not become a hypochondriac, to use Lucy's term, because of a discrete trauma; he simply *is* a hypochondriac. Lucy begins her analysis with no prior knowledge of the king's "nature" or "habits," and such a knowledge is not necessary, for the king—through his visible "signs" or "characters" or "hieroglyphics"—is continually displaying what is always true about him. No probing of memory is necessary, for no real development can occur. Rather than an informative analepsis about this king, we are presented with a visual sketch: the "constitutional" has, through the signs of his body, replaced the developmental.[63]

Precisely the same logic of fixing is applied to Brontë's major characters. Reminiscence is defused because it is not in any real way different from what is occuring in the present, as Crimsworth shows when he addresses a letter to an old schoolmate:

"Still, out of school hours we walked and talked continually together; when the theme of conversation was our companions or our masters we understood each other, and when I recurred to some sentiment of affection, some vague love of an excellent or beautiful object, whether in animate or in inanimate nature, your sardonic coldness did not move me. I felt myself superior to that check *then* as I do *now*." (*P*, 39)

"Then" and "now" are nicely, and explicitly, elided, and early in *The Professor* we are furnished with a clue that although Crimsworth's exterior situation may change throughout the narrative, his character will not alter. Far from being records of self-discovery or psychic growth, Brontë's narratives are records of the collisions and vicissitudes of fully formed, static, fixed psyches searching for the niches that will best accommodate their hardened contours. This antimnemonic personality—a form of the "amnesiac selfhood" whose origins lie in the depathologizing of nostalgia but that is here based on the body's own amnesia—is constructed, as can be best seen through Lucy's discussion of the king of Labassecour, by a continual coalescence of the five phrenological tasks I have been discussing. Rarely if ever are any of these five functions (surfacing, taxonomizing, decontextualizing, detaching, and fixing) to be found divorced from the others; together, they help structure the antimnemonic psyches of Brontë's fiction, and they play a major role in the extended discussions of two of Brontë's novels that follow.

The Professor: Memory and Mastery

At the end of 1845, Charlotte Brontë was engaged in two writing projects: a short semiautobiographical novel, later to be called *The Professor*, and a series of unanswered letters to Constantin Heger, her former teacher and employer in Brussels from 1842 to 1843. The letters, whose frank confessions of lingering romantic attachment led to their being largely excised from Gaskell's biography, end with a final effort, from November 18, 1845, in which Brontë laments her inability to suppress memories of Heger:

> I have done everything, I have sought occupations, I have absolutely forbidden myself the pleasure of speaking about you—even to Emily, but I have not been able to overcome either my regrets or my impatience—and that is truly humiliating—not to know how to get the mastery over one's thoughts, to be the slave of a regret, a memory, the slave of a dominant and fixed idea which has become a tyrant over one's mind.[64]

The ideas running through the letter—which, like the opening letter of William Crimsworth's story, will not lead to an actual correspondence—are thoroughly mapped out by *The Professor*. Memory as a tyrant, a "master"; a reluctance to be a "slave" to the past; the potential of memory to overwhelm a personality unless practical steps are taken—in short, memory as a masterful burden that must in turn be mastered: these are the constitutive elements of William Crimsworth's stern narrative. Brontë's letter introduces us to a world of "mastery," in which the tyrant/slave dynamic is continually operative, and thus provides a good introduction to her earliest novel, in which memory is the primary obstacle to achieving a "mastery over one's thoughts." In *The Professor*, the successful evasion of mental enslavement is achieved through the often tyrannical processes of phrenological, or clinical, sight.

It would at first seem that remembrance is no threat in Brontë's novel, since so little of its space is devoted to acts of memory. Although Crimsworth darkly promises his sadistic brother, the mill-owner Edward, that "you will find I have a good memory" (*P*, 52), there is no real evidence of such a faculty, and no real need to produce it. The narrative begins in an industrial town, a "mushroom-place . . . concerning whose inhabitants it was proverbially said, that not one in a thousand knew his own grandfather" (*P*, 61). From there it progresses to Brussels, where Crimsworth finds employment, gradual success, and a wife; but the city, insofar as it presents him with no past associations, no relations, and no similarities to his native Britain, is not a threat to his mental equilibrium. At each moment of the text, its narrator is occupying a radically *new* space: a modern mill-town, an Ostend coach, a Belgian pensionnat; and the energy of the narrative is directed toward describing the effects of new sensations and experiences (Catholic mores, the Continental female, the act of teaching) on its narrator. With one notable exception, Crimsworth's friend Hunsden Yorke Hunsden, characters disappear from the text and are not resurrected. The narrative is, therefore, a record of discarded attempts to find a social role, and the discarding is abrupt and violent; having left Britain, Crimsworth does not continue communication with his brother, and his maternal uncles having been offended at the novel's outset by his willingness to take employment in trade, they refuse any further contact with their nephew. Although the text ends with a return to Britain, that return is propelled by Crimsworth's wife Frances, who has never set foot on British soil, while the true expatriates—Crimsworth and Hunsden—are either silent about the British virtues she trumpets or openly contemptuous of them. Her attempts to create an "English" atmosphere for Crimsworth are ineffectual; when she asks if her preparation of tea reminds him of "home," he responds: "If I had a home in England, I believe it would recall it" (*P*, 201). A return to previous connections and past options is rigidly foreclosed by the logic of the novel.

If the narrative's broader path refuses returns and remembrances, the psychic cast of its characters reinforces this inability to turn back. "As to the fact of my brother assuming towards me the bearing of a proud, harsh master," Crimsworth thinks during his short-lived employment in Edward's mill, "the fault is his, not mine, and shall his injustice, his bad feeling, turn me at once aside from the path I have chosen? No; at least, ere I deviate, I will advance far enough to see whither my career tends. As yet I am only pressing in at the entrance — a strait gate enough; it ought to have a good terminus" (*P*, 53). A narrative concerned with newness and the shocks of inaugural experiences is reflected in Crimsworth's mindset; rather than considering himself tied to various exits — from his boyhood home, from Eton, from his maternal relations — Crimsworth formulates each moment as an entrance, a passage into an unprecedented set of events. Such a psyche will inevitably form projects, or prospects, rather than retrospects. Frances Henri, in disclosing her idea for founding a school in Britain, discusses the difficulties such an action would encounter, but adds: "Pourtant j'ai mon projet" (*P*, 170). A long-cherished plan, evidently — one nursed in silence, and fiercely defended — occupies Frances's mental energy, supplanting any regrets for her native Switzerland. Like Crimsworth, she is an orphan who plans much and remembers little, a personality that is continually shaping new projects for advancement. Such a structure of experience is relentlessly *active*: the text depicts the efforts to find employment, learn new trades, succeed at new occupations, decipher new situations. The leisure for retrospect, as well as the stuff of retrospect (parents, relations, native landscapes), is not to be found.

Perhaps the other immediately visible fact about *The Professor* is its saturation in phrenological and quasi-phrenological vocabulary. When Crimsworth expresses doubts about moving to Brussels, Hunsden reproves him by scientizing him: "There speaks the organ of caution" (*P*, 84). Portrayals of minor characters, such as the aforementioned analysis of Juanna Trista's head, are explicitly phrenological. Given the prevalence of Spurzheim's and Combe's lexicon, it is difficult to read references to "faculties" as entirely nonphrenological; when Crimsworth declares that his "Conscience" speaks, it is difficult to know whether he is using a familiar trope, or referring to a phrenological organ — perhaps that of Conscientiousness, which Combe tells us instills a "love of truth" — or mixing both discursive registers.[65] When Crimsworth advises Frances to "cultivate the faculties that God and nature have bestowed on you" (*P*, 165), he alludes not only to her capacities but also, and more strictly, to her phrenological profile.

These two peculiarities of the narrative — its retrospect-free logic, and its incorporation of phrenological language — are intimately related. If memory has been successfully fended off by Crimsworth and others, it is because the clinical gaze as I have defined it acts as an ample shield. The very presentness of looking is often simply enough to deflect memory; meeting his brother for the first time since childhood, the grown William comments: "I still retained some confused recollection of Edward as he was ten years ago—a tall, wiry, raw youth; *now*, as I rose from my seat and turned toward the library door, I saw a fine-looking and powerful man, light-complexioned, well-made, and of athletic proportions" (*P*, 43). Insofar as the "now," constituted by Crimsworth's intent, evaluative gaze, can trace no link to the past, his "confused recollection" is useless; the sentence's syntax, abruptly leaping from past to surprising present, denies any hypotactic connection between mnemonic image and present sight. But such a simple conquering of the past by present seeing is not always possible, and at these moments the processes of phrenological or clinical sight come into play.

The primary mnemonic image of the novel is an heirloom—a portrait of Crimsworth's dead mother that hangs, at first, in his brother Edward's dining room. We have already seen Hunsden subject this picture to an explicitly phrenological analysis, but for him no retrospect is stirred by it; for Crimsworth, who before it is threatened by rueful recollections—his mother's penury and early death—there is more of a need for distancing rhetoric and evasive visual techniques. His first study of the picture reveals certain clinical processes: "The face, I remembered, had pleased me as a boy, but *then* I did not understand it; *now* I knew how rare that class of face is in the world, and I appreciated keenly its thoughtful, yet gentle expression. The serious grey eye possessed for me a strong charm, as did certain lines in the features indicative of most true and tender feeling" (*P*, 47). It is first notable that no specific memory, not even a particularized emotion, is mentioned by Crimsworth, save a connoisseur's "pleasure" and "appreciation"; his mother's face has been decontextualized from the remembrances for which it might have metonymically stood, detached from a field of mnemonic data. Furthermore, and most remarkably, this maternal image is immediately taxonomized, placed in a "class of face" that enables Crimsworth's appreciation. The ability to class a face is more crucial, in terms of understanding the image before him, than being able to claim kinship, or at least a set of shared memories, with it. And as so often in the novel, "then" and "now" are put in explicit opposition: previous incomprehension is contrasted with current knowledge, and memory is obscured by the activity of present "reading." Rather than recalling his mother, in short, Crimsworth performs a reading of her face—the present, clinically influenced gaze supplants remembrance.

Crimsworth still finds the image compelling and disturbing, and seeks it out again to further analyze it:

My mother, I perceived, had bequeathed to me much of her features and countenance — her forehead, her eyes, her complexion. No regular beauty pleases egotistical human beings as much as a softened and refined likeness of themselves; for this reason, fathers regard their daughters' faces, where frequently their own similitude is found flatteringly associated with softness of hue and delicacy of outline. I was just wondering how that picture, so interesting to me, would strike an impartial spectator, when . . . (P, 57)

Hunsden interrupts this reverie, but the process of evasion has already occurred. Although the passage begins with an admission of descent, Crimsworth performs a neat figural reversal: the mother/son relationship is replaced by a father/daughter comparison, whereby Crimsworth can place himself in a position of *priority* to his own mother; he is, for a moment, his mother's progenitor, gazing not at an older version of himself but at a younger, softened one. Thanks to this bit of temporal juggling, he arrives at enough of a distance from the portrait that he can begin the work of decontextualizing himself from it, figuring himself no longer as a father to a daughter — which is still a compelling relation, if one of priority — but as an "impartial spectator" to an interesting, if not emotionally charged, spectacle. Once again, present sight, and in particular a sight focused on the body, deflects memory. Brontë follows up these interestingly fraught moments where retrospect is evaded; much later in the novel, when Crimsworth is preparing to marry Frances, Hunsden purchases the portrait from the estate sale of the bankrupt Edward and brings it to William in Brussels. There Crimsworth takes it out of its crate, unwraps it, gazes at it for a few moments — and then places it under his bed, from which it will not emerge in the text; we hear no more of it.

Memory is, as is evident from the preceding passages, allied to the pictorial, but in such a way that memory is itself limited, stripped of its emotional power.[66] The portrait of Crimsworth's mother does not enable memory to be produced, but instead enables its reduction. Later, as Crimsworth searches futilely for Frances — who has left her place at the female pensionnat at which he teaches — through the streets and suburbs of Brussels, he classifies his activity as a pursuit for "an ample space of brow and a large, dark, and serious eye, with a fine but decided line of eyebrow traced above" (P, 191); as Sally Shuttleworth has remarked, it is a search for a phrenological profile, not a particular woman, and by remaining focused on Frances's profile Crimsworth is able to forget, for the time being, the circumstances of their courtship, the details of his dalliance with the pensionnat's proprietor, Mademoiselle Reuter, and in fact his own poverty.[67] The focus of his attention has narrowed to a clinically tinged visuality. The visualities of pictorial art and phrenology are almost identical in the text:

the maternal portrait is read phrenologically, and phrenological readings are proclaimed as works of pictorial art. Shortly before the lengthy, and explicitly phrenological, reading of Juanna Trista, Crimsworth exhorts his readers to "look here while I open my portfolio and show them a sketch or two, pencilled after nature" (*P*, 126). Sketches are open to infiltration by clinical methods of sight, while in turn the act of phrenological reading is billed as sketching. Both are brief, depthless, visual modes of apprehension, and both, significantly, preclude any intrusion of remembrance.

Even when memory is openly invoked, its alliance to visuality drains it of specificity, as in Crimsworth's brief life-summary before his entrance into Belgium:

> Three — nay, four — pictures line the four-walled cell where are stored for me the records of the past. First, Eton. All in that picture is in far perspective, receding, diminutive; but freshly coloured, green, dewy, with a spring sky, piled with glittering yet showery clouds; for my childhood was not all sunshine — it had its overcast, its cold, its stormy hours. Second, X —, huge, dingy; the canvas cracked and smoked; a yellow sky, sooty clouds; no sun, no azure; the verdure of the suburbs blighted and sullied — a very dreary scene.
>
> Third, Belgium; and I will pause before this landscape. (*P*, 86)

It is difficult to know whether the descriptions offered are literal memories — recollections of the mill-town might indeed contain sooty clouds and sullied verdure — or tropes, and that difficulty is tremendously productive: it enables these mnemonic images to be detached from specific moments and generalized, indeed fixed, made static: a time period, Crimsworth implies, is consistent and easily summarizable, easily contained in a mental landscape. Much like phrenological "sketches," these "sketches" drain memory of its particularity and contain it safely — within a frame, within a "four-walled cell," within a set of visual practices. Visuality encloses memory, seals it, and prevents its eruption into vivid retrospects; it replaces a diachronic series of remembered actions or events with a synchronic "picture." Images of shutting or sealing proliferate throughout Brontë's text; there is a careful mapping of doors, partitions, and barriers in the schools in which Crimsworth works, and his mental images are suffused by acts of closure. Commenting that Mademoiselle Reuter had sprung the lid of his heart, he asks the reader to guess "whether she stole and broke it, or whether the lid shut again with a snap on her fingers" (*P*, 134); later, fantasizing about returning the bills with which Frances had paid him for his English lessons, he imagines how he "could have thrust them back into her little hand, and shut the small, taper fingers over them" (*P*, 190). These "closural" images usually refer, however, to remembrance. Briefly recalling the scenes of his first night in London before his Channel crossing, Crimsworth invokes the missing phrenological faculty: "treasure them, Memory; seal them in urns, and keep them in safe niches!" (*P*, 88). As for thoughts of Frances's disappearance from the pensionnat, he does not allow them "to monopolize the whole space of my heart; I pent them, on the contrary, in one strait and secret nook" (*P*, 187). Ultimately, these tropes coalesce around one of Crimsworth's favorite terms of approbation: *propriety*. The personality of "propriety" treats its psychic material as "property," to be safely pent up, to be contained and, ultimately, mastered. Whether within frames, cells, urns, or nooks, mnemonic "property" must be visually reduced and protected from outbursts.

Why must memory be so contained—why is all this work, through "sketching" and sealing, necessary? The dark hints of cloudy childhood days offered here provide one clue, and we are briefly offered, in the novel's opening pages, an account of the bankruptcy of Crimsworth's father and the subsequent misery and death of his mother. There is also Crimsworth's mysterious collapse from "Hypochondria" shortly following his engagement to Frances, a disease that, as he tells us, "had been my acquaintance, nay, my guest, once before in boyhood" (*P*, 253).[68] Here we meet the idea of mastery that Brontë's letter to Heger opened up, the reluctance to become a "slave of a regret, a memory," the refusal to submit to the possibly all-consuming energies of the past. In Crimsworth's case, the idea of mastery is linked as well to all social and professional exchanges—public spaces in which memory is not only a distraction but a handicap, and in which only a swift and nimble application of clinically informed sight, of body-reading, can truly succeed. Mastery is containing memory through sight; it is also mastering others through seeing them clinically, and avoiding slavery by avoiding the gazes of others. When Crimsworth discovers that his employer, M. Pelet, is carrying on a flirtation with Mademoiselle Reuter, he proclaims: "I thanked heaven that I had last night opened my window and read by the light of a full moon the true meaning of that guileful countenance. I felt half his master, because the reality of his nature was now known to me" (*P*, 142).

There are, speaking generally, two kinds of spaces in *The Professor*: the private, claustrophobic spaces of bedroom and closet, metaphorically reappearing in the cells or niches of Crimsworth's own mind, and the public, dramatic spaces of workroom and classroom, theatres in which power struggles are manifest. In both categories, gazes are used to achieve mastery and deflect the inferiority—both social and psychological—that comes with the past. Even in drawing-rooms, Crimsworth's gaze is always evaluative, and the purpose of that evaluation is usually to answer a simple question: can I be mastered by this person? "As an animal, Edward excelled me far," he muses; "should he prove as paramount in mind as in person I must be a slave" (*P*, 49). Such a comment is habitual; but the evaluative gaze does not always turn upon physical strength. More commonly, in fact, it turns upon a kind of visual vulnerability: can this person read me, and in doing so, master me? As Crimsworth testifies later, even the delicate Mademoiselle Reuter is capable of this kind of mastery:

> Her glances were not given in full, but out of the corners, so quietly, so stealthily, yet I think I lost not one. I watched her as keenly as she watched me; I perceived soon that she was feeling after my real character; she was searching for salient points, and weak points, and eccentric points; she was applying now this test, now that, hoping in the end to find some chink, some niche, where she could put in her little firm foot and stand upon my neck — mistress of my nature. (*P*, 118)

What Mademoiselle Reuter is performing is, despite the lack of obviously clinical vocabulary, a clincal reading. She attempts to fix Crimsworth's character ("my real character") and to detach aspects of his character from others ("salient points, and weak points, and eccentric points"), all in the service of gaining control over him. The tactile, sadistic character of her glances — feeling, testing, even placing her "little firm foot" upon his neck — suggests as well the mixture of the tactile and visual in phrenological practice, in which visual examination could often be supplemented by the use of calipers or direct application of the hands. Mastery, that is, is not only achieved through the application of clinical gazing on objects such as a portrait of a mother, for that gaze can also be leveled at oneself; if Crimsworth is vulnerable to incursions of memory from such "heirlooms" as his mother's portrait, he is equally vulnerable to the hostile, well-trained facial readings of others.

It is in public spaces, however, that issues of control — centering around body-readings — become paramount. Encountering the scenes of instruction with which *The Professor* is full, we might very well echo the cynicism of M. Pelet, who asserts that "dans l'instruction, l'adresse fait tout autant que le savoir" (*P*, 95). Very little seems to be imparted when Crimsworth faces his students; what does occur is, continually, a dynamic of mastery and submission, and Crimsworth usually compels submission through a phrenologically tinged gaze that at once exposes his students and masks himself. The "adresse" or tact that conquers "savoir" or knowledge is, in fact, the tact of clinical assessment. A paradigmatic switch occurs when Crimsworth first faces female students: his initial glance is not clinically armed and is therefore vulnerable; his subsequent glances employ clinical methods and therefore both protect him and threaten his students. He is, at the outset, unprepared, for he sees that good features, ruddy, blooming complexions, large and brilliant eyes, forms full, even to solidity, seemed to abound. I did not bear the first view like a stoic; I was dazzled, my eyes fell, and in a voice somewhat low I murmured —

"Prenez vos cahiers de dictée, mesdemoiselles."

Not so had I bid the boys at Pelet's take their reading-books. A rustle followed, and an opening of desks; behind the lifted lids which momentarily screened the heads bent down to search for exercise-books, I heard tittering and whispers. (P, 113)

Crimsworth notices aspects of form — complexion, eyes, figure — that are not immediately susceptible to phrenological or clinical assessment, and thus his mastery dissipates; he is not reading, he is being read. His female students have the upper hand, and have read him already; one whispers that he is "un véritable blanc-bec," a real greenhorn (P, 114). What is apparent, due to Crimsworth's unprepared gaze, is his pedagogical inexperience, his foreignness, and his lack of acquaintance with women — all aspects of his past, and all aspects the text has conditioned us to accept as real, and as real handicaps. Crimsworth's aim is to mask these conditioned facts about himself (facts that derive from his past) and to present himself anew; this he can only do by claiming the privileges of clinical sight.

Immediately gathering himself, he trains upon his students a new gaze. First, he isolates the three most troublesome students, who happen to be the most attractive: Eulalie, Hortense, and Caroline. Then he proceeds to read them: "Eulalie was tall, and very finely shaped: she was fair, and her features were those of a Low-Country Madonna; many a 'figure de Vierge' have I seen in Dutch pictures exactly resembling hers; there were no angles in her shape or in her face, all was curve and roundness — neither thought, sentiment, nor passion disturbed by line or flush the equality of her pale, clear skin" (P, 114). As for Hortense, "consistency and good sense she might possess," Crimsworth ironically notes, "but none of her features betokened those qualities" (P, 114). Caroline, we are told, "was sensual now, and in ten years' time she would be coarse — promise plain was written in her face of much future folly" (P, 115). Suddenly the features of these girls are being subjected to an analysis of *signification*, not merely an aesthetic evaluation; and the plenitude that Crimsworth had previously seen ("large and brilliant eyes, forms full") is replaced by an emptiness — the smooth silences of Eulalie's and Hortense's faces — or by a foreboding meaning, as in the prophetic signs Caroline has "written on her face."

What of the "tasks" of the clinical gaze? They are evident here, certainly; Caroline's future is fixed, her character made static, by virtue of her sinister signs, an analysis that leaves little room for the ameliorative effects of Crimsworth's teaching; and a definite taxonomizing is occurring, as Eulalie becomes a "Low-Country Madonna" and Caroline becomes merely "sensual." Yet in a surprising reversal, the true aim of the clinical "tasks" I have mapped is Crimsworth himself. Whereas the clinical gaze usually taxonomizes or fixes the seen object, here it is the gazing subject who is transformed. Through the process of isolating three "sketches," Crimsworth has in the eyes of his students decontextualized himself from his origins and nationality, detached his new, sterner demeanor from his initial hesitation, fixed himself as a disciplinarian, and made himself into the embodiment of a certain taxonomical category: the Professor. He has eliminated any interiority, any past, that might again open him up to the cruel but accurate ridicule that greeted him. With a changed gaze Crimsworth changes his own face; his next act, to stride off his podium and tear Eulalie's dictation into fragments, is empowered by his clincally informed readings, which act on himself as much as his students.

This is a strategy Crimsworth will continue; the extraordinary reading of Juanna Trista's head is but one instance of the technique of phrenological control, which produces Crimsworth as Professor, as Master. It is important to note that Crimsworth's mastery begins with a comfort in phrenological language — this insures his comfort in his literal occupation, which is the teaching of a language (English); we might also note that his first occupation, in his brother Edward's mill, was also translation, the rendering of English into French or German. It is not surprising then that Crimsworth will marry a woman whom he will have to tutor in English, and not at all surprising that when she accepts his marriage proposal in French, he imperiously demands, "Speak English now, Frances" (*P*, 248). That is, Crimsworth's growing proficiency in *translation* — English to French, French to English — mirrors his mastery of phrenological discourse, into which the potential difficulties of everyday encounters can be translated. It is also important to note the obscurity of phrenological language (recall Juanna's organ of "adhesiveness," which requires a phrenological gloss), an obscurity that further insures the power of those who use it.[69] The esoteric phrenological lexicon engendered a distinction between its "masters" and the illiterate "subjects" of that lexicon, subjects such as Juanna, Caroline, and even Frances. Need we look for further evidence of the link between Crimsworth's profession as translator and his phrenological "translations," we can turn to Edward's ridicule of his brother's "useless trash of college learning — Greek, Latin, and so forth" (*P*, 51), which immediately precedes Crimsworth's proud claim of facial invulnerability: "I showed him my countenance with the confidence that one would show an unlearned man a letter written in Greek; he might see lines, and trace characters, but he could make nothing of them; my nature was not his nature, and its signs were to him like the words of an unknown tongue" (*P*, 53). By using an obscure language of facial reading, a language that, furthermore, shrouds and seals the past, Crimsworth achieves his elevation into a static, professorial categorization. Everything in his past that does not feed into this new identity is summarily forgotten, including the maternal portrait, left by the narration under a bed in a Brussels boardinghouse.

Yet in the end this path of mastery through clinically tinged gazing is not entirely satisfying; the novel has been, one might say, too honest in portraying education *as* discipline — or too forthright in being an education *in* discipline — for the phrenological evasions of the past to seem attractive. We are left, that is, with Crimsworth's life as a series of negations and refusals, with the clinical mindset as a tremendously difficult practice of cutting off and shutting in, of detachments and separations, all of which are barely compensated for by his marriage to the evidently cowed Frances Henri, who, when asked for her assent to Crimsworth's marraige proposal, can only stammer, "Master, I consent to pass my life with you" (*P*, 249). Insofar as the phrenological psyche is concerned, Brontë's next task will be to graft the forces of desire, of eros, onto the phrenological structure — to make the actions of taxonomizing, detaching, and surfacing not merely negative acts that cut off the past but positive acts of erotic choice. It is not until *Villette* that we see the positive side of Crimsworth's all-too-negative image.

Villette: Memory and Desire

Brontë's juvenilia are dotted with verbal portraits. Her early tales, in fact, seem to lead to moments of great descriptive intensity; upon her major Angrian characters she lavishes a painterly attention that is far from the terseness of her later clinical practices. One early description of her Byronic hero Zamorna, from the 1834 tale "My Angria and the Angrians," sufficiently demonstrates the different register of her adolescent work:

> He seemed to be in the full bloom of youth: his figure was toweringly, overbearingly lofty, moulded in statue-like perfection, and invested with something which I cannot describe — something superb, impetuous, resistless, something, in short, no single word can altogether express. His hair was intensely black, curled luxuriantly, but the forehead locks, looked white and smooth as ivory. His eyebrows were black and broad, but his long eyelashes and large clear eyes were deep sepia brown. The wreathes on his temples were brought so low as to meet the profusely curled raven whiskers and mustachios which hid his mouth and chin and shadowed his fair complexioned cheeks.[70]

Her narrator's eye lingers over Zamorna's hair, and is attuned primarily to color; only the broadness of his eyebrows bears any relation to a phrenological report. Most remarkably, the clinical propensity for taxonomizing or naming is inapplicable here, denied by the sublimity of Zamorna's looks —"no single word can altogether express" the "something" that radiates from his figure. Zamorna's body might mean much, but precisely what it means is not accessible through this gaze, which can only evoke an erotic interest in curves, tints, and hinted significances.

Therefore when Brontë takes a formal leave of Angria and her adolescent writing, she describes her farewell as a farewell to pictorialized faces, which is also a farewell to memory. "My readers," she states in "The Last of Angria," "have been habituated to one set of features, which they have seen now in profile, now in full face, now in outline, and again in finished painting — varied but by the change of feeling or temper or age . . . but we must change, for the eye is tired of the picture so oft recurring and now so familiar." As for the future, it holds no such combination of remembrance and the pictorial: "When I depart from these I feel almost as if I stood on the threshold of a home and were bidding farewell to its inmates. When I strive to conjure up new inmates I feel as if I had got into a distant country where every face was unknown and the character of the population an enigma which it would take much study to comprehend and much talent to expound."[71] The pattern mapped in Brontë's juvenilia — a pattern of which, as this citation shows, she was very much aware — is as follows: from a world of familiar, eroticized faces, bodies that might be called *mnemonic*, to the world of what I call the "amnesiac body," a world that is at once foreign, no longer pictorial, and literally studied. Brontë's new faces will demand study from her and will in turn reflect that effort; they may be striking, but more often they will be imperfect, jarring, harsh. In considering this overlooked pattern in Brontë's career, we must be reminded of both *The Professor* and *Villette*, novels in which familiar faces are replaced by foreign scenes (Belgium, Labassecour), study (the teaching of English), and harsher, less picturesque faces (Crimsworth's students, M. Paul) — above all, novels in which faces that remind are replaced by faces that challenge. Phrenology is both an effect of this change and a cause of it; its foreign lexicon, its elimination of the painterly in favor of the clinical, the study demanded of its adepts, and the frequent harshness of its assessments all coalesce to produce amnesiac bodies, and are all at the same time called forth by the foreign faces Brontë's plots encounter once they leave Britain behind.

Such is the pattern that *Villette* continually dramatizes: from the eroticized, pictorialized faces of memory to phrenologized faces that contain no memory. The surprise of the novel, and one reason for its oddity, is that desire is then wedded to these newer, foreign faces, thereby defusing the threat of the still-attractive faces of memory. If *Villette* is, as Janice Carlisle has memorably phrased it, "a carapace of defenses against the almost intolerable pain of memory," then one of these defenses, and by no means the least important, is Lucy Snowe's ability to eroticize a new type of body, one that contains in it no reminders of what Carlisle calls "a record of losses and humiliations."[72] Lucy Snowe's past is, it seems, even more threatening than William Crimsworth's. Her childhood can only be described in terms of a shipwreck; all we are told is that "the ship was lost, the crew perished" (*V*, 94). An object-lesson is provided by Miss Marchmont, Lucy's early employer, who proclaims proudly "I love Memory to-night" (*V*, 98) and then proceeds to die — as if the flood of painful recollections she evokes is linked to, if not a cause of, mortality. Lucy's own withholdings are famous enough in the long history of perverse narrators: her refusal to tell us that "Dr. John" is in fact the Graham Bretton of the novel's early chapters, and her refusal to describe the disappearance of her closest relations, are both notable instances of how retrospection is deflected. "Unutterable loathing of a desolate existence past forbade return" (*V*, 110), Lucy tells us, and it forbids as well too many acts of remembrance. While the old Lucy Snowe, with white hair underneath her cap, withholds memories, the young Lucy Snowe avoids them by searching out new faces and new ways of seeing faces. Mnemonic bodies, with all their requisite potential for futile desire and disappointment, are replaced by amnesiac bodies, much as Brontë's juvenilia had predicted.

The replacement can be seen, in microcosm, in the seventh chapter of *Villette* — called, appropriately enough, "Villette." The chapter concludes with the initial reading of Lucy's face by M. Paul, but its beginning is curiously different. Attempting to reclaim her missing trunk from a coach, Lucy enlists the help of a fellow passenger in whose French she detects an English accent. This gentleman is, of course, the grown Graham Bretton; Lucy is as yet ignorant of his identity, but she catches a glimpse of him by the light of a street lamp: "I saw that he was a young, distinguished, and handsome man; he might be a lord, for anything I knew: nature had made him good enough for a prince, I thought. His face was very pleasant; he looked high but not arrogant, manly but not overbearing. I was turning away, in the deep consciousness of all absence of claim to look for further help from such a one as he" (*V*, 124). Much like the more breathless description of Zamorna, this depiction of the English stranger works directly against any sort of clinical gaze. Height and beauty are Lucy's determinants here — nothing more nor less than the traditional dyad of tall and handsome. Furthermore, Lucy's language loses its characteristic acerbity and veers oddly close to trite, almost obsolete terminology, such as "lord" and "prince." Although she as yet does not recognize him as Graham Bretton, Lucy associates this face with memory nonetheless: memory of England. And the face itself sticks in her memory: "The remembrance of his countenance, which I am sure wore a light not unbenignant to the friendless—

the sound in my ear of his voice, which spoke a nature chivalric to the needy and feeble, as well as the youthful and fair—were a sort of cordial to me long after. He was a true young English gentleman" (V, 125). What must be gleaned from this passage, however, is the disadvantage it creates in Lucy. Methodologically disarmed, having to fall back on a mode of description familiar from Brontë's juvenilia of the 1830s, Lucy finds herself in the inferior position, barely able to ask for help from this magisterial figure. Although she is helped by him, Lucy has lost her voice; this face of memory, at first a national and subsequently a personal memory, disarms her. The falseness and insecurity of the language is evident, for we find Lucy's prose swooning over this both mnemonic and pictorial face, over "the remembrance of his countenance."

From here Lucy finds her way to the pensionnat, where, as I have already shown, M. Paul trains on Lucy an explicitly clinical gaze. Merely a "small, dark and spare man, in spectacles" (V, 128), M. Paul's face is an index to no national memory, to no personal retrospects, and to no familiar canons of male beauty. He is, in fact, synecdochically reduced to a pair of glasses. He is also capable of being read—unlike Graham's face, which creates in Lucy the temptation to turn away, the "compression of the lips, and gathering of the brow" in M. Paul's visage leads Lucy to the conclusion that "he meant to see through me, and that a veil would be no veil for him" (V, 128). Whereas Graham's body can only be described in general terms— a "pleasant" face, a "manly" countenance—Lucy meets this new face with the usual phrenological maneuver of detaching, denying to M. Paul's lips and brow even a possessive pronoun. Here we see the foreign face Brontë predicted in "The Last of Angria," a face that demands study. If we do not read carefully, we might also find in this new face a switch from the flush of pleasure created by Graham to the discomfort of a clinical examination.

The error is to read the switch from Graham to M. Paul, from idealized portrait to phrenological reading, as a loss of eros and a loss of security. Few enough critics have been willing to acknowledge that the Lucy who faces M. Paul is not only more secure than the Lucy who gazes at Graham but also that the Lucy whose skull is being visually interrogated by M. Paul is experiencing an erotic thrill as compelling as that presented by the handsome English stranger.[73] It is the thrill of being seen that is recorded in Lucy's first encounter with Paul Emanuel. Graham, like so many others in the novel, does not truly see Lucy; with him she will remain futilely viewing. With M. Paul, under the auspices of a phrenological reading, desire is produced in surplus, a desire that can actually be reciprocated. This is perhaps the novel's central paradox: only through the most brutally scientific of gazes will desire be fulfilled. What seems like a severe disadvantage—Lucy squirming under the scrutiny of those spectacles—is in fact a step toward the advantageous, for Lucy and M. Paul share the phrenological language and can therefore reach a position of relative parity. For Graham, who cannot truly see Lucy, she is nothing; for Paul Emanuel, who can see through her, she will become a force to reckon with. With the phrenological gaze — with which she both reads and is read in her first minutes at the pensionnat — Lucy both avoids the inferiority implied by the mnemonic face (I am no longer in England, I cannot attract this man, etc.) and discovers a new form of eros, one that is crucially not founded on childhood cathexes but rather on an adult process of reading, counter-reading, attribution, and denial, the process of visual and verbal argumentation that constitutes her relations with M. Paul. Phrenological gazing in *Villette*, in short, does not merely contain or elide memory — it also makes this containment or elision erotic.[74]

Brontë's novel sets up for itself a prehistory — the interactions of Lucy, little Polly Home, the young Graham Bretton, and his mother, who is also Lucy's godmother, in England — and then demonstrates how Lucy avoids the attractions and patterns of these interactions once she is in Labassecour. In order to illustrate the difficulty of this process, Lucy will rediscover her childhood nexus in her new Continental home; unlike William Crimsworth, she is not provided the luxury of a clean break with her British past. She is, therefore, continually presented with mnemonic faces, particularly those of Graham and Polly — faces that are both beautiful and associative of a host of retrospects: England, love for Graham, loss of family. It is germane here that Bretton, the name of Graham and his mother, is the name of their English town; like Polly and her father, "home" is literally inscribed upon them, is constitutive of their identity. Graham and Polly are certainly foremost among these mnemonic bodies, bodies sufficient in and of themselves, bodies full of health and the promise of pleasure, bodies that are too English, and too perfect, to inspire a phrenological reading. While these bodies are themselves reminders, the possessors of these bodies always act in accordance with previous patterns; unlike Lucy, they are bound firmly to the prehistory sketched in the novel's opening chapters; their behavior is deeply repetitive.

Polly is the novel's clearest example of the body that cannot be phrenologically viewed wedded to a psyche that cannot break free of older cathexes. Lucy's first evaluation of the grown Polly, now Paulina Mary Home de Bassompierre, is a glance that cannot find a clinical foothold, that must return to the painterly:

> As I folded back her plentiful yet fine hair, so shining and so soft, and so exquisitely tended, I had under my observation a young, pale, weary, but high-bred face. The brow was smooth and clear; the eyebrows were distinct, but soft, and melting to a mere trace at the temples; the eyes were a rich gift of nature. . . . Her skin was perfectly fair, the neck and hands veined finely like the petals of a flower. (*V*, 346)

Polly's brow, once revealed by Lucy's hand, is not a phrenological brow; rather than being broad, or ample, or powerfully reflective, it is "high-bred": an index to ancestry. This face cannot be taxonomized, or separated into significant, legible units. Its beauty is possibly a poverty—a poverty of meaning—but this poverty is unassailable; part of the lesson Brontë's novel imparts is that the resources of the beautiful body are immense. Even Ginevra Fanshawe, whose opacity to reason is worlds away from Polly's self-awareness and containment, is impervious to embarrassment and—more crucially—to the threats of the past. There is no need for these women to avoid memory at all costs. Polly, for her part, enjoys the pastime of a quiet afternoon with Lucy, discussing the far-off days of Bretton, which she remembers distinctly; "Paulina," Lucy admits, "loved the Past" (V, 374).

This enjoyment is Wordsworthian: Polly the child is mother to Paulina the young adult, her days linked each to each by natural, consistent affection for her father and for Graham.[75] Our first glimpse of Polly the child is of a tableau of homesickness, of eighteenth-century nostalgia; her face is clearly, agonizingly mnemonic: "no furrowed face of adult exile, longing for Europe and Europe's antipodes, ever bore more legibly the signs of home sickness than did her infant visage" (V, 69). Sitting alone, crying for her absent Papa, Polly is emblematic of a Wordsworthian piety—to Lucy she appears to be like "some precocious fanatic or untimely saint" (V, 69)—that Lucy cannot afford and does not possess. Lucy's judgment is, interestingly enough, a phrenological one: "This, I perceived, was a one-idead [sic] nature; betraying that monomaniac tendency I have ever thought the most unfortunate with which man or woman can be cursed" (V, 69). Monomania, as some commentators have pointed out, was a phrenological diagnosis, for no particular faculty could control other faculties except under the pathologized condition of monomania; what in the Wordsworthian, poetic tradition is an understandable, laudable, and indeed inspirational piety toward the past is in the phrenological viewpoint an abnormality. The path of Polly's affections, so neatly transferred from father to paternalized mate, is a further illustration of Polly's backward-turning reverence, for unlike Lucy she will never have to be wrenched from her past and transferred to a world of foreign faces. A delicate, floral beauty combines with an emotional reliance on retrospect in Polly's character; both are attributes that defeat Lucy, who can only look enviably on Polly's physical charms and unmarred past. Indeed, memory—both Polly's and Lucy's—is written on the mature Polly's face: "Having only once seen that sort of face, with that cast of fine and delicate featuring," Lucy states, "I could not but know her" (V, 358). Know her, that is, as the child she was and continues to be.

Graham's face is much the same, too perfect to be detached into phrenological parts:

[p]erhaps his eye glanced from face to face rather too vividly, too quickly, and too often, but it had a most pleasant character, and so had his mouth; his chin was full, cleft, Grecian, and perfect. As to his smile, one could not in a hurry make up one's mind as to the descriptive epithet it merited; there was something in it that pleased, but something too that brought surging up into the mind all one's foibles and weak points. (*V*, 160)

Again there is the failure of taxonomical language — no "descriptive epithet" fully encompasses Graham's enigmatic smile; and there is a replacement of clinical attributes with self-consciously artistic terms (a "Grecian" chin). Furthermore, like all faces that return from Lucy's past, this one lays open her faults, places her in a position of insecurity far more perilous and exposed than that created by M. Paul's spectacles. Gazing at his "hair, whiskers, and complexion," Lucy realizes that "Dr. John" and Graham Bretton are the same person; his face, rather than any slip of the tongue or personality trait, brings her English past forcefully before her in her newer Continental surroundings. The threat of this face is registered by Lucy in a conversation with Polly, in which she claims to "never see" Graham: "I looked at him twice or thrice about a year ago, before he recognized me, and then I shut my eyes; and if he were to cross their balls twelve times between each day's sunset and sunrise, except from memory, I should hardly know what shape had gone by." To Polly's stunned expression of wonder, Lucy explains that "I value vision, and dread being struck stone blind" (*V*, 520).

Being blind: what Lucy seems to mean by this is the loss of one's idiosyncratic language before the object, the effacement of a newer, precariously constructed self when presented with so powerful an object of memory. Surely we can read here the struggle to disown a well-established desire, but we can also read here the peril of being critically disabled or methodologically impaired. If the face stands out as a series of eroticized, painterly, familiar fragments — a cleft chin, an English profile, a pair of lips — and not as a series of phrenological, legible units, or as an object of putatively disinterested study, then one has been struck blind. The fear of blindness, of self-effacement before a beautiful object of memory, had been depicted by Brontë sixteen years earlier, in "The Return of Zamorna," when the faithful Mary Percy reencounters Zamorna after a long absence: "Mary saw him turn and fix on her, so eager, so hawklike a glance while the classic lips curled with such a fond and sunny smile, that dizzy with the tumultuous feelings, the wild pulsations, the burning and impatient wishes that smile and glance excited, she closed her eyes in momentary blindness."[76]

Part of the novel's avoidance of these mnemonic selves consists in demonstrating their obvious repetition of previous erotic structures or in registering a dislike for their engagement with memory. Young Graham's first conversation with the child Polly is an obvious enough parody of flirtatious politesse, but the couple never seems to progress much beyond that model. By the time of their adult courtship the children still speak through the adults, except for the heavy breathing of the simulated sexual encounter; Graham's feeding a cup of "old October" to Polly is merely a return to the games of tempting and withholding that had constituted their relations as children. And lest we think that this repetitious behavior — the playing out of an unchanged cathexis — is unself-conscious, we have Polly's prolonged rumination on Graham's mnemonic power:

> Paulina would tell me how wonderful and curious it was to discover the richness and accuracy of his memory in this matter. How, while he was looking at her, recollections would seem to be suddenly quickened in his mind. He reminded her that she had once gathered his head in her arms, caressed his leonine graces, and cried out, "Graham, I *do* like you!" He told her how she would set a footstool beside him, and climb by its aid to his knee. And this day he could still recall the sensation of her little hands smoothing his cheek, or burying themselves in his thick mane. He remembered the touch of her small forefinger. (*V*, 519)

Memory precisely *is* the attraction between Polly and Graham; their very gazing is based on it. At bottom, the mnemonic body is always a palimpsest, always revealing further layers of recollections, always yielding to previous sensations and images. Polly's beauty is both a surface repletion that combats clinical detaching and taxonomizing, as well as a depth that contains years of stored erotic energy. To Lucy these reflections of Polly's are at once a source of regret — for she has been excluded from Graham's memories — and of vague ridicule; Lucy's defense is to condemn this powerful bond between doctor and Wordsworthian young woman as merely a repetition, merely a playing out of childishness. So Lucy closes her eyes to Graham — she will not be blinded by beauty or memory.

One possible way to contain the disadvantage and threat that Graham's face represents is to read it phrenologically. Thus it is potentially important when, after an argument about Ginevra, Lucy reports to us of Graham that "the sympathetic faculty was not prominent in him" (*V*, 264). But this mode cannot continue for long, insofar as Graham does not read back phrenologically; he continues to overlook Lucy completely, producing diagnostic banalities such as "happiness is the cure — a cheerful mind the preventive: cultivate both" (*V*, 330). The clinical gaze provokes a countergaze, a response; the irony is that the novel's only professional physician cannot produce the clinical elision of memory that Lucy needs to avoid her damaged and hidden past. Lucy's clinical assessment of Graham's "sympathetic faculty" had two goals: to reclaim her voice from the silence his face compels and to induce a clinical response, to create a model of desire that would differ from, and possibly supercede, his heavily retrospective attraction to Polly. The second goal fails, which helps to explain the plot's shift, so delicately handled by Brontë, to the world of M. Paul and his synecdochic spectacles. Gradually, with Lucy's desire still putatively focused on Graham, the short, austere man with the forceful brow begins to dominate pages and scenes; and as this occurs, the novel shifts into a new realm, a metaphorical "distant country" in which unknown faces "take much study to comprehend and much talent to expound."

When Lucy, having been rescued from her dangerous long vacation swoon, rises from her bed at La Terrasse — itself merely a reconstruction of long-gone Bretton — and hears the name "Graham" repeated, she comments: "The plot was but thickening, the wonder but culminating" (*V*, 243). Part of the work of Brontë's novels is the *thinning* of a potentially thick plot — for what is a thick plot but a plot thick with memory, with recurrences and revenants, past complications and future consequences? Much like *Jane Eyre*'s elimination of Bertha Mason's attic, or *The Professor*'s avoidance of Crimsworth's brother and maternal relations, *Villette*'s plot introduces a possible thickening, in the form of a return of the Brettons and the Homes, only to reduce that thickness to a thin sideplot; what is potentially central must be marginalized, what creates wonder must be replaced by faces that create firm assertions and challenges. Lucy looks at Graham's face with "an inexpressible sense of wonder" (*V*, 219), but wonder is not a part of the all-knowing clinical gaze. The "thick" past, bound up with idealized beauty, wonder, and above all painful memories, must be replaced by a "thinner," surfaced gaze, and that is precisely why M. Paul's countenance, which is usually reduced synecdochically to a brow or a pair of spectacles, takes command of the novel. All the potential thicknesses of *Villette*, from a reunion with Graham to the legend of the buried nun, are thinned out; the ghostly nun becomes a fop in disguise, and Graham yields to the "dark little man" whose brow is "pungent and austere" (*V*, 197).

What does the gaze of M. Paul perform? In its purest form, it produces a series of attributions; it carries out the familiar clinical task of "fixing" by attaching names to Lucy's behavior. Whereas Graham's diagnoses, however professionally achieved, end in platitudes about the cultivation of happiness, M. Paul's diagnoses are resolutely personal and temporally immutable. They are, whether explicitly phrenological or not, clinical in form — they make Lucy's character static, and they are based on visual investigation, as in one of his first evaluations: "One ought to be 'dur' with you. You are one of those beings who must be kept down. I know you! I know you! Other people in this house see you pass, and think that a colourless shadow has gone by. As for me, I scrutinized your face once, and it sufficed." (*V*, 226) Bearing no reference to Lucy's past, this assertion at once fixes (the static "ought" and "must be kept down") and taxonomizes ("one of those beings") her character, on the basis of a single, sufficient clinical glance. In a world of surveillance — and such is the world of Madame Beck's pensionnat — mistakes in evaluation are constantly produced, and M. Paul can occasionally overreach his powers and arrive at incorrect conclusions; yet his mistakes are fortuitous, and his errors open up vistas.[77] A later string of terms for Lucy—"Petite chatte, doucerette, coquette! . . . Sauvage!"— imputes to her a calculation and possibly even a hidden malice that, if present, are merely components of a more complex unity; the clinical gaze necessarily misses several nuances. Lucy, however, claims these terms as her own: "Oui; j'ai la flamme à l'âme, et je dois l'avoir!" (*V*, 404). Confusion may exist for Lucy, but nuance — a careful evaluation of qualities, a balancing of opposites, an effort to reconcile the disparate — signifies the loss of cathexis. The affixing of names — or, more precisely, the attribution of fixed, atemporal names — is a value in *Villette*. The phrenological "reader" presents a caricature, in which the qualities of the read object are distorted, magnified, and liberated from a developmental past; the pleasure that arises out of the encounter with this caricature is seeing oneself freed from trauma or memory, lifted into the melodramatic clarity of clinical certainty. The pleasure, that is, does not arise from the success or failure of the reading but in the fact of being read at all, and the particular, nonmnemonic manner in which the reading takes place. Away from Graham's features, and faced with M. Paul's spectacles, Lucy is free to become a spectacle: dramatic, nameable, present.

The clinical gaze does not merely taxonomize and fix in *Villette*, however; it also challenges. The challenge is always more or less the same: choose between past reticences or present opportunity. Madame Beck, herself a good phrenological reader, scrutinizes Lucy before asking her to teach; having read a latent capacity, she then offers Lucy the choice between teaching and not teaching, between progress and regress:

> "Will you," said she, "go backward or forward?" indicating with her hand, first, the small door of communication with the dwelling-house, and then the great double portals of the classes or school-rooms.
> "En avant," I said. (*V*, 141)

Insofar as the clinical gaze does make character immediately present and fixed, it also makes character a challenge, and throws the burden of personality into the future; it is adversarial, and it forces the read object to act.

With M. Paul, Lucy is literally forced to "act": his investigation of her "moyens" through her "skull" produces a similar challenge:

"There is no time to be lost," he went on now speaking in French; "and let us thrust to the wall all reluctance, all excuses, all minauderies. You must take a part."

"In the vaudeville?"

"In the vaudeville. You have said it."

I gasped, horror-struck. *What* did the little man mean?

"Listen!" he said. "The case shall be stated, and you shall then answer me Yes, or No; and according to your answer shall I ever after estimate you." (*V*, 202)

The clinical gaze in general, and phrenology in particular, is the novel's language for progressive choice; through phrenological attribution the public and private realms are blurred. Lucy must enter the classroom and the stage; in exposing her faculties, Madame Beck and M. Paul have insured her further exposure. Lucy's body, the brute biology of her skull formation, has betrayed her, and will continue to betray her, to M. Paul, and that betrayal — always taking place slightly beyond the realm of consciousness — produces, in yet another paradox, both the high degree of vulnerability Lucy feels in these scenes of harsh reading, and the firm decisions she reaches through them.[78]

It is not enough that, as the novel proceeds, Lucy comes to desire M. Paul; what the novel must enact is the process of coming to find M. Paul's type of interaction — clinically immediate, harshly taxonomic, melodramatically unnuanced — *desirable*. The new faces of Labassecour must not only replace the old faces of Bretton and "Home," but the new ways of seeing that erupt once Lucy arrives in Villette must replace old ways of seeing. The replacement is, finally, the replacement of memory by a vivid presentness, a presentness that is in the end figured as a new form of inscription:

I lifted my happy eyes: they were happy now, or they would have been no interpreters of my heart.

"Well," said he, after some seconds' scrutiny, "there is no denying that signature: Constancy wrote it; her pen is of iron. Was the record painful?"

"Severely painful," I said, with truth. "Withdraw her hand, monsieur; I can bear its inscribing force no more." (*V*, 583)

Desire is the replacement of an old language, with its Wordsworthian, pictorial, wondering rhetoric, with a new language, however painful its attributive inscriptions: the newer language of faculties, signifying faces, and challenges. Although the novel is forthright about the lingering attractions of old bodies, with their beautiful indistinctness, it ends with desire for an amnesiac body: M. Paul. It ends as well by having created Lucy anew as an amnesiac body herself, the perfect summary of phrenological theory and practice from Gall to Combe. "To follow, to seek out, to remind, to recall—" Lucy states with only slight irony near the novel's end—"for these things I had no faculty" (*V*, 539). If Lucy knows that she can still remember, she knows as well that she literally lacks the faculty of remembrance; by the end of *Villette*, that lack has been constituted as the basis of an erotic choice and thus of a whole world.

Toward Broca and the Modern

The dispersal of memory: what begins as a phrenological tenet ends by becoming the cornerstone of late-nineteenth-century neurology and modern neuroscience. The process begins most openly with Paul Broca, surgeon at the Hopital Bicêtre and founder, in 1859, of the Paris Société d'Anthropologie. In 1861, an elderly patient at Bicêtre with a severe aphasia came to Broca's attention. The patient, known to posterity as "Tan" for the only word he was able to form, was autopsied by Broca in April of that year, and what Broca found would change neurology immediately. Tan's brain contained an infection in the posterior part of the third frontal convolution— precisely where, sixty years earlier and without the benefit of pathological evidence, Gall had placed the organ of language. Broca's conclusion was that he had confirmed the dream of Gall, Spurzheim, and Combe by finding firm evidence for the localization of brain function—and, more important, by localizing linguistic memory, with which Gall had, as we have seen, begun his own researches. A vista opened up for neurologists and latter-day phrenologists: a complete and empirically verifiable map of the brain in which memory too could find a place. Gall's vision, which had been silenced by respectable medical theory for forty years, burst again into view.[79] "The localization project of neurology," Ian Hacking has recently written, "derives in part from phrenology"; but the neurological project was a crucial widening of the original phrenological mandate, for it included in its mental map a place for memory.[80] Indeed, one of the consequences of Broca's discovery was that memory now seemed localizable; it could be reclaimed from its phrenological absence and incorporated into a newer, more accurate, more comprehensive diagram. The world of Spurzheim and Combe—which is, as I have argued, also the world of Charlotte Brontë—was, it seemed, to be superceded by Broca's world, in which the body again could be mnemonic.

Such, however, is not the case. Broca's fixing of the legendary "memory of words" to the third left frontal convolution opened the way not to an accurate fixing of memory in the brain but instead to the paradoxical revelation that memory could not be localized. "By physically pinpointing the areas of sensorial (visual, auditive) as opposed to motor (graphic, verbal) dysfunctions," Matt Matsuda has claimed, "Broca and his successors revealed the awesomely complex multiplicity of ways in which the brain and body remember."[81] The more precisely the brain could be mapped, therefore—the more Gall's original vision was carried out with experimental rigor—the less memory could indeed be localized. Gall's decision to refuse memory a place, to disperse it among all the faculties, seemed more and more prescient, and in the end neurology despaired of finding a mnemonic "center." Memory could not be a single entity; it could only be a series of activities, connections, passings; the brain was no longer a storehouse or even a collection of small storehouses but a series of pathways with infinite branchings. It is with this neurological context that Henri Bergson could, in his 1896 *Matière et mémoire*, press his famous argument that memory is not to be found in the body. Phrenology had produced its legacy: the return of the amnesiac body.

The lasting effect of the phrenological dispersion of memory is the complication of remembrance; more than its "respectable" associationist peers, as exemplified by Sir Benjamin Brodie or Alexander Bain, phrenology determined the fraught way we see memory today. The amnesiac bodies of Brontë's characters lead, through a devious historical process, to the dispersed, fragmented memories of twentieth-century novelistic psyches. Memory does indeed make a return to fiction, and later narratives contained a recognition of remembrance that Brontë's texts could not and did not encompass; but thanks to the amnesiac bodies proposed by phrenologists, this memory could never again be simple and could never again be placed in a bodily center. William Crimsworth's and Lucy Snowe's fictional heirs would remember more, and more frequently, but the evasions and elisions of memory exemplified by *The Professor* and *Villette* bore their fruit in the difficult and unsure relation to remembrance that is so familiar to us from twentieth-century narratives. If Gall and Spurzheim could lead to Bergson and Freud via Broca's work, so too could Brontë's selective amnesias lead to Joyce, Proust, and Woolf—the modern.

THREE

Associated Fictions

DICKENS, THACKERAY, AND MID-CENTURY
FICTIONAL AUTOBIOGRAPHY

"That's the effect of living backwards," the Queen said kindly:
"it always makes one a little giddy at first—"
"Living backwards!" Alice repeated in great astonishment.
"I never heard of such a thing!"
"—but there's one great advantage in it, that one's memory works both ways."
"I'm sure mine only works one way," Alice remarked.
"I ca'n't remember things before they happen."
"It's a poor sort of memory that only works backwards," the Queen remarked.
—*Lewis Carroll,* Through the Looking Glass

Early in *The History of Henry Esmond*, William Makepeace Thackeray's eponymous hero comes into possession of a troubling piece of paper: one that proves him to be the rightful, no longer illegitimate, heir of Lord Francis Castlewood, a paper that would at one blow divest the current Lord Francis, his sister Beatrix, and his mother Rachel—Esmond's adopted family—of fortune and estate in favor of Esmond's claims.[1] Almost immediately Esmond decides to burn the proof of his identity and inheritance. In a novel putatively devoted to the operations of retrospect, to the maneuvers and contours of memory, Esmond's remembrance of the paper's immolation is treated with careful attention:

> Esmond went to the fire, and threw the paper into it. 'Twas a great chimney with glazed Dutch tiles. How we remember such trifles in such awful moments!—the scrap of the book that we have read in a great grief—the taste of that last dish that we have eaten before a duel or some such supreme meeting or parting. On the Dutch tiles at the bagnio was a rude picture representing Jacob in hairy gloves, cheating Isaac of Esau's birthright. The burning paper lighted it up. (*HE*, 162)[2]

What we have here is an absolutely paradigmatic memory for the British fiction of the mid-nineteenth century: a memory that posits a peripheral, diffuse recall of the kind familiar to us from Wordsworth —"the scrap of the book that we have read in a great grief," "the taste of that last dish that we have eaten before a duel"— but that instead is rigidly emblematic, anything *but* diffuse; the past that is retained here is symbolically relevant, thematically connected to the largest narratives of Esmond's life, particularly to the narrative of fraternal rivalry and displacement that the Dutch tile signals. The tile representing Jacob and Esau is by no means a "trifle"; it is remembered because it stands in an integral relation — here, a relation of allusion and symbol — to the central act, the burning of the birthright, which Esmond has performed. This is not a memory that records trifles; this is a memory that always *signifies*.[3] Keeping in mind *Henry Esmond*'s status as a narrative of full recollection and its place in a canon of voluminous nineteenth-century retrospective fictions, this textual sleight of hand — offering us a strictly symbolic and coherent memory in the guise of a fortuitous, accidental reminiscence — is both surprising and significant. The questions to ask, then, are the following: to what extent is the sort of memory depicted and theorized in the mid–nineteenth century incapable of recording desultory details or "trifles"? To what extent is it capable of recording only what is thoroughly selected, narrativized, even predictive: only what is symbolically or proleptically Important?

What is at stake here is the kind of consciousness envisioned by nineteenth-century fiction, and its possible similarity to or difference from the fictional or autobiographical consciousnesses more temporally, and perhaps temperamentally, closer to us. In Wordsworth's *Prelude*— whose 1850 publication predates Esmond's recollections by only two years — we find this familiar reminiscence, from the poet's sixth year, of the view from a lonely prospect:

> A naked pool that lay beneath the hills,
> The beacon on the summit, and more near,
> A girl who bore a pitcher on her head,
> And seemed with difficult steps to force her way
> Against the blowing wind. (12.249–253)[4]

Should we seek an easy cognitive or thematic context for these details, we are certain to fail, or at least to feel that our answer is only one of many possible divinations; the content of Wordsworth's memories remains persistently enigmatic, unassimilable to any quick categorization. Indeed, the almost photographic nature of this recall, much like the "taste of that last dish" that Esmond hypothetically savors, seems to defeat our initial efforts to explain why *these* details have been chosen, why *these* mental flashes (a pool, a beacon, a girl, wind) have been registered. The *effet du réel* of Wordsworthian memory may remind us, from our vantage point, of the similarly ample recollections of Proustian, or Joycean, fiction. But it is not what we find in Thackeray's novel, where even in the midst of a proclamation of a full, pure memory, we find nothing but a highly selected, relevant, and *classified* retrospect. The Jacob and Esau picture does not so much burst upon this scene as confirm its already obvious resonances of usurpation and illegitimacy—and therefore Esmond's more streamlined memory seems to proceed in a manner very different from the Wordsworthian recovery of the past.

If we attempted to find a dispersed and diffuse reminiscence in the British novel of the Victorian era, however, we would most likely find it in the period's many fictional autobiographies, those "Fictitious Biographies" that, as Carlyle wrote in 1832, "the greener mind in these days inditeth"; if we were, in other words, to find within Victorian fiction the representation of a fully mnemonic consciousness, one that was periodically confronting pieces of an as yet unassimilated, still troubling past, we would find it in the many Victorian narratives that present, through a first-person narration, the story of what is essentially a life of memories.[5] And indeed, from 1847 to roughly 1860 we can detect an extraordinary flowering of such autobiographical narratives, many of which have come to be constitutive of what we now consider the Victorian novel as such. In 1847 we have the arrival of Charlotte Brontë's *Jane Eyre* and G. H. Lewes's *Ranthorpe*; Charles Kingsley's *Alton Locke* followed in 1850, during which year Thackeray's *Pendennis* and Dickens's *David Copperfield* carried out their famous serial rivalry. William Harrison Ainsworth's *Mervyn Clitheroe* achieved some success in 1851, and the aforementioned *Henry Esmond* was published, set in a lavish physical mimicry of eighteenth-century texts, in 1852. Brontë's *Villette*, in 1853, seems to have brought this brief but intense period of fictional retrospect to a close, yet shortly after this six-year fad we find Dickens's *Great Expectations*, in 1860, and George Meredith's *Evan Harrington*, in 1861. Add to this such concurrent phenomena as the 1848 appearance of John Henry Newman's *Loss and Gain*, and what emerges is the picture of a sustained cultural interest in autobiographical memory. But the drama of remembrance that these texts enact, as I will argue, is precisely *not* the drama of dispersed, diffuse, detail-rich memory. What these texts offer is the spectacle of a rigidly coherent memory that remembers only what it can *turn to account*: as in the example from Thackeray's novel, only what can be either a symbol of the narrative's larger motifs or what can stand in a predictive relation to the narrative's present tense.[6] The answer as to why this might be the case—why even the period's loose, baggy, and monstrous autobiographical fiction does not contain the thematically and psychically dispersed retrospects of twentieth-century fiction—can be largely found in the period's most prevalent theory for memory and the psychic construction of identity: association psychology.

Why the necessary link between association psychology — something much more commonly thought of in connection with the eighteenth century — and the fictional autobiographies of High Victoriana? A preliminary response might simply note that until almost 1880 British psychology was firmly in the grip of associationist theory; its principles went unchallenged, and the work of theoretical psychology was devoted to refining its insights; the reign of what was termed "analytic psychology," which included the work of James and John Stuart Mill, Alexander Bain, and Sir William Hamilton, was in fact a continuation and development of the dominance that associationist theory had enjoyed since the 1748 publication of David Hartley's *Observations on Man*.[7] It might only be necessary to establish the undoubted hegemony that associationism had in the nineteenth century to explain its importance to the increasingly "psychologized" novel of the time. More crucially, however, the temporal intersection of two cultural facts — association psychology and the mid-nineteenth-century fictional autobiography — has implications beyond the issue of where to locate the boundaries of "psychology" in the 1850s. The project of nineteenth-century associationism, and the projects of such texts as *David Copperfield*, *Pendennis*, and *Henry Esmond*, which will be considered later in detail, can be summarized as the effort to plot the mind, and to *plot memory*, in such a way as to insure a newly coherent, newly organized psyche; and these projects can be detected in fictional texts that, in their artful connections between past and present, category and instance, mirror the mind they seek to construct. Furthermore, these mid-century novels use associationist terms and structures to psychologize their own coherence and continuity; rather than partaking in any older justification for internal coherence, they turn instead to the period's dominant mental philosophy. The operating premise here is as follows: in the associationist theory of Bain or Hamilton we see a turning away from the enigmas of Wordsworthian memory and a turning toward a cleansed, organized mind free of such uncategorizable detail. If we would explain how Henry Esmond's memory works, then, we should begin with the theories that sought explicitly to halt the possibility of a "trifling" mind — and to manage and reduce the hold memory might have on consciousness.

What Was Associationist Memory?

Summarizing his influential 1870 study of the state of British psychological thought, *La psychologie anglaise contemporaine*, the French clinician and theorist Théodule Ribot states that associationism is "the truly fundamental phenomenon" of English theories of mind and is the key to understanding the work of John Stuart Mill, Alexander Bain, and others.[8] Standing at the edge of a new world—which he would help to create, along with such names as Janet, Ebbinghaus, Breuer, and Freud—Ribot looks back at more than a century of psychological work and sees it all as a process of unlocking the secrets contained in the writings of Locke and Hartley. Sir Walter Scott may have once derisively termed associationism "the universal pick-lock of all metaphysical difficulties," but Ribot—as well as the mainstream of British psychology—would have chosen to keep Scott's phrase while rejecting Scott's skepticism.[9] At the higher edge of Victorian epistemological theory, then, was an idea that went back to Hartley's claim that the mind is structured by innumerable learned or acquired associations between sensations and ideas, or between ideas themselves. It was an idea whose infiltration into realms of polite learning was as thorough as its hold on more abstruse forms of dialogue; Dickens, we know, owned Dugald Stewart's 1792 associationist masterwork *Elements of the Philosophy of the Human Mind*.[10]

But how can nineteenth-century associationist theory have licensed a memory that, as we have seen in the Jacob and Esau tile from *Henry Esmond*, is incapable of fortuitous, contextless retrospects, desultory memories; that is too coherent for dispersed reminiscences; that can recall only a set of rigorously selected, symbolically or narratively relevant details? For this must not be, surely, the form of the theory that is more familiar to literary history, the form that has become "associated," most prominently perhaps, with Sterne's more freely associative fictions. In *Tristram Shandy* we can find numerous examples of truly incoherent associative remembrance; Walter Shandy's habit, for instance, of spending his Sunday evenings in the pursuit of clock-windings and "other little family concernments" leads to the following explanation:

> It was attended with but one misfortune, which, in a great measure, fell upon myself, and the effects of which I fear I shall carry with me to my grave; namely, that from an unhappy association of ideas which have no connection in nature, it so fell out at length, that my poor mother could never hear the said clock wound up,—but the thoughts of some other things unavoidably popped into her head—& *vice versa*:—which strange combination of ideas, the sagacious Locke, who certainly understood the nature of these things better than most men, affirms to have produced more wry actions than all other sources of prejudice whatsoever.
> But this by the bye.[11]

This, surely, is precisely what Esmond's Jacob and Esau memory is not: a comical and thoroughly dispersed juxtaposition, which leads to the dispersal of animal spirits that so bedevils Walter Shandy and his son; a purely irrelevant connection of two facts whose irrelevance is precisely the point. That is, the form of associative theory familiar to Sterne, and derived seemingly directly from Locke, seems to license instead a form of mnemonic madness.

In fact, the associative incoherence that seemed to be a consequence of Locke and Hartley was not an uncharitable interpretation; Hartley admitted that it is difficult, under the associationist theory, to explain the difference between imagination and recollection and that "all men are sometimes at a loss to know whether clusters of ideas that strike the fancy strongly, and succeed each other readily and immediately, be recollections, or mere reveries."[12] Locke — whose chapter "On the Association of Ideas" in his 1690 *Essay Concerning Human Understanding* founded the theory — begins his investigation of mental associations with a discussion of the madness to which they seem to lead: "I shall be pardon'd," he writes, "for calling it by so harsh a name as *Madness*, when it is considered, that opposition to Reason deserves that Name, and is really Madness; and there is scarce a Man so free from it, but that if he should always on all occasions argue or do as in some cases he constantly does, would not be thought fitter for *Bedlam*, than Civil Conversation."[13] The high associationism of the eighteenth century could and often did describe a mind unmoored from the sequence of past events, their relative importance, or indeed any governing context at all; substantively, that is, the workings of madness were not different than the workings of normative consciousness. As a result, eighteenth-century associationism did not study dementia of any variety, insofar as the association of ideas already provided the necessary theoretical armature to define what dementia might be.

This is not, however, the associationism of Esmond — not the associationism of Thackeray, Dickens, and the fictional selves of the mid–nineteenth century, and it is important to stress that from this Sternean dispersal the nineteenth-century version departs. Victorian psychology has usually been considered as the long, dull expiration of a limited eighteenth-century theory, as the crabbed and brittle annotations to a no longer vibrant, if still pervasively accepted, notion of mental functioning; or, perhaps, as psychology's long sleep between the Scottish common-sense school and Viennese innovations. This perception is accurate only in its largest sense — as Ribot saw, Victorian mental theorists were not engaged in open contestation with their associationist forebears and did base their work on this foundation; but what occurred was a thorough revision of the "associative madness" we can with some justice ascribe to the original association psychologists. The revision — which can be detected in the work of Dugald Stewart, James Mill, Jeremy Bentham, and Alexander Bain, who comprised the greater part of latter-day British associationism — is in the direction of eliminating the madness, the desultory, from associative memories.

It is interested instead in codifying the rules of associationism, firming them up, so to speak, in order to produce a rigidly bounded and internally consistent psychic sense of self; a self that classifies *as irrelevant* those reminiscences that might disrupt or disperse the paths of autobiographical memory. This self can be found in texts as diverse as Stewart's aforementioned *Elements*, Mill's 1829 *Analysis of the Phenomena of the Human Mind*, Sir William Hamilton's 1860 *Lectures on Metaphysics and Logic*, and perhaps most notably Bain's 1855 *The Senses and the Intellect*, which brought associationist theory to its fruition and, in a sense, its conclusion. To this constellation of texts it is necessary to turn, in order to establish the new plotting of memory that they sought to construct.

For nineteenth-century associationists, the laws of mental connections were neatly reduced to two: what were usually termed the Law of Contiguity and the Law of Similarity.[14] Bain's explanations are the clearest and most telling. Contiguity, Bain writes, can be defined as follows: "Actions, Sensations, and States of Feeling, occurring together or in close succession, tend to grow together or cohere, in such a way that, when any one of them is afterwards presented to the mind, the others are apt to be brought up in idea."[15] As for Similarity, it can be expressed as this law: "*Present* Actions, Sensations, Thoughts, or Emotions tend to revive their *like* among *previous* Impressions, or States."[16] Sensations that "cohere," thoughts that revive their "like": what we can detect here is a strong *binding* of mental operations; whether the memories elicited by a given sensation are contiguous (in original time) or similar (in thematic contour), they will not be mysterious or enigmatic. Esmond's Jacob and Esau tile is both contiguous in time with the burning of his birthright and thematically similar to that act, while Wordsworth's pool and beacon remain slightly out of the reach of Bain's coherences. The laws of nineteenth-century association were, therefore, constructed to either explain or eliminate memories that remain resistant to meditation, to bind and classify mental contortions.

Bain's summary of this newer, classificatory self is worth citing in detail:

> Our past life may, therefore, be conceived as a vast stream of spectacle, action, feeling, volition, desire,—intermingled and complicated in every way, and rendered adherent by its unbroken continuity. It is impossible, however, to associate equally all the details, so as to recover them at pleasure; only the more impressive facts remain strung together in recollection. The larger epochs and the stirring incidents readily come to our recollection, when we go back to some early starting point; while the minor events fail to appear on the simple thread of sequence in time, and are recalled only by the presence of other circumstances that serve to link them with the present.[17]

What is striking in this passage is a tendency roughly similar to that present in the moment from *Henry Esmond*: a recognition of the *possible* dispersal of memory ("a vast stream of spectacle, action, feeling, volition, desire"), of the innumerable possible "trifles" that *might* resurrect themselves, which is then superseded, or covered, by an assertion that the contrary is, in fact, the case: that memory does not "trifle" at all. For Bain the "vast stream" of the past resolves itself into a rather smaller and more tightly channeled series of remembrances that record the significant moments—that is, moments chosen retrospectively for their relevance to the present—of a life full of relatively insignificant, or as Bain would claim, already forgotten, detail. This is a psychic structure that is continually making distinctions between major and minor, useful and useless; that might edit out, for instance, the meal Esmond has before his birthright-burning but that retains as significant the emblematic Dutch tile that was briefly and tellingly illuminated by the fire.

The reason for this newly bound self begins with the associative madness of Locke and Hartley, which by the time of Dugald Stewart's 1792 *Elements* was increasingly seen as a threat to mental health—a threat because of its unpredictability, its capacity to unsettle the orderliness of present-time functioning. For Stewart, the principal alteration that had to be performed to the older concept of associationism is to add the "idea of the past": the notion that an association must also include the realization that this association is in some sense *already over*, a relic of a disappeared past; and that we can locate this association, understand its context, and therefore understand (and limit) its hold on our present activity. We must stress, Stewart writes, the "power of recognizing, as former objects of attention, the thoughts that from time to time occur to us; a power which is not implied in that law of our nature which is called the association of ideas."[18] Locating associations in the past is, for Stewart, a way of containing their potential for disruption. Remove that location, and the rememberer becomes like "some old men, who retain pretty exactly the information which they receive, but are sometimes unable to recollect in what manner the particulars which they find connected together in their thoughts at first came into the mind; whether they occurred to them in a dream, or were communicated to them in conversation."[19] Stewart's vision of senescence is not dissimilar from Sterne's depiction of a more ludic, although still somewhat mentally crippling, path of unavoidable and unaccountable mental connections. What has changed between *Tristram Shandy* and Stewart's work—which inaugurated the concerns of nineteenth-century theorists—is the attitude taken to these aleatory associations.

By terming unbound, unregulated associative activity "crippling," however, one begs the question: crippling to what? The answer, as found in James Mill's work, is narrative. Throughout Mill's *Analysis of the Phe-*

nomena of the Human Mind there runs the following theme: that selfhood is guaranteed by a continual narrating of the past, a narrating that although instantaneous is nonetheless carefully linked, thoroughly causal, temporally unidirectional, moving from past to present rather than back and forth. Lockean associations threaten the comforting uniformity of this process, make it difficult to maintain, disengage it from occurring. Mill's explanation of the process reads unlike any eighteenth-century associative account:

> What happens at the moment of memory? The mind runs back from that moment to the moment of perception. That is to say, it runs over the intervening states of consciousness, called up by association. But "to run over a number of states of consciousness, called up by association," is but another mode of saying that, "we associate them;" and in this case we associate them so rapidly and closely, that they run, as it were, into a single point of consciousness, to which the name of MEMORY is assigned.[20]

Memory is, neurologically speaking, a *narrative function* in Mill's account —it does not pluck out of the stream of the past randomly "associated" facts or events but instead takes a relevant past fact and then instantly—at the moment of mnemonic activity—narrates the intervening moments between that memory and the present. We might say, in fact, that Mill's process is the Victorian fictional autobiography in miniature: a linear travel from past to present that explains how that (narrated) past became this (narrating) present.[21]

So nineteenth-century associative memory, as in Bain, selects and winnows; as in Stewart, it always recognizes the past as past; and as in Mill, it narrates, explains, binds. It is possible to go one step further and say that it always *wills* recollection as well. For most theorists of the time, the possibility of fortuitous or involuntary memory was acknowledged only to be ignored. Stewart, in a move that would become second nature to later writers, split memory into "recollection," or recalling "in consequence of an effort of our will," and "memory," or spontaneous recall, for which he laments that the English language has no other word.[22] Hamilton's tremendously influential *Lectures* defined the split as that between "Recollection and Reminiscence" and "Spontaneous Suggestion, or Suggestion merely"—and like Stewart's *Elements* proceeds to concentrate only on the willed variety.[23] What twentieth-century psychological theories considered memory in its purest form, and what eighteenth-century associationism began, in a preliminary way, to describe, is precisely what is left out of Victorian analytic psychology; unwilled recollection is the lacuna that defines what remains. To return to Esmond's birthright-burning, the Jacob and

Esau tile is a carefully selected memory, in some sense explanatory, and, one might say, willed by Esmond for its acutely symbolic aspects; it is nineteenth-century associative memory perfectly exemplified.

The new nineteenth-century plot of memory will not, therefore, be a Sternean one and will not follow the path *Tristram Shandy* laid down. Nor will it be Wordsworthian, for, as we have seen, the associationist theory that comes out of Stewart, Mill, Bain, and Hamilton limits everywhere the possible enigmas of recollection, seeking instead to resolve them into instantly perceptible "coherences."[24] It will instead seek everywhere to turn chance recollections into rule-bound ones, "trifles" into significant thematic comments, and temporal juggling into linear processes. The form that evolved around this particular self was the Victorian fictional autobiography—a form that could produce a causally bound psyche ringed by Significant Events and Pivotal Moments rather than incoherent trifles; a form characterized by the instantly comprehensible, and by no means comically unaccountable, memories organized around a vividly memorable proper name (David, Jane, Pen). To understand why this form would be so congenial to associationist regulations, one must first excavate the parallel processes that mid-Victorian fiction, and psychological theory, carried out.

Principles of Remembrance: Three Facets

How, then, does the late-associationist mind perform these feats of regulation? It is possible to identify in both the period's fictional autobiographies and its associationist manuals three principles, as I will call them, of mnemonic functioning: three rules under which the dispersed data of the past can be winnowed, organized, stored, and reproduced or retold: the principles of *relevance*, *concordance*, and *integrity*, which I have extracted and named because they are nowhere stated in associationist theory, although everywhere evident. The word "principle" is apt precisely because the collective import of these rules is both cognitive (how the mind *does* work) and ethical (how the mind *should* work): I would stress that it is difficult to disentangle the more purely analytic strain of these rules from their admonitory aspects (that is, how the mind *should* order the past). Each principle is describing not only the normal conditions of remembrance but its optimal conditions, and both the normative and the ideal cohere in a vision of a mind that can tell a highly organized and pruned version of the past, one with the proper narrative virtues of cause and effect, an economy of detail, and a concatenation of prolepses and informative analepses.

The first such principle, the principle of relevance, is the idea that details from the past are selected according to their immediate, and immediately lucid, symbolic or explanatory relation to the present. Each mental theorist of the time who worked on memory inevitably stated this principle in his own fashion: for Alexander Bain, it was the law that "what is indifferent passes away"; as Bain would elsewhere claim, this principle of retrospective selection mitigates against flashes of dissimilarity being revived in memory:

> When in some new impression of a thing, the original form is muffled, obscured, distorted, disguised, or in any way altered, it is a chance whether or not we identify it: the amount of likeness that remains will have a reviving power, or a certain amount of reinstating energy; but the points of difference or unlikeness will operate to resist the supervention of the old state, and will tend to revive objects *like themselves*."[25]

Associative memory does not merely find relevances to the present moment; it then proceeds to taxonomize these memories; for his part, Stewart states that memory "spontaneously and insensibly *classifies* (or, as the Abbé de Longuerue expressed it, *puts in its proper place*) every particular fact at the moment when it is first presented to the mind."[26]

"Cut us off from Narrative," Carlyle exclaimed in 1830, "how would the stream of conversation, even among the wisest, languish into detached handfuls, and among the foolish utterly evaporate!"[27] Let there be no mistake: the principle of relevance is a Victorian narrative virtue, binding past to present even in the absence of directly causal connections; and this narrative virtue is grounded in what is the serious priority association theory ascribes to the remembering self, over the more defective knowledge of the remembered self.[28] The psyche, then, does spontaneously what the increasingly aestheticized novel of the mid–nineteenth century does laboriously: rejects unnecessary detail in order to leave behind a surface that might always either be useful (for the psyche) or thematically significant (for the novel). Of course the principle of relevance presented association theorists with a methodological problem: if it was possible to provide an example of an entirely irrelevant (or fortuitous, or desultory) recollection—the recollection as snapshot—then the very law of associations would be overthrown; thus the tenacity with which the principle of relevance, as I have called it, was defended and explained.[29] But since by nineteenth-century definition no associative memory is ever irrelevant, this dilemma was unlikely to seriously unsettle theoreticians of remembrance.

To see how this principle might operate within the space of a novel, we might turn to *David Copperfield*, when the permanent arrival of Mr. Murdstone is announced:

"Master Davy," said Peggotty, untying her bonnet with a shaking hand, and speaking in a breathless sort of way. "What do you think? You have got a Pa!"

I trembled, and turned white. Something—I don't know what, or how—connected with the grave in the churchyard, and the raising of the dead, seemed to strike me like an unwholesome wind. (42)[30]

The train of associations here—from "Pa," the general term, to the grave of David's biological father, to the forbidding aspect of Mr. Murdstone, which in turn leads to the word "gravestone"—is sufficiently obvious, and, of course, sufficiently *relevant*: fear and the father figure, death and paternity, are clearly linked in David's story. Characteristic here is also the claim "I don't know what, or how": as if the very obvious associative workings of the mind, as in my example from Thackeray, needed to be covered with an expression of bewilderment before the mind's pathways. At times the relevances of mnemonic juxtaposition are unannounced; on first seeing Mr. Murdstone David is reminded "of the waxwork that had travelled into our neighborhood some half-a-year before" (22)—but the comparison of objects, however striking, amusing, or unexpected, is not particularly enigmatic. Here I think we can see that what is remembered (a grave, a churchyard) is remembered for a reason, and a very good reason indeed.

The reason is not only generally associative (paternity with death) but *predictive* as well: David recalls a grave at the precise moment of Mr. Murdstone's arrival in the family because that arrival will herald not only a general gloom but, in fact, the death of his mother and her newborn child. Here we arrive at the second associative principle: the principle of concordance or circularity. Broadly speaking, this is the idea of proleptic memory: that what is remembered is remembered *because it will recur*; we recall the origin of what will also be an end; we remember in the light not only of past relevance but, more important, in the light of future relevance; what has happened once need not have happened at all and thus need not be remembered at all. Singularity is not the watchword of associative memory; repetition is. "In the transactions of the world," Bain writes, "great and small, there is so much of repetition, that a new history is in reality a various reading of some old one."[31] The mind edits the data of the past, therefore, with an eye toward possible future recurrence. Thus David vividly recalls Steerforth at sleep, with his head lying upon his arm, at the moment when Steerforth's dead body washes ashore in precisely that same position: that early, deeply felt scene retains its place in the text, and in the text's psychic order, because it predicts or foretells a later repetition: "I saw him lying with his head upon his arm," David tells us, "as I had often seen him lie at school" (795).[32] David continually narrates even highly unusual or unprecedented actions as slightly ironic, or surprising, repetitions—while on his desperate pilgrimage from London to the Kentish shore, he passes by his old school, Salem House: "So I crept away from the wall as Mr. Creakle's boys were getting up, and struck into the long dusty track which I had first known to be the Dover Road when I was one of them, and when I little expected that any eyes would ever see me the wayfarer I was now, upon it" (182). Repetition with a difference is still repetition insofar as it is narrated as such, as a return, as a circular journey. The associative mind is thus strictly economical, not capacious enough to retain a fragment of memory that cannot be eventually recycled.

The idea of a memory based on *scarcity*, on relevant categories and the potential reuse of mental material, brings me to the final principle: the principle of integrity. What is remembered, so the associationist claim runs, is remembered only insofar as it confirms this monad that I call my self.[33] What might disperse this identity—a surprising, fortuitous recollection, a sundered bit of the past—cannot be recalled, precisely because it is I, "me now," that is doing the recalling. Memory is both the evidence of a single, integral self, and the guarantor of that self, since it protects against any more diffuse recollections, any deeply alien reminiscences. Starting with Mill's *Analysis*, the idea of memory as the immediate link between what Mill calls "the idea of my present self" and "the idea of my past self" is, as we have seen, emphasized continually by association theorists; and, of course, it is the operations of the memory along the axes of relevance and concordance that help to guarantee that the link between past and present is not at all frayed. If memory can guarantee one's own self, it can guarantee the selves of others as well: for when David's mother dies, we hear this:

> From the moment of my knowing of the death of my mother, the idea of her as she had been of late had vanished from me. I remembered her, from that instant, only as the young mother of my earliest impressions, who had been used to wind her bright curls round and round her finger, and to dance with me at twilight in the parlour. What Peggotty had told me now, was so far from bringing me back to the later period, that it rooted the earlier image in my mind. (133)

The self is one, and an associative memory will only confirm this fact, summarizing one's own life into Significant Moments and their relevant cognates, while summarizing the lives of others into epitomes, epitaphs, condensed versions. We might recall here Paul de Man's assertion that the heart of autobiography is the trope of prosopopeia, the trope by which, de Man says, "one's name is made as intelligible and memorable as a face"; the principle of integrity insures the same result: a diluted and summarizable self, memorable, as de Man says, because memory itself is doing the diluting and summarizing.[34]

But a reference to de Man's analysis should only go so far here; while we might also remember his assertion that autobiography exemplifies the impossibility of a totalizing, or closural, dilution, we should keep in mind that mid-Victorian psychology—and mid-Victorian fictional autobiography—was interested in precisely what de Man denies: a self that continually produces closure, resolution, concordance, fixity. While the cracks that might undermine this structure, such as involuntary memory, or memories slightly aslant of immediate relevance, are detectable (even to the theorists themselves), the goal nonetheless stands, and nonetheless alters the form that fiction, and fictional lives, took in the middle decades of the nineteenth century. To some of these fictional lives it is now necessary to turn, to see how the interlocked wheels of relevance, concordance, and integrity propelled the shape of personal pasts.

Already Seen, Already Foreseen: *David Copperfield*

I begin with a single word, the word "association" or "associated"; it is rife within *David Copperfield*, and it serves as the pivot to countless passages that describe the shifts and routes of memory. Here, for instance, is David explaining his familiar (and rather infamous) linkage of Agnes with a church window: "I cannot call to mind where or when, in my childhood, I had seen a stained glass window in a church. Nor do I recollect its subject. But I know that when I saw her turn round, in the grave light of the old staircase, and wait for us, above, I thought of that window; and I *associated* something of its tranquil brightness with Agnes Wickfield ever afterwards" (223).[35] Or David's description of Ham Peggotty, as Ham relates the story of Little Em'ly's flight: "The face he turned up to the troubled sky, the quivering of his clasped hands, the agony of his figure, remain *associated* with that lonely waste, in my remembrance, to this hour" (451). When Mr. Omer, the aging undertaker, announces that he has read David's first book and that it didn't "at all" make him sleepy, we hear this: "I laughingly expressed my satisfaction, but I must confess that I thought this *association of ideas* significant" (734). Our narrator is not the only associationist in the text; Julia Mills, the heartbroken young diarist and confidante of David's first wife Dora, records this instance of Dora's first fight with David and of Dora's attentions to her dog Jip: "Monday. My sweet D. still much depressed. Headache. Called attention to J. as being beautifully sleek. D. fondled J. *Association* thus awakened, opened floodgates of sorrow. Rush of grief admitted. (Are tears the dewdrops of the heart? J. M.)"

(560). There is also Mr. Micawber, who revels in describing David as "an individual linked by strong *associations* to the altar of our domestic life" (530).

We should remember, in perusing these passages and the many others that operate in similar ways, that to "associate" was still, when used of mental operations, a term that referred narrowly and specifically to association psychology; not until the twentieth century, when the theory's scientific obsolescence was clear, could one speak of one idea being "associated" with another without calling up the echoes of associationist theory.[36] The very word "association" in the mid–nineteenth century was part of what might be called, to use a term of Gillian Beer, a "passive vocabulary" of analytic psychology that had thoroughly infiltrated the formally educated classes of Victorian Britain, much as Darwinian or Freudian language would over the next several decades — and its constant presence in *David Copperfield* is a sign both of the shadowy presence of this psychological language and its ability to express a generally understood cultural idea.[37] That is, Dickens's text continually refers, in both playful and deeply earnest tones, to what was the accepted account of mnemonic activity, and when Dickens employs the word "associate"— as he does persistently in *David Copperfield*— he certainly does it with the expectation that the lay reader of his novel will understand what the word signifies. When David says of Agnes that "I cannot say at what stage of my grief it first became *associated* with the reflection that, in my wayward boyhood, I had thrown away the treasure of her love" (817), the syntax of the sentence requires the reader to know the post-Lockean sense of the word — this despite the fact that the work of Bain, Hamilton, and Mill was never disseminated in popular form in the manner of phrenology or mesmerism. Rather, the centrality of associationism to the representation of mental processes in the mid-nineteenth-century novel gets its power from the degree to which memory itself was then understood through a general and diffuse, though also still professionally viable, psychological theory. In a text so committed to understanding the processes of loss and the mental recovery of a sundered past, the workings of "associations" function as the highest and most readily credible form of psychic realism available to Dickens.

The use by Dickens of the word "associate" throughout *David Copperfield* is only the most explicit invocation of the processes of remembrance of mid-century fictional autobiography, however; David-as-narrator, as well as David-as-child, is continually "associating" even when the word itself is not present. Describing the inverted boat that functions as Mr. Peggotty's house, David evokes an association: "On the walls there were some common coloured pictures, framed and glazed, of scripture subjects; such as I have never seen since in the hands of pedlars, without seeing the whole interior of Peggotty's brother's house again, at one view" (30). Associations linger in objects, such as Peggotty's "Crocodile book," even when perused years after childhood: "I find it very curious to see my own infant face, looking up at me from the Crocodile stories; and to be reminded by it of my old acquaintance Brooks of Sheffield" (874). As pervasive as the word "associate" may be, the process of associating is even more so—and all in the service, as we have seen in our survey of nineteenth-century analytic psychology, of removing the potentially disruptive force of desultory, sudden recollections.

But how can this be so? Admit the presence of associative psychology and vocabulary in Dickens's text, admit furthermore the constant reliance on "associations" as models for mental actions; yet is there not still the deeply reminiscential tone of the novel, its lavishly recovered details and its elaborately constructed vision of childhood? How can this blatantly retrospective—and finally very *wordy*—text be engaged in forming only bound memories, only those recollections that are relevant, concordant, and integral? *David Copperfield*'s status as a text of complete and detailed memory, after all, has only been strengthened by its place in the early memories of so many of its readers. Doubts like these gain some of their impetus from Dickens's famous pronouncements on the ethical imperatives of remembrance; there is the ringing, if slightly ambiguous, motto of the Christmas story "The Haunted Man," intoned by the protagonist Redlaw: "Lord, keep my memory green!"[38] Indeed, the names Wordsworth and Proust are found in close juxtaposition to Dickens in many critical discussions of the novel—far more so, one might add, than the names Thackeray, Brontë, or Collins.[39] It would seem at first that Dickens, perhaps more than any other Victorian novelist, prized memory as both thematic material and inspirational source.

Furthermore, *David Copperfield* is populated by a series of rememberers, a cast of psyches organized around, or defending against, a painful or at the very least uncomfortable memory: there is Mr. Wickfield's lingering cathexis for a long-dead wife; Mrs. Gummidge and her frequent invocations of "the old 'un"; Mr. Dick, whose unnamed trauma is represented by the figure of King Charles's head, which creeps into his "Memorial"; and the aforementioned Julia Mills, who, in the aftermath of a failed adolescent affair, continually sings about "the slumbering echoes in the caverns of Memory" (485). Here, however, we would do well to pause, for these characters are not the text's paradigms of health—I would claim instead that these instances should stand not as miniature exemplars of the text's own mnemonic motions but, in their insistence on an either seriously traumatic (or comically obsessive) relation to a still-troubling past, as negative examples for the kind of relevant, circular, and integral associative psyche David's own narration is engaged in constructing. And indeed, instead of the radically discontinuous relation to the past that these characters present, David's own relation is continually posited as a linked series, a chain, a comprehensible story.[40] The "associativeness" of the text is no epiphenomenal appearance of a philosophical lexicon. It is the text's own way of managing the tremendous amount of mnemonic data that David has to contend with, of binding it into a chain far stronger, and far more consistent—one might say, far more *narratable*—than the traumas of Mr. Dick and Mr. Wickfield. Indeed, if it is Dickens's habit to build into his narratives a collection of vivid counterexamples to healthy remembrance, from *Great Expectations*'s Miss Havisham to *Little Dorrit*'s Mrs. Clennam, it is because his source of value does not lie with such hypermnesiac psyches.[41] His source of value is with the tightly bound chains of associative remembrance: with David and his pruned "retrospects."

The novel famously contains four chapters called "retrospects"—"A Retrospect," "Another Retrospect" twice, and "A Last Retrospect"—narrated in the present tense and, putatively, told as immersions in certain periods in David's life. Their *summary* nature, however, is not accidental: they exist to bind links in David's chain, and they themselves are posed as chains out of which certain emblematic links can be extracted. Thus David begins his first "retrospect," of an adolescent love affair with "the eldest Miss Larkins": "My school days! The silent gliding on of my existence—the unseen, unfelt progress of my life—from childhood up to youth! Let me think, as I look back upon that flowing water, now a dry channel overgrown with leaves, whether there are any marks along its course, by which I can remember how it ran" (265). If we examine David's metaphor, we find that it is not far from Bain's explanation of the nature of memory, a "vast stream" of material winnowed down to "only the more impressive facts"; we see, therefore, that even these chapters that advertise themselves as present-tense regressions into the past are already highly selected, already "marks" by which a "progress"—nothing more *relevant* to the present than the progress of the past!—can be charted. These retrospect chapters, so often adduced as evidence of the novel's memory-rich texture, are in fact perfect instances of the reductive, binding nature of associative memory, and they perform this reduction in several complementary ways. First, insofar as they bind gaps in David's narrative—here, the gap from boyhood to early adulthood—they make his narrative more consistent, more explanatory (no lacunas allowed); second, insofar as they reduce the detail of these gaps to a breezy summary, they defuse the potentially troubling power that a mnemonic gap might have; third, they focus only on events that will later recur in more serious form: they are predictive. David's typically ludicrous adolescent infatuation for Miss Larkins, complete with a decorative ring and cosmetic applications of bear's grease, is in the end reminiscent of nothing so much as the later, fuller attraction to Dora—reminiscent, that is, of a later development; the reader, having reached the final concords of the novel, can look back on "the eldest Miss Larkins" as a memory of David's that in turn recalls a later repetition. No wonder, then, that this "retrospect" chapter, having achieved its goal of bridging and reducing the gaps of David's life, ends on a fade-out; David-as-youth forgets Miss Larkins, and the text leaves her behind with only a couple of metonymic objects, or textual souvenirs, to stand for her: "This, and the resumption of my ring, as well as of the bear's grease in moderation, are the last marks I can discern, now, in my progress to seventeen" (272). Elaborate acts of recovery these chapters are not; they are instead acts of leavetaking—David dispenses with these life-gaps except for those predictive elements that will later recur.

One might point with equal justice to the third of David's "retrospects," the narrative of Dora's death, in which the strands of David's relation to Dora are tied together neatly, in order to be condensed, made into a symbol of itself: "Ever rising from the sea of my remembrance, is the image of the dear child as I knew her first, graced by my young love, and by her own, with every fascination wherein such love is rich. Would it, indeed, have been better if we had loved each other as a boy and girl, and forgotten it? Undisciplined heart, reply!" (768). Thus David in Dora's death throes. To the final question—which might be rephrased: would it have been better if my relation to you had been exactly like that to Miss Larkins?—the answer is an unequivocal yes. Forgetting is better, when it can be achieved; and note here how Dora's illness is "forgotten," at the moment of its acutest phase, through the insistently recurring image of her "first" appearance. It is at once an act of concord—tying together Dora's beginning in this narrative, and her end—and an act of elimination, since the dispersed facts of his marriage to Dora (debt, mutual incomprehension, regret) are elided in this memory of love at first sight.[42] This "retrospect" concludes, in fact, on the image of Agnes "pointing upward"—to the death-room upstairs—which is an image that actually signals both backward (to the stained-glass window) and forward (to David's next, and final, marriage) rather than to the life of Dora. The novel functions, therefore, through visual condensations or metonymies that tie together significant strands of memory and elide troubling or more "dispersed" recollections—metonymies like the stained-glass window "pointing upward," or Peggotty's workbox with the picture of St. Paul's painted on the top. Bain's *Senses and the Intellect* offers a similar description of memory: "The ploughman's active day is partly summed up on the furrowed field that is pictured in his mind in the evening retrospect. Hence remembered actions may be to a great extent remembered appearances."[43] Dickens's fictional "retrospects" are "summed up" in an analogous fashion, so successfully that, just as one does not ask what in the ploughman's day is *not* summarized in the image of his final *telos* or success, one does not ask what is elided in David's visual metonymies.[44]

The "retrospect" chapters are crucial because they exemplify the rigidly coherent and bound nature of David's fictional memory—bound one to another in a narrative, bound to the future of the narrative, ultimately to David and Agnes's union. The text's largest contrary instance is also instructive. Here is David at the moment of the famous "Tempest," the storm that will kill Ham Peggotty:

> There was that jumble in my thoughts and recollections, that I had lost the clear arrangement of time and distance. Thus, if I had gone out into the town, I should not have been surprised, I think, to encounter some one who I knew must then be in London. So to speak, there was in these respects a curious inattention in my mind. Yet it was busy, too, with all the remembrances the place naturally awakened; and they were particularly distinct and vivid. (789)

The terms here are precisely the opposite of the associative order I have been sketching: a "jumble" in David's recollections; a confusion of sequence (David would not be surprised to meet someone he had just left in London); "vivid" and "distinct" memories floating without being fixed to any relevant context or predictive order; what might be called an hypermnesia. No wonder, then, that this stands as David's closest approach to mental instability in the text; and no wonder that it is matched with a natural disorder—the sea-storm—that is ultimately catastrophic. Dickens marshals the power of eighteenth-century associationist mental disarray at the moment when the text is most engaged in evoking disaster. What the novel does elsewhere, however, is much closer to what I have called visual metonymies, to nineteenth-century associative recall. Is it also much closer to what contemporary psychologists have considered a sign of mental malfunction but that, in the terms of nineteenth-century associative order, is a sign of mnemonic health: the phenomenon of déjà vu.

Some contemporary critics, Hillis Miller among them, have discussed the text's occasional recourse to déjà vu as an instance of the novel's proto-Proustian interest in the lingering power of the past; but déjà vu is the text's clearest possible account of how a narratively linked, nontraumatic memory would work; of how associative memory might be explained in almost neurological terms; of how, in short, relevance, concordance, and integrity could psychologically coalesce.[45] One such scene is particularly illustrative. During David's courtship with Dora, Mr. Micawber—who has thus far only been introduced to Dora through David's references to a "D"—meets Agnes Wickfield; maintaining David's alphabetical delicacy, he says that were it not for "D," he would suppose "A" to be David's love interest. Immediately déjà vu enters:

We have all some experience of a feeling, that comes over us occasionally, of what we are saying and doing having been said and done before, in a remote time — of our having been surrounded, dim ages ago, by the same faces, objects, and circumstances — of our knowing perfectly what will be said next, as if we suddenly remembered it! I never had this mysterious impression more strongly in my life, than before he uttered those words. (566)

If we read this scene with the three principles of associative memory in mind, the following should become clear: first, how the memory evoked by Micawber's playful indiscretion is so strongly *relevant* to the text's present as to be, in the way of déjà vu, almost identical to it; second, how the impossible-to-grasp origin of this scene (the shadowy memory) leads neatly, with a perfect (because mysterious) *concordance* back to the present; and three, how the relentless sameness of memory and sensation — the same faces, the same objects, the same circumstances — insures an *integral* self. The past does not burst with any vivid particularity upon the present because it is merely a recapitulation of that present. Here we see an attempt at psychic realism — the accurate noting and recording of passing mental states and transitions — that incorporates, in an embedded fashion, the underlying principles of associationist memory. These are principles that are summarized by Aunt Betsey Trotwood: "It's in vain, Trot, to recall the past, unless it works some influence upon the present" (347).

Déjà vu offers us, I would suggest, a way to see — in a condensed and almost caricatured manner — the workings of a textual memory, and a mid-nineteenth-century psychic structure, that insists on turning every bit of mnemonic data *to account* and dispenses with what threatens to destabilize the oneness of self and cognition.[46] Instances of instability abound in the novel, as I have said — most memorably with Mr. Dick, the most poignant of failed autobiographers — but the central figure of the text, its voice and eyes, is ordered through a memory that almost ceases to be a memory, and certainly ceases to be a regression to the past, so thorough is its identification with the present. Sleeping safely with the Wickfields in Canterbury, David recalls — what else? — his first, solitary trek through the town, but only in order to register the dramatic irony of that first walk's proleptic relation to his current place of rest: "In the course of the evening I had rambled down to the door, and a little way along the street, that I might have another peep at the old houses, and the grey Cathedral; and might think of my passing the very house I lived in, without knowing it" (224–225). This is a metaphorical instance of déjà vu, insofar as the memory is summoned up in order to say "I have already seen what I am now seeing." Thus even when David's memory does not announce itself as déjà vu, it functions in an analogous fashion, binding past and present through relevance, concordance (the circular motion of David's passage through, and then back to, Canterbury), and integrity. During a purely nostalgic visit to his mother's grave, he recalls his boyhood subjectivity: "My reflections at these times were always associated with the figure I was to make in life, and the distinguished things I was to do" (320). The familiar presence here of the word "associated" mixes well with the temporal juggling, the nineteenth-century associative juggling, the sentence performs: David remembers, from a position of greater eminence, a boyhood yearning for that eminence, and both what James Mill called the "idea of the present self" and the "idea of the past self" meet in a perfect mnemonic concord, which leaves nothing—no fact, no object—unincorporated.

Dickens's text does, therefore, turn to the past continually, with a highly developed sense of the possibility of regression, and it is often enough that David claims to see a past object, past love, past landscape before him again; but through the example of déjà vu we can see that these hinted regressions are in fact eclipsed by a carefully worked out idea that no matter how vividly the past returns, it returns only in the context of a relevant, concordant, and integral memory—only as a memory that binds the self. Déjà vu is only the most obviously signaled version of this mental mechanism. Continually David's recollections are set in a context of a *significant pattern*; a moment is recalled because its emblematic nature would seem to promise a later, revealed importance, or a moment calls forth a memory of an earlier, almost identical moment that would have predicted (had David been able then to understand it) the present. An example from David's encounter with the marital life of his teacher Dr. Strong and his wife Annie, which is throughout complicated by the presence of Annie's childhood love Jack Maldon, will make this clear. Seeing Annie kneeling in a supplicatory posture before Dr. Strong, David tells us this: "It made a great impression on me, and I remembered it a long time afterwards, as I shall have occasion to narrate when the time comes" (246). It "made an impression" because it seemed to promise at the time what in fact it ended up delivering: a hint of the future relations between Annie and her elderly husband; and it is mentioned because of that later relation. David-as-child carefully notes the scene for future reference, and David-as-adult recalls it when that future reference finally arrives—when the Strong marriage reaches a crisis. That is, David's recollections are set in a context of past-and-future concatenation; his memory flips backward and forward, cross-referencing and indexing his mnemonic data.

As we have seen with déjà vu, origins refer immediately to ends in David's text; what was first will be last, what began will finish. Like James Mill's chain or series of recollections that the mind passes through, from start to conclusion, David's memories always either inaugurate or finish a series. Observing Mrs. Steerforth and Rosa before Steerforth's death has closed the series of memories dealing with them, David evokes this recollection:

> As I moved away from them along the terrace, I could not help observing how steadily they both sat gazing on the prospect, and how it thickened and closed around them. Here and there, some early lamps were seen to twinkle in the distant city; and in the eastern quarter of the sky the lurid light still hovered. But, from the greater part of the broad valley interposed, a mist was rising from the sea, which, mingling with the darkness, made it seem as if the gathering waters would encompass them. I have reason to remember this, and think of it with awe; for before I looked upon these two again, a stormy sea had risen to their feet. (673–674)

"I have reason to remember this": what better reason than that it will return, that the rising sea will transform into the sea that literally takes Steerforth's life, the sea that will then metaphorically engulf both mother and friend? No irrelevant memory this, its referential quality to Steerforth's death makes it worthy of recollection; no discontinuous memory this, insofar as it ties together a hint and its fruition, a premonition and its later fulfillment.

Primarily, of course, the function of this "reason to remember" is to comfort readers who expect a high level of continuity and coherence in the fictions they read. Ultimately, however, the *reasoning* behind this "reason" is the maintenance of a self that undergoes no significant alterations, a self whose present and past are directly, and causally, linked — a self, in fact, whose experiences that do not contribute to this linkage are then forgotten. David's memory contains few seeds that fail to grow; very few events are without their companions and repetitions. The effect of all this chainlike concordance and integrity is, however, to reduce the capacity of experience to alter a life.[47] Everything, it seems, can be foretold by an earlier memory — and therefore all memories can potentially be reducible to a single term, which in David's case is clearly the maternal term. If early memories have a hold on David, it is not because of their fascinating, ineffable difference from the present, but rather their ability to seem most "real," their ability to supersede any later memories that might complicate or disperse the path of his consciousness. This tendency is notable even early in the novel; when the Murdstones disappear briefly from his house, David, gazing at pictures in the household fire, says: "I almost believed that I had never been away; that Mr. and Mrs. Murdstone were such pictures, and would vanish when the fire got low; and that there was nothing real in all that I remembered, save my mother, Peggotty, and I" (112). What he here tentatively suggests the novel will later confirm: David might remember many things, many "trifles," but what is *real* in these remembrances will be severely limited — limited to what expresses only relevance, concordance, and integrity.

An integral self presumes a structure of déjà vu, since if something has been seen once it will be seen again; for the completely integral self everything has already been seen. The best illustration of this associative selfhood is a memory of David's that, if not a pure instance of déjà vu, neatly encapsulates his text's continual recourse to the mechanisms of that oh-so-familiar mental phenomenon: "We stood together in the same old-fashioned window at night, when the moon was shining; Agnes with her quiet eyes raised up to it; I following her glance. Long miles of road then opened out before my mind; and, toiling on, I saw a ragged way-worn boy forsaken and neglected, who should come to call even the heart now beating against mine, his own" (863). Here, with the two figures of David — way-worn boy and proud husband — meeting in a seemingly spontaneous act of memory, we see the complex weaving of tenses and pronouns that characterize associative memory. "I saw" becomes "should come to call"; "mine" meets "his own"; looking upward, David-as-adult sees backward, back to David-as-child, who is, of course, toiling, and presumably looking, forward. The scene's déjà vu — the ragged boy we have "already *seen*" — meets what might be called "déjà prévu," since that ragged boy has "already *foreseen*" the present that remembers him. We have earlier seen how, in Thackeray's *Henry Esmond*, memory edits the past with an eye toward the possible symbolic or explanatory relevance it may have to the present; in Dickens's text, we see an even more extreme version, in which memory edits the past with an eye toward those components of the past that foretell the recollective moment. Within this strict and circular mnemonic system, there is no place for the sort of dispersed, diffuse, unbound recollections that have become hallmarks of modernist fiction, as well as hallmarks of what we have come to consider as "real" mental processing or "pure" memory. David himself, at the end of his text, is explicit about this associative concord of memory: "And now, indeed, I began to think that in my old association of her with the stained-glass window in the church, a prophetic foreshadowing of what she would be to me, in the calamity that was to happen in the fulness of time, had found a way into my mind" (769).

It should come as no surprise, given the rigidly bound nature of *David Copperfield*'s "associations," that this text ends just as the more explicitly amnesiac texts of Austen and Brontë do: on a series of cancellations of the imperfect past. Mrs. Micawber strikes the appropriate note on the eve of her husband's departure for Australia: "the time is come," she announces of her family's quarrel with her husband, "when the past should be buried in oblivion" (772). And so it is. Old, unsolved disappointments and latent cathexes are brought back to be rectified, with an economy native to Victorian fiction: Uriah Heep is caught and imprisoned; Martha Endell marries in Australia, far even from colonial outposts; and even Mr. Mell, the dismissed schoolteacher of David's Salem House days, reappears in the "Port Middlebay Times" as "Doctor Mell (of Colonial Salem-House Grammar School, Port Middlebay)" (871). Even the incorrigibly melancholy Mrs. Gummidge has revived, through a sudden ability to forget—the characteristically Dickensian cure of the obsessive rememberer: "And thinking of the old 'un," Mr. Peggotty reports to David, "is a thing she never done, I do assure you, since she left England!" (870). Leavetakings, both physical and psychic, are scattered across *Copperfield*'s final pages, and we could say, with some justice, that the counterparts of the mnemonic bindings and linkages that organize David's text are the willed amnesias that eliminate what cannot be so bound and linked together. Just as nineteenth-century associationism promised to cleanse the eighteenth-century associative mind of its scattered madness, so Dickens's fictional autobiography reworks the architecture of a personal past to construct a more organized, more classified, more coherent self. *Copperfield*'s nineteenth-century associations, in other words, are no free associations.

Memory's Habitués: *Pendennis*

Writing on Thackeray in 1913—a time when, after a drastic fall in his reputation, Thackeray's mid-century fictions could for the first time be looked back to with affectionate distance—G. K. Chesterton explained his generation's nostalgia for such texts as *Pendennis* as a formal effect of the fiction: "It may be said, in approximate summary, that Thackeray is the novelist of memory—of our memories as well as his own. Dickens seems to expect all his characters, like amusing strangers arriving at lunch: as if they gave him not only pleasure, but surprise. But Thackeray is everybody's past—is everybody's youth."[48] Chesterton's comment inaugurated a familiar critical stance: to see Thackeray as, preeminently, the Victorian novelist of the personal past.[49] But if we look closer at Chesterton's comment, we can detect the vagueness of Thackeray's fictional memories; for how can any text embody "everybody's past" or "everybody's youth" without necessarily losing specificity? In fact, might it not be appropriate to say that in order to be the novelist of communal nostalgia, a nostalgia so intense that the "everybody" who shares in it can extend sixty years into the future, a certain washing-out of detail is a prerequisite? If Arthur Pendennis is to be the "everybody" of memory, he can least of all be an utterly unique "somebody"—he must exemplify the mean, the expected, the hazy: everybody's memories. Being the novelist of memory might mean, in fact, avoiding the particulars of remembrance, preferring a predictable Memory to the surprises of memories.

Turn to *Pendennis*, whose serial publication from 1849 to 1850 over-lapped with Dickens's *Copperfield*, and that suspicion is continually confirmed. Take this description of the young Pen's first love, his comical attraction to the provincial actress Emily Costigan (whose stage name is Emily Fotheringay):

> I suppose there is scarcely any man who reads this or any other novel but has been balked in love some time or the other, by fate and cir-cumstance, by falsehood of women, or his own fault. Let that worthy friend recall his own sensations under the circumstances, and apply them as illustrative of Mr. Pen's anguish. Ah, what weary nights and sickening fevers! Ah, what mad desires dashing up against some rock of obstruction or indifference, and flung back again from the unim-pressionable granite! (*P*, 165)

Rather than describe the peculiarities of Pen's own initiation into desire, Thackeray prefers to set up an open space of description—one that can only be filled by the insertion of the reader's recollections, which the nar-rator is sure the reader possesses insofar as the category of experience under question here, "love problems," is so commonplace as to be almost not worthy of mention. The absolute predictability of this type of experience obviates any need for a narrative about Pen and can lead only to a quick, al-most tired, certainly ironized summary. The sense of repetition is so per-vasive here as to infect even the text's own claim to uniqueness—Pen can be understood by a reader of "this or any other novel," as if even the status of Thackeray's own novel, and his own readers, is nothing special; and the various subgenres of "love problems" ("by fate and circumstance, by false-hood of women, or his own fault") are listed only in order to establish how they all, in the end, come to the same thing. Caught in this web of mun-dane certainty, the reader, Pen, and Thackeray's weary narrator can, it seems, only speak memories so drearily familiar that they need not be men-tioned at all.

What of the privilege of the individual, however—what of the right of reader, and character, to claim a personal experience so precious and invi-olable that no sense of repetitiveness can spoil it? Thackeray's well-known emphasis on psychic isolation would seem to insure at least some space for fresh private memories; but even these moments are undercut by repeti-tiveness. Speaking of such inner isolations, *Pendennis*'s narrator brings forth this instance: "The old grandmother crooning in the corner and bound to another world within a few months, has some business or cares which are quite private and her own—very likely she is thinking of fifty years back, and that night when she made such an impression, and danced a cotillon with the captain before your father proposed for her" (*P*, 184). First the inaccessibility of another person's memory is posited, only to be undermined by the "very likely" memories she is having—stereotyped recollections of first courtship and marriage. One can always guess what someone else's memory is: such is the power not of Thackeray's narrator (this is no extreme omniscience) but of the repetitiveness of retrospect in general.

The significance of Chesterton's "everybody's past" opens up when we consider how thoroughly this "everybody" rules *Pendennis*'s mechanisms of remembrance. If *David Copperfield* offered us an instance of how associative memory could organize, winnow, or *plot* a highly detailed set of remembrances into a coherent self, *Pendennis* offers us another version of the effects of associations on retrospect: the degradation of relevance, concordance, and integrity into what might be called "the usual" or "the expected." If every memory is relevant to the present, surprise is ruled out in favor of predictable memories; if, further still, every memory can in some sense predict or govern later actions, then our very motions become stereotyped, not at all eccentric, indeed deeply, even problematically, forecasted. And as Thackeray's success—as well as Chesterton's resonant comment—tell us, this repetitiveness is not limited to one individual: it is the repetitiveness or familiarity of every reader; we are all "everybodies." In Thackeray's fictionalized autobiography, the effort of nineteenth-century associative memory to plot experience is revealed as having the potential effect of making all experience seem *already plotted*.

Lest we think the utter familiarity of memory was an unintended byproduct of associative theories, we can read the theorists themselves, who were only too happy to point out the reassuringly "used" quality of our recollections. As Bain put it, a "present incident will revive former incidents of a like character, at whatever times they may have occurred"—and if we wonder how "like" this "character" is, Bain offers us a metaphor from history, in which he states that "each nation repeats itself through its successive epochs," a repetition that insures "the coherent tissue of recollected events."[50] The regularity of recollection was crucial to associative theorists, since memory could then become didactic: "It was before observed," Stewart writes, "that the great use of the faculty of memory, is to enable us to treasure up for the future regulation of our conduct, the results of our past experience, and of our past reflections. But in every case in which we judge of the future from the past, we must proceed on the belief that there is in the course of events, a certain degree at least of uniformity." And indeed such is the case: "In the moral world, the course of events does not appear to be equally regular [as in the material world], but still it is regular, to so great a degree as to afford us many rules of importance in the conduct of life."[51] In the terms I have outlined here, the relevance of associative memory is dependent on its ability to be concordant and integral; if experience suddenly assumed an unpredictable quality, then no memory could truly be relevant. Thomas Reid explained this rule in a different fashion: "Our first acquaintance with any object of thought cannot be by remembrance. Memory can only produce a continuance or renewal of a former acquaintance with the thing remembered."[52] On its surface the comment is perfectly obvious — memory is not the same as perception — but its deeper significance is that memory can never be the source of insight, can never be revised; we can never, that is, see a memory in a new light, recall an event with a new set of assumptions or interpretations. Memory can only confirm what is already known.

There is no evidence that Thackeray, unlike Dickens, read association psychologists or took any interest in analytic psychology, but there need not be.[53] The importance of associationist memory to Thackeray's work is largely analogical — one important cultural field mirroring another — although perhaps, and more obscurely, causal, insofar as theorists such as Bain seem to be describing the mind Thackeray depicts just as surely as Thackeray seems to be producing fictional memories along associationist lines. In the larger cultural space that might be called "autobiographical theory," Thackeray and the associationists work side by side, each constructing deeply routinized psyches. Thus our experience of *Pendennis* should be informed throughout by how persistently ordinary its protagonist is meant to be, his memories never meant to surprise but only to allude to what our own memories already are. When Pen considers marrying the morally suspect Blanche Amory, for which he will receive an income and a seat in Parliament, we hear this: "And if every woman and man in this kingdom, who has sold her or himself for money or position, as Mr. Pendennis was about to do, would but purchase a copy of his memoirs, what tons of volumes Messrs. Bradbury and Evans would sell!" (*P*, 839). The leveling claim, the *tu quoque* assertion that shades into the more blandly accepting tones of "we've all been there": these are the recognizable features of *Pendennis*'s narrative voice, one that never insists on the singularity of the narrative it relates. Thus Pen's progress, from young man with an inappropriate affection for an actress of Irish descent, to callow Oxbridgian, to London hack journalist, to novelist, to husband of his saintly adopted sister Laura Bell, is always told as one instance of a very familiar series.[54] The items that led to Pen's college debts? "All which items the reader may fill in at his pleasure — such accounts have been inspected by the parents of many University youth" (*P*, 245). Pen's possibly exciting experiences in the London literary world? "We know how the life of any hack, legal or literary, in a curacy, or in a marching regiment, or at a merchant's desk, is dull of routine, and tedious of description" (*P*, 449). The Grand Tour Pen takes with his family? "It is not our purpose to describe this oft-travelled tour" (*P*, 716). Quite often the blandness of the novel's retrospections, its almost somnolent avoidance of specificity, shades into a denigration of any possible melodrama; of "the Fotheringay," we hear both a reduction of her possible stature and therefore a not-so-subtle mockery of Pen's attraction to her: "She was not grateful, or ungrateful, or unkind, or ill-humoured. She was only stupid; and Pen was madly in love with her" (P, 74). Thus the associativeness of Thackeray's novel: the thoroughly bound and relevant memories of nineteenth-century associationism lend to *Pendennis* its air of instant familiarity, its collection of deeply habituated characters.

For *habit*—the repetitive relevance of associative memory carried to a psychic principle—is *Pendennis*'s true topic, its underlying process. We might hear of a vivid recollection, but we hear of it only in the context of many later repetitions, so many repetitions that the freshness of the first experience is irrecoverable. Pen's first visit to a London theater is one such instance:

> The lights and the music, the crowd and the gaiety, charmed and exhilarated Pen, as those sights will do young fellows from college and the country, to whom they are tolerably new. He laughed at the jokes; he applauded the songs, to the delight of some of the dreary old *habitués* of the boxes, who had ceased long ago to find the least excitement in their place of nightly resort, and were pleased to see anyone so fresh, and so much amused. . . . What tired frequenter of the London *pavé* is there that cannot remember having had similar early delusions, and would not call them back again? (P, 351–352)

The scene is recollective, but only as a series—one should be reminded here of James Mill's associative chain, and how the first term in a series necessarily inaugurates the remembrance of the rest of the series. It is a series, furthermore, of wearying, repetitive, integral memories (the same sorts of plays, the same jokes, the same venues), so strongly relevant to each other as to have become indistinguishable. And yet, of course, the elder spectators keep returning. What we see here is the associative rememberer as *habitué*, habituated to the same memories and sensations: the melancholy side of a bound identity that *Copperfield* does not explore.

That memory is habit is not merely a Thackerayan comment on the eventual blandness of urban delights; it is a structure, throughout the text, that owes much to the classifying, organizing psyches of associative theory. When Pen himself remembers in the novel, he does so based on strict categories, and he therefore defuses the power that his various pasts might have over him. When he meets Captain Costigan, Emily's improvident, charming father, many years after *l'affaire Fotheringay* has ended, Pen has already learned to make his early love not a traumatic cathexis but a general, and rather run-of-the-mill, cultural instance. Costigan's Irish tales spark this: "Pen—as he heard these oft-told well-remembered legends—recollected the time when he had given a sort of credence to them, and had a certain respect for the captain. Emily and first love, and the little room at Chatteris, and the kind talk with Bows on the bridge came back to him" (*P*, 621). Note here how the individual memory, "Emily," is immediately set in the context of the general category—"first love"—that she instantiates. As Dugald Stewart claimed, Pen has learned to "spontaneously and insensibly classify" his memory, and the effect of the classification is a noticeable drop in emotional temperature. Everything is old, familiar ("those oft-told well-remembered tales"), slightly worn in the repetition and therefore no longer of much interest; or only of the sort of poignant, reflective, somewhat self-absorbed interest of the London *habitués* of which Pen is now a member. We might call this "disillusionment," of the sort familiar to us, perhaps, from Balzac's Lucien de Rubempré or Stendhal's Julien Sorel, except that Pen's disillusionment is less a process of violent social disjunction—a too-rapid rise and an equally precipitous fall—and more a comment on how memory, once the first term of a series has been installed, habituates the self to the new fact and then makes it lose any luster it might have had. Pen, for instance, does see Emily act after their affair ends, in her newly prestigious London surroundings, but as the narrator tells us, his former pleasure is gone—"he recollected it rather than renewed it" (*P*, 233). Memory is inevitably a process of, one might say, progressive boredom.

Of interest here is D. A. Miller's analysis of Trollope's account of "usual" experience, and of the purpose of eliciting a reader's boredom: "But boredom, as the example of pornography perhaps best illustrates, overtakes not what is intrinsically dull, but what is 'interesting' to excess. Far from the simple reflex-response to banality, boredom hysterically converts into yawning affectlessness what would otherwise be outright panic."[55] The Thackerayan process is roughly analogous. Thus the potential scandals of Pen's maturation—debt, a growing cynicism about writing, potentially illicit liaisons, such as Pen's flirtation with the very young, very uneducated Fanny Bolton: the silent side of nineteenth-century bachelorhood—are transferred into "everybody's past" and therefore become too dull to discuss in detail. When Thackeray, in one of the more infamous examples of Victorian self-censorship, refuses to discuss Pen's Oxbridge career, saying that "the life of such boys does not bear telling altogether," he offers as explanation not Pen's extraordinary folly but instead his ordinariness: "I would not wish to say of poor Arthur Pendennis that he was worse than his neighbours, only that his neighbours are bad for the most part. Let us have the candour to own as much at least. Can you point out ten spotless men of your acquaintance? Mine is pretty large, but I can't find ten saints in the list" (*P*, 211–212). In remembrance, former sources of anxiety are transformed, through the habituating nature of memory, into commonplaces.

Even the act of fictional autobiography becomes a developmental cliché, as in the lengthy discussion of the writing, editing, and publication of Pen's own effort, *Leaves from the Life-Book of Walter Lorraine*. The early version, written in the midst of his affair with Emily, was a strongly felt mnemonic record, but looking at it in early adulthood, Pen's associative memory reduces it to a bland *roman à clef*. Much like David Copperfield's "marked" retrospects, or Bain's "stream" out of which only the most telling moments have been preserved, the original manuscript of *Walter Lorraine* has been "marked" by Pen's adolescent tears, which blot the most important pages. But what do these associations, plucked out of the stream of the past, mean now? For the more mature Pen, very little:

> As he mused over certain lines he recollected the place and hour where he wrote them: the ghost of the dead feeling came back as he mused, and he blushed to review the faint image. And what meant those blots on the page? As you come in the desert to a ground where camels' hoofs are marked in the clay, and trace of withered herbage are yet visible, you know that water was there once; so the place in Pen's mind was no longer green, and the *fons lacrymarum* was dried up. (*P*, 518)

So Pen takes his souvenir of a lost time and several dead emotions — he finds it among his "old shooting-jackets, old Oxbridge scribbling books, his old surplice, and battered cap and gown, and other memorials of youth, school, and home" (*P*, 518) — and sets about converting it into a publishable novel, Arthur Pendennis writing a version of *Pendennis*. Continually in the process of revision, Pen is struck by how little his childhood memories now mean: "'By Jove!' said Pen, thumping down his papers, 'when I think that these were written only a very few years ago, I am ashamed of my memory'" (*P*, 519). Under the tutelage of his older, even more severely disillusioned friend Warrington, he attempts to "add a little comedy, and cheerfulness, and satire, and that sort of thing," to "prune" it (*P*, 523).[56] Eventually *Walter Lorraine* is published and achieves a minor success, but its function within *Pendennis* has been to dramatize the text's own conditions of production — or more precisely, to undo any "drama" that might attach to the act of fictional autobiography, to demonstrate how its writing is in reality a process of leaving the past behind, how its necessary conditions are not a renewed cathexis to the past but instead a willingness to *forget* it, to convert it into career capital. The pervasiveness of Thackeray's own ironized memory is nowhere clearer than in these scenes when Pen and Warrington work over, edit, remake, and market Pen's past.

Given all of this ordinariness, given the manner in which Thackeray's version of associative memory becomes a habituating rather than a destabilizing influence on selfhood, one might ask the following: how can a vision of memory as endless reiteration find a place in one of the earliest, largest, and most ambitious examples of the Victorian *Bildungsroman*? Put another way, what is its *ethical* function—what does it ask us to understand about youth and development? Perhaps the clearest answer is the one provided in the three principles of associative remembrance: that development is itself a misnomer.[57] *Pendennis* is a vast tribute to the notion that the Self is One and that not only will experience hopefully not alter that stability but that experience—insofar as it is filtered through a categorizing, plotting memory—is *powerless* to alter it. If Thackeray is enamored of reductive or synthesizing modes of thought, it is because memory itself (and we here can take seriously the idea of Thackeray as a "novelist of memory") is reductive and synthesizing. *Plus ça change*: "A college tutor, or a nobleman's toady, who appears one fine day as my right reverend lord, in a silk apron and a shovel-hat, and assumes benedictory airs over me, is still the same man we remember at Oxbridge, when he was truckling to the tufts, and bullying the poor undergraduates in the lecture room" (*P*, 796). What memory recalls and what perception sees is nothing but complete persistence, despite the easily ignored alterations in appearance or station.

The idea is evident in the many characters in the novel who reappear in a new guise while performing the same narrative role; the mechanism, which might be called "repetitive function," is employed throughout. Take the figure of Mr. Bows, the old music teacher whose unrequited, faintly poignant attraction to Emily Costigan is disrupted by Pen's more impetuous efforts; when Bows reenters the text, he is in the almost identical position of Fanny Bolton's older admirer and protector, again warning Pen (who is now much older) about his flirtation. Captain Costigan, who is introduced to us in the role of Emily's drunken father, is reintroduced as Fanny's drunken father figure, again slyly drawing Pen into a disreputable entanglement. Repetitive function, in other words, works to expose the identical nature of various characters despite the alterations in circumstance that the plot demands they undergo; similarly, it asks us to see the same person under various names, most vividly in the example of Blanche Amory's shady father, who moves from "John Armstrong" to "J. Amory" and then "Colonel Altamont," or, as the perceptive Captain Strong calls him, "Jack Alias" (*P*, 975). The epistemological justification for fictional autobiography, in other words, is the absolute consistency of character under every possible change in outward situation. Time, that is, passes with very little effect except for an increased weariness about its repetitive stagings; things change, but the change is noted only as an amusing irrelevancy.[58]

Thackeray's ultimate explanation of this system is presented in one of the novel's bravura passages, a *tour de force* of what we might call "associative prose"—a prose that seeks, in the mid-nineteenth-century manner, to associate past and present, memory and perception, so strongly as to make them identical. We begin with the newly passive Pen, who wonders at his being, only a year earlier, deeply in love:

> Yes, it was the same Pendennis, and time had brought to him, as to the rest of us, its ordinary consequences, consolations, developments. We alter very little. When we talk of this man or that woman being no longer the same person whom we remember in youth, and remark (of course to deplore) changes in friends, we don't, perhaps, calculate that circumstance only brings out the latent defect or quality, and does not create it. (P, 766–767)

Thus far so good: when we remember, we are remembering what may look different but is, in fact, the same thing. And Pen, well into his eponymous text, has not changed from the Pen who opens it. Then the passage shifts, with a burst of Thackerayan melancholy, to the reader:

> Are you not awe-stricken, you, friendly reader, who, taking this page up for a moment's light reading, lay it down, perchance, for a graver reflection,— to think how you,— who have consummated your success or your disaster, may be holding marked station, or a hopeless and nameless place in the crowd—who have passed through how many struggles of defeat, success, crime, remorse, to yourself only known!—who may have loved and grown cold, wept and laughed again, how often!—to think how you are the same *You*, whom in childhood you remember, before the voyage of life began? It has been prosperous, and you are riding into port, the people huzzaing and the guns saluting,— and the lucky captain bows from the ship's side, and there is a care under the star on his breast which nobody knows of: or you are wrecked, and lashed, and hopeless, to a solitary spar out at sea:— the sinking man and the successful one are thinking each about home, very likely, and remembering the time when they were children; alone on the hopeless spar, drowning out of sight; alone in the midst of the crowd applauding you. (P, 767)

Memory here is nothing more than confirmation, but the success of the passage is its ability to insert this confirmation (elsewhere so productive of ordinariness, boredom) into the largest categories of melodrama: pinnacles of success, death. All intermediate terms in the series of a life are, as James Mill claimed, run over in quick succession—"defeat, success, crime, remorse"—but what counts, the only term that counts, is the first one. The image here is of a self so deeply habituated by the earliest recollections that even the most severe later shocks, or the most drastic later changes of position, do nothing but force the self back upon an isolating consideration of how unchanged we all are. "You are the same *You*, whom in childhood you remember": this coalescence of memory, the integrity of the self, and the insistence that no later occurrences can alter it, summarizes the associative fictions of the mid–nineteenth century.

Memory is a narrative, and narrative is a forgetting. This, at any rate, is how we are left in *Pendennis*, where even Pen's own setbacks are immediately remembered as "stories" that then defuse any disappointment, stories that are already familiar. Pen receiving Blanche Amory's goodbye missive: "He turned over and over the musky gilt-edged riddle. It amused his humour: he enjoyed it as if it had been a funny story" (*P*, 924). Pen remembering his life in grandly narrative, grandly summary terms: "The train carried Arthur only too quickly to Tunbridge, though he had time to review all the circumstances of his life as he made the brief journey; and to acknowledge to what sad conclusions his selfishness and waywardness had led him" (*P*, 932). No matter the irony in "selfishness and waywardness," since Pen has been able — even in a brief suburban train ride — to encapsulate his life, wash it clean of troubling detail, and tell it whole. "The past is broken away," Pen tells Laura. "The morrow is before us" (*P*, 942). The sentiment is familiar to us from so many Victorian closural condensations and nostalgic forgettings; but the unique lesson of Pendennis's text is that tomorrow, given the mechanisms of memory, will be very much like yesterday.

Life as Summary: *Henry Esmond*

Associationist memory: the concordance of past, present, future. But what would produce this concordance better than death? "I wish I had died," David Copperfield tells us. "I wish I had died then, with that feeling in my heart! I should have been more fit for Heaven than I have ever been since" (109). It is not the only time David wishes on himself a premature death and in doing so wishes for the kind of instantaneous sense-making that its closure can provide, that it perhaps can provide far more thoroughly than mere remembrance. In dying, particularly in dying at the right moment, life might achieve a more complete narrative concordance than associative memory can ever generate — unless, that is, associative memory is a sort of dying. Thackeray's *Henry Esmond*, which has been read as a response to the wild success of *David Copperfield*'s first-person narration, confirms this suspicion: Esmond's memories are narrated throughout as if they are remembered at the point, or even *beyond* the point, of death — the point at which a life can be summarized, its relevant details retained, its irrelevant details lost, and all details formed into a coherent whole.[59] If *Pendennis* illuminates the buried tedium and routinization of memory that association theory implied, *Henry Esmond* brings into focus the summarizing force of associationist memory, its tendency to (metaphorically) kill off a life in order to better encapsulate it. If memory here does not predict the future, as in *Copperfield*, it is because there is no more future to predict.

What *Esmond* does is to offer us that strangest of all textual maneuvers: an autobiography for which the death of the narrating voice is often figured as the *terminus ad quem*.[60] At times that death is only guessed at, as in this memory of Esmond's grim Huguenot childhood:

> The unhappiness of those days is long forgiven, though they cast a shade of melancholy over the child's youth, which will accompany him, no doubt, to the end of his days: as those tender twigs are bent the trees grow afterward; and he, at least, who has suffered as a child, and is not quite perverted in that early school of unhappiness, learns to be gentle and long-suffering with little children. (*HE*, 30)

At other times that death is mentioned as a promise, a vow of mnemonic faithfulness: "He will remember to his life's end the delights of those days" (*HE*, 31). Still more frequently, however, Esmond's narrating voice leaves open the possibility that that death has already happened: "To the very last hour of his life, Esmond remembered the lady as she then spoke and looked, the rings on her fair hands, the very scent of her robe, the beam of her eyes lighting up with surprise and kindness, her lips blooming in a smile, the sun making a golden halo round her hair" (*HE*, 17–18). Thus Esmond's first meeting with the viscountess Lady Rachel Castlewood, at first his guardian, later his wife. Were we to wonder how Esmond can assert that this memory will survive to the last hour of his life — if we read the syntax as a promise and not, as it literally indicates, a description — we might say this: the memory will last because its content (an emblematic vision of Rachel) does not confuse the facts of Esmond's life but in fact makes sense of them. The most binding memory of all, his first vision of Rachel *must* coincide with the last moment of his life, since it *explains* that life. The same goes for the first citation here, which if not as important to Esmond as his love for Rachel, is still crucially explanatory: his early melancholy determines his later melancholy as surely as a heavy storm bends permanently the tenderer twigs. These memories are certainly relevant (insofar as they explain a life) and integral (insofar as they explain *one*, continuous life) — and they can be nothing so much as concordant, since they will recur at the last moment of Esmond's existence. That is to say, they *summarize*.

"He remembers," Esmond says of his reaction to the demise of Lord Thomas Castlewood at the Battle of the Boyne, "and must to his dying day, the thoughts and tears of that long night, the hours tolling through it. Who was he and what?" (*HE*, 70). The answer is, of course, that he is the person who remembers, and will *always* remember, that crisis of identity. He is the person who is now able, through remembrance, to put a "he" to the past: to turn his life into a stable enough narrative that a third-person pronoun can be used to describe it. If the text occasionally slips into a first-person immersion in past events, it more commonly stays with a third-person distance from them—the past transformed into a detached story, a story that although descriptive of its teller is now over, finished, particularly as its teller is so often figured as a man on the verge of death. To ask "who was he" of oneself is quite different than to ask "who am I" or even "who was I"—as the "he" seals off the rippling uncertainty of the question, preventing its application to the present. The question, therefore, is not permitted to be a live one; it is answered even before it is asked by the assertion that it will be remembered "to his dying day." A moment where identity seems in peril is surrounded, in fact syntactically prefaced, by the claim that Esmond's identity is so flawlessly integral that its relevant events will recur, in summary fashion, at the instant of his death.

What of these summary, after-death memories—why are they important for a consideration of *Esmond*? Perhaps because it has continually been read as the nineteenth century's ultimate Book of Memory, a text so attuned to the past in various ways (celebratory, regretful, fixated) that it offers us an uncanny preview of twentieth-century fictions. Its initial publication form, in three volumes deliberately set in an "antique" eighteenth-century typeface and complete with a dedication to a patron—rather than the modern serial form of *Pendennis* or *Vanity Fair*—seemingly confirms its status, alongside *David Copperfield* and *The Mill on the Floss*, as one of the most serious Victorian expressions of the power of constant, complete, detailed memory over an individual life.[61] Indeed, its air of personal retrospection tends to overshadow its status as a historical novel. But if it is thoroughly reminiscential, it reminisces only in order to produce a summarizable self. No twentieth-century desultory retrospects play over the surface of Esmond's mind; no eighteenth-century associative linkages, unpredictable in their range and context, link past to present in Esmond's text. What we have here is, instead, a novel that—as we can see in the Jacob and Esau tile with which my investigation began—posits a detailed and dispersed memory only in order to condense it, to demonstrate how all the various chords of a life can end in a final harmony. It is a harmony that, as nineteenth-century associationists might have said, is finally a healthy one, both musically and medicinally *tonic*.

Let us take one of Esmond's more obviously advertised memories, one that might seem to confirm what J. Hillis Miller has called "the Wordsworthian nature of Henry's enterprise."[62] When Francis Castlewood, Rachel's first husband, says farewell to his departing houseguest Lord Mohun—after having planned to meet again in London in order to consummate a duel, which will be fatal to Castlewood—Esmond is as yet ignorant of any strife between the two. But a faint foreboding hangs over the parting. Esmond's recollection of the moment is, in the way of a Wordsworthian spot of time, exact:

> There was in the court a peculiar silence somehow; and the scene remained long in Esmond's memory;—the sky bright overhead; the buttresses of the building and the sundial casting shadow over the gilt *memento mori* inscribed underneath; the two dogs, a black greyhound and a spaniel nearly white, the one with his face up to the sun, and the other snuffing amongst the grass and stones, and my lord leaning over the fountain, which was plashing audibly. 'Tis strange how that scene and the sound of that fountain remain fixed on the memory of a man who has beheld a hundred sights of splendour, and danger too, of which he has kept no account. (*HE*, 149)

Strange? What could be strange about the juxtaposition of Francis Castlewood, having recently set himself on the vindictive course that will end his life, and a shadow darkly cast over a "gilt *memento mori*"? Why is it strange that this moment of "already foretelling" a death is preserved over other "sights of splendour, and danger too," when Castlewood's death will have the largest possible resonances to Esmond, the most important of which is the clearing of the way for his (eventual) marriage to Rachel? Even the two dogs, planted in the scene as misleading indices of a photographic recall, are so strongly referential—black and white, Mohun and Castlewood—as to be almost embarrassingly symbolic. Esmond recalls this over other moments of which he has kept "no account," because this scene forms a strict "account" of his life; it explains his eventual rise in this family from bastard protégé to husband and father: it leads directly to Castlewood's slaying, his revelation of Esmond's true pedigree, and, eventually, to the frank eroticization of his relationship to Rachel. Nothing here is desultory, nothing here is accidental or noted purely for the "effect of the real"—even if it bills itself as such.

If there is anything strange about such a memory, it is, of course, that Esmond should register it *before* he knows of its significance, before he even knows of the duel he will later witness. This is, however, one of the most strongly associationist elements of the text: that details are selected by the mind with reference to their possible later recurrences or significance, and that this selection is not only *retroactive* (throwing out the memories that are no longer useful, ridding the mind of obsolescent recollections) but also, in an occult fashion, *simultaneous* with the event: we are likely to remember only what will later be, in a narrative context, important, and we can sense this as an event occurs. The mental mechanism is not only present in Esmond's theatrically staged memories, such as the one just discussed; it influences the novel's relation to its "historical" past, in particular to its mode of introducing the grand historical figures of the era. "Dick" Steele, "Joe" Addison, even Louis XIV: what so famously maddened Georg Lukács is the offhand, deflationary way these characters enter the text, but what might be of more interest is why they are even there in the first place.[63] The answer is, often enough, a strange kind of simultaneous categorization of individuals into the unimportant and the will-be-important. That is, Esmond mentions his acquaintance with these figures not only because they are of interest to his later readers, as might be the case with any autobiographer, but because — or so the text would have us believe — Esmond has a preternatural sense of what will be historically, as well as personally, significant. These individuals would seem to have been innocuous at the time of their intersection with Esmond's life (particularly Steele, who enters as "Dick the Scholar," learned but drunken and penniless), but the winnowing process of memory selects these innocuous individuals, and not others, for later recollection. Esmond's meeting with men such as Swift may have been accidental, but the memory of these men is no accident: "Dick the Scholar" is plucked out of the stream of Esmond's childhood because he will later become Richard Steele. It is the novel's historical version of the sortings and editings of personal memory, and if it seems curiously unrealistic for Esmond to have mingled in such famous company, we should remember that associationist memory itself is not "realistic"— not, that is, photographically exact, not uninflected by what will later be Significant.

What we are left with is a vision of a life in which beginning and end, past importance and subsequent judgment of that importance, coincide with a neat perfection. The novel's Horatian epigraph —"See it be wrought on one consistent plan / And end the same creation it began" (*HE*, 467) — is a promise, one the novel successfully fulfills; it does so through a fictionalized memory that is largely a memory of promises kept. Throughout the text, in moments of self-review, Esmond summarizes his past as a process of *keeping a promise*, and it might be said in addition that the very fact that the promises have been kept, rather than neglected or forgotten, makes his life that much more summarizable. Life is, like the text itself, a plan, which has no troubling excrescences or diversions, and memory is a charting of that plan's successful conclusion, even possibly a mode of enabling that plan to arrive at a successful conclusion. The vow typically remembered, the vow on which all other mnemonic details hang, is Esmond's early promise to stay faithful to Rachel, and the novel is not shy about recalling it: "If the lady looked forward — as what fond woman does not? — toward the future, she had no plans from which Harry Esmond was left out; and a thousand and a thousand times in his passionate and impetuous way he vowed that no power should separate him from his mistress, and only asked for some chance to happen by which he might show his fidelity to her." Thus the memory of the vow. And the standpoint of the rememberer? "Now, at the close of his life, as he sits and recalls in tranquillity the happy and busy scenes of it, he can think, not ungratefully, that he has been faithful to that early vow" (*HE*, 74). If *Pendennis*'s recollections spring from a memory so habituated to what it remembers that only boredom is the result, *Esmond*'s recollections are spurred by a memory glad to find that what it predicted would happen has happened, that what it promised has been carried out. In both versions, of course, memory cannot encounter what falls outside repetition, what escapes fulfilled promises, or what, in short, escapes the significance of a fully concordant life. Esmond may move his family to Virginia as a result of the final defeat of the Stuarts, but it will be to a "new Castlewood," the novel moving from its origin to an end that will be made as similar as possible.

"We forget nothing"— so Esmond asserts; but the claim is immediately set in the context of the kind of summary-memory that has been the text's hallmark. "The memory sleeps, but awakens again; I often think how it shall be when, after the last sleep of death, the réveillé shall arouse us for ever, and the past in one flash of self-consciousness rush back, like the soul, revivified" (*HE*, 394). The "History" of Henry Esmond is, in other words, a history with a claim to total knowability, and knowability in a "flash"; like the last judgments that Esmond postulates, the mnemonic judgments of the novel operate in order to make the self's past almost *formulaic*, easily recountable. What Esmond alludes to here, as well as in the countless other moments of "after-death" memory, is the familiar idea of the "life passing before one's eyes" at the point of death.[64] But the life that passes in this way is never a series of disconnected items, each encased in its own time; it is instead integrally united, a single stream with a single driving force, single origin, and single outcome. Even the more tranquilly recollective moments Esmond can afford achieve this same flashlike, summarized notion of the past:

> In tears of not unmanly emotion, with prayers of submission to the awful Dispenser of death and life, of good and evil fortune, Mr. Esmond passed a part of that first night at Castlewood, lying awake for many hours as the clock kept tolling (in tones so well remembered), looking back, as all men will, that revisit their home of childhood, over the great gulf of time, and surveying himself on the distant bank yonder, a sad little melancholy boy, with his lord still alive — his dear mistress, a girl yet, her children sporting around her. Years ago, a boy on that very bed, when she had blessed him and called him her knight, he had made a vow to be faithful and never desert her dear service. Had he kept that fond boyish promise? Yes, before Heaven; yes, praise be to God! (*HE*, 392)

What we have here is the associative stream of life, in which the beginning of the chain, the vow to Rachel, accords neatly with the end of the chain. As a result, there is no dissonance in Esmond's return to Castlewood, no sense of a sundered past—the clock tolls the hours as it always has, the promise is as operative, and as significant to Esmond's life, as it always has been. If the repetitive concords between past and present are celebrated here with a sense of relief and not, as in *Pendennis*, lamented as part of memory's anesthetic routine, the very idea of concord has not changed. Lest we forget that Esmond's life is a series of fulfillments and returns rather than discrete steps in a forward-looking progress, the novel continually reminds us through such reviews as these; we are not permitted to elide the fact that the Esmond we first met is Esmond still. After his satisfying life-review, Esmond's sleep permits even more concordances between past and present: "All night long he was dreaming his boyhood over again, and waking fitfully; he half fancied he heard Father Holt calling to him from the next chamber, and that he was coming in and out from the mysterious window" (*HE*, 392). Dreaming his boyhood over again in preparation for reliving it: not much later the same window, which Esmond's Jesuit teacher used for quick escapes, will be used to let in the Old Pretender so that he may pursue Beatrix Castlewood.

Memory does saturate *Esmond*, but in a peculiar way, and with a clearly nineteenth-century style. The memory permitted into the text is only that which confirms identity and fulfills vows and not any memory that might, in the way of a Wordsworthian spot of time or a Sternean accidental association, be opaque or troubling to a dying man (or to a live reader). What *Esmond* means for us is that the mid–nineteenth century fictional autobiography, no matter the amount of transfigured personal detail or historical research that went into its composition, chooses not to imagine an enigmatic self; neither, as we have seen, does nineteenth-century analytic psychology, for which the immediate clarity of every mind is continually reaffirmed by the clarifying force of associationist memory.[65] Over and throughout both mid-century psychology and mid-century fiction plays a mind that functions, perhaps, like a machine: winnowing and sorting, eliminating and arranging, turning the past into the story that always only confirms our sense of the present. If we should wonder what would happen if the machine breaks, that wondering will not be satisfied. Ruptures of the chain of associationist memory are difficult indeed to find in mid-century fiction, in which, as we have seen, what is remembered is remembered, in a sense, because it has never been forgotten: it is only (but why "only"?) what one always knows about oneself. So says Esmond, who in asserting the permanence of memory actually asserts the impossibility of actual re-collection, re-membrance: "Parting and forgetting! What faithful heart can do these? Our great thoughts, our great affections, the Truths of our life, never leave us" (*HE*, 383). Mid-century autobiographical memory is—as presented to us in *Copperfield*, *Pendennis*, and *Esmond*—about precisely this: a memory that never has to re-member. The cultural space called "autobiographical theory," occupied by both lengthy novels and equally dense psychological tracts, presents us with no recoveries, no insoluble enigmas, but instead minds, and memories, lifted into lucidity.

After Associationism
(The Broken Past)

A memory that disables remembering, or makes remembrance unnecessary —such is the theme of the mid-century "associative" fictional autobiography. It is a theme that will have an afterlife of some importance in the history of the English novel. Take *Great Expectations* (1861), which is newly concerned with ideas of memory *in extremis*—with amnesias, hypermnesias, identity confusions, explosive memories—but which returns to this slightly older idea of diluted memory as if by habit, as when Pip asks Joe Gargery if he wants to know the story of Magwitch:

> "If you would like to hear, Joe—" I was beginning, when Joe got up and came to my sofa.
> "Lookee here, old chap," said Joe, bending over me. "Ever the best of friends; ain't us, Pip?"
> I was ashamed to answer him.
> "Wery good, then," said Joe, as if I *had* answered; "that's all right, that's agreed upon. Then why go into subjects, old chap, which as betwixt two sech must be for ever onnecessary? There's subjects enough as betwixt two sech, without onnecessary ones. Lord! To think of your poor sister and her Rampages! And don't you remember Tickler?"[66]

The typically Victorian closural assertion here is a relic of sorts, in a novel that is moving to more late-century concerns with sick or obsessive remembrances: a relic of the rationale behind mid-century associationist memory. A still dangerous "onnecessary" memory is dismissed—Pip later comments on "the delicacy with which Joe dismissed this theme"[67]—and a safer "necessary" topic introduced in the interests of self-justification (Joe explaining how powerless he was to keep his wife's attacks on Pip at bay) and of familial binding, as the older memory is adduced to bring Pip back to the Pip with which the novel starts. It is a classic instance of the sort of mental structure that pervades *Copperfield*, *Pendennis*, and *Esmond*, in which the mind continually separates the "necessary" from the "onnecessary," albeit at a less fully conscious level than Joe's carefully prefaced forgetting.

That is, in fact, the fate of associationist editings in the Victorian novel—the more explicit they become, the less thoroughly they influence the shape of narrative.

But the afterlife of associationist memory is only so long. What replaces it, in fact what is its conceptual opposite, is the form of remembrance in which the past is still too powerful to be edited, in which the self cannot even fully know what has passed: trauma. Whereas the mind of Bain, Mill, and Hamilton is always perfectly assimilated to its past, the traumatic self encounters a past that is as yet ungrasped (and possibly ungraspable), unknown, and yet determining. The crisis of trauma is a crisis of knowledge. The most persuasive recent accounts of trauma insist upon this aspect: Cathy Caruth, for instance, has argued that "trauma is not locatable in the simple violent or original event in an individual's past, but rather in the way that its very unassimilated nature—the way it was precisely not known in the first instance—returns to haunt the survivor later on." When the past is mystified by trauma, categories become inoperable; the mind cannot categorize what cannot be known. The traumatic past is always *relevant*, of course, but relevant in an occult and always surprising fashion; it is *concordant* with the present and future, but only in the form of uncontrollable repetitions, which for Freud were the primary symptoms of traumatic neuroses; and it can never produce an *integral* self, since it is, as Caruth has claimed, "a break in the mind's experience of time."[68]

Realizing that the reign of traumatic memory succeeds the reign of associationist memory not only sets a limit to the period I have outlined but also helps illuminate, through a glimpse of what nineteenth-century associationism is *not*, what it *is*—what it *does*. If trauma is, to use Caruth's term, "unclaimed experience," associationist memory is the mind's ability to claim experience, to put it to use, to turn it to account, to make it productive. It is memory that does not need to recollect, since what is useful of the past is all around us, already retained, part of our habits, our set of explanatory "experiences" that, far from being obscure, are on the tips of our tongues. Whereas trauma is the difficulty of not being able to remember, associative memory is the lack of a need to; detailed remembrance is, in the terms of nineteenth-century associationism, unnecessary. David's predictive memories, Pen's habituated recollections, Esmond's fulfilled vows: in all of them we find not trauma but *work*—the spectacle of remembrance as work, the work of confirming the self's decisions, of defusing the glamour of the past.

Reading backward from the constantly narrated traumas of the twentieth century, we discover in the Victorian fictional autobiography a mind before trauma's contours were taken to define memory as a whole, before the advent of what Benjamin has called the "traumatophile."[69] Prior to Freud or Janet, there is a large corpus of psychological theory that not only ignores trauma but describes a mind impervious to it, the mind that we find in mid-century Victorian fiction. I would suggest that those texts, those *names* that cluster around the middle years of the nineteenth century — Jane Eyre, Arthur Pendennis, and, of course, David Copperfield — work to reduce the threat (a threat to narrative clarity, a threat to psychic sanity) that a particularized and vivid memory, or traumatic fixation, might present. Progressive in the extreme, these texts "associate" not backward but forward, projecting the past into the present and future, sternly dividing the data of memory into the useful (that which retains crucial and predictive "associations") and the useless. And these texts, therefore, furnish us with a clue to the generally *amnesiac* character of mid-Victorian selfhood, a selfhood that continually converts memory into action, remembrance into prediction, the past into promise.

FOUR

The Birth of Amnesia

COLLINS, SENSATION, FORGETTING

"Perhaps you would kindly give me a sketch of the course
of events from memory."
"Certainly, though I cannot guarantee that I carry all the facts in my mind.
Intense mental concentration has a curious way of blotting out what has
passed. The barrister who has his case at his fingers' end, and is able to argue
with an expert upon his own subject, finds that a week or two of the courts will
drive it all out of his head once more. So each of my cases displaces the last,
and Mlle Carère has blurred my recollection of Baskerville Hall."
—Arthur Conan Doyle, The Hound of the Baskervilles

Our record of the reactions to Collins's sensation novels of the 1860s reads
like a record of forgettings.[1] Responding to the 1860 publication in book
form of *The Woman in White*, an anonymous reviewer in the *Saturday Review* describes the consumable nature of Collins's mysteries, which, like
yesterday's meals, leave little memory behind them: "Nobody ever leaves
his tales unfinished. This is a great compliment to his skill. But then very
few feel at all inclined to read them a second time. Our curiosity once
satisfied, the charm is gone."[2] As a reviewer of *The Moonstone* remarked in
the *Nation*, the only remembrance these texts leave behind is a regret for
the empty activity they occasioned: "We do not know of any books of
which it is truer than of Mr. Collins's to make the damaging remark, that
nobody reads them twice, and that when the end of the first perusal is
reached, everybody thinks his time has been wasted."[3] If the complex plots
and nervous, edgy affects of Collins's novels are difficult to retain in the
memory for readers and lose their appeal once those nervous sensations
have ceased, they might have left similarly few traces on Collins himself;
having composed *The Moonstone* with almost constant help from laudanum, Collins received a copy of the finished work with pleased surprise,
finding himself unable to recall the planning of the narrative.[4] The earliest
responses to Collins's work, and to adjacent sensation novels by Reade,

Braddon, and others, register the fungible, erasable nature of their melo-dramatic shocks and climaxes, which are forgotten as soon as they arrive, and which turn their consumers into amnesiac compulsives who, having immediately absorbed one plot, turn with hungry attention to another. It is as if the triadic motto famously ascribed to Collins—"make 'em laugh, make 'em cry, make 'em wait"—could very well contain a fourth item: "make 'em forget."

Forget they do, not simply in the commercial world of Victorian pub-lishing (which by the 1880s would already have "forgotten" the sensation novel and its craze) but in Collins's own plots, which are littered with am-nesiacs. The instances from two novels of the 1860s are striking in their va-riety and their centrality to their narratives: in *The Woman in White* we find Laura Fairlie, whose amnesia is both specific—an inability to recall the date she was transferred, under the control of Count Fosco, from Blackwater Park to London—and traumatically general, as she cannot recall anything of her treatment in the asylum in which Fosco placed her. This amnesia is not a simple example of drug-induced obliviousness but something far more pathological, a real mental *disease*, and much of the novel's final third is an attempt to cure it. In *The Moonstone* we have Franklin Blake, whose opium-induced inability to remember one night, the night in which the fa-bled Moonstone is stolen, drives the entire mystery; we also can find there Mr. Candy, the elderly local doctor whose fever-induced amnesia wipes away his entire memory, thus rendering the mystery insoluble until his as-sistant, Ezra Jennings, discovers a method for extracting facts from Mr. Candy's disconnected ravings. Alongside these vivid examples of various forms of amnesia (the traumatic, the pharmacological, the senescent) are a host of characters who, in ordinary and unexceptional—if still obfusca-tory—ways, cannot recall significant details, find facts slipping out of their minds, and rely on a host of secondary devices to keep their fast-fading memories intact. If the novels of Austen, Brontë, Dickens, and Thackeray contain characters who choose not to remember or for whom remem-brance is *useless*, as well as narratives that look to evade the past in various ways, in Collins's texts of the 1860s this generalized amnesia has become pathological or diseased and has become a widespread *problem*. Simple criminal acts go unpunished because crucial memories about the act have been erased; central characters find themselves crippled by mnemonic gaps and elisions. The general and more or less genial nostalgic erasures of pre-vious nineteenth-century fiction become explicit in Collins's work—the amnesiac self, one might say, becomes *thematized*. And if earlier Victorian texts sought a reader for whom nostalgic generalities replaced specific reminiscence, Collins's novels seek a reader who might forget having read the text itself, for whom even the amnesiacs within the novels are quickly forgotten.

The general lesson here — that Collins's texts thematize the Victorian novel's construction of sensibilities freed of burdensome remembrance — depends on a deeper systematics within Collins's work: the constant alliance between "sensation" (which in its extreme forms becomes "shock") and amnesia. We may start with *The Moonstone*, which, although not usually categorized as a "sensation novel," shares nonetheless with Collins's more sensationalistic fiction a dynamic interchange between sensation and forgetting. Franklin Blake — who has no recollection of having stolen the novel's eponymous gem — finds the thief's long-hidden nightgown with the telltale paint smear on it, only to discover that the nightgown is his own:

> I have not a word to say about my own sensations.
>
> My impression is, that the shock inflicted on me completely suspended my thinking and feeling power. I certainly could not have known what I was about, when Betteredge joined me — for I have it on his authority that I laughed, when he asked what was the matter, and, putting the nightgown into his hands, told him to read the riddle for himself.
>
> Of what was said between us on the beach, I have not the faintest recollection. (*M*, 359)[5]

The sudden amnesia continues for several moments: Blake forgets his resolution never to enter Rachel Verinder's house and does enter it, in order to be seated and collect himself; he then forgets that he is carrying a letter from Rosanna Spearman in his pocket, which he has to be reminded of before he takes it out and reads it. Walking in a trance, unable to retain his actions and words, forgetting his motives and his physical surroundings, Blake is a man *sensationalized* — made newly amnesiac by virtue of the overwhelming power of exterior shock. The apparatus of the nervous system ("sensations," "impression," "shock") is mobilized to contain and defend against the new, and for the time being unassimilable, information from without; in the process, basic operations of remembrance are suspended. With the physiological acuity so frequently found in sensation fiction, the process of "being shocked" by new information shades into the process of "going into shock" — and in this area where a conceptual shock meets a cerebrospinal shock, amnesia is the common term. We forget, in other words, because we have sensations.

The linkage is so familiar to readers of sensation novels and so deeply embedded in these novels's modes of description (the ever-familiar moments of "surprise" and "excitement") that it can pass unnoticed; the texture of Collins's work is often constructed out of momentary amnesias produced by sensation. *Armadale* opens with a Scotsman, Mr. Neal, being convinced to transcribe the novel's foundational narrative — the dying Mathew Wrentmore's confession — because of his sudden attraction for the dying man's wife, an attraction that is sensational in both its immediacy and its strangeness, insofar as the wife is of mixed blood: "For the first time in his life, the Scotchman was taken by surprise. Every self-preservative word that he had been meditating but an instant since, dropped out of his memory" (*A*, 14). That is all: a shock (beauty, racial otherness), an amnesia (of formulaic denials, polite refusals). The pattern is constant in Collins's novels and should lead us to the following general observation: that if amnesia is so prevalent in Collins's sensation fiction, it is because for Collins, and — as I will show — for late-Victorian physiology, sensation was necessarily amnesiac. Any text that attempted to elicit "sensations," therefore, must inevitably elicit forgetfulness as well. Thus the strange spectacle of Collins's plots from the 1860s, in which a constant and pervasive forgetfulness allows the mystery in question to be prolonged and intractable, and in which so many serious amnesiacs find their diseases becoming central matters of inquiry.

The first phenomenon to note about Collins's amnesiacs is, then, this most basic (or most physiological) fact: that the readerly response of forgetting, so continually noted in contemporary reviews of Collins's work, is already encoded in the novels *as a necessary byproduct of sensation itself.* Well before any theorizations of wartime traumas or "shell shock," the sensation novel had already described a world in which the reactions of the nervous system in extreme situations dictate an automatic amnesia, whether of the everyday or the morbid varieties — an amnesia that metastasizes from the text to the compulsive reader of sensation novels, who, as contemporary descriptions had it, might remember no more of a given sensation novel than the fact of having read it. The second and complementary phenomenon to note here is how Collins's sensationalized amnesiacs represent *a sudden pathologization of the Victorian amnesiac self.* Victorian narratives had, as we have seen, long depended on a psyche capable of revising, diluting, or even erasing past cathexes and previous mistakes in the name of a communicable, generalizable nostalgia; in Collins, this psyche becomes an illness, its contours become symptoms. In fact, what might be suggested by Collins's amnesiacs is the closing of a circle: what started in Austen's work as the depathologizing of "nostalgia," its shift from medical dilemma to cultural virtue, is in Collins's work repathologized, transferred again into the realm of the problematic, the potentially dangerous. An oblivion that was seen as a blessed release from the past, and that was licensed by countless closural moments in Victorian fiction, becomes *morbid* once more. But this shift from a general virtue to a pathology should not blind us to the value amnesia has for sensation fiction — it is the *necessary foundation of a sensation plot*; it forms the necessary conditions for "sensation" itself to occur. In short, the pathological amnesias of these novels mirror the lucid amnesias of Austen, Brontë, Dickens, or Thackeray; what we see in Collins's novels of the 1860s is the Victorian amnesiac self in its later phase, when the actions of a "nervous" physiology begin to interact with the elisions of a nostalgic psyche. But forgetting — whether in its extreme or in its everyday senses — is as necessary to Collins's intricate mysteries as to the pleasant dispositions of Austen's social unions.

Alongside these claims I would place a further, more broadly historical one: that Collins's amnesiac sensations, and plots of amnesia, are the sign of a genesis: the *birth of amnesia* as a cultural and scientific fact. Amnesia itself had yet to become a topic of psychology, physiology, or mental philosophy and was far from being considered the key to the mind's dynamics; as a word it scarcely existed in English. Collins's work represents not only a pathologizing of a general cultural structure but also an anticipation, by at least a decade, of the importance of that pathology — thus, perhaps, the silence that has so often surrounded the forgettings in Collins's work. By using amnesia to bring both *The Woman in White* (1860) and *The Moonstone* (1868) into relation, my study admittedly collapses the distinction between "sensation novel" and "mystery novel," but does so in order to reveal Collins's construction, in the 1860s, of a category that spans both genres: the amnesiac plot of sensations. In investigating the function of amnesia in Collins's two most popular texts, we may be, in fact, reconstructing a time before amnesia itself became the norm for psychological study — before, that is, amnesia inaugurated a wholesale cultural obsession with memory; we are also investigating a time, and a cultural formation, that laid the foundations for our contemporary emphasis on the pathologies of amnesia and the pathologies of narrative.

The Birth of Amnesia:
The Music Box

Collins's novels are nothing if not medically *up to date* — citing the best and most respected physiologists of the time, offering advanced theories for various psychic anomalies, situating themselves in surgeries, asylums, and sickrooms. *The Woman in White* contains a prolonged debate, won by Count Fosco, on how Marian Halcombe's fever symptoms should be treated, along with Laura Fairlie's incarceration in a London asylum; *The Moonstone*, most famously, contains citations from both John Elliotson's 1840 *Human Physiology* and William Carpenter's 1842 *Principles of Human Physiology*, both considered among the crucial medical texts of their time. Even if the novels are occasionally at pains to veil this scientific background, the saturation in physiological research is clear.[6] It was evident to contemporary critics, who, like Margaret Oliphant in a well-known 1862 review of Collins's work in *Blackwood's*, spoke of the "violent stimulant of serial publication," thereby turning Collins into one of the shady physicians he depicts, dispensing potentially dangerous substances to an easily gulled public; evident as well to recent readers of Collins, although perhaps too evident to seem to need further discussion.[7] The extent of Collins's reading in the Victorian sciences of mind would seem to have been extensive, yet understanding the import of that reading has, perhaps due to its very extensiveness, been an undertaking rarely attempted and not considered particularly urgent. If Collins's interest in Victorian medicine has been noted, therefore, it has also been largely ignored, precisely because it seems too obviously a *debt* to Victorian medicine, particularly a debt to confused, and only briefly tenable, medical notions.[8]

But Collins's relation to Victorian psychology and physiology is not a debt so simple as one we might repay by somewhat perfunctorily acknowledging it. What the idea of amnesia brings into focus for us is Victorian medicine's possible debt *to Collins*—for rather than passively and even shoddily incorporating the medical reading he most likely did, Collins's stress on the conditions and possibilities of forgetfulness predates the psychological emphasis on amnesia that we find in the late nineteenth century. Collins's amnesiacs are not stock medical figures in the 1860s, straight out of physiological textbooks, but are instead *new cultural formations*, rearrangements and refashionings of the earlier Victorian amnesiac self in the light of an emergent physiological concentration on "nervousness," "shock," and what came to be called "biological memory." When Collins's amnesiacs have been noted by readers—as in Ian Hacking's recent study of multiple personality disorder—their strange advance on contemporary psychology has been missed.[9] Collins's role in this regard was to produce, more than a decade before psychological research could fully catch up, the new cultural category of "amnesia."

It is a word that does not enter familiar English usage until at least the late 1860s and does not become a recognized medical term until the 1870s; although the term *amnésie* had been accepted in French since a 1771 translation of Francisco Boissier de Sauvages's nosology, its transplantation into English was long in coming.[10] In large part, the delay of acceptance of the word "amnesia" is due to its marginal status—although English psychology and physiology were aware of the existence of pathologized states of forgetfulness, no real importance was accorded to these instances, which remained anecdotal and unsystematized. "Memory," as part of a statistical, neurological, and pathological matrix, was not yet an object of science. And in the period before memory could be so situated, its opposite was rarely discussed and not yet given its modern name. If, as William Carpenter claimed in his *Principles of Human Physiology*—in the same section from which Collins's Ezra Jennings quotes—"no single term can express the various effects of accident, disease, or decay, upon this faculty [memory]," it is because the organizing category of "amnesia" was not yet in existence; until the scattered phenomena long noticed by physiologists (forgetfulness of language, of the recent past, of the distant past; through apoplexy, injury, age, lack of attention, or drug use) could be condensed into a recognizable figure with a set of familiar symptoms and a discernible profile, or what might be called a *cultural function*, the category of "amnesia" could not emerge.[11] What Collins's novels of the 1860s perform is the delineation of this category—a delineation so successful that the pathology of Laura Fairlie or Mr. Candy reads as immediately, almost too readily, familiar.

How amnesia did in fact arrive as a frequent, indeed eventually dominant, object of psychological inquiry has much to tell us of how its contours in Collins's fiction can be read, and what Collins brought to the older, implicit Victorian tradition of the amnesiac self—through what avenues, in other words, that older tradition could be explicitly thematized and repathologized. What lies between Fanny Price and Laura Fairlie, or even between Laura and Lucy Snowe, is the intervention of the body itself, the intervention of "sensation," a sensation that is now rooted not in a hypothetical "sensorium" but in the nervous system: the spinal cord, the cerebellum, the body's network of *nerves*. And as memory gains a mechanical apparatus, it gains the ability to break down. This is a process that Collins adumbrates from the outset of his fictional career, particularly in *The Dead Secret* (1857): the novel's Uncle Joseph, the small, excitable German carpenter who takes in his fleeing niece, Sarah Leeson, and helps promote her final acknowledgment of her long-forsaken daughter, is continually praised for his nearly eidetic memory; but what accompanies him, what in fact comes to metonymically displace this vaunted memory, is a small music box. The melody of the box—"Batti, batti" from *Don Giovanni*—accompanies his every appearance in the text and perfectly expresses his automatically sentimental memories: "What depths of sorrow there were now in those few simple notes! What mournful melodies of past times gathered and swelled in the heart at the bidding of that one little plaintive melody!" (*DS*, 222). The box—both a figure for Uncle Joseph's memory and a memory itself for the novel's readers, given how often it appears—might seem to be the perfect souvenir, but the crucial difference is that it is a machine; it can stop, it can run out, its chain will end. Having opened the box to comfort his niece, Uncle Joseph's mnemonic reverie comes suddenly to an end:

> The stop had not been set, and the melody, after it had come to an
> end, began again. But now, after the first few bars, the notes suc-

ceeded one another more and more slowly—the air grew less and less recognisable—dropped at last to three notes, following each other at long intervals—then ceased altogether. The chain that had governed the action of the machinery had all run out: Mozart's farewell song was silenced on a sudden, like a voice that had broken down.

The old man started, looked earnestly at his niece, and threw the leather-case over the box as if he desired to shut out the sight of it. "The music stopped so," he whispered to himself, in his own language, "when little Joseph died!" (*DS*, 223)

On the note of a buried trauma (the death of a son) this genial fount of reminiscence, with its "mournful memories of past times," ceases *because of a mechanical process*. The music box is an early, hesitant, but still very apt image for the kind of physiologized memory Collins will later thoroughly explore: a memory that is at once *physicalized* and *mechanized* and because of its mechanization prone to, indeed dependent on, stoppage, failure, even possibly *breakage*. The box is also, and perhaps most important, *automatic*—even if it is "the one memorial left that reminded him of all the joys and sorrows, the simple family interests and affections of his past life" (*DS*, 352), it reminds in the most automatic of ways, both in Uncle Joseph's own actions (opening the box when needing comfort, shutting it in moments of agitation) and the box's own mechanisms: it can never play any other song; it can only cease to be able to play that song. The memory described by the music box is closer, perhaps, to *reflex* than to the willed nostalgias of Austen or Dickens.

That is precisely, in fact, what happened to notions of memory in and through nineteenth-century physiology: as remembrance becomes increasingly physiologized, increasingly linked to the physical facts of brain and spinal cord, it is increasingly pathologized; as it is discussed more and more in terms of bodily "sensation," it is figured more and more in terms of failure. Making memory "nervous"—making it part of the nervous system, particularly part of the newly theorized autonomic nervous system— makes it, paradoxically, much less reliable. The process is part of a more general and systemic shift in nineteenth-century psychology and anatomical theory, in which an almost complete reversal of former ideas of brain function took place; whereas earlier notions of the nervous system and the spinal cord considered it as a degraded version of the brain's higher faculties, nineteenth-century physiology began to see the brain as merely a derivation of the spinal cord. All mental functions, that is, were increasingly seen as based on the reflex actions of the nervous system.[12] It was William Carpenter's central idea—the idea that lent his *Human Physiology* its distinction, even if it was not so much innovative as constructed out of the surmises of others—that the cerebrum might have a "reflex" action as well as the spinal cord and that various cerebral functions might be better understood if conceptualized as forms of reflex action; the notion went a long way toward eventually eliminating, and making quaintly anachronistic, the familiar linkage of cerebrum with intellect and spinal cord with reflex.

The state of physiology and psychology in the 1860s, however, was not quite so advanced yet—and this is precisely the interest of Collins's amnesiacs: that his picture of a "music box" memory, at once mechanical, automatic, and potentially broken, predated the eventual shift in nineteenth-century sciences of mind, or perhaps *produced the necessary conditions* for that later shift to occur. Alexander Bain's 1855 *Senses and the Intellect* is one example of the as yet troubled and murky relations between cerebral function and bodily sensation that predated later physiologists, for whom every mental function was inescapably organic and thus inescapably linked to decay (and thus, perhaps, better studied through that decay). Bain was not a physiologist as such, and his intellectual debts were more oriented, as we have seen in relation to Dickens and Thackeray, toward traditional associationist psychology, but his work begins with an intensive mapping of the nervous system, of nerve matter, ganglion cells, the physical foundations of mind; a start that seemed to promise an entirely new, physiologized associationism, a start that broke with the more philosophically oriented work of James Mill or Sir William Hamilton and that promised to elucidate the "thorough-going concomitance of physical processes with mental."[13] But this emphasis is short-lived in the text, which turns quickly to its more familiar, if comprehensively presented, associationism.[14] And as the opening claim to be presenting a physiologized, integrated picture of mind and body fades, descriptions of sensation and descriptions of memory are situated as opposites, as if neither phenomenon had anything to say about the other. Bain's account is fairly specific:

> By Sensations, in the strict meaning, we understand the mental impressions, feelings, or states of consciousness, following on the action of external things on some part of the body, called on that account sensitive. Such are the feelings caused by tastes, smells, sounds, or sights. These are the influences said to be external to the mental organisation; they are distinguished from influences originating within, as, for example, spontaneous activity (the case we have already considered), the remembrance of the past, or the anticipation of the future.[15]

What is "sensation"? The answer, for Bain—who represented the mainstream of nineteenth-century psychology and whose attempt to marry associationism to physiology was seen as breaking new ground—was: the opposite of memory. Even if, as he goes on to state, the "simplicity and purity" of our sensations have been diluted through the habits of civilized life, they "continue to have one feature that keeps them distinct from the thought-processes,—namely, they owe their being to actual contact with the outside world, while Memory, for example, is independent of such origin."[16] That is, at the time when Collins's fictional career began and at the time when most of his personal reading in physiology would have been conducted—immediately prior to, that is, the publication of *The Woman in White* and *The Moonstone*—Victorian physiology did not yet consider memory an organic fact and thus did not yet consider memory in its relation to failure and disappearance.

One further instance of the state of physiology at the time of the inception of the "sensation novel" will help to make this point clear. G. H. Lewes's 1860 *Physiology of Common Life* mentions a series of French experiments, by the physicians M. J. P. Flourens and Jean Baptiste Bouillaud, in which the cerebrum of a fowl is removed to determine what functions are possible without it. Flourens had claimed that the fowl so treated could have neither sensation nor memory; Lewes disagrees, because for him sensation is still a property of the spinal axis, memory of the cerebrum, the two systems perhaps overlapping but not at all identical in locus or manner of operation. Bouillaud's report of the experiment, in which the fowl was roused by a slight irritation of the skin and tried to escape its cage, is for Lewes more accurate. The fowl, says Lewes, would still show evidence of sensation—touch, pain—if not easy movement: "It is true that she stumbled against objects, and knew not how to avoid them; but having lost all *memory*, that is intelligible."[17] Remove the brain, Lewes implies, and memory disappears, while sensation is still possible—an experimental result that confirms the still-present dualism of mind and body, in which however much memory is admitted to be located in the brain, to be in that sense *material*, its linkage to more "primitive" processes, to the automatic actions of the spinal cord and nerve ganglia, is denied. For Lewes, as for Bain, the result is that a truly physiological exposition must ignore memory (of which Lewes provides no account), while a true account of memory would largely dispense with physiological facts. To use the terms of Michael Kearns, mid-century sciences of mind were caught between "simple reflex actions," or sensation, and "mature reflection," or remembrance, and no middle term existed to mediate between the two.[18] Such is the state of Victorian physiology in the year of the publication of *The Woman in White*, in which pathological amnesia makes its first dramatic appearance in British fiction.

It is not a state that would last long, of course; the controversy over the experiments Lewes cites makes it clear that to what extent mental functioning could be equated with cerebral functioning—and to what extent it might be equated with the cerebrospinal system as a whole—was becoming an open question. But throughout the 1860s, when the sensation novel reached its cultural peak, British physiology did not yet physicalize memory and thus did not yet consider amnesia a fact worthy of research, analysis, or systematization. The "music box" conception of memory, in which an automatic, physical process implies the always present threat of cessation or breakage, had not yet arrived, and would not for more than a decade. The eventual pivot was separated from *The Woman in White* by twenty years and a national, and natural, border; "amnesia" as an object of psychological inquiry would not truly arrive until the 1881 publication of Théodule Ribot's *Les maladies de la mémoire*.

Ribot's seminal work, the first systematic treatment of amnesia, has received increased attention in recent years, most notably for what it presaged, and for its later contribution to European intellectual history; it has been cited, for instance, as an influence on Nietzsche's *Genealogy of Morals*.[19] But for my purposes the interest of Ribot's work is the light it casts backward—back, that is, to Collins's fiction, which had already surmised and implemented the most basic assumptions of Ribot's system. Ribot's task was to insist on the music box model of mnemonic functioning and to claim that the data best suited to confirm the alliance between memory and automatic, physicalized mental functioning was provided by amnesia. The logic is so familiar that its force has, perhaps, been lost to us, but its uniqueness was glaringly apparent to Ribot's readers: the linkage between body (sensation, the nervous system) and mind (memory) can only be persuasively made by reference to memory in its negative states— forgetting, erasure, oblivion of a morbid nature. Ribot's manifesto begins with this point: "La pathologie de la mémoire complète sa physiologie [The pathology of memory completes its physiology]," he claims, although the work's more fundamental point is that the memory considered in its pathological aspects *proves* the physiological nature of memory.[20] If we would link memory to sensation, to the body, to what Ribot calls "actions automatique secondaires," or "secondary automatic actions," we must consider amnesia. Forgetting and having sensations—amnesia and the "sensationalized" body—are, in Ribot's work, indissolubly linked. If we would believe, as Ribot would have us believe, that "la mémoire est, par essence, un fait biologique; par accident, un fait psychologique [memory is essentially a biological fact, and only by accident a fact of psychology]," we must take amnesia seriously.[21]

The logic is nothing if not familiar to a reader of Collins's sensation fiction, for whom the entire project of a "nervous" fiction, designed to expose the reader to shock, suspense, irritation of the nerves, is dependent on forgettings of a more or less pathological nature—the forgettings of characters within the plot, the temporary oblivion of the outside world (its "suspension") during a particularly suspenseful passage, the eventual forgetting of the novel once it has been read. If in Austen's fiction the ability to forget is evidence of the mind's liberation from the world of pathology, in Collins the tendency of the mind to erase the past is evidence of its renewed dependence on the body. Ribot, for instance, would eventually reduce the etiology of amnesia to defects in nutrition or circulation of the blood, to causes embedded, eventually, in the health of nerves themselves; memory is suddenly lodged in the fabric of the nervous system and thereby exposed to decay, disturbance, shock. Collins, in other words, provides not only a fictional depiction of Ribot's central thesis — through his Laura Fairlies and Franklin Blakes — but creates a fictional form that acts on the reader in such a manner as to validate that very thesis *in the act of reading*. Read, become nervous, forget: a system that would have been thoroughly understood by Ribot and by late-century physiologists.

It would have been less thoroughly grasped by the physiologists of Collins's most productive years. As late as 1880, the most prominent work on mental pathology, Henry Maudsley's *Pathology of Mind*, did not discuss amnesia or any forms of forgetting; while hysteria, epilepsy, and somnambulism — that *cause célèbre* of Collins critics and an important part of *The Moonstone*'s thematics — are discussed at length, memory of any form is not even mentioned. Maudsley's earlier essay *Body and Mind* (1873) does open the door to a sensationalized memory, however, claiming that "the acquired functions of the spinal cord, and of the sensory ganglia, obviously imply the existence of memory," considering habit as the key datum that might bring memory and the nervous system together, and Maudsley's definition of memory as "the organic registration of the effects of impressions" is not far from Ribot or Collins; but the centrality of amnesia to the physiologization of memory is not a central part of Maudsley's work.[22] Only Carpenter, whose early work would appear in edited form in *The Moonstone*, appeared to grasp what Ribot would later canonize; "the relation between the Psychical phenomena of Memory and the Physical condition of the Brain," Carpenter writes in his *Principles of Mental Physiology*, "is further shown by the effect of fatigue and of the impaired nutrition of old age in *weakening* the Memory; and of disease and injury of the brain in *impairing* it or *destroying* it."[23] But this passage was published in 1874, six years after *The Moonstone*'s senescent Mr. Candy, fourteen years after *The Woman in White*'s traumatized Laura Fairlie. Note as well that the etiologies of memory loss adduced here (fatigue, age, disease, injury) are significantly less varied than the categories offered by Collins's own fiction; in Collins we can find, in addition to these explanations, amnesia through trauma (Laura) and through opiates (Franklin Blake). The lesson here is that if we would seek to find a source or set of sources for Collins's interest in amnesia, we are bound to fail — unless we look outside of the strictly physiological and turn back to the novelistic tradition in which Collins was so well schooled. With his amnesiacs, Collins brings the Victorian amnesiac self into collision with the new science of the nervous system and produces through this juxtaposition a category that contemporary science could not yet envision.

The result is a fiction that, in the first place, persistently medicalizes suspense. *The Moonstone*'s Gabriel Betteredge, relating Franklin Blake's advice for Rachel Verinder after the theft of the gem, is typical: "From what he said to my lady, while I was in the room at breakfast-time, he appeared to think that Miss Rachel—if the suspense about the Moonstone was not soon set at rest—might stand in urgent need of the best medical advice at our disposal" (*M*, 132). The second result is a fiction that brings forth this newly medicalized body (in such suspense that a doctor is required) in order to explain the erasure of the past, whether in momentary ways—shock leading to a temporary amnesia—or in a more thoroughgoing fashion. If the phrenological system as present in Brontë's novels elevated certain aspects of the body (skull, head, facial features) to elide the workings of memory, Collins's physiologized texts work in a similar manner, using the body (nerves, senses) to explain their own more explicit amnesias. "Surely you forget," Blake asks the Verinder family attorney, Mr. Bruff, "that the whole thing is essentially a matter of the past—so far as I am concerned?" (*M*, 405). "A matter of the past": the phrase is usually cited as an example of Collins's plotting of memory, his obsession with past crimes, "dead secrets," prior mysteries. But the "matter of the past" that drives these narratives, and that—as we shall see—concludes them, is the past's erasure. The "matter" Blake refers to is his amnesia, the amnesias of everyone around him, a forgetfulness so extensive that it is the ground of the entire tale and also the place where an investigation of Collins's own oblivions should begin.

Cultures of Forgetfulness

No one in *The Woman in White*, it seems, can remember very well. There are claims to the contrary—Count Fosco speaks of "my memory which forgets nothing" (*WW*, 548) and earlier compliments Marian Halcombe's diary for the "wonderful power of memory" it evinces (*WW*, 308). But these vaunted faculties are exceptions to the continual current of forgetfulness that runs throughout the narrative, that indeed propels it. For as the novel's earliest reviewers commented, the plot eventually hinges on an inability to remember the date on which Laura Fairlie, under the power of Count Fosco and his wife, is transported to London from Blackwater Park under the delusion that she will meet Marian there; were the date known, it could be proved that the journey occurred after Laura's alleged "death" and that therefore the living "Anne Catherick" is really the former Lady Glyde, née Fairlie.[24] It is an inability to remember shared by Laura, by the housekeeper at Blackwater Park, by the cook at Count Fosco's London residence, by a host of personnel who surround the novel's central event. The cook's response, when asked if she can recall the date, is characteristic: "She was to come that day, as well as I can remember — but, whatever you do, don't trust my memory in the matter. I am sorry to say it's no use asking me about days of the month, and such-like" (*WW*, 367). Mr. Fairlie's comment, when asked for a date that might help fix the date of Laura's arrival in London, protests with characteristic peevishness: "I am told to remember dates. Good Heavens! I never did such a thing in my life — how am I to begin now?" (*WW*, 310). Other facts are just as elusive. What can Laura remember of her fellow student, childhood acquaintance, and eventual double Anne Catherick? "Miss Fairlie's recollections of the little scholar at Limmeridge were, however, only of the most vague and general kind" (*WW*, 52). Anne Catherick's own recollections are no more secure, as we learn when she relates her guardian Mrs. Clements's first promise to "take care of you": "Kind words, were they not? I suppose I remember them because they were kind. It's little enough I remember besides — little enough, little enough!" (*WW*, 87)

The inhabitants of *The Moonstone* fare no better; within it admissions of memory loss, however minor and temporary, are even more frequent. Competence and memory are directly related in this protodetective novel, and the instances of incompetence are constant. Mr. Bruff, when one of the mysterious Indians comes to ask for advice and presents a card, lets details escape: "I looked at the card. There was a foreign name written on it, which has escaped my memory" (*M*, 323). A trifle, perhaps, but as the novel's Sergeant Cuff so famously declares, within the closed system of a mystery (the scene of the crime closed to onlookers, a house closed to strangers, a book closed by its covers) there are no trifles — and it is this mnemonic incompetence, an inability to retain trifles, that condemns the typically bumbling Superintendent Seagrave, particularly in relation to the telltale smudge on Rachel Verinder's painted door; asked if he had noticed it, Seagrave's response is clearly inadequate: "Mr Superintendent looked a little taken aback; but he made the best of it. 'I can't charge my memory, Sergeant,' he said, 'a mere trifle — a mere trifle'" (*M*, 136). If the memories of Gabriel Betteredge (the scene's narrator) and Superintendent Seagrave do not retain "trifles," that fact has now become a *problem*. It is as if a collection of Pendennises and Copperfields, with only the most broadly categorizing and edited memories, have stumbled into a crime scene, where their relevant, concordant, and integral memories, so thoroughly based on elisions and forgettings, will no longer *do*.

The result is what can be broadly called a "culture of forgetfulness," which Collins's texts from the 1860s not only employ but *assume*, as a given of his new genre. Collins shows us a genial cultural habit of mnemonic elision that has become a bit diseased, almost compulsive, certainly anxious; and the shift is registered through a constant notation of the small, everyday "trifles" that his characters cannot remember. Collins addresses the "amnesiac self" from the standpoint of a pathology: his amnesiacs cannot help themselves, and they can find company everywhere they look, but they recognize nonetheless that they are a problem, and the tones of apology are sounded by them almost reflexively. As for those of Collins's characters who can remember, the methods they take to do so are as revealing as the helplessness of their peers. The extended apology by Mrs. Michelson, the Blackwater Park housekeeper, is one of *The Woman in White*'s most revealing instances:

> In the second place, I desire to express my regret at my own inability to remember the precise day on which Lady Glyde left Blackwater Park for London. I am told that it is of the last importance to ascertain the exact date of that lamentable journey; and I have anxiously taxed my memory to recal it. The effort has been in vain. I can only remember now that it was towards the latter part of July. We all know the difficulty, after a lapse of time, of fixing precisely on a past date, unless it has been previously written down. That difficulty is greatly increased, in my case, by the alarming and confusing events which took place about the period of Lady Glyde's departure. I heartily wish I had made a memorandum at the time. (*M*, 366)

The paradigmatic features are all here — the obligatory memory failure; the apologetic frame; the claim that this kind of memory failure is more common than not ("we all know the difficulty . . ."). What is of the utmost importance here, however, is the suggested solution: "unless it has been previously written down." A "memorandum"— that is Mrs. Michelson's mnemonic safeguard, which she has been (*felix culpa*) remiss in keeping. But Collins's more "reliable" characters are not so careless; if they remember accurately, in fact, they do so not because of any native power, but because their lives are surrounded with written notes, memoranda, records, *texts of memory*. Like the modern urbanite whose every move is written — in the face of an overtaxed, overstimulated memory— in a pocketbook or calendar, Collins's central characters write because they fear an incipient forgetting.

Let us peruse the most obvious evidence, which — like the "exhibits" in a murder trial— is tagged for us by Collins's narrative schemes. *The Moonstone*'s inset books are numerous: the washing-book at the Verinder house, which verifies the continued absence of the telltale nightgown; Ezra Jennings's diary, which records for a skeptical posterity his "experiment" with

Franklin Blake; and the diary of Gabriel Betteredge's daughter Penelope, without which, we are occasionally reminded, Betteredge's own precise narration could not be composed: "On summoning up my own recollections—and on getting Penelope to help me, by consulting her journal . . ." (*M*, 82) There are also more surprising "journals"; Mr. Bruff, upon being advised by the colonial traveler Murthwaite to expect "news" of the Moonstone-pursuing Indians a year after the earliest possible date the gem might have been pawned, immediately turns to his pocketbook: "I made a note of the date, and it may not be amiss if I close my narrative by repeating that note here." The note? "June, 'forty nine. Expect news of the Indians, towards the end of the month" (*M*, 338). Alongside these textual "appointments," there are a series of sealed letters that linger in the text, keeping the mystery in action: Rosanna Spearman's letters, Lady Julia's will, Ezra Jennings's secret notes on Mr. Candy's dissociated ravings. But it is *The Woman in White* that offers us the most extreme instance of this tendency—at times, in fact, it can seem that the novel itself is assembled out of the pocketbook of Walter Hartright. Within this capacious item can be found Marian's recollections of the Glyde family history—"I noted them down carefully, in the event of their proving to be of importance at any future period" (*M*, 421)—and Mrs. Catherick's letter of congratulation upon the death of Sir Percival Glyde, which at first Hartright considers burning, until "a consideration suggested itself" and "I sealed up the letter, and put it away carefully in my pocket-book" (*M*, 501). Later we will encounter the order-book of the carriage-driver that eventually confirms the date of Laura's arrival in London, and Marian's diary, which sets down with a stenographic exactitude the conversations, movements, and overheard plottings of Fosco and Sir Percival. Even the church registry that proves Sir Percival's illegitimacy, however doctored it may be, yields to the "true" copy, which can stand as the most secure form of evidence Hartright needs.[25]

It is as if remembering were necessary to the positive outcomes of these plots, and the only way to remember well is to note down, to record, to fix into text. What a Collins novel is, in fact, is a tissue of memoranda, usually composed—as in the instances of Gabriel Betteredge's "Narrative" in *The Moonstone*, or Marian Halcombe's diary in *The Woman in White*—as either transcriptions of diaries or loose, embellished versions of a journal's terser, if more reliable, entries. The anxiety surrounding memory is a central affect of these texts; in each there are tense moments in which the need to remember what is passing is juxtaposed with the panicked realization that memory may not be so easy to come by. Marian and Laura, at one point during their nerve-racking stay at Blackwater with Fosco and Percival, have a brief, whispered debate: when Percival asked Laura for money and then suddenly relented, is it possible that he could have given bills at three months to raise the sum instead? What was it that his lawyer, overheard by Marian, told Percival? The answer is not to be found in memory alone; Marian is relieved to find her recollection supported by her diary, adding that "it is hard to say what future interests may not depend upon the regularity of the entries in my journal, and upon the reliability of my recollection at the time when I make them" (*WW*, 259). Yes, Marian's memory functions well enough; yes, text here only verifies that memory; but the anxiety evoked here is an anxiety fundamental to the sensation novel: what if memory should fail? Lest we think the anxiety unfounded, the novel will proceed to confirm it, in the way that any suspenseful narration must at least partially confirm (if only to eventually disprove) our worst fears: Laura does end up "forgetting" the entire intermediate period between her removal to London and her rescue from the asylum; and Marian's memory of the events that led up to her illness is only guaranteed by her journal, since that very illness incapacitated those memories that were not written down. "I recal the impulse that awakened in me to preserve those words in writing," Marian relates, "exactly as they were spoken, while the time was my own, and while my memory retained them" (*WW*, 306). The anxiety is a race to the finish: what will happen first, the disappearance of the memory, or its translation into text (at which point any amnesia is safely irrelevant: I can forget it now because it is written down)? Even dissemblers and villains, such as *Armadale*'s Lydia Gwilt, feel the need to transcribe their schemes into written form lest their intricacies be lost. The anxiety is so constant that it can often seem parodic; when Marian tells Hartright to exact a personal revenge on Fosco, he responds that he will keep a letter of Fosco's, insolently written to Marian, "to help my memory when the time comes" (*WW*, 413). What could possibly, we might wonder, make Hartright worry that he would *forget* such a dislike — why is it necessary to keep a memorandum of the most personal (and dangerous) animosity of his life? The gesture is oddly superfluous, but its very superfluity, its almost compulsive repetition, should at least alert us to the presence of a *symptom*.

The function of Collins's proliferation of memoranda, then — at least in terms of the sensation novel's production of anxious affect — is to elicit a nervous attention to the constant presence of forgetfulness. Memoranda imply their opposite, the cultural surround that necessitates their very existence: amnesia. Let us take this one step further and refer to Marian and Laura's relieved consultation of Marian's diary. "On looking back to the entry referring to the lawyer's visit," Marian begins: is this a prepositional phrase or a suggestion? If we take the proffered hint, we will not be disappointed — we, too (since we are "in possession" of Marian's diary) can look back to that entry and satisfy our own doubtful memories. The sensation novel, that is, produces memoranda not only in order to evoke an anxiety surrounding all acts of remembrance but also to aid its reader's own possibly flimsy recollections; for after all, reading quickly under conditions of suspense, we might in fact be oblivious to much that passes (or, that is, have suffered some momentary "oblivions"). Feeling nervous, feeling anxious, the sensation novel reader would not read carefully—more accurately, would not read mnemonically. The "culture of forgetfulness" that envelops the novel's miniature societies extends, with an inevitable logic, to the implied reader of these texts. So Collins provides his readers with memoranda, with readerly "reminders."

What to do when your reader's memory is fungible, unsteady, possibly overburdened? The answer is to compose prose shaped like this, from *The Moonstone*: "If you will look back, you will find that, in first presenting Rosanna Spearman to your notice, I have described her as occasionally varying her walk to the Shivering Sand, by a visit to some friends of hers at Cobb's Hole" (*M*, 162–163). Thus Betteredge's narrative. The tendency, within *The Moonstone*'s complex plot, is constant, and handled with an almost unembarrassed obviousness: "My daughter," relates Betteredge again, "reminded me of Mr Candy's illness, owing (as you may remember) to the chill he had caught on the night of the dinner-party" (*M*, 187). At which point the sentence has done its work; it has recalled Mr. Candy to our attention, which—to a particularly acute reader—might promise the eventual importance that dinner-party illness will have to the central mystery. Franklin Blake uses his own frequently posited forgetfulness to aid the reader's own: "On our way to the Shivering Sand, I applied to Betteredge to revive my memory of events (as affecting Rosanna Spearman) at the period of Sergeant Cuff's inquiry. With my old friend's help, I soon had the succession of circumstances clearly registered in my mind" (*M*, 355). Upon which, of course, the circumstances are duly summarized for us. The pressures here are, of course, pressures forced on the novelist by serial publication; "reminding" was one of the formal techniques any serial novelist would had to have learned, if not mastered. The exigencies of serial form should not, however, obscure the central point at stake here: that Collins's fiction is continually engaged in fighting off his reader's own forgetfulness, just as his characters produce texts (which eventually become the novel itself) in order to stave off their own lurking amnesias.

This is not, to be sure, the sort of clinical amnesia that Ribot would later codify and that Collins's own narratives did so much to outline; but it is the general, rather unfocused, if still visible basis for the more strictly defined amnesias to which the plots of these novels eventually turn. If this pervasive forgetfulness is problematized and apologized for, it is also—in the manner of previous Victorian fiction—a virtue, perhaps even a necessity for sensation novels. In Collins the references to forgetting are so explicit that we cannot help but know how often this culture forgets, how much of its everyday energies (writing down, filing away) are devoted to the maintenance of an at least functional memory; and we are shown this cultural forgetting in texts that make forgetting somewhat allowable for the reader: if we forget a character, a plot point, a scene, it will later be rehearsed for us by one of the novel's similarly absent-minded characters, a luxury that permits a certain amount of scanning — scanning, that is, for *sensations*. Sensations that are themselves a cause of forgetting.

Forgetting, the Forgotten, the Forgettable

As the periodicals of the 1860s struggled to come to terms with the sensation novel, their attention turned again and again to the evanescent nature of these texts, which seemed meant to be consumed and then discarded. Sensation fiction appeared initially as something fairly new in literary culture: a commercialized form designed to leave behind only the appetite for more of the same. Whether they were described as food or as drugs, sensation novels could barely be classed with other fiction, simply because their digestible nature represented a new, perhaps more patent commodification of literary labor.[26] When the contemporary critic felt it necessary to comment on this trend, the part of the sensation novel fixated on was, inevitably, the plot. "His are works not so much for the library as for the circulating library," the *Saturday Review*'s aforementioned anonymous review of *The Woman in White* said. "We should prefer hiring them out as we hire out a Chinese conjuror — for the night. As soon as we have found out the secret of his tricks, and admired the clever way in which he does them, we send him home again. Just so it is necessary to the enjoyment of Mr. Wilkie Collins' writing that we should not have read them before, or should have forgotten all about them since the first perusal."[27] Come to them clean — with no obfuscatory memory — or with that memory erased: the two modes in which Collins's fiction is best experienced.

We would do well to take this early complaint as not only perceptive about the significance of sensation fiction within an expanding publishing market but as also suggestive about how Collins's plots work to erase memory and mnemonic fixation, how they depend on various erasures of the past — both pathological and ordinary — and, in the end, work toward that erasure, although in a more "nostalgic" register. In other words, a plot that asks us not to remember it — that works only if we do not remember it — might be a plot made up of refusals or inabilities to remember and might end with the refusal to remember as a final resting point. We have already considered the most obvious instances of amnesia driving a plot: in *The Woman in White* we saw a plot hinging on a collective inability to re-

member a specific date, and in *The Moonstone* we saw a mystery whose solution is obscure only so long as two figures, Franklin Blake and Mr.
Candy, retain their amnesias. But what needs to be explored is the odd coalescence of a new, narrative virtue (the necessity of forgetting for the project of suspense and shock) and an older, more familiar fictional value, the
value of nostalgic erasures. Can the two coexist in the same text—can a
plot that, as we have seen earlier, hinges on a problematized and increasingly pathologized amnesia work toward the production of a classic closural nostalgia, in the mode of Austen, Brontë, or Dickens?

Let us turn to specifics. *The Moonstone*, like so many of Collins's texts,
contains an intriguing list of troublingly divided characters, figures split
between an obscure and presumably sundered past and a placid if resigned
present; characters such as Rosanna Spearman and Ezra Jennings, each of
whom is, in the curiously appropriate Victorian phrase, a "forgotten" person. Rosanna Spearman dies by her own hand, Ezra Jennings by an unnamed but sinister disease; each is, by the end of the text, *erased*. Jennings,
for his part, insists that the erasure be total: "He asked me to do one other
thing for him—which it cost me a hard struggle to comply with. He said,
'Let my grave be forgotten. Give me your word of honour that you will
allow no monument of any sort—not even the commonest tombstone—
to mark the place of my burial. Let me sleep, nameless. Let me rest, unknown'" (*M*, 516). It is a willed, posthumous amnesia, as complete in its
way as Rosanna's suicide in the Shivering Sands, the local whirlpool. These
erasures are curiously complete (even if both leave behind letters and diaries to help explicate the mystery at hand); the question is, what do they
have to do with the sort of plot-forgetting that the *Saturday Review* so
strongly critiqued?

To answer this question, let us turn back to the reviews—to another
typical complaint about Collins, this from the *Westminster Review*'s survey
of *Armadale* in 1866: "The way in which the story is put together is certainly ingenious, but to admire the plot and forget the characters is like admiring the frame instead of enjoying the picture."[28] Collins "forgetting"
the characters, characters who are either "forgotten" or "forgettable"—
these three aspects of Collins's narratives are in a tight relation.[29] A text
driven by plot mechanics of amnesia; a text containing socially ambiguous
or liminal figures; a text containing bland, barely distinguishable characters
—forgetting, the forgotten, the forgettable. This much can be surmised:
that Collins's dependence on a plot mechanics driven by amnesia necessitates two further erasures—the erasure or self-erasure of those characters
who might be termed "memorable," troubling, unique, inimitable, ambiguous; and the production of characters whose blandness will not detract
from the workings of suspense and shock. The project of a suspenseful
text dependent on protopathological amnesia leads, then—as suggested

earlier — to familiar "nostalgic" erasures, when characters such as Ezra Jennings and Rosanna Spearman, who cannot stand in a comfortably nostalgic relation to their past, are silenced and forgotten, and characters whose only defining trait is a nostalgic blandness (Walter Hartright, Laura Fairlie, Franklin Blake) are permitted to remain and speak the usual closural leave-takings. The system of an amnesiac plot may be new — the *sensationalization* of the amnesiac self may be an innovation — but the ultimate values of the sensation novel are identical to those of Austen or Brontë: the silencing of a vexed relation to the past and the elevation of a genial, nostalgic relation. The only technical difference, of course, is that in Collins a splitting occurs; whereas in Austen certain characters, most notably Marianne Dashwood, are permitted space to revise their own mnemonic functioning, in Collins's sensation fiction there is a rigid division between the "forgotten" characters such as Rosanna Spearman — who cries out to the eminently bland Betteredge that "the stain is taken off," but "the place shows, Mr Betteredge — the place shows!" (*M*, 57) — and the "forgettable" characters such as Hartright.

A plot system constructed around forgetting, which we may with Patrick Brantlinger call a "structural amnesia," leads back to a value system based on nostalgic erasure.[30] If we would for a moment remember Collins's characters, the way in which they are then forgotten or erased will become clearer — and the best figure to begin with is, of course, *The Woman in White*'s Count Fosco. From his first appearance he is so "memorable" that Marian cannot get rid of his image; like a reader of the novel itself, she can remember his contours far more clearly than those of any other inhabitant of the text: "It absolutely startles me, now he is in my mind, to find how plainly I see him! — how much more plainly than I see Sir Percival, or Mr. Fairlie, or Walter Hartright, or any other absent person of whom I think, with the one exception of Laura herself! I can hear his voice, as if he was speaking at this moment. I know what his conversation was yesterday, as well as if I was hearing it now" (*WW*, 196). His corpulence, his orotund manner of speaking, his mice, his suspicious politesse — these "vivid" qualities make him instantly memorable, in a manner unapproachable by any other character here save, perhaps, Marian herself, whose gender hybridity also acts as a memorable marker. In fact, Marian is precisely right, her readerly response accurate: compared to Fosco, the novel's other figures — particularly the bland if resolute Hartright, who cannot rival Fosco in charisma — are ciphers or in fact more or less functional entities, distinguishable one from another only by the most blandly repetitive habits or "hobbies" (Gabriel Betteredge's love for *Robinson Crusoe*, Walter Hartright's drawing talent).[31] And if Fosco is memorable, he is also a man of memory; his is the only mind in the novel capable of retaining an intricate plot without committing it to writing —

until Hartright forces him to, at which point the plot can be solved and forgotten.

What the novel must do to Fosco is to "forget" him—to erase him from its concluding dispositions precisely because he is not easily forgotten; his final appearance as a naked corpse, "unowned, unknown; exposed to the flippant curiosity of a French mob" (*WW*, 581), after he has had to go into disguise and renounce his instantly memorable characteristics, helps to reduce this troubling instance of a figure that sticks in the memory. Reduce and replace, if not completely eliminate: reduce him through a literal "exposure," replace him with the newly united trio of Hartright, Laura, and Marian. The novel culminates, in fact, with a literal erasure—the erasure of Laura's tombstone inscription and its replacement by a terse name and date: "Anne Catherick, July 25th, 1850" (*WW*, 577). If we do remember Fosco when we recall *The Woman in White*, the reading process itself helps to defuse that memorability—as well as the memorability of Anne Catherick—through a gradual, and then explosive, process of erasure: killing him, burying her. More to the point, perhaps, the elimination of this most memorable of villains enables a classic, almost Austenian closural nostalgia, a turn away from the past that—upon Marian and Laura's return to Limmeridge—is as rule-explicit as Elizabeth Bennet's "philosophy" in *Pride and Prejudice*. When Hartright expresses surprise at their return, Laura and Marian both speak the conclusion of the sensation novel's progression from the pervasive *forgettings* of the plot to the erasures of *unforgettable* characters to the resumption of a happily, if blandly, *forgettable* life:

> "My darling Walter," she said, "must we really account for our boldness in coming here? I am afraid, love, I can only explain it by breaking through our rule, and referring to the past."
> "There is not the least necessity for doing anything of the kind," said Marian. "We can be just as explicit, and much more interesting, by referring to the future." (*WW*, 583)

At which point Hartright's child by Laura—the "Heir of Limmeridge"—is held up in Marian's arms.

While no one would argue that Fosco is forgotten entirely by the reader after the novel's conclusion, the mechanics of *The Woman in White*'s closure operate to at least half-forget him, to leave behind the threat he represented and to strip him of his "memorable" characteristics. The paradox of such a traditionally nostalgic closure, so explicitly reliant on an elision of the past, is that *it is precisely that mental function*—forgetting—that has spurred the plot all along and that has made the novel's dénouement so long in coming. "Finally," Jenny Bourne Taylor perceptively claims, "*The Woman in White* depends upon transforming particular patterns of suspense into the means of closure."[32] If we put the novel in its belated relation to earlier Victorian nostalgias, we might say instead that it depends on transforming a familiar means of closure (nostalgic elision) into a means of suspense, all the while retaining its original use as a means of closure. Collins's plots of the 1860s, that is, run throughout on the principle of a problematized, constant forgetting, then turn near the novel's close to forgetfulness as a means of *ending* the narrative — of "forgetting" those individuals whose status, interest, or danger might make them "memorable."

The phrase "plots of the 1860s" is apt precisely insofar as it removes the often spurious division between sensation novel and mystery novel, categories far more fluid in that decade than they would be twenty years later; in *The Moonstone*, for instance, we can see an almost identical process in operation, whereby what is difficult to forget, what might blossom into a cathexis, is exactly what must be erased — in the case of Ezra Jennings, erased without a trace. The influence of the mysterious, sickly doctor's assistant is nearly obsessive for Franklin Blake, who in idle moments cannot resist a compulsive sketching of the assistant's features:

> I sat idly drawing likenesses from memory of Mr Candy's remarkable-
> looking assistant, on the sheet of paper which I had vowed to dedi-
> cate to Betteredge — until it suddenly occurred to me that here was
> the irrepressible Ezra Jennings getting in my way again! I threw a
> dozen portraits, at least, of the man with the piebald hair (the hair in
> every case, remarkably like), into the waste-paper basket — and then
> and there, wrote my answer to Betteredge. (*M*, 409)

A "memorable" character indeed, one who can be drawn from memory with precision. The same might be said of Rosanna Spearman and her mysterious criminal past: a "forgotten woman" who "gets in the way" of Cuff's inquiry, Blake's and Rachel's reconciliation, and the mystery's solution. The answer in each case, of course, is that these vivid characters are forsaken: in the first case by a self-dictated erasure, and in the second case by a nostalgic sundering carried out by Blake himself, who after Rosanna's suicide makes her part of the "past" prior to announcing that past's conclusion:

> The retrospect is now complete. I may leave the miserable story of
> Rosanna Spearman — to which, even at this distance of time, I cannot
> revert without a pang of distress — to suggest for itself all that is here
> purposely left unsaid. I may pass from the suicide at the Shivering
> Sand, with its strange and terrible influence on my present position
> and future prospects, to interests which concern the living people of
> this narrative, and to events which were already paving my way for the
> slow and toilsome journey from the darkness to the light. (*M*, 380)

A strangely ungrateful farewell, given that Rosanna had done more than any other individual caught up in the theft of the gem—more than Cuff himself, perhaps less than only Jennings—to point out the thief and thus to "pave the way" for the narrative's conclusion; but perhaps gratitude is less the issue than the logic of Collins's plots, which turn forgetfulness to multiple uses: a pharmacological forgetfulness on Blake's part that keeps his crime hidden, and a nostalgic forgetfulness that helps end any possible cathexes upon the fascinating Ezra Jennings and the all too suggestively named Rosanna Spearman. The aptness of Blake composing this disconnection of past and cleansed present should be apparent if we remember that at various points he needs Betteredge to remind him if he had ever walked in his sleep as a boy, if he was intoxicated on the night the gem was stolen, what his family's relationship to his uncle, John Herncastle, had been, among other points of murky recollection. A habitual amnesiac, and the novel's organizing figure, erases these lives so that the plot might find its proper, more or less amnesiac, conclusion. Forgetting, the forgotten, and the forgettable all exist here in a continuum, as Collins's novels of the 1860s refuse to settle exactly on one use or meaning of memory's failures.

Collins's texts, that is, both expand the older notion of an amnesiac self into new, more anxious territory—the idea of a "culture of forgetfulness" that might start to approach a pathological amnesia—and retain its former usage as a closural method and a personal virtue, as a novelistic *telos*, as what I have called nostalgia. If his plots seem to lose energy as their conclusions approach and as various memorable characters are progressively torn out of the narrative fabric, that is because the nervous energy of forgetting is being transmuted back into its original value and function in Victorian fiction—nostalgia; and the resultant loss of affect, or relaxation of the nerves, reads like nothing so much as exhaustion (the exhaustion, perhaps, of the overexcited reader, finally numb to further sensation). But to investigate the deepest layer of Collins's construction of "amnesia," at once his most interesting innovation and his most hidden contribution to what might be called a history of consciousness, it is necessary to turn back from his unexpectedly conventional closures and to look at the very production of "sensation" in these texts and how that "sensation" leads us to the beginning of a truly pathologized amnesia.

Shock, Reflex, Oblivion

The Woman in White—as well as much of the critical commentary it has received—begins with a sensation: Walter Hartright's first meeting with the white-robed fugitive Anne Catherick. Having just left Hampstead Heath, pondering what his future drawing students will look like, "every drop of blood in my body was brought to a stop by the touch of a hand laid lightly and suddenly on my shoulder from behind me" (*WW*, 15). The moment's power and suggestiveness have much to do with the fact that it combines so many of the elements of what we now term the "sensational": mystery, sexual suggestiveness, hints of crime — and, most fundamentally, a sensation, a touch.[33] What happens to consciousness as a result of this sensation? Something very close to "shock" sets in: "It was like a dream," Hartright relates. "Was I Walter Hartright? Was this the well-known, uneventful road, where holiday people strolled on Sundays? Had I really left, little more than an hour since, the quiet, decent, conventionally-domestic atmosphere of my mother's cottage?" (*WW*, 18). The shock instantly destabilizes memory, even to the point of making personal identity precarious; the security of the recent past totters under the influence of this one, unexpected touch, whose tremors — like any "surprise" that springs nervous reflexes — continue to ripple long after the scene has begun to unfold in more predictable ways (a helpless woman, an appeal to Hartright's honor). The sensation is amnesiac, not only in the immediate manner of not understanding its origin but also in the *contagious* manner of making previous, unrelated memories fungible. The progression might best be described as a textual reflex: a touch, an instant "shock," an involuntary contraction of the body (Hartright turns with his fingers "tightening round the handle of my stick" [*WW*, 15]), an inability to remember.

The class of sensations that might induce such a neuropathic response, in which the reflex contraction of a hand works like the contraction of a temporary mental illness, is not limited to touch alone. Any surprise, even the most genteel, has an instant (and usually noted) amnesiac consequence. Let us take Hartright's first sight of Limmeridge House, which occurs the morning after this initial shock:

> The view was such a surprise, and such a change to me, after my weary London experience of brick and mortar landscape, that I seemed to burst into a new life and a new set of thoughts the moment I looked at it. A confused sensation of having suddenly lost my familiarity with the past, without acquiring any additional clearness of idea in reference to the present or the future, took possession of my mind. Circumstances that were but a few days old, faded back in my memory, as if they happened months and months since. Pesca's quaint announcement of the means by which he had procured me my present employment; the farewell evening I had passed with my mother and sister; even my mysterious adventure on the way home from Hampstead, had all become like events which might have occurred at some former epoch of my existence. Although the woman in white was still in my mind, the image of her seemed to have grown dull and faint already. (*WW*, 24)

It is, again, a reflex reaction: as soon as the surprise occurs the elision of the past begins involuntarily, like a physiological process that runs from the sensory registration of change ("such a surprise") to a cerebral, or more precisely *cerebrospinal*, amnesia (a "confused sensation of having suddenly lost my familiarity with the past"). If we step back a bit and consider the scene's deeply traditional contours, the historical significance of this reflexive amnesia might become a bit clearer. Arriving at a new location having left an older phase of life behind, the itinerant but genteel individual (tourist, governess, teacher) gazing for the first time upon the property that is initially the site of wage-labor but will eventually be possessed in full: Hartright has as predecessors Elizabeth Bennet gazing upon Pemberley, Jane Eyre encountering Thornfield Hall, Esther Summerson taking a tour of Bleak House. A highly *generic* scene, then, derived from a genre in which a separation from the past—from socioeconomic struggles or from solitude—is always, more or less explicitly, at stake; the genre is an essentially amnesiac one, insofar as it presumes the ability to cut the unwanted past off without pain, particularly insofar as it throws the weight of narrative interest forward, toward the "new" locale. In all of this Collins has scripted his moment with faithfulness to the generic tradition, with the exception of two alterations: the gender of the anticipatory character, and the relation of this heretofore *social* amnesia to the body.[34] It is the latter alteration that interests me here.

The passage's encoding of this traditionally "forgetful" scene is explicit, and it is physiological. Explicit in that it scrupulously records all the events that seem to have disappeared from Hartright's mind, as well as its lengthy notation of bewilderment at this sudden divorce from the past (a divorce that usually is assumed: Austen need not tell us that Elizabeth Bennet, looking at the Pemberley prospect, has forgotten "home"). Its physiological emphasis is related in a lexicon just short of professional: a "confused sensation" that takes "possession of my mind," making mnemonic images "dull and faint." In short, what we can only metaphorically (and anachronistically) call "amnesia" in earlier British fiction has become very close to a true modern instance of amnesia, however much the scenes themselves may be generically similar. Collins turns this familiar moment of disempowered arrival into a sensation, a "surprise" in the sense of "shock"—and throughout Collins's work, the effort to make "sensational" a given social or sexual narrative depends, necessarily, on the production of a memory loss, because *bodily sensation implies the erasure of memory*. Here Collins not only anticipates later physiology but inaugurates the cultural category of "amnesia," which largely begins with the effort to create a novel of sensations.

This is perhaps what lies behind Jenny Bourne Taylor's perceptive comment that, for Collins, "suspense and indeterminacy also need to arise from *within* the process of memory"— a comment worth citing, since readings of Collins tend to ignore sensations as such, which tend, literally or otherwise, to be prefaced by the adjective "empty," as if sensation itself needed to be contrasted to whatever thematic line is "really" at stake.[35] It is as if the implicit question — where do "sensations" *lead*? — has usually been answered, nowhere in particular; but in Collins's physiology, which would later become Victorian physiology, sensations lead *through an automatic response* to the erasure of memory. The process in Collins is so prevalent and so instantaneous that it can be rightly called a reflex; and if the very automatism of reflexes usually make them immune to being "read," that very automatism (the way they eliminate "thought," memory) is enormously crucial to an understanding of Collins. It is perhaps to the notion of reflex — what reflex meant for physiology — that we must briefly turn in order to excavate how, precisely, sensation and amnesia became systemically linked.

An automatized amnesia: although the idea seems present in *The Woman in White*, the sort of psychology current at the time of the novel's publication had not yet integrated recent developments in the study of reflexive mechanisms — most notably, the concept of the "reflex arc" pioneered by Marshall Hall's 1837 *Memoirs of the Nervous System* — with any sort of conceptualization of memory.[36] Typical in this regard is J. D. Morell's *Elements of Psychology* (1853), a pedestrian, comprehensive, and rather Hegelian textbook whose description of memory avoids any mention of amnesia and explicitly rejects any automatism to remembrance: "To say, therefore, that memory is a renewed sensation, or a prolonged sensation, or any kind of sensation, is wholly incorrect. We can neither prolong nor revive our sensation. They come and they go; they fill up the experience of a given moment, and then disappear for ever. What we reproduce is simply the product of the mind's free activity."[37] This hierarchized vision of the psyche, in which sensation and automatic response provides only a remote basis for advanced activity such as memory, imagination, and reason, was fated to be experimentally debunked by later physiological work, but its significance here lies in its utter difference from Collins's sensationalized amnesiacs.

The seeds for a reflexive memory (and therefore a reflexive amnesia) are laid by a combination of Hall's work on the reflex and by William Carpenter's hesitant conceptualization of an automatized cerebrum, one that might itself register memories in a reflexive fashion, one that might be a neurological organ in precisely the same manner as the spinal ganglia. Carpenter's importance — aside from his status as one of the authorities cited by *The Moonstone*'s Ezra Jennings, alongside the mesmerist John Elliotson and Thomas De Quincey — is the suggestive manner in which he arrives at what he will, by the mid-1870s, call the "cerebral reflex": through an increasing consideration of memory failure.[38] In the *Principles of Human Physiology* from 1842, the formulations are as yet tentative; after a partial list of forms of memory loss, Carpenter ventures the following: "When we take all these phenomena into consideration, we can scarcely resist the conclusion that every act of ideational consciousness produces a certain modification in the nutrition of the Cerebrum."[39] This is not a voluntary mental action — one feels here the dawning impulse to organicize consciousness and memory — but it is not yet a "reflex."

That development waited until 1874 for its full exposition, when Carpenter's aforementioned *Mental Physiology* would produce a much lengthier catalogue of mnemonic failures, including one of the first British investigations of aphasia; these failures of memory lead Carpenter to the following conclusion: "Memory is essentially an *automatic* form of Mental activity. By far the larger part of our Psychical operations depend on the mechanism by which past states of consciousness *spontaneously* reproduce themselves."[40] Carpenter's term for this automatic memory is "the reflex action of the cerebrum," a term that announces the linkage of remembrance and the autonomic nervous system. The music box paradigm, in other words, was at this point fully sanctioned by one of the most prominent British neural researchers. The logic to grasp here is the following: a "sensational" memory, a memory that is linked to sensations and the nervous system, arises out of an investigation of amnesia; the instantaneous reactions of the nervous system to threat or overstimulation (surprise, shock, contractions) are analogous to the automatic reactions of memory (aphasias arising out of head trauma, a loss of the ability to retain verbal information arising out of apoplexy or epilepsy). To discover a healthy reflex, one strikes the leg; to discover the reflexive nature of memory, its automatic or organic nature, one studies amnesia. To be sure, the automatic memory Carpenter advocated was supposed to work most of the time; but like the reflex motions only discovered through radical surgical or experimental procedure (such as the fowls studied by Flourens and Bouillaud), an automatic memory-system is only discoverable, really only present, in the cases in which it is under threat. What threatens it most, aside from illness or aging, is an excess of information, an excess of stimuli. When the stimuli presented are excessive, the mind automatically, or reflexively, shuts down memory: thus a physiological, pathological explanation for amnesia. With Carpenter's cerebral reflex the study of memory is prepared for all manner of later developments, from the statistical analysis of Ebbinghaus to the psychodynamics of the unconscious — a later form of "automatic" forgetting — espoused by Freud, Breuer, Janet.

But as early as Collins's 1857 *The Dead Secret*, Carpenter's long-delayed acceptance of the cerebral reflex, based on amnesia, has been anticipated. Being "touched" by her mother Sarah Leeson (disguised as the nurse "Mrs.

Jazeph"), Rosamond Treverton — as yet ignorant of the nurse's identity — finds the sensation mentally disruptive: "Mrs. Jazeph's touch, light and tender as it was, had such a strangely disconcerting effect on her, that she could not succeed, for the moment, in collecting her thoughts so as to reply, except in the briefest manner" (*DS*, 117). The process does not only relate to touches of an unexpectedly tender nature; more fundamentally, it is involved with those moments of heightened suspense in which the workings of a restricted number of senses become so engulfing that a temporary mental "oblivion" — analogous to the obliviousness of the engrossed reader — is the necessary physiological result. When Sarah Leeson reenters the Myrtle Room of Porthgenna Tower, where years earlier she had hidden proof of her motherhood, in order to take the proof and destroy it, she anticipates a resentful ghost, and the usual machinery of Gothic terror is mixed with a physiologized description: "She forgot the suspicious numbering of the doors; she became insensible to the lapse of time, unconscious of the risk of discovery. All exercise of her other faculties was now merged in the exercise of the one faculty of listening" (*DS*, 192). Just as, presumably, all our faculties are ideally merged in the one act of reading, having forgotten the circumambient world, being ready to later forget the act of reading itself. The importance to the sensation novel's production of suspense of this particular physiologized, involuntary process — sensation, shock, or its anticipation, an excess of stimulation, leading directly to a temporary amnesia — is evident.

Not that it is limited to classic moments of suspense such as opening a locked door or being accosted by an unknown figure. Its uses are varied throughout Collins's fiction and often parodically employed; when *The Moonstone*'s famous evangelist, the tract-dropping Miss Clack, is "touched" by Godfrey Ablewhite — whose power of attraction over Miss Clack parodies the novel's frequent use of "open secrets" — we find this self-deluded, humorous, but still physiologized moment: "He led me to a chair. I have an indistinct remembrance that he was very affectionate. I don't think he put his arm round my waist to support me — but I am not sure. I was quite helpless, and his ways with ladies were very endearing. At any rate, we sat down. I can answer for that, if I can answer for nothing more" (*M*, 296). For Walter Hartright, the process can shade into the more familiar narrative of the socially disadvantaged male letting his sexual attraction to his employer (a series of furtive "sensations") dictate "forgetting" his status: "Yes! Let me acknowledge that, on this first day, I let the charm of her presence lure me from the recollection of myself and my position" (*WW*, 44). That said, Collins's production of these automatic memory failures are located at those moments when the necessity for suspense-reactions are at their greatest, particularly the most suspenseful activity of all: waiting. Therefore the sensation novel can sensationalize even its dead moments, even its resting periods. Waiting restlessly for the soon-to-be-eavesdropped conversation between Fosco and Sir Percival to begin, Marian cannot write, cannot think, cannot remember: "In this perverse state of my mind, the recollection of what had passed since the morning would not come back to me; and there was no resource but to close my journal and to get away from it for a little while" (*WW*, 289). *The Moonstone*'s Gabriel Betteredge finds waiting for Sergeant Cuff's investigation the most difficult act of all:

> Here again, I find it impossible to give anything like a clear account of the state of my mind in the interval after Sergeant Cuff had left us. A curious and stupefying restlessness got possession of me. I did a dozen different needless things in and out of the house, not one of which I can remember. I don't even know how long it was after the Sergeant had gone to the sands, when Duffy came running back with a message for me (*M*, 195).

This interval need not be narrated, but when Collins does seek to fill gaps in this manner, the best way to do it is through a sensationalized gap: a waiting so suspenseful that it can only relate what it failed to notice or remember.

The novel as stimulant: it is worth returning to Margaret Oliphant, whose earlier-cited description of the "violent stimulant of serial publication" was more perceptive than mere name-calling. Her recognition of the physiological process both depicted and enacted by sensation fiction is highly acute; in her fear for the effects of this new form — a fear that interestingly presages the constant worries of a culture of "addiction"— she understands the demands of the sensation novel–reader: surprise me, make me forget. Even genial Betteredge, with his taste for Defoe and a relaxing pipe, is not immune to this need:

> "Before I go to London," I began, "I have two questions to ask you. They relate to myself, and I believe they will rather surprise you."
>
> "If they will put that poor creature's letter out of my head, Mr Franklin, they may do anything else they like with me. Please to begin surprising me, sir, as soon as you can." (*M*, 381)

The demand here is not for a "memorable" story but for one that enables forgetting, one so "surprising" that Betteredge *cannot help but forget* what he would like to forget. It is the involuntary quality, the "cannot help but," that so worried Mrs. Oliphant and that so caught the taste of the public in the 1860s: the depiction of a world of automatic responses, which are in this case amnesiac — forgettings physiologically dictated by the very nature of memory itself, which was, for the first time in British fiction, depicted as a physical, organic, unwilled function, tied inevitably to sensations, shocks, disruptions. The consequence of this change is that Collins ends up supplying, in the latter phases of both *The Woman in White* and *The Moonstone*, an entirely new genre: the case study. The novels undergo a strange kind of formal metamorphosis, in which the vagaries of a "culture of forgetfulness" and the momentary reflexes of sensationalized amnesiacs yield to a prolonged investigation by various authorities of one single, seemingly incurable case of clinical amnesia. The spectacle of Collins's closures are oddly mixed: on the one hand, closural nostalgias of the most traditional kind; on the other hand, the attempted cure of an amnesiac straight out of Ribot's later studies. These medical detective stories—how did the amnesia occur? how far has it gone? what can be done?—are Collins's most modern trait. It is as if in response to the readerly demand that has propelled so much of the novel (surprise me, make me forget), Collins brings forward two examples of what too much forgetting can mean, and in the instance of Laura Fairlie, what too much surprise can mean.

Case Studies

Laura's first words when reunited with Hartright, before her false gravestone, begin her case study narrative: "They have tried to make me forget everything, Walter; but I remember Marian, and I remember *you*" (*WW*, 380–381). Who "they" might be, how they "tried" to induce amnesia, and what that "everything" might be—an "everything" that excludes only Laura's two caretaking figures—are now open questions, and *The Woman in White* shifts from domestic drama to a hunt: a hunt for proof of Fosco and Percival's conspiracy, and a hunt for what Laura's missing memories might contain. First the outlines of this amnesia are drawn. Laura's memory is not entirely missing, and the class of data that she has lost is not conceptual (words, a language, a place) but temporal: the gap of time, as Hartright will later explain, "from the period of her leaving Blackwater Park to the period of our meeting in the burial-ground of Limmeridge church, was lost beyond all hope of recovery. At the slightest reference to that time, she changed and trembled still; her words became confused; her memory wandered and lost itself as helplessly as ever" (*WW*, 517). A time of trauma, a time whose exact content will never be related. Glance at the form of this suddenly contorted plot, and one thing becomes clear: Laura in her posttraumatic phase is now an *object of investigation*. The narrative now starts a process of asking questions about the missing mnemonic information: who did what to Laura at the asylum? Why can she not recall it? How might we induce her to remember what she cannot (or chooses not to) remember? If previous Victorian texts have shown us various selves in the act of letting go of a defective past—Jane Eyre leaving Lowood School, for instance—*The Woman in White* takes matters from the other end and shows us a *process of inquiry* into why that past has been forgotten and how, or under what conditions, it might be recovered.

Continually after Laura's rescue from the asylum she is subjected to questioning, probing, excavating. Spiriting Laura away from the asylum in a cab, Marian begins the research, and is met by obstacles: "Miss Halcombe was able to collect such remembrances of the past as her sister's confused and weakened memory was able to recal. The terrible story of the conspiracy so obtained, was presented in fragments, sadly incoherent in themselves, and widely detached from each other" (*WW*, 390). The questions Marian most likely asks are those already posed by the narrative, which sets itself up as an investigation parallel to Marian's own unquoted queries: on what day was Laura transported to London by Fosco? Who met Fosco at the station, and by what means did they arrive at Fosco's house? What did Fosco say when asked for Marian's whereabouts? "From this point," Marian ruefully admits, "her recollections were found to be confused, fragmentary, and difficult to reconcile with any reasonable probability" (*WW*, 393). As for the unnamed horrors of the asylum, Marian attempts a bit more tact, refusing to press Laura directly on them, hoping that more indirect measures will eventually cause the traumas to emerge. Which of course they never do: much of what "they" have tried to "make" Laura forget remains forgotten, only to be supplied by whatever detailed horror we choose to invent for her. Still, the narrative keeps asking questions just as Hartright and Marian try ever more subtle approaches. Hartright tries the therapeutic avenue of starting with positive recollections, encouraging the memory of "the little trivial domestic events" of Limmeridge, showing her the souvenir sketch of the Limmeridge summerhouse she had one day made, trying to revive her interest in drawing—attempting, in short, to restore a former state of existence. Having realized that Laura cannot be directly questioned, Hartright tries to lull her into a nerveless placidity while he carries on his investigation elsewhere, an investigation that is largely *a substitute for Laura's diseased memory*: he goes elsewhere because Laura cannot, or will not, remember. "The one remaining chance, which I had at first thought might be trusted to serve us—the chance of appealing to her recollection of persons and events with which no impostor could be familiar, was proved, by the sad test of our later experience, to be hopeless" (*WW*, 400).

The fact is important to keep in mind: both *The Woman in White* and *The Moonstone* end as protracted attempts to solve an amnesia that the patient cannot solve alone. This is important because it is well in advance of psychology at the time of the novel's publication, which had yet to recognize "amnesia" as a unique category of pathology, but important above all for this reason: that although more familiar forms of forgetting, particularly a familiar nostalgic closural process, do coexist in these texts with these "case studies," Collins with his pathologized amnesias *hardens into one form* all the various means of forgetting his novels record and then *makes it available to study*. The amnesias of Laura Fairlie and Mr. Candy dramatize, condense, and ratify the diffuse amnesias of a "culture of forgetfulness"— they turn these novels's dispersed analyses of forgetting into the creation of a type, the amnesiac. By making amnesia not only a dispersed pathology, found everywhere in his texts, but also an object of investigation toward which the text increasingly moves, Collins makes it available for a more widespread cultural and scientific investigation, one that, as I have been arguing, did not exist before Collins's first sensation novels.

What *was* present at the time, and what has often been read as the overriding topic of Collins's texts as a result of its cultural presence, was what went by the term "double consciousness": the splitting of the self into two completely independent halves, as evidenced by the presence of two competing mnemonic systems. The most typical example, cited by Carpenter among others, is that of an inebriate who can recall, when drunk, where an object was placed during an earlier bout of drinking but who cannot, when sober, recall even being in possession of the object.[41] Coleridge's famous example from the *Biographia Literaria* was often adduced as well: an illiterate German woman, Coleridge relates, contracted a fever, during which she could recite Latin, Greek, and Hebrew. Inquiry demonstrated that she learned these ancient texts from a former employer, a pastor, who had been in the habit of reading out loud; but the lesson here is of a memory that does not always know what it knows until an alteration in the body (alcohol, disease) forces the hidden set of mnemonic data to emerge.[42] Double consciousness, according to Ian Hacking, was central to British psychology and physiology in the years prior to the 1870s simply because memory was not yet their focus. "Memory and forgetting were simply unimportant to what was known, in the English-speaking world, as double consciousness," Hacking states; its symptoms — a *memory that does not know what it knows* — were part of a preamnesiac pathology, in which if something is forgotten, it must be stored in a doubled version of the self, recoverable through a sudden or fortuitous switch back to that doubled self.[43] Double consciousness, that is, was a way of exploring the odd appearances and disappearances of mental information before amnesia was a possible way of explaining those phenomena. Perhaps that is why the earliest writers on amnesia were so contemptuous of double consciousness; Ribot, for his part, says sardonically that it is "fort à la mode" before dismissing it.[44]

It is not that Collins was incurious about double consciousness and its subsidiary conditions, such as somnambulism, opiates, and the like; it is that at the end of *The Woman in White* and *The Moonstone* he turns to a condition that was not yet sanctioned by British physiology and that was, in fact, an entirely new cultural phenomenon, one that would eventually end the period of double consciousness and begin the study of memory in Britain: amnesia. Laura Fairlie or Mr. Candy can never be put in a situation where they will become re-cognizant of their missing recollections or missing double self; their amnesias can only be solved by either a patient investigation, as in the case of Hartright, or a curious reconstruction, as in the case of Mr. Candy's disconnected ramblings. The amnesiac is now not two mutually coherent, if split, selves, like the somnambulist or the drunkard, but one self that knows it doesn't remember and cannot help that fact. The significance is precisely this: Collins does not entirely rely on an older psychic category but instead ends his novels on the production of a new one, one that makes memory, its loss and recovery, the explicit topic of narrative in a way that double consciousness could never achieve. For the sufferer from double consciousness, memory is unproblematic, assumed, uninteresting: of course they might remember; how the "two selves" might be integrated is the question. For Collins's characters there is no "of course" to memory any more. Double consciousness becomes amnesia in Collins's narratives of the 1860s, and Collins therefore anticipates a later, fundamental shift in the sciences of mind of the later nineteenth century.

It is a shift that can then produce the figure of *The Moonstone*'s Ezra Jennings, physiological investigator and theorist, who is "writing a book, addressed to the members of my profession—a book on the intricate and delicate subject of the nervous system" (*M*, 423). Although his book will never be published, or even cited by the novel that contains and is analogous to it, Jennings's consideration of amnesia as a phenomenon to be studied and solved, one susceptible to rational explanation, would eventually—and outside Collins's text—become normative psychological practice. Jennings is, in other words, a prefiguration of Ribot's innovative attempt to classify all amnesias and find a general etiology for each one—a prefiguration which then takes over the novel's "mystery". In *The Moonstone*, that is, the mechanics of a detective-plot (who stole the gem, and how can it be recovered?) eventually coalesce with the mechanics of a physiological investigation: the secret of who stole the gem hinges on the solution of an instance of amnesia, which can then become a "case" both in the scientific and the criminal senses. For it is Mr. Candy's inability to remember having playfully drugged Franklin Blake on the night of the theft that makes the precise details of the theft unavailable to investigation. Unlike so many later mystery narratives, where physical objects—a cigarette butt, a fingerprint—speak what the criminal cannot or will not, *The Moonstone*'s plot is resolvable only through the recovery of memory; the famous paint-smear on Franklin Blake's nightgown is not enough. It may point to the correct "criminal," but of course that indication is only the beginning of the larger enigma of how, and why, the gem was taken by Blake. Meaning that can be fixed, in the way of closural solutions to a crime, is only available here through the intervention of a physiological theory into a field of amnesia.

When Blake first visits Mr. Candy after his illness, the results of his questioning are baffling, seemingly intractable. All that can be detected is the presence of some valued memory that remains out of reach: Blake tells us that "it was plain, pitiably plain, that he was aware of his own defect of memory, and that he was bent on concealing it from the observation of his friends" (*M*, 415). Asked delicately if he has made any "memorandum" of the famous birthday dinner that might aid his remembrance, Mr. Candy explodes—"I require no memorandums, Mr Blake" (*M*, 415)—in a way that only emphasizes the importance of written aids to memory in Collins's texts. What must be stressed here is how this strange figure—a doctor prostrate with amnesia, whose missing memories are the core of a plot of suspense—is unprecedented in both fictional and psychological texts; what must be further stressed is how the novel produces a complementary and similarly unprecedented figure, the physiological theorist, to cope with the dilemma this amnesia produces.

Jennings's theory runs as follows: take the ravings of Mr. Candy that followed his illness, which were duly transcribed, and read them as a text that makes perfect sense but contains gaps. "In plainer words," Jennings explains, "after putting the broken sentences together I found the superior faculty of thinking going on, more or less connectedly, in my patient's mind, while the inferior faculty of expression was in a state of almost complete incapacity and confusion"; Jennings therefore can fill in the blanks, so to speak, or penetrate "through the obstacle of the disconnected expression, to the thought which was underlying it connectedly all the time" (*M*, 437). The method essentially treats Mr. Candy's amnesia as a case of aphasia, in which the memory is there and retrieval is possible but the translation of that retrieval into a communicable form is disabled; more important, the method makes the attending physician—in this instance Ezra Jennings—the only figure who can excavate the memory. If we return to "double consciousness" for a moment, we can see the difference: in the case of the drunken man, or Coleridge's illiterate servant, the production of a "lost" memory (the location of an object) is dependent on a physiological switch (alcoholic stupor) that is largely fortuitous, that medical intervention can only hope to induce. The famous "recreation" experiment at the end of *The Moonstone*, in which opium is administered to Blake in order to activate his "second self" that will recall how the gem was stolen, is much like an instance of double consciousness; but the solution of Mr. Candy's amnesia is entirely different and owes little to double consciousness and its "switching" between selves. Here a physician assumes one coherent self (a self that means what it says and knows what that meaning should be), then sets about supplying information to fill the gaps that the amnesia has left in that self's expression: thus "five and twenty minims . . . without his knowing it . . . to-morrow morning" is transformed, in Jennings's clear account, into "Give him five and twenty minims of laudanum to-night, without his knowing it; and then call to-morrow morning" (*M*, 436–437). The *method* itself is not picked up by later physiologists, but the *methodology*, one might say, is: the idea that amnesia is a field for rational inquiry and rational solution, the notion that amnesias can be classified, the axiom that there are layers of mental activity (thought, expression) into which amnesias can penetrate more or less deeply. A "case study" indeed: Mr. Candy is at once a "case" for all of the novel's amateur detectives and criminologists, and the focus of a "study" that will at once unravel a missing memory and lead the novel's enigma to its resolution.

So Collins's most obvious amnesiacs, Laura Fairlie and Mr. Candy, ossify the various amnesias of these texts into one form in order to make that form susceptible to study. But it should be noted that these amnesias do not entirely lose contact with the "amnesiac self" as we have previously seen it, as Jennings himself shows us in a diagnosis that veers from the clinical to the nostalgic:

> "His memory of events, at that past time, is hopelessly enfeebled," said Ezra Jennings. "It is almost to be deplored, poor fellow, that even the wreck of it remains. While he remembers dimly plans that he formed — things, here and there, that he had to say or do, before his illness — he is perfectly incapable of recalling what the plans were, or what the thing was that he had to say or do. He is painfully conscious of his own deficiency, and painfully anxious, as you must have seen, to hide it from observation. If he could only have recovered in a complete state of oblivion as to the past, he would have been a happier man. Perhaps we should all be happier," he added, with a sad smile, "if we could but completely forget!" (*M*, 418–419)

The range of *codes* in play here — medical, psychological, romantic — is entirely characteristic of Collins's diverse and not entirely coherent suffusion in forgetfulness and its possibilities. We have a precocious, and rather sophisticated, delineation of the class of Mr. Candy's amnesia, in which categories are recalled without their attendant content, a classification Ribot would have recognized; we have a psychological analysis of Mr. Candy's attempts to cover up this amnesia; and finally we have the traditionally closural note of Victorian fiction, the desire to "completely forget" in the service of a more complete happiness — a nostalgic formulation that is, crucially, now voiced by a physiologist.[45] In Mr. Candy's illness and its treatment by Jennings, we have then a hardening or condensation of the general forgettings of the sensation novel into one pathologized instance of amnesia, but a condensation that also maintains its links to a fictional tradition of nostalgic remembrance. The instance, that is, gives us not only a modern "case" of amnesia but also a familiar nostalgic ethos, all mediated through the figure of a physiologist, who is at once the theorist of mnemonic failure and the figure who will request to be totally forgotten, buried under a nameless tombstone with his writings enclosed with him.

Under the auspices of a still highly nostalgic physiology, then, "amnesia" as a clinical entity enters British fiction, transforming that nostalgic tradition while still retaining an affinity for its more familiar formulations. The problem with Mr. Candy's illness, Jennings says, is not that it has erased memory but that it has not erased enough memory; in much the same manner, for instance, Jane Eyre's first attempt at marrying Mr. Rochester is not flawed because of its erasure of the past but because that erasure was incomplete. What the physiological transformation of forgetting has done, however, is to once again root forgetting in the body as an automatic response, to make this forgetting reflexive: both instantaneous, and capable of theorization, self-reflection. After Laura Fairlie and Mr. Candy come a succession of cultural narratives or "case studies," too numerous to mention, in which the root of a problem is an inability to remember, an inability that must be corrected, a gap that must be filled. To the "state of oblivion as to the past" that Jennings recommends has been added the idea of *morbidity* — and the "culture of forgetfulness" has metamorphosed into its modern counterpart, the culture of amnesia. The distinction between those two cultures — both anxious over memory lapses, but only the latter having construed those lapses into a field of scientific labor — aptly summarizes the force, for later theories of mind and for the cultural function of those theories, that Collins's sensation novels would have.

Mind and Machine

Collins's novels begin increasingly to depict *machinery*: the gas-chamber mechanism by which *Armadale*'s Lydia Gwilt kills herself, the trap door by which assassins in *The Moonstone* enter Godfrey Ablewhite's hotel room to smother him with a pillow, the telegraph that summons Sergeant Cuff to the scene of the Moonstone's theft. One might think as well of the plot "machinery" that was supposed, according to his earliest reviewers, to afflict Collins's novels, which displayed their structural supports and joints as brazenly as modern architecture. But the most prevalent machine in the sensation novel is the mind itself. So often in Collins do we see consciousness working only on the level of the habitual, the "absent-minded," the possessed—working, that is, according to the dictates of the autonomic nervous system, whether in a shocked trance or the heightened states of suspense—that we might overlook the mental machinery so constantly brought forward for us. The manner in which we see Hartright, shortly after he has first met the Woman in White, is typical: "Ten minutes, or more, had passed. I was still on the same side of the way; now mechanically walking forward a few paces; now stopping again absently" (*WW*, 21). Having been surprised, struggling to assimilate that surprise, Hartright begins to work automatically; or perhaps we should say "continues" to work automatically, given that his reactions to the encounter as it occurred, characterized by the tightening of his fingers around his stick, are nothing if not reflexive, mechanical. Even Anne Catherick herself is rather machine-like, with her "curiously still and mechanical" voice (*WW*, 15). What we see here is, in fact, a succession of involuntary actions and reactions: a chain of effects controlled by nerves (spasms, contractions, repetitious movements), a mind that does not need the intervention of will to operate.

When reaction replaces reflection as thoroughly as it does for Collins's characters—who are accustomed to note not a train of thoughts but an automatic bodily reaction, as when *The Moonstone*'s Betteredge records that his "heart couldn't have thumped much harder than it did now, if I had been five-and-twenty again" (*M*, 172)—we see memory itself, which had heretofore been considered among the most immaterial of all mental functions, turn toward the automatic as well. Such is perhaps the ultimate lesson of Collins's new amnesiacs, of his sensationalized memory: the reflexivity of memory. No longer is something like nostalgia, with its elaborately willed, shaped, and streamlined retrospects, at the center of narrative; the elisions of nostalgia, which triumph over the body's pathological reactions to loss, are transformed into amnesia, which is itself a *reaction* to overstimulation, suspense, anxiety. With this innovation in the fictional representation of memory, Collins presages the eventual fate of physiologized memory in European science, the path that the investigation of a "nervous" memory would take: the conditioned reflex studies of Pavlov.[46]

Memory as machine: when discussing Collins's amnesia it is impossible not to refer to "processes," "functions," "systems," to the inevitable and unconscious workings of a physiological machine. Be shocked, feel a sensation, forget—Collins's automatized memory is not far, in the broadest terms, from Pavlov's famous path whereby a recurrent sensation leads to a recurrent, reflexive recollection. Collins's fiction centers on memory loss and "amnesia" as firmly as do Austen or Brontë's prephysiological texts, but if anything is most distinctive about Collins's amnesias it is this reflexive quality that his novels so continually depict and depend on, the same reflexivity that enables Collins's readers to forget the outside world, to forget elements in the narrative that will then surprise them later, to forget the novel itself and then to desire another one. If in studying Austen's nostalgics we feel as if we are excavating the conditions and reasonings behind a series of choices, in studying Collins's amnesiacs we are peering into the workings of a mechanism, the memory-as-machine.

FIVE

The Unremembered Past

ELIOT'S *ROMOLA* AND AMNESIAC HISTORIES

The past forgets that it is past; and at this price, plays upon the present.
—*Paul Valéry*

George Eliot's attempt to recapture a distant past in all its specificity—
through extensive researches, reading, and philological investigation—persists as perhaps the most "memorable" fact about her 1863 historical novel
Romola.[1] Accounts of the novel seem incomplete without a turn to its difficult, library-laden genesis, which is elaborately described in Eliot's own letters and journals, where the minutiae of Florentine history become subject
to an effort of recovery that can seem wearying and almost spectacularly
excessive. Writing to the novel's illustrator, Frederic Leighton, Eliot ex-
pounds in a typical manner on the details of Florentine dress:

> Since I saw you I have confirmed by renewed reference my conclusion
> that gamurra was the equivalent of our *gown*, i.e. the constant outer
> garb of femininity, varying in length and cut according to rank and
> age. The poets and novelists give it alike to the peasant and the "city
> woman," and speak of the *girdle* around it. Perhaps it would have
> been better to call Tessa's gown a *gamurrina*, the word sometimes
> used and indicating, I imagine, just that abbreviation of petticoat that
> active work demands.[2]

Detail is the ostensible object of Eliot's preparation for writing *Romola*: a
detail so complete and so demandingly faithful to a vanished reality that it

can scarcely be classed with the vagaries of "nostalgia." If from Austen's work onward nostalgia implies a vague, disconnected pleasure in a vanished time, Eliot's process in composing a historical novel seems instead the effort to reconnect to the present (often through translations such as "gamurra" into "gown") a deeply particularized, fully real or revivified past, one that implies as well a certain degree of pain — the pain of the overwhelmed researcher. If, as Eliot later claimed, she began *Romola* a young woman and finished it an old woman, it is because the effort at a nonnostalgic historical reconstruction resembled the traumas of the eighteenth-century nostalgic, too attached to a past reality and its particularities to adapt well to present tasks.[3] Eliot's difficulty in beginning the writing of the novel is well recorded, as if the pull of historical recovery itself, despite the pain of the accumulation of detail, superseded the act of transforming the detail into a narrative. "When you see her," G. H. Lewes implored her publisher John Blackwood, "mind your care is to discountenance the idea of a Romance being the product of an Encyclopaedia."[4]

The Victorian historical novel, then, as exemplified by *Romola*, would seem to be in direct contrast to the workings of nostalgic remembrance and nostalgic amnesias that characterize Austen's social fiction, Brontë's narratives of progress, the fictional autobiographies of Dickens and Thackeray, or Collins's sensation fiction. When we consider nineteenth-century historical fiction, we are largely presented with a spectacle of waste: the waste of pain and effort, of years of research and composition, devoted to now underread texts such as Dickens's *Barnaby Rudge* (1841), Thackeray's *The Virginians* (1857–59), or Pater's *Marius the Epicurean* (1885) — a pain often associated with the dense particularity of these narratives, so different from the genial sentimentalities and closural dilutions of other genres of Victorian fiction.[5] Vast attempts to recover a past in all its lived complexity, Victorian historical fiction performed on the level of history what no good nostalgic — neither Fanny Price nor Henry Esmond nor Franklin Blake — would do on the level of personal memory: the reconstruction of a detailed and particular past. While nostalgic recollection aims always at a winnowing of fact into a named, stable, communal meaning, these texts were, as Lewes described Eliot's Florentine knowledge, *encyclopedic*, glorying in a multiplicity of researched recovery of a disappeared milieu. Gowns and gamurras, petticoats and gamurrinas — these texts offer themselves as perhaps the most vivid possible contrast to the principles of nostalgic remembrance. Historical fiction, it would seem, operated without reference to the idea of remembering only what is pleasant or vague.

But this general picture is complicated, indeed entirely altered, if we look to one of the most fascinating elements of these Victorian historical narratives, and *Romola* in particular: the presence within them of either familiar nostalgic characters, or even characters who are explicit amnesiacs;

and in *Romola*, in perhaps the most interesting instance of this trend, the amnesiac in question is himself a scholar and antiquarian, a devotee of the historical past, whose learning and scholarly memory is subject to a pathological erasure of a kind analogous to Collins's sensationalized memory losses. The amnesiac in question is Baldassare Calvo, adoptive father of Romola's egoist husband Tito Melema. An enigmatic illness, contracted while enslaved at Corinth, has explicitly removed all the skills and recollections that Eliot herself would have used in the novel's own composition, and the novel, as here, is at pains to describe and work over this antiquarian amnesia:

> He was in one of his most wretched moments of conscious helplessness: he had been poring, while it was light, over the book that lay open beside him; then he had been trying to recall the names of his jewels, and the symbols engraved in them; and though at certain other times he had recovered some of those names and symbols, tonight they were all gone into darkness. And this effort at inward seeing had seemed to end in utter paralysis of memory. He was reduced to a sort of mad consciousness that he was a solitary pulse of just rage in a world filled with defiant baseness. (378)[6]

We see here a pathology and narrative logic that might remind us of Collins, in which amnesia functions as an extreme instance of a more general novelistic forgetting: Baldassare, through his mental disfunction, is "reduced" to a single function — revenge — and his consciousness is drastically, and pathologically, streamlined to only the most relevant, concordant, and integral memories, only those that relate to his son's denial, betrayal, and ingratitude. If, unlike Collins's Laura Fairlie, Baldassare *can* recall the unpleasant and *cannot* remember his formerly pleasurable, vast knowledge, the general effect is similar, in that Baldassare's amnesia reduces the complexity of memory to only what is meaningful, what can emotively signify. Particulars drop out of Baldassare's recollection — the particulars of language, of place, of objects: amnesia restores to him only the most significant generalities (betrayal, justice, a wounded pride). He cannot even recall what it is that he cannot recall: all that is left is "the vague aching of an unremembered past within him" (335).

Yet this instance of pathologized amnesia is not simply an infiltration of the sensation novel and its mechanics — a pervasive forgetfulness, a plotted murder — into an otherwise seriously "historical" narrative; what it tells us is somewhat more specific, more deeply tied to the project of historical fiction itself. It is how Baldassare's amnesia is uniquely *thematized* that must capture our attention. His inability to remember is, again and again, an inability to remember *precisely those things that make historical fiction pos-*

sible: skills of language (we hear most about Baldassare's inability to recall his Greek), historical facts (the names of ancient cities and writers), methods of identification (names, images, ways of contextualizing and specifying objects). Baldassare's traumatic mental fissure separates him from the most readily apparent, and most often castigated, elements of historical fiction, from its emphasis on a scrupulous faithfulness of detail, from its continual recourse to lexicographical research such as "gamurras" and "gamurrinas," from its very *historicity*. What amnesia leaves Baldassare, as I will show in greater detail, is only his *personal* history, and only its more general outlines.

The phenomenon to note, then, and the phenomenon that must serve as the starting point for an inquiry into the effect of Victorian styles of nostalgia on the period's historical fiction, is the intersection of personal amnesias of various sorts with large historical projects of recovery.[7] We misunderstand the mnemonic contours of these texts if we concentrate solely on the dense fabric of research and scholarship that went into their composition; what requires further study is the way this detailed research, most visibly in the example of *Romola*, is transformed and even negated through the use of a panoply of amnesiac or more traditionally nostalgic characters, from the extreme and telling Baldassare, an antiquarian who forgets everything he has learned, to Romola's father Bardo, a scholar whose blindness and social irrelevance marks his capacious textual memory as ultimately useless, to Romola herself, who revises the dispersed facts of her past into a stable, vague "legend." Personal nostalgia reworks and replaces the specificities of historical memory.[8] A particularized recovery of the past, the genesis of *Romola*, becomes in its negotiation through narrative a nostalgic retrospect, which eliminates a "useless" past and activates a "useful" past into present perception and present value.

This, finally, is the deepest contribution of the historical novel to Victorian notions of memory—not the elimination of a "useless" past, which we have seen from Austen to Dickens, but the conversion of a portion of the past into present perception, the *activation* of a small remainder of the past into a present fact or object, a past that is "unremembered" because it is no longer to be remembered: it is merely, and only, a part of the present.[9] As I will show, a complex account of present perception and the ways in which it can eliminate the pastness of the past, which I will term "recognition," is worked out in *Romola*, so that an active memory becomes unnecessary in the Florentine world Eliot depicts: what is useless of the past disappears through amnesia, loss, or nostalgic revision, and what is still of value in that past loses its "pastness." This is not, it should be made clear, the mnemonic landscape that seems promised by such obsessively precise research as Eliot's novel demonstrates; but it is nonetheless the fashion in which *Romola* functions, the narrative fate of Eliot's historical reconstruction. Before the process of "unremembering" the past can be described, however, it is perhaps necessary to look at how the very acts of historical memory within Eliot's novel are subject to the erasures of personal forgetting.

From Book to Body

The idea of research: it is never very far from the reading experience of *Romola*, particularly when the novel's grand-historical figures — Savonarola, Machiavelli, Piero di Cosimo — enter the text. How Eliot assembled the materials of the past is often as legible as the narrative of the past itself: "Savonarola rose and turned to his desk as he spoke. He took from it a letter on which Tito could see, but not read, an address in the Frate's own minute and exquisite handwriting, still to be seen covering the margins of his Bibles" (618). At the same time that we learn the rather picturesque detail about Savonarola's handwriting — indicative, perhaps, of an ambitious and controlling personality? — we learn the *source* of Eliot's description; lest we think that the detail is an authorial invention, we have a proof that it is not, that a record of this handwriting survives and that our author has consulted it. The past, in all its specificity (no more meaningful or evidentiary, perhaps, than any handwriting analysis), survives, and often enough *Romola* is a testament to this fact. It is even more significant that this authenticating detail is a text, for Eliot's process of reconstruction came primarily, and necessarily, from texts. Reading *Romola*, aware as we cannot help but be of the memory encased in texts and how much our author has learned from them, we are very quickly taught the value of textual transmission, of scholarship, of historical memory — so much so that critics have not hesitated to accuse Eliot of a Casaubon-like narrowness.[10] Henry James's retrospective judgment remains, like so many of James's comments, a keynote: "It is overladen with learning, it smells of the lamp, it tastes just perceptibly of pedantry. . . . A twentieth part of the erudition would have sufficed, would have given us the feeling and colour of the time, if there had been more of the breath of the Florentine streets, more of the faculty of optical evocation, a greater saturation of the senses with the elements of the adorable little city."[11] The feminized "adorable little city" of Florence is for James unwarrantably diluted by a masculinized "erudition" — and the novel itself lodges erudition in masculine hands; it is as if Eliot's research, designed to provide *Romola* with a weight and ballast that might be denied to narratives based on "mere" personal recollections (the Hayslope of *Adam Bede*, the St. Ogg's of *The Mill on the Floss*), has ended up sinking the novel instead.

But there is more to this animosity to Eliot's all too visible research than a critical misogyny or a bibliophobic aversion to a novel with "sources" or "background." Eliot had, after all, merely transferred a newly energized historiographical confidence in textual sources—sparked by Macaulay's *History of England*, whose impact on the increasingly commonplace historical novel was crucial—to fiction.[12] In fact, the common dislike of Eliot's research, the aversion to the idea of research and antiquarianism in fiction that persists into contemporary accounts of *Romola*, might have much to do with what, as we have seen, was a long established Victorian preference in matters of memory: a preference for the inexplicit, the vague, the generalizable, the nostalgic. If Eliot's novel seemed too "researched," too dense with particularity, it therefore failed to gratify those tastes, which expected from fiction something much closer to Austen's closural dilutions or Dickens's always relevant, always concordant retrospects. The extent to which Eliot herself saw historical reconstruction on this scale as an issue of personal memory is evident from a chance remark lodged in her journal in July 1861, during the initial preparatory work for *Romola*: "Busied myself with a plan of rational mnemonics in history."[13]

It is mnemonics—or, as it was more commonly termed, "mnemotechnics"—that stands as far as possible from the ethics of remembrance that pervades Victorian fiction. A detailed, and possibly exact, recollection of dispersed facts, mnemonics or memorization receives only negative attention in the period's fiction, as in the humorously useless memorization exercises undergone by *Mansfield Park*'s Bertram sisters. Unable to separate the relevant from the irrelevant, unwilling to eliminate detail, incapable of converting mnemonic data into useful information: such is the usual judgment of mnemotechnics, which Eliot doubtlessly employed in her long journey through Florentine history. The notebook in which Eliot recorded much of her research, known now as the "Quarry for *Romola*," is an example of the kind of detailed mnemonics she maintained—categories such as "Fairs," "Imports," "Banners," and even "Laws about Food, 1472" multiply within it, as if no fact could go unremembered.[14] Rational mnemonics indeed—the very effort at remembering the reading she managed to do seeps into *Romola*, making it highly susceptible to criticism arising out of a preference for a more nostalgic, more vague, more disconnected and more effortless memory. If one can critique such lavish and painstakingly constructed tableaux as Eliot's description of the nativity procession of Saint John the Baptist, one can perhaps only do so from the standpoint of the "pain" such an effort implies—the pain of memorization, the pain, as we have seen in other Victorian narratives, so thoroughly associated with a particularized memory.

That is, much of the criticism leveled at the novel's research targets its insufficiently vague mnemonic texture, a specificity that implies difficulty or trauma. When Trollope wonders, in a letter to Eliot, at "the toil you must have endured in getting up your work," it is the toil of detailed recollection to which he alludes.[15] For even later critics, such as Georg Lukács, the density of recovered fact in historical fiction is culpable not because of its affront to canons of vagueness but because of its necessary lack of relevance to either the present or the past described; writing on Flaubert's similarly researched *Salammbô*, Lukács famously indicts "this frozen, lunar landscape of archaeological precision": "He chooses an historical subject whose inner social-historical nature is of no concern to him and to which he can only lend the appearance of reality in an external, decorative, picturesque manner by means of the conscientious application of archaeology."[16] But on a certain level it does not matter whether the critique be from the standpoint of the vague and pleasurable or from the standpoint of the relevant—they both coalesce in being a critique of a certain kind of memory, the detailed memory of antiquarians, of scholars, of mnemotechnics. The idea of research is directly opposed to the idea of nostalgia: a densely recovered past guaranteed by an athletic memory stands against a leavetaking of the past and its resonances.

What then to make of the novel's own antiquarians? What to do with Bardo di'Bardi, blind scholar, who tells Romola that "even when I could see, it was with the great dead that I lived; while the living often seemed to me mere spectres—shadows dispossessed of true feeling and intelligence" (96); what to do with his functional counterpart, Baldassare, who gains his prominence in the novel at precisely the moment Bardo's death vacates the role and who exhibits an even more extreme version of Bardo's general impotence: amnesia? Bardo's extensive library is called a "precious relic" (310), his passion for it a "collector's mania" (118); Baldassare's knowledge, which is termed a "mental empire" (406) when it briefly returns to him, is yet another example of the sort of power and the type of endeavor that explicitly mirrors the novelist's own pursuit, that explicitly addresses the idea of research, the idea of "collecting," codifying, and recalling the materials, from magnificent relic to detritus, of the past. Set against these figures is Romola herself, who, according to her father's peevish and misogynistic complaints, has little of the scholar's memory for details; he speaks of "the capriciousness of my daughter's memory, which grasps certain objects with tenacity, and lets fall all those minutiae whereon depends accuracy, the very soul of scholarship" (110). How to explain the strange ineffectuality of scholarly work and memory within the novel, and the equally strange beneficence of a "capricious" recollection? Can Bardo's criticism of Romola's memory be recovered as a positive value?

In the broadest possible terms, *Romola* performs the following: it *converts* the question of historical memory and scholarship to a matter of personal memory, then *assesses* the types of personal memory created by that conversion through the familiar Victorian values of nostalgic remembrance. The seemingly impersonal endeavors of Bardo or Baldassare, such as the preservation of a classical past for the greater good of Florentine scholarship or the maintenance of Greek learning, are related in the terms of personal recollection — Bardo's antiquarianism comes to seem like nothing so much as a nonnostalgic cathexis to the past, as the obsession of one "who sat among his books and his marble fragments of the past, and saw them only by the light of those far-off younger days which still shone in his memory" (92); a scholar, perhaps, but a scholar in the mode of Miss Havisham. As for Baldassare, the question of whether his Greek learning is worthwhile is entirely superseded by the issue of amnesia, a personal amnesia that continually frustrates his revenge on Tito and complicates his own identity. What Baldassare largely forgets is his Greek, the magical "black marks" on a page; but the narrative emphasis is on the forgetting rather than the Greek. If we hesitate to discuss Eliot's illness-inducing Florentine research in the context of personal memory, we have the novel itself to reassure us, as it continually ties the value of scholarship to the quality of the personal memory exhibited by the scholar in question, or the quality of personal memory demanded by scholarship itself. Once that conversion has been made, the novel considers these instances of personal memory in the light of nostalgic retrospect.

This, then, is the deeper import of Bardo's complaint about Romola's memory, which he continually presents as a gendered critique: "Something perhaps were to be wished in thy capacity of attention and memory, not incompatible even with the feminine mind" (100). "Feminine" as such memory lapses may be in *Romola*, their very femininity, as in the tradition of Austen's heroines or Brontë's narrators, helps to guarantee their nostalgic value. Let us consider the possible cultural meaning of a memory that "grasps certain objects with tenacity, and lets fall all those minutiae whereon depends accuracy, the very soul of scholarship": is this not a formula for nostalgia itself? A winnowing process whereby certain objects — pleasurable ones — are retained at the expense of a not-very-vague "accuracy" is one of the central virtues (if traditionally *closural* virtues) of Victorian fiction. The constant particularities of scholarly memory, so far from nostalgic "capriciousness," are negated in Romola's person through her dependable capacity for inattention and forgetfulness — forgetfulness of detail.[17] Loyalty to the large facts of the past is certainly a strength of hers, but there runs next to them a constant elision of a more detailed past.

What of Baldassare? His presence in the novel has been ignored to the extent that it has been seen as, for Eliot, unusually clinical; one early reviewer in the *Home and Foreign Review* mocked the "psychologico-medical study of Baldassare," and if his amnesia has seemed to come from the world of the sensation novel, that has been license enough to separate him from the novel's main thematic lines.[18] But the pathological amnesiac and the novel's eponymous heroine share a function: the conversion of historical remembrance into terms taken from personal memory (amnesia, inattention), and the reduction of personal memory according to the canons of nostalgia. For this is the effect of Baldassare's amnesia: "As he had recovered his strength of body, he had recovered his self-command and the energy of his will; he had recovered the memory of all that part of his life which was closely enwrought with his emotions; and he had felt more and more constantly and painfully the uneasy sense of lost knowledge" (335–356). The source is not a "capricious" memory but a sick one; the result, however, is the same—a psyche that dilutes the past according to what is relevant ("his emotions"), concordant (the sense of past betrayal by Tito that will become future vengeance), and integral (his "life" is retained, his "knowledge" gone). Baldassare can function—can plot Tito's death, can discover Tito's mistress Tessa and her children, can negotiate Florence; what he cannot do is disperse his mental functions among the wider range of cultural memory and scholarly proficiency. The illness that took his literacy has narrowed, but not neutralized, his passion: "But there are deep draughts in this world for hatred and revenge," he tells himself. "I have memory left for that" (339). The novel's amnesiac is a potential murderer, while Romola's inattention is of course far less threatening; but the logic structuring these two dilutions of memory is the same. Both figures lose (through illness or "capriciousness") a useless set of memories, and in both cases the memories situated as useless are precisely those required for the construction of historical fiction: a comprehensive literacy, an ability to retain dispersed facts, a fixation on language.

Through the novel's major nonhistorical persons—Romola, Tito, Bardo, Baldassare—Eliot is engaged in the elimination, *through a careful mapping of memory loss*, of the conditions of historical fiction, the very conditions that have usually been cited as the reasons for the novel's failure: research, textual denseness, overwhelming detail. That this logic has gone largely unnoticed might have something to do with the novel's explicit argument between Romola and Tito, the reason for their first estrangement: Tito's decision to sell and disperse Bardo's library. Romola's anger and feeling of betrayal at this act (a mirror of Baldassare's feeling of betrayal by Tito) and her abortive efforts to reclaim the library begin her growth and lead her into the historical controversies of the narrative; her separation from Tito takes her to Savonarola, which takes her into the center of the novel's thematics. If we accept the claim that Romola's outraged defense of the sanctity of Bardo's library—the sanctity, that is, of both familial and cultural memory and its integrity—is the beginning of her liberation, we must also accept the failure of that outrage; Romola's liberation is secured while the library itself, and the immensity of the past that it contains and that demands a caretaker, is lost beyond hope of retrieval, dispersed among buyers from Milan and France. The liberation, that is, is explicitly from Tito's cavalier attitude toward the past but implicitly from that past itself; Romola is permitted the feeling of injured family piety while denied the numbing task of maintaining the specificities — books, relics, antiquities — which constituted it.[19] Thus a certain sleight-of-hand nostalgia occurs: Romola can venerate and miss the past *only when it has disappeared*. It is not that Eliot avoids the difficult moral dilemma of how Bardo's request to save the library could be lived; it is that the novel locates its morality in a nostalgia that combines an appreciation of the past and a separation (or, to use my earlier term, *disconnection*) from the particularities of that past. Romola's sanctified memory of her father is more possible when the dispersed objects of his life have fled out of the city, when, therefore, that memory can be condensed into a vague image of beneficent paternity and wounded family pride.

So, the forgetting or leavetaking of particularized forms of the past: such is the structure that links Baldassare's pathology to Romola's "inattention" or "capriciousness," her regret for a terminally disconnected past. How, in general, does such a disconnection occur — what replaces the particularized past? The question first arises when Bardo, excited at the news that the mysterious Greek stranger who has come to him for employment has been on expeditions, asks if Tito can make a written record of his travels; Tito "must recall everything, to the minutest trace left in your memory," Bardo demands (114). In particular, Bardo wants — in the way typical of antiquarians, in a manner that might remind us of Eliot's gamurras and gamurrinas — a record of any texts or inscriptions Tito might have seen. Tito, however, replies that "in the case of inscriptions copied in memorable scenes, rendered doubly impressive by the sense of risk and adventure, it may have happened that my retention of written characters has been weakened" (111). The "memorable," which here is limited to sight and the body (the body's risks and exposure), does not include the "written characters" so dear to Bardo's scholarship. The paradigm set up here — the body as center of the memorable, texts as fungible, erasable, difficult to "retain"— is carried out rigidly throughout the novel. The etiology of Baldassare's own disease, his strange recovery and relapse, is dependent on it.

Baldassare does, famously, recover his Greek literacy at one point — crucially, immediately after a failed attack on Tito, in which his dagger has broken and he has been tossed to the ground. The exertion the attack requires, and the consequent exhaustion, leads directly to a fortuitous and unexpected mnemonic recovery: "But in that bodily helplessness he sat surrounded, not by the habitual dimness and vanishing shadows, but by the clear images of the past; he was living again in an unbroken course through that life which seemed a long preparation for the taste of bitterness" (404). At which point, he glances at a volume of Pausanias he had bought in an attempt to restore his memory: "an hour or two ago he had been looking hopelessly at that page, and it had suggested no more meaning to him than if the letters had been black weather-marks on a wall; but at this moment they were once more the magic signs that conjure up a world" (405). When his body is negated by failure and exhaustion, his memory suddenly returns; more than ever helpless physically, Baldassare is restored to his recollections, both of a personal kind—the "unbroken course through that life"—and of a scholarly kind. Memory and the body, it seems, are in direct opposition, each emerging as a result of the other's feebleness. When the resumption of a fully mnemonic life relapses into amnesia, it is because of the renewed claims of the body; when Tito once again denies him, at the pivotal supper in the Rucellai Gardens, Baldassare feels a "shock of rage," a "strange bodily effect" (423) that issues in the return of his amnesia.

All of which turns Baldassare into the most vivid example the novel produces of an amnesiac dependent on the body, on vision and immediate image, and on, above all, sensation. We might recall at this point Collins's sensationalized amnesiacs, but of even greater relevance is the system presented to us by Brontë's narratives, where the legible signs of the body obviate the need for memory or mnemonic excavation. The stress in *Romola* is less upon the legibility of the body, however, than its inherent ability to make memory waver, to make it unnecessary. Thus the importance of Baldassare reaching into his tunic and fingering the poniard intended for Tito, "feeling the edge abstractedly, as if he needed the sensation to keep alive his ideas" (533); thus the significance of Tito's inability to recall written texts while the sensations of danger and sublimity from his travels remain with him. The very presentness of the body, its sensations and its perceptions, are continually overtaking the power of memory in the novel, as if a weakened retrospect must yield to the force of the still-active. We see it in Savonarola's fierce bodily imagination, picturing the flames of the trial by fire; we see it in Baldassare's inability to remember Tito's name, because the "very force with which the image of Tito pressed upon him seemed to expel any verbal sign" (460).

Thus the contradiction of this historical narrative, whereby what is not available to bodily sensation, bodily imagination, bodily perception—in general, texts, cultural memory, historical fact—becomes ever more difficult for characters within the novel to access. We may start with the "book," with perhaps the unrolling parchments that Romola's brother Dino warns her of in describing his vision, but we continually come back to the body, to a collection of images and objects (Tito's face, a large fire, a poniard) that are not parts of the past but active parts of the present, active in the way that they implicate, threaten, or assuage the body—the way a poniard can pierce, a fire can burn, a face can stare back. This most general fact about the mnemonic processes of *Romola*—the way the "idea of research" or a particularized memory gives way to the body's presentness—takes us some of the way to an investigation of how Eliot's historical fiction lifts the past into the present, making memory itself unnecessary. To continue, however, it is useful to look more closely at those objects that surround her characters: if the novel is interested in the erasure of texts, we must keep in mind that the texts so erased or negated are only part of a larger class of objects that might be similarly threatening.

Souvenirs, Relics, the Antimemorial

What might be the status of objects in the historical novel? If nineteenth-century realism depends on a certain density of recognizable, familiarized objects to validate its transparency, what occurs when that density is transferred to a past world—often more polarized, violent, or exotic than the world *realism* usually describes—where objects are inescapably markers of (historical, personal) memory? Those objects that stand out, then, can never be merely neutral, merely part of an *effet du réel*; they are carriers of remembrance and as such bear the burden of how remembrance is to be negotiated. Attempts to taxonomize historical fiction usually turn on the meaning of objects within it, as in Avrom Fleishman's definition: "But what is the characteristic of historical fiction that distinguishes it from other kinds of poesis? This must be the particularity of the past which it treats: it is, after all, a novel, filled with named objects which create a virtual world, as populated as the past world it represents."[20] But insofar as these "particular" objects are also past objects, their presence creates a problem for the Victorian novel, which tends to use objects, such as Fanny Price's souvenirs, to signal the cancellation of the past and which tends to work against any threatening "particularity" of memory.

Indeed, that is the way we see objects functioning in perhaps the initial British historical novel, Scott's 1814 *Waverley*, where the souvenir governs the plot's closural motions. Under disguise, Edward Waverley slips into Edinburgh, where he meets the former landlady of his Highland compatriot, Fergus Mac-Ivor or Vich Ian Vohr; he accepts her invitation to stay the night:

> When he entered the parlour, his heart swelled to see Fergus' bonnet, with the white cockade, hanging beside the little mirror.
> "Ay," said Mrs Flockhart, sighing, as she observed the direction of his eyes, "the poor Colonel bought a new ane just the day before the march, and I winna let them tak that ane doon, but just to brush it

ilka day mysell, and whiles I look at it till I just think I hear him cry to
Callum to bring him his bonnet, as he used to do when he was gang-
ing out.—It's unco silly—the neighbours ca' me a Jacobite—but they
may say their say—I am sure it's no for that—but he was as kind-
hearted a gentleman as ever lived, and as weel-fa'rd too."[21]

When Fergus has been thus condensed to a souvenir, the souvenir acts to
disconnect not only Waverley from his Jacobite past—he experiences a
nostalgic regret on seeing it, because it will never be worn again—but also
to disconnect Fergus from political strife; Mrs. Flockhart announces that
she does not keep the bonnet out of any factional sympathy but because
"he was as kind-hearted a gentleman as ever lived," the past tense (a bit in
advance of Fergus's actual demise) serving to put Fergus in the past as far
as the narrative is concerned: *that*—civil strife, national upheaval, illicit
cathexes of various sorts—is, the souvenir announces, over. Not content
with one closural souvenir, Scott gives us several, including the famous
painting of Fergus and Waverley in their Highland dress that hangs in
Tully-Veolan, the estate of the Bradwardine family, into which Waverley
marries; alongside it hang "the arms which Waverley had borne in the unfortunate civil war."[22] Like no other souvenir, perhaps, the weapons—
which Waverley expressly arranges to preserve—announce the cancellation
of the past; they will not be taken off the wall, they will not be used, and in
their purely personal, purely poignant interest, they imply the passage of
Jacobite unrest into nostalgic memory.

Thus one solution to the problem of how particular, charged objects
that persist over time—that, in fact, speak of a troubling past—can be altered or situated in historical fiction in order to defuse the glamour, appeal,
or consequence of that past: the souvenir. It is the common solution to the
problem of objects, not simply in British historical fiction but in the Victorian social novel, where objects end their narrative careers as signs of their
own obsolescence. In the middle of *Romola*, however, we see that solution
in the process of being revised. In Eliot's historical fiction, objects are not allowed to rest as mere markers of the past's conclusion, inert in themselves,
but must be transferred from the world of memory to the world of present
activity and use; no significant object remains a souvenir or memorial, insofar as the past must be continually lifted into the present. If a souvenir is
a sign of the past's cancellation, Eliot's objects are usually signs of the past's
absence: if nothing is "past," memory is bypassed, unable to create uncomfortable chasms between previous pleasures and current dilemmas.

The object that first opens the way to the novel's theorizing about objects and memory is Romola's wedding ring, which she considers taking
off and returning to Tito before her first, unsuccessful attempt to flee Florence.[23] A contrary thought briefly occurs to her: why not turn the wed-

ding ring into a keepsake? "If that beloved Tito who had placed the be-
trothal ring on her finger was not in any valid sense the same Tito whom
she had ceased to love, why should she return to him the sign of their
union, and not rather retain it as a memorial?" (391). Why indeed? The answer is that no memorial can exist if nothing is "past"; the postulated two
Titos, a vanished faithful one and a present feckless one, cannot maintain
their separation: Tito is one, and thus to "memorialize" some prior version
of Tito is a logical fallacy. That is the conclusion Romola reaches as she de-
clines keeping the ring as a memorial and instead returns it to Tito in a
sealed envelope. Of course that envelope never reaches its destination —
Savonarola intercepts Romola's flight, compelling her to return to Florence and resume her marriage — thus further maintaining the object in its
space of actual use. The decision is of great thematic importance: it announces the novel's dominant attitude toward the object-world, which
might be termed the "antimemorial." Objects appear in the text not as signs
of the past's haunting presence or, in the way of souvenirs, as signs of the
past's cancellation, but as elements of the past *lifted into present use and import*, drained of their "pastness."

It is a rigidly unsentimental attitude, but not unsentimental in a manner that implies hardheartedness to the past's significance, beneficence, or
pathos; it simply rejects the notion that objects have a past life; it concentrates instead on present utility, present meaning. The process can be detected in many of the text's well-known objects — indeed, the narrative can
be said to be propelled by objects: by the wedding ring, by a lock of Tito's
hair that Tessa innocently shows Romola, by the necklace of Tessa's that
enables Romola to identify her after Tito's death, by Dino's crucifix, which
Romola stubbornly refuses to lock in Tito's tabernacle, preferring instead
to wear it as a sign of her continuing sympathy and identification with
Savonarola's movement. Tito's "shrine," built to encase and to in some sense
memorialize Dino's crucifix (memorialize it to deaden its power) is precisely the wrong gesture; when Romola takes it out of the painted tabernacle to wear it, she *activates* its symbolic and social potential, making it
meaningful in the current spheres of religious and political controversy
that she then turns to inhabit. Baldassare himself, who might be thought
to consider old objects as possible keys to his missing memory, resolutely
plumbs his souvenirs for something that can be converted to active life and
use. Finding his *breve*, a parchment pouch he has worn since boyhood, he
resolves to open it, despite the fact that it "was part of the piety associated
with such brevi, that they should never be opened" (340). The process of
activation is rapid and violent:

> It all rushed through his mind — the long years he had worn it, the
> far-off sunny balcony at Naples looking towards the blue waters,

where he had leaned against his mother's knee; but it made no moment of hesitation: all piety now was transmuted into a just revenge. He bit and tore till the doubles of parchment were laid open, and then — it was a sight that made him pant — there *was* an amulet. It was very small, but it was as blue as those far-off waters; it was an engraved sapphire, which must be worth some gold ducats. Baldassare no sooner saw those possible ducats than he saw some of them exchanged for a gold poniard. (340)

Which he in fact does: the amulet is sold and the poniard obtained. No more vivid example is offered in the text of the way the past-life of objects is *exchanged*, either literally or figuratively, for a life that can be effective in the present. Significant as well is the essentially timeless nature of so many of the objects here (although the exotic *breve* is an exception): a wedding ring, a lock of hair, a necklace, none of them so redolent of a vanished Florentine way of life that their historical meaning would overwhelm their personal meanings for Eliot's characters. They point, in fact, toward a romance or even folklore tradition, so drained of historicity are these objects; they have the totemistic quality of what Vladimir Propp termed "magical agents."[24] If an object does have a bit of antiquarian interest, such as the *breve*, it is converted quickly into a more homely, more thrilling — or more sensational — object: a dagger.[25]

Ultimately, however, the negotiation of objects in Eliot's novel is more subtle than Baldassare's physical exchange; the narrative of one such object, Tito's onyx ring, given to him by Baldassare, leads us to the more complex idea of *recognition*, the present's conquering of the past, which *Romola* uses as structure and motif. The story of the onyx ring reminds us of the idea of an "unremembered past": a past whose continual reentrance into present activity negates its very pastness, negates the need to "remember" it. It begins with Tito's sudden discovery of the ring in his wallet, which he opens to find a bauble to satisfy Tessa: "'Ah, my ring!' he exclaimed, slipping it on the forefinger of his right hand. 'I forgot to put it on again this morning. Strange, I never missed it!'" (162). With the note of *resumption* we first see it: it enters the text in the process of being resurrected, brought back to active use, and this switch from forgotten absence to sudden use will characterize its frequent appearances in the rest of the text.

Through his wearing it, Tito is recognized by Romola's brother Dino, who carries with him a slip of paper — reading "Tito Melema, aged twenty-three, with a dark, beautiful face, long dark curls, the brightest smile, and a large onyx ring on his right forefinger" (164) — which identifies Tito and permits Dino to give him a message from the still-alive Baldassare. Through the sale of the ring, an attempt of Tito's to avoid any further recognition, Baldassare sees it on the hand of a stranger at Genoa, enabling him to begin the inquiries that lead to his location of Tito in Florence and that lead as well to his first suspicions that his adopted son has not cared to ransom him out of slavery. In short, the ring in its passages from Tito's hand to the hand of Bratti the pedlar to the hand of the Genovese stranger keeps Baldassare and Tito in a present-day collision course, permitting Tito's betrayal to escape the realm of the merely mnemonic (an affair of conscience) and allowing it to take a repeatedly active shape in the streets and loggias of Florence. In each case that the ring *resumes* its role in the plot, it functions as a memory lifted immediately into active use and consequence — as soon as it is "recognized," future plans are made, future intersections sketched out. Baldassare's recognition of the ring, which "stirred the dominant fibres" (337) of his recollective faculties, allows him to achieve his first purposeful action of the narrative: a journey to Florence and a search for his son. What is most noticeable about this vexed ring is not its power of turning plot attention backward — indeed it elicits no specific reminiscences other than the fact of its having been given to Tito by Baldassare — but its power of *propelling narrative forward*. However much the ring forces a return of the repressed, one must also bear in mind that these returns elicit no narrative flashbacks of any detail; instead, a series of tactical decisions relating to the future take over. The ring's power is, more specifically, the power of turning elements of the more or less distant past (a father–child relationship, a gift, a betrayal) into current, embodied realities. In this the ring merely condenses the novel's dominant practice.

The lesson of the ring can be found within Tito's self-deluding reasoning before his decision to sell it:

> Why should he keep the ring? It had been a mere sentiment, a mere fancy, that had prevented him from selling it with the other gems; if he had been wiser and had sold it, he might perhaps have escaped that identification by Fra Luca. It was true that it had been taken from Baldassare's finger and put on his own as soon as his young hand had grown to the needful size; but there was really no valid good to anybody in those superstitious scruples about inanimate objects. The ring had helped towards the recognition of him. Tito had begun to dislike recognition, which was a claim from the past. (196)

But what kind of "claim from the past" is this? It is a precisely a claim on present activity: it forces the "recognized" to recognize, above all, the refusal of the past to be past, and it therefore shortcircuits any particularized memory; what, after all, does anyone "remember" about the onyx ring? No specificities or detailed recollections spring from its "claim," which is a sort of memory that retains *only what is of immediate and present concern*. Tito does not remember any details (words, sentiments) about the original passing on of the ring but recalls only the threat (a threat to bodily safety as well as social prestige) that continued recognition might present. If the attempt to eliminate recognition by selling the ring fails, it is because of the tightly conservative energies of Eliot's narrative, in which — with a neat circularity that should remind us of Dickens's concordances — if an object is remembered, it is because it will reappear, as the ring does in Genoa, or at least be converted to an object with more present-oriented potential.

This is not the system set up by Scott's closural mementos or Austen's souvenirs, where objects dead-end any retrospects associated with them; in the world of Eliot's historical narrative memory is swept aside by the activating force of reemerging artifacts, which enter the text not as archeological finds — as enigmatic fragments of a rich past whose buried presence they imply — but as suddenly useful and vibrant objects, whose import lies ahead rather than behind. "Mrs. Lewes is very well and buried in musty old antiquities," Lewes wrote in late 1861 to John Blackwood, "which she will have to vivify."[26] It is a picture of Eliot that has persisted in critical commentary; but in the common emphasis on the weight of scholarly detail in *Romola*, the process of vivification, which Lewes suggested Eliot would "have" to perform, has remained more mysterious and less understood. It is enough to remember, however, that the objects in Eliot's narrative are antimemorials that work against the mustiness of antiquities and toward the resurrection of "recognition," which stretches beyond the object-world to influence the novel's deepest accounts of perception and remembrance.

Recognition, Reactivation

Describing a painting suggested by Tito's looks, Piero di Cosimo describes the fear that he feels Tito's features so readily accomodate: "He's seeing a ghost — that fine young man. I shall finish it [the painting] some day, when I have settled what sort of ghost is the most terrible — whether it should look solid, like a dead man come to life, or half transparent, like a mist" (247). The answer that we are by this point in the narrative prepared for — having just heard of an adoptive father of Tito's — is the solid ghost, the dead man come to life; and indeed that might be the most accurate way to describe Eliot's turn away from particular, personal memory in *Romola*: toward a present-moment *solidity* of the past, where only the still-solid facts of memory, those available to actual perception, can enter narrative.[27]

Let us begin with a thought experiment from *Romola*'s own pages. Walking in the daylight of Florence, Tito, engaged as an aide to a political meeting between Florentine and French emissaries, is greeted by a chaos of perceptual details: the decoration of a piazza, the laughter of a crowd, the effort to translate Tuscan jokes into inoffensive but humorous French, and, from a corner of the scene, a procession of three prisoners, being led by

French soliders through the streets. The atmosphere leaves little room for interiorized comment or elaborate acts of consciousness—everything in the scene (quite painterly in its composition) is devoted to the simpler motions of sight and sound, an urban perception that is sufficiently complex and varied to occupy the individuals within it. At that moment the general dispersal of the scene concentrates in one burst of noise and blur: the escape of the prisoners from their fetters; all three flee, but one, the most visibly aged, moves directly up to Tito and his group and grabs Tito by the arm.

> It was Tito Melema who felt that clutch. He turned his head, and saw the face of his adoptive father, Baldassare Calvo, close to his own.
> The two men looked at each other, silent as death: Baldassare, with dark fierceness and a tightening grip of the soiled worn hands on the velvet-clad arm; Tito, with cheeks and lips all bloodless, fascinated by terror. It seemed a long while to them—it was but a moment.
> The first sound Tito heard was the short laugh of Piero di Cosimo, who stood close by him and was the only person that could see his face.
> "Ha, ha! I know what a ghost should be now."
> "This is another escaped prisoner," said Lorenzo Tornabuoni. "Who is he, I wonder?"
> "*Some madman, surely*," said Tito. (283)

It is the scene of recognition to which *Romola* has built since its inception, and it is skilfully managed. The question to ask of it is this: what sort of memory is this, that issues in the materialization of a father whose permanent disappearance (through death or slavery) had been presumed? What sort of memory is it that fills the gap left by Tito's first shocked recognition of Baldassare?

The more general version of this question would run as follows: what sort of memory is it that is identical with perception? In recognizing his father, Tito merges a past fact that he had thought confined to recollection with present reality; in the process, memory itself is conspicuously disabled. The "shock of recognition," as it is commonly called, that makes mnemonic image and perceptual reality merge, excises any specific memory itself; like a small-scale trauma, recognition makes available to consciousness only that *memory that is identical with what is being perceived*. As a result, only the most deeply habitual impulses of character ensue; Tito, as is consistent with his self-preserving habit of thought, immediately—without the kind of retrospect-filled pause of misgiving or regret that might have occurred had the memory presented to him not been so perceptually real—utters a lie plausible enough that no spark of recollection can be noticed by any other member of the scene. A lie that is not only effective at the present moment but instrumental in the future: it enables Baldassare to be captured and taken to a Florentine "asylum," and it sets off in Baldassare enough self-doubts about the effect of amnesia on his own sanity that the term "madman" becomes, perversely, more and more accurate.

I have called the scene a "thought experiment" not merely to abstract it momentarily from the narrative in which it is the initial climax but to stress how its elaborately lengthened and carefully structured arrangement — the set-piece quality of the chapter, with its movement from a lavishly detailed perceptual chaos to a single moment of glance and reaction — is in fact posing a question and providing an answer that the rest of the novel will repeat in various ways. The question posed is, what kind of memory — what form of the past's manifestation — is most common in this world? The answer is, as we have seen, a form of memory that wedges *only that part of the past that can be activated in perception* into the fabric of the narrative.[28] What the scene initiates is a wide-ranging consideration of the possible forms this "recognition" might take and its many possible ethical consequences, for it is slightly misleading to introduce the idea of "recognition" in the context of a moment of denial. Romola shortly before has had her own moment of recognition, when her dying brother Dino, under his Dominican name Fra Luca, asks her to visit him: "The next moment her eyes met Fra Luca's as they looked up at her from the crucifix, and she was absorbed in that pang of recognition which identified this monkish emaciated form with the image of her fair young brother" (209). A discontinuity of experience is overcome by a mnemonic style that sees persistence and identity, that "recognizes" rather than identifying the lost or the sundered. Whether the recognition issue in callous denial or a poignant renewal of affection, the memory presented to us in these scenes is confined to that which is *still present*. It is, one might say, an account on the perceptual level of the relevance, concordance, and integrity of the fictional autobiography. It is perhaps experientially different from our definition of nostalgia, but it functions in a similar manner: if nostalgic remembrance disconnects a threateningly attractive past in order to make free the psyche for the present and its demands, Eliot's "recognition" works to simply eliminate any form of remembrance that even acknowledges a past not still part of a perceptual present.[29]

This is the overall task of Eliot's historical fictions, which we have seen in miniature in her arrangement of objects in *Romola*: to dememorialize the past through its activation in the present. It is an objective large enough to motivate historical fiction itself and specific enough to govern the actions of plot and character within the fictions, as in this example from the later *Felix Holt* (1866), when Esther Lyon thinks of her love for the imprisoned Felix:

She began to look on all that had passed between herself and Felix as something not buried, but embalmed and kept as a relic in a private sanctuary. The very entireness of her preoccupation about him, the perpetual repetition in her memory of all that had passed between them, tended to produce this effect. She lived with him in the past; in the future she seemed shut out from him.[30]

So the logic of *Felix Holt*'s narrative, therefore, is to take this "relic" and dememorialize it, to make it live again — to take what might have been consigned to the past (and might therefore harden into a thwarted desire, a cathexis denied discharge) and make it reemerge in the present of the narrative. It is a process identical to that which controls *Romola*, but the passage from *Felix Holt* is worth citing here because of its strange and telling terminology. In essence, what we see in Esther's thoughts and *Romola*'s narrative is a neat reversal of the logic of nostalgia in order to achieve the identical end. Whereas an Austenian nostalgic like Fanny Price collects relics in order to disable the pull of the past that they symbolize — to condense the particularities of memory into one object that might then cancel those particularities — Eliot's historical characters refuse literal or figurative "relics" and insist instead on the activation of the past in present perception; and if they seem resigned to a memory of "relics," the machinery of the narrative will relieve them of that fate, restoring to them that which they thought was past. But the aim of both these styles of remembrance is the same: the elimination of a memory of alluring, traumatic, or otherwise detailed facts and emotions in favor of a memory that works in the service of the present moment.

It is such a consistent process in *Romola* that even the memory of an emotion will create an identical version of that emotion, shifting the mental process in question from memory to repetition. When Romola returns, much later in the novel, to the scene of her initial "recognition" of Dino as Fra Luca, she does not remember the event so much as *activate* it as a present impulse:

> Once more looked at by those sad frescoed figures which had seemed to be mourning with her at the death of her brother Dino, it was inevitable that something of that scene should come back to her; but the intense occupation of her mind with the present made the remembrance less a retrospect than an indistinct recurrence of impressions which blended themselves with her agitating fears, as if her actual anxiety were a revival of the strong yearning she had once before brought to this spot — to be repelled by marble rigidity. (571)

The "intense occupation of her mind with the present": less an aberration occasioned by the crisis in Florentine affairs that brings her to Savonarola's headquarters than an accurate, general description of not only character but plot within Eliot's historical fiction. It is a present-oriented process that, as here, transforms "retrospect" into a (crucially) "indistinct recurrence" of the past—indistinct because the past itself loses its details and precise contours when it is manifested only in present perception and not in any mental imaging. If nostalgia turns the past into vague, formulaic, named units, Eliot's "recognition" makes the past indistinguishable entirely; how to separate the strands of past and present that converge in the "recognition" of Baldassare by Tito, or the "recognition" of Dino by Romola? As with a more traditionally nostalgic narrative, but through a different process, recognition-as-memory achieves a washing-out of the past's specificities. This is not, of course, what is promised by the heavily *researched* nature of the text, but as we have seen through the pivotal examples of Baldassare and Bardo, the novel's turn to personal memory as the key level of recollection helps to negate the particularized forms of memory that historical research implies.

Recognition does not merely save the novel and its inhabitants from antiquarian, particularized, painful, or perilously attractive memories; it also opens the novel up to the sort of overtly symbolic texture that elsewhere—in the pastoral realism of *Adam Bede* or the more studied, scientized version of *Middlemarch*—Eliot works hard to excise. When Romola is washed ashore in a plague-afflicted village after her attempt at oblivion at sea, the first few villagers who see her (a tall, elegant woman carrying a child) "recognize" her, at least initially, as the Madonna and Child. "She carries a pitcher in her hand—to fetch water for the sick," a young man thinks as she approaches. "It is the Holy Mother, come to take care of the people who have the pestilence" (644). It is a verdict that the novel is in no hurry to deny. It is also rooted not in a feverish mysticism but in a rather more hardheaded acceptance of the uncanny: the village priest who eventually sees Romola is struck by the strange, iconic resemblance, all the while believing that he is witnessing a less-than-supernatural woman and child; but the peculiar mixture implied by "recognition" persists, in which a past image or field of images (the symbology of the Holy Mother) is *activated* in the present simply through perception. Romola is not the Madonna, nor is the child she carries the Christ; but the collective imagery of the Virgin merges with her, making it difficult to separate, perceptually, the activated (or "recognized") symbol from the more prosaic woman, the tenor from the vehicle. Which is to say that the same mechanism that protects the novel from a particularized past propels it toward a very *general* realm of symbolic connotation—if anything is strange about this scene, it is the way it contrasts so sharply with the densely particularized world that historical novels are supposed to represent.

There is a sense, therefore, that recognition is deeply allied to abstraction: although it makes the past *real*, it makes the past real by draining it of precisely those more specific elements that contextualize it as the past. It is a process close enough to the modern neuropsychological term "source amnesia," noted earlier in its relation to associationist memory: the inability to locate a mental image as fact or fantasy, as actual perception or secondhand imagination. Recognition as, through its abstracting tendency, a form of amnesia: that is the conclusion to which we are led; a "forgetting" of the distance between Baldassare-as-father and Baldassare-as-prisoner, a "forgetting" of Dino's desertion from the Bardi family through identifying him as that same long-lost brother; a forgetting, that is, of the lost, painful, particular past in the process of seeing a revivified, if somewhat abstracted, present. All the pervasive recognitions of *Romola* act to keep objects (rings, daggers) and characters (Baldassare, Dino) relatively abstract, their histories less important than the immediate impact they have when they reenter the narrative in bursts of sudden, dramatic action. If Romola is recognized as the Holy Mother, we similarly "recognize" Baldassare as Revenge, or Dino as Mysticism, or Tito as Betrayal; their pasts, the complicated turnings of fortune that lead them to their positions in the narrative, are obscured in favor of the narrative's "intense occupation with the present," the present as mirror image of an abstracted, activated past.

Romola's Fading

Everywhere we look in *Romola* we see Florence in the process of losing its luster: cracking, chipping, fading, wearing away. When Nello the barber takes Tito on a brief tour of the city, we are shown Ghiberti's famous Baptistery doors, "the quaint octagon of San Giovanni in front of them, showing its unique gates of storied bronze, which still bore the somewhat dimmed glory of their original gilding. The inlaid marbles were then fresher in their pink, and white, and purple, than they are now, when the winters of four centuries have turned their white to the rich ochre of well-mellowed meerschaum" (76). That is the Florence of Tito and Romola: halfway along its life-span from "original gilding" to current decrepitude, with the direction of the trajectory already evident — nothing here will get fresher; it will only continue to age.[31] Taken inside Bardo's library, we see his "books and antiquities":

> The colour of these objects was chiefly pale or sombre: the vellum bindings, with their deep-ridged backs, gave little relief to the marble, livid with long burial; the once splendid patch of carpet at the farther end of the room had long been worn to dimness; the dark bronzes wanted sunlight upon them to bring out their tinge of green, and the

sun was not yet high enough to send gleams of brightness through the narrow windows that looked on the Via de'Bardi. (93)

This is not, on the face of it, the vivid activation of Eliot's "recognition," which would seem to be something else. And indeed, just as Collins's sensation novels arise out of the intersection between a familiarly nostalgic closure and amnesiac characters who pathologize that nostalgia, Eliot's novel reverses the process of nostalgic vagueness through recognition while retaining nostalgic vagueness as a method of finally ending the constant, often violent shocks of recognition that propel the bulk of the narrative. Behind the activations of the past in the present there is a world of fading, of increasing vagueness and indistinctness, signaled by the soon-to-be-mellowed Florentine architecture and antiquities but increasingly present in the world of human affairs. Eliot describes several parades, processions, and festivals in the course of the novel—it is dotted with them, with a frequency her other texts usually reserve for seasonal changes—but as *Romola* proceeds, we see these urban occasions with a greater sense of *blur*: facts and individuals are beginning to be combined together; the vague starts to become a fact of narrative presentation. Let us consider the procession that carries the Tabernacle of the Madonna dell'Impruneta into the city, in which various groups walk, with particular identities hidden, obscured, or blurred by the very act of walking in the mass. First come a selection of Florentine youth; then the mysterious Companies of Discipline, wearing a costume that revealed only the eyes:

> Every one knew that these mysterious forms were Florentine citizens of various ranks, who might be seen at ordinary times going about the business of the shop, the counting-house, or the State; but no member now was discernible as son, husband, or father. They had dropped their personality, and walked as symbols of a common vow. (453)

Then the groups come in faster succession—the Benedictines, the Franciscans, the Augustinians, the Carmelites, and finally the Dominicans: "One black mantle parted by white after another, one tonsured head after another" (454). Moving faster and faster, the event starts to generate a rate too quick to yield to a more specific gaze, and particularities (of dress, of stature, of expression) fade into general categories. Just as Austen's nostalgic closures insist on general names to seal off the troubling details of the past—even the past of the novel itself—Eliot's historical narrative begins to drain off particularities gradually, so that large combinations of action and character are discernible rather than any smaller scale disruptions. After all, when Tito and Baldassare are found dead, Baldassare having strangled Tito and lost his life in the process, they can no longer be dissociated. "It was not possible to separate them" (639), we are told of the bodies in a combined grip, which can also be said for the characters's functions as well: they are to be remembered as one, Betrayal and Revenge, no longer analyzable by memory into discrete units. The text leaves them as a single entity, part of the grouping process—a process of indistinctness as well—that nostalgic closures habitually bring about. They are, that is, no longer "recognizable"—no longer capable of being brought to life, activated in any sense—and therefore can be left to the disconnecting elisions of nostalgic vagueness: a communal nostalgia as well, for the bodies are brought back into the city "that notice might be given to the Eight" (639). We pass, that is, from the complexly "unremembered" past of recognition, in which the past needs no remembering because it is identical to perception, to the "unremembered" past of nostalgia, in which the past calls for no recollection because it is firmly sundered from the present.

If we would investigate further this switch from recognition back to nostalgic naming, disconnection, vagueness, and communality, there is no better place to look than the enigmatic passages in which Romola slips out of Florence on a boat, arrives at the plague-stricken village, nurses its inhabitants back to life, and returns to Florence once again. No other part of Eliot's novel has inspired a greater variety of intriguing, if often bewildered, commentary—the bewilderment stemming from the strangely ahistorical nature of the scenes, which suddenly lose the support of the research and antiquarian detail that seems elsewhere almost too evident. Perhaps Miriam Bailin has expressed the general critical sentiment best:

> Given the well-known difficulty George Eliot experienced in the composition of *Romola* and the vast accumulation of historical information and detail by which she continually postponed its commencement, there is something breathtaking about the way she so utterly levels the huge, variegated edifice built up by her own labors and renders its complexity nugatory in her symbolic representation of human relations in the stricken village.[32]

If such self-negating gestures, such sudden changes of technique, are breathtaking, it is because they are so difficult to understand: why would Eliot, one of the nineteenth century's more self-aware and cautious novelists, script such a disjunction of styles within one text; or, having scripted it, why would she not be at more pains to hide the fissure? The sort of language that inspires such commentary might be illustrated by the following instance of Romola's time in the village:

> So they all went together down the slope, and that morning the sufferers saw help come to them in their despair. There were hardly

more than a score alive in the whole valley; but all of these were comforted, most were saved, and the dead were buried.

In this way days, weeks, and months passed with Romola till the men were digging and sowing again, till the women smiled at her as they carried their great vases on their heads to the well, and the Hebrew baby was a tottering tumbling Christian, Benedetto by name, having been baptised in the church on the mountain-side. (649)

When Lukács raised "the question of *language* in the historical novel," he spoke of the "modernizing of feelings, ideas and thoughts, combined with archaeological faithfulness towards things and customs of no concern to us"— a symptom familiar enough, perhaps, elsewhere in the text; the problem with this passage is that it fits into no recognizable "question of language" in historical fiction at all.[33] The restriction to general nouns, to the vaguest possible terms of quantity (*all* were comforted, *some* were saved), and to units of time whose mounting imprecision frustrates any chronological framework— days, weeks, months— is from, one senses, a discourse directly opposed to the specificities normally demanded of a historicized narrative. Add to this a catalogue of actions, such as succoring, feeding, and nursing, whose symbolics are obvious, and what seems to be occuring here is a generic shift: from the historical novel to some other kind of language.

Therefore the number of terms attached to this section of *Romola* has multiplied. For George Levine, in a lucid argument, the plague-village scenes are a "fable"; for Margaret Homans they are Romola's "apotheosis"; for Gillian Beer they are part of Eliot's "testamental simplicity"; for Susan Winnett they comprise a "legend."[34] All of these attempts, however carefully mapped or tonally accurate, fail to see the connection between the strange "fading" of Eliot's concluding movements and the processes of the rest of the text; rather than resolving or bridging the disjunction of styles, these readings insist on that disjunction as a way of preserving the uniqueness of the plague-village moments, their stylistic courageousness. What I would suggest that we are seeing here instead is a continuation of the Victorian preference for nostalgic dilution or fading at closural moments— an extension of the novel's concern, which is shared with the other Victorian fictions I have up to this point considered, to eliminate the specificities and nagging details of memory in favor of something more generally *useful*. Up to this point in the text that work has been carried out by the process of "recognition," which can be considered as a sort of recycling machine for memory, whereby what had been an element of the past is brought back into active perception so that it can be understood quickly, handled, transformed from disabling trauma or obsessive reminiscence to utility. With the plague scenes Eliot turns back to the nostalgic solutions of Austen, to the language-formations we have learned to identify with nostalgic vagueness, albeit with a severance from the more densely realist context that surrounded Austen's closural dilutions. The import of both "recognition" and "fading away," however, are the same. As she guides the plot to its conclusion, Eliot guides the reader *back* to an earlier novelistic solution to particularized memory rather than *forward* to an experimental or innovative style. Indeed, if any part of *Romola* could be considered truly in advance of contemporary fictional technique, the account of memory-as-perception, and the way such an account offers a complex and highly sensationalized way to describe *a consciousness without obsessive or continual remembering*, is perhaps the facet of the text least determined by previous fictional solutions, and it points the way to the more dramatic condensations of perception, object, and memory in Hardy's mature work.

But in the chapters called "Drifting Away" and "Romola's Waking" we are on more familiar ground. Romola is inspired by a story of Boccaccio, read in childhood, to take to the sea and leave her fate in its hands; when she first leaves the shore, however, the result is disappointment: "Had she found anything like the dream of her girlhood? No. Memories hung upon her like the weight of broken wings that could never be lifted -- memories of human sympathy which even in its pains leaves a thirst that the Great Mother has no milk to still" (590). What is at stake here is a search for an amnesia of a sort — one that would efface the signs of narrative Romola has up to this point undergone, as if once that past was canceled its determining influence on the present would no longer be felt; it is a nostalgic cleansing that Romola is after, and that the novel will provide. A renewal in present utility, a safety in the past's vague summary: if Romola's nursing a plague village is not where heroines from Austen or Brontë would find such salvation, the nostalgic formula is the same.

For when Romola wakes in her boat, having landed on a strange shore, the formula has become a reality:

> She lay motionless, hardly watching the scene; rather, feeling simply the presence of peace and beauty. While we are in our youth there can always come, in our early waking, moments when mere passive existence is itself a Lethe, when the exquisiteness of subtle indefinite sensation creates a bliss which is without memory and without desire. As the soft warmth penetrated Romola's young limbs, as her eyes rested on this sequestered luxuriance, it seemed that the agitating past had glided away like that dark scene in the Bargello, and that the afternoon dreams of her girlhood had really come back to her. (640–641)

This, then, is the rationale behind the fablelike tone of the upcoming scenes in the plague village: the replacement of specific, and consequential (most likely deforming), recollections by "subtle indefinite sensations." What Romola *was* was outlined by her father and filled in by Tito and Savonarola — was, that is, an inevitable outcome of the often passive experiences she had undergone in the past; what Romola *will be* is now a free space, open to definition because the claims of the past have been suspended. In its broadest terms nostalgia is a leavetaking of the past's resonances; this is what Romola arrives to find.[35]

We may find it difficult to read this heavily symbolic set of scenes, invested as they are in images of divine maternity, as owing something to Austenian methods; but when we arrive at the novel's concluding scene, a tableau in which Romola explains her own narrative to Lillo, the son of Tessa and Tito, we feel fully the impress of Victorian nostalgic closure. There is the requirement of Austenian "life-review," in which the major character (or characters) offers a brief and heavily diluted version of the past to others, giving a portable or easily communicable, easily named account of events so that the complexities of the narrative itself can become vaguer, nostalgized. There is also the requirement that this review assert a disconnection from the past narrated, that its past tense be in some real sense *terminal*. Echoes of Anne Elliot's final proclamations can be heard within Romola's assessment of Tito's conduct:

> There was a man to whom I was very near, so that I could see a great deal of his life, who made almost every one fond of him, for he was young, and clever, and beautiful, and his manners to all were gentle and kind. I believe, when I first knew him, he never thought of anything cruel or base. But because he tried to slip away from everything that was unpleasant, and cared for nothing else so much as his own safety, he came at last to commit some of the basest deeds — such as make men infamous. He denied his father, and left him to misery; he betrayed every trust that was reposed in him, that he might keep himself safe and get rich and prosperous. Yet calamity overtook him. (675)

What could be stranger — and yet, in the terms of Victorian fiction, more necessary — than that a richly researched historical narrative, putatively devoted to recovering a distant past with a certain level of veracious detail, should end on a note of such detached, vague, summarizable personal retrospect? Like the fading of Ghiberti's Baptistery doors, Romola's own memories have here achieved the same sort of named ("the basest deeds," "calamity"), vague ("he betrayed every trust"), communal, even pleasurable (insofar as the story has its just ethical conclusion) status that Austen's social concords always produced. Historical detail yields to personal memory throughout Eliot's novel, and that personal memory is allowed the final word, a word that is as stable and drained of specificity as possible. No single instance, no single fact, disturbs Romola's concluding meditation; and as for the antiquarian research with which the novel's composition started, that has receded into silence.

Memory against History

"Memory and history," Pierre Nora has recently written, "far from being synonymous, are thus in many respects opposed."[36] Even though this dichotomy is contested from a variety of disciplines and methodological positions, its force remains, and it seems to encapsulate a widely shared, even vernacularized, assumption.[37] When, one might ask, did this opposition begin? What cultural forces or vectors, what institutions, first severed the link between remembrance and historical record? A first glance would suggest that the historical novel, an enormous part of the historical consciousness of the nineteenth century, predated this division. The strange confidence that one could, through a mastery of texts, documents, minutiae of all sorts, reconstruct a vanished world — the operational starting-point, one assumes, of such efforts as *Romola* — points backward to a time when the mnemonic and the historical might not have been in such opposition. Lewes noted that Eliot's knowledge of fifteenth-century Florence was quite as personal to her, in its way, as her knowledge of the world of Silas Marner — a claim that, no matter how accurate, reflects a conceptual merging of memory (rural England) and history (Renaissance Italy).[38] Despite the severe effects that the "idea of research" could have on the body and mind of a novelist, it would seem that the idea itself demanded an alliance between the two terms: if its method was historical, its object was the recovery of a mass (cultural, national, racial) memory.

But this is merely what the historical novel *predicates* — its origin, not its completion. For in the range of cultural objects that may have inaugurated the thoroughgoing separation between personal memory and historical consciousness, the nineteenth-century historical novel must count as one prominent member. Not out of its avowed goal of recreation through detail but through its more deeply embedded narrative values, in which that detail is canceled by amnesiac or nostalgic characters and replaced by a series of purely personal, highly diluted summarizations — by, to use the crucial term, nostalgia. What is a nostalgic history like? Precisely a history that constructs two categories: a dangerous, useless, unwanted accumulation of detail (which one might, with Nora, call "history") and a safe, cleansed, vague personal memory, which in its very generalizable capacity can be retold, opened out to others. In *Romola*, we find those characters who represent the former category either exposed as maimed and ineffective or neutralized through an extreme amnesia, while the latter category is voiced through the sudden turn of the narrative away from physical concretion and social realism and toward the symbolic, the summary. The amnesias of the novel—both Baldassare's pathological version and Romola's nostalgic retention of only the outlines of Tito's narrative—split memory and history apart, turning the former into a method of self-construction, like Austen's heroines and their leavetakings, and the latter into an irrelevancy. When Nora wonders at the severance of memory and history, he wonders at the work performed by a *nostalgic* history, at the way in which the nineteenth century's "amnesiac selves" undo the determining link between past and present.

For as we have seen in Austen's nostalgic closures as well as *Romola*'s "recognitions," a nostalgic history is finally in the service of the future, of freeing it from the claims of the past: fixing the past in vague outline so that the constant work of adjustment and assimilation can continue, rejecting "history" and its intellectual processes. It is a theme Eliot would eventually return to in an explicit manner, in her *Impressions of Theophrastus Such*: "I at least am a modern with some interest in advocating tolerance," her narrator explains, "and notwithstanding an inborn beguilement which carries my affection and regret continually into an imagined past, I am aware that I must lose all sense of moral proportion unless I keep alive a stronger attachment to what is near, and a power of admiring what I best know and understand."[39] The quality of the "regret" here, as well as the "attachment," encapsulates not only the general workings of nineteenth-century nostalgia but also the effect of mixing that nostalgia with a historical project: a turn to the past that is immediately balanced by a stronger, more pressing turn to what is "near." A form of memory that is oddly future-directed dispenses with history: such is the strange, unexpected cultural work carried out by the historical novel, using a familiar nostalgia to negate the influence of the very history it set out to explore.

What, then, of Savonarola, the grand-historical figure who first captured Eliot's attention and interest? His confession, we are told, is a hopeless muddle of textual inaccuracy, scribal interpolation, personal wavering, incomprehensible formulae—nothing can be learned from it; no worthy evidence exists for Romola, who reads all accounts of Savonarola's final acts with little hope that anything can be gained from them. History, which we have learned throughout to associate with the transmission of texts, has nothing, finally, to offer, no clue to what passes in the mind of the novel's only possible historical hero. Even in the novel's concluding moments, a personal and highly vague memory of Romola's—perhaps, she wonders, "I should never have learned to love him if he had not helped me when I was in great need" (676)—replaces anything of greater scope or specificity. Savonarola's lesson, then, is his own disappearance, his own yielding to the logic of personal nostalgia. Silent and reserved as his final moments pass, he is the image of Nora's familiar dichotomy: history dissolving into the vague gratitude in Romola's remembrance, vividness passing into the generality of nostalgic memory.

CONCLUSION

Nostalgic Reading

Society from time to time obligates people not just to reproduce in thought previous events of their lives, but also to touch them up, to shorten them, or to complete them so that, however convinced we are that our memories are exact, we give them a prestige that reality did not possess.
—*Maurice Halbwachs*

A nostalgic looking-backward is, as I have argued throughout this book, necessarily a looking-forward — a dilution and disconnection of the past in the service of an encroaching future.[1] It would be odd, then, to write a history of nostalgia's emergence in nineteenth-century fiction without a look toward the future that nostalgic retrospection always implies. What was the future of nostalgia? One answer is its own cancellation: its replacement, at the end of the nineteenth century, by a host of psychologies and narrative techniques that restore an active, particularized memory to consciousness. Some of these cancellations have been mentioned previously, such as the turn that phrenological compartmentalization took toward a neurological search for the location of memory and memory failures or, more crucially, the development of a science of amnesia out of a novelistic consideration of cultural forgetfulness. Each of the preceding chapters has concluded with a brief glimpse of the later developments and alterations to the psychic structures they describe. The general picture suggested by these ventures into later psychological constructs is the closing of a circle: what had begun, in Austen's fiction, as the depathologization of a disease of memory ends by the reimposition of pathology. If this historical narrative can be called a progress, however, it is a progress-through-regress, in which the medicalized memories of eighteenth-century "nostalgia" reemerge in more contemporary and, for us, familiar guises: trauma, fixation, patho-logical amnesia. Insofar as the nostalgia of the nineteenth century led back to the pathologies it sought to erase, it prepared the way for its own disappearance — and thus our relation to the amnesiac self of the nine-teenth-century novel becomes itself nostalgic, as we wistfully recognize our separation from that vanished psychic structure.

But this is not the whole story; our relation to Victorian nostalgia is not solely *post festum*. Alongside this historical narrative of nostalgia's dis-appearance there is another narrative that must be considered, if the com-plexity of cultural history is to be respected: the persistence of nostalgia, and even its spread to adjacent spheres, that has been the work of the Vic-torian novel in our own time. Reading nostalgia means, in other words, studying nostalgic reading — a form of reading, and reception, that does not perish with the nineteenth century and that lives on today in the con-tinuing interaction between reader and novel. Victorian fiction does not merely give us access to a vanished mnemonic mode. It still teaches us the cultural habit of nostalgia, and teaches it with such success that much modern nostalgia is, in fact, a nostalgia for the Victorian. It is scarcely nec-essary to point to the various current phenomena, from television and film productions of nineteenth-century fiction to magazines illustrating Victo-rian decoration, that appeal to a seemingly inexhaustible nostalgia for the British nineteenth century. We misunderstand this nostalgia, however, if we search for the various *contents* of "Victoriana" that constitute its appeal; what most produces this nostalgia are the *processes* of nostalgic remem-brance instituted by Victorian fiction, which continues to teach us so effec-tively to remember that fiction in the pleasurably, and vaguely, discon-nected ways of nostalgic recollection. Next to a history of nostalgia, which would account for its rise to and fall from cultural dominance, a poetics of nostalgia — a way of explaining its continued efficacy in and through the Victorian novel — is necessary and has formed one of the goals of this book.

Understanding nostalgia as one of the primary end-products of the nineteenth-century novel, as part of the work performed by what Frederic Jameson has called the "coherent functional operation" of a text, solves several critical problems associated with Victorian fiction.[2] It solves ini-tially the mystery, however gratifying or professionally beneficial that mys-tery has been, of the persistent appeal of these novels, which have not needed much in the way of academic advocacy to maintain their popular-ity. It also solves the related problem of how these novels have managed to remain popular despite the difficulty a reader has in remembering them, in maintaining a mnemonic grasp of their difficult, detail-laden textures. This is a problem only insofar as one hypostatizes an academic or even New Critical reading habit, one interested in weaving dense thematic and mo-

NOSTALGIC READING   237

tivic connections, into the reading these novels ideally seek; if these novels instead work toward a genially forgetful, nostalgized retrospect, their density ceases to become a barrier to mass popularity.[3] Finally, one abiding problem of the Victorian novel — how its frequent claims to speak for the oppressed of various sorts fall victim to a meliorizing vision of social progress and closural happiness — is at least partially resolved when one understands the nostalgic processes of replacing painful particularities with pleasurable vagaries that shape these narratives.[4]

What I am making explicit here is a claim that has implicitly guided this book as a whole: the final target of the nostalgia of the Victorian novel is its reader. Not the least important thing that "happens" to readers of Brontë, Dickens, Collins, or even (to stretch backward) Austen is their placement in a strategy of nostalgic remembrance, whereby what they are asked to recall is by no means some "whole" of a text, or even its partial representative, but a carefully whittled-down, diluted set of vague facts that then work retrospectively to cast a haze over the mistakes, chaos, and loss that might have been a part of the narrative's fabric. The reader leaves one of these novels only after witnessing acts of forgetfulness and willed amnesia, and those acts are always, with more or less obviousness, models for the reader's own recollections. "Think only of the past as its remembrance gives you pleasure": the admonition echoes for the reader of *Pride and Prejudice*, and that admonition continues to function in other, very different, nineteenth-century narratives, down to Marian Halcombe's claim, in *The Woman in White*, that there is not the least necessity, nor even interest, in referring to the past. The theories of reading that we have, from Jameson's account of a text's "process of production" to the different reception-theories of Wolfgang Iser and Hans Robert Jauss, vary widely, from accounts of public efficacy, such as Jauss's well-known "horizon of expectation," to phenomenology; an implicit divide has persisted between studies of the individual reader and studies of the cultural contexts in which reading is shaped.[5] It is a divide that continues to preoccupy theories of reception and histories of affect. In nostalgia — as a subjectivity that is also a social injunction, or a social strategy enacted psychologically — we find a common ground, where a phenomenology of reading meets a culturally sensitive account of reception. The individual nostalgic reader is also a reader in contact with, even constituted by, a cultural habit of nostalgic remembrance; and the primary location for a reader to learn this cultural habit is the nineteenth-century novel. Nostalgia, in short, is a socially oriented affective response, the production of which is part of the usual aim of Victorian narrative.[6]

Part of my reason for making this point explicit is to indicate how infrequently it is explicit within the novels I have examined. Elizabeth Bennet's proclamation is aimed at Darcy, for instance, and Marian Halcombe's at Walter Hartright; rarely does a novel in this tradition turn directly toward the reader and beg for her forgetfulness. Rarely, but not never. One mid-Victorian novel that does make the turn to a readerly nostalgia more explicit and that in the process recapitulates in summary fashion the entire history of Victorian nostalgia is Anthony Trollope's *Can You Forgive Her?* (1864–65). Trollope's novel is an ideal place to conclude an account of nostalgia and nineteenth-century narrative, not simply because of its encapsulation of the development of "nostalgia" from eighteenth-century sickness to nineteenth-century therapeutics but also because of its addition of a key twist: a demand, often in direct address, for the reader's nostalgic forgetting and an admission that without this forgetting the novel's aims have been defeated.[7] Reading Trollope's novel, we cannot help but be aware of all that we are asked not only to forgive, but to forget—a forgetting that the narrative will assist in various, familiar ways; what is perhaps less immediately obvious is how the novel's requests for nostalgic erasure of the past are only more explicit versions of a procedure characteristic of the narrative tradition Trollope knew so well.

In the "her" that we are asked to forgive, Alice Vavasor, we are presented with a portmanteau character in relation to memory: both a Marianne Dashwood, unable to release herself from past cathexes and sickening from that inability, and an Elizabeth Bennet, Anne Elliot, or even Lucy Snowe, desiring nothing so much as a freedom from that past and its consequences. Her initial memory-sickness is a continual remembrance of past scenes of affection, and flirtation, with her cousin George Vavasor, a remembrance that threatens to overwhelm her newer, and thus less initially alluring, attachment to the all too gentlemanly John Grey. She is goaded toward these recollections by George's sister Kate, whose primary talent seems to be that of "constantly making allusion to those past occurrences, which all of them should have striven to forget."[8] But what will form the greatest mnemonic temptation to Alice, and what will be the immediate cause behind her first barely forgivable offense—the ending of her engagement to John Grey—is an evening with George, while on a Swiss vacation, spent talking freely about their past. What better detail, in terms of a history of nostalgia, than that this scene should take place in Basel, the city out of which Johannes Hofer published his 1688 dissertation that brought the term into European consciousness? And what more fitting result of this journey to Basel than a subsequent diagnosis of Alice as a nostalgic sufferer?

The diagnosis is provided by Grey upon Alice's return, and in its terms we can catch a history of nostalgia unrolling itself again:

"I learned, love, that something had been said or done during your journey,—or perhaps only something thought, that had made you melancholy, and filled your mind for a while with those unsubstantial and indefinable regrets for the past which we are all apt to feel at certain moments of our life. There are few of us who do not encounter, now and again, some of that irrational spirit of sadness which, when over-indulged, drives men to madness and self-destruction." (145)

Grey follows this diagnosis with a request to be Alice's "nurse"; when Alice responds that she is not ill, Grey answers that she is not ill "with any defined illness. You do not shake with ague, nor does your head rack you with aching; but yet you may be ill" (147). Trollope will not dismiss the diagnosis, referring to it as "that theory of bodily ailment as the cause and origin of her conduct" (185), and as "a malady for which no name was known" (637). No name, that is, that remains in British medicine, given that by 1864 "nostalgia" has, as we know, been so successfully depathologized as to have passed out of clinical usage; but that "no name" also masks the term for the very strategies that will rescue Alice from her illness and that will be passed along to the novel's reader. Alice's disease is even explicitly situated in terms of physical distance: "It was her special fault, that when at Rome she longed for Tibur, and when at Tibur she regretted Rome" (177–178). In Alice's Swiss malady, Grey's diagnosis, and Trollope's inability to find the right term for this disease, we can see the diluted remembrance of eighteenth-century "nostalgia" that was symptomatic of British narrative in the 1860s.

Diluted remembrance, in fact, becomes the dominant procedure of the novel's middle sections, which are devoted to two overlapping cases of cathexes that need to be left behind: not only Alice's attachment to George but the potentially adulterous liaison, produced by a powerful erotic and emotional memory, of Lady Glencora Palliser and the penniless, and fast deteriorating, Burgo Fitzgerald. In each case the dangerous recollected content has to be both partially remembered — remembered, however, as past — and forgotten, insofar as its ability to become an active part of the present must be halted. We march through, that is, the familiar processes of detaching and diluting that the trajectory of Austen to Collins makes so evident. Trollope even provides us with apt physical analogues for these nostalgic processes, such as the fate of the engagement ring George almost manages to offer to Alice. Balked in his proposal to Alice, who has been somewhat cured of her mnemonic sickness, George throws the ring behind the fire-grate of Alice's room; Alice retrieves it, but only partially — one of its diamonds has been knocked out, and Alice consents to its disappearance into the dust-heaps of London — while the remainder is carefully folded in paper and hidden in a desk drawer. Its most valuable part missing, its damaged setting relegated to a place of sentimental inactivity, the ring can now only testify to a past that bears little real relation to the future. As with small things, so with great: Lady Glencora's admission of her love for Burgo to her husband, Plantagenet Palliser, is followed immediately by a husbandly forgiveness that tacitly, and skillfully, detaches Burgo from their marriage and places him in a similarly discreet space of obsolescent memories.

Forgiveness, after all, is the novel's key goal, its interrogatory title expressing rather more anxiety about a negative response than the studied neutrality of Trollopian narration usually permits. But the old linkage of forgiveness and forgetfulness is continually being raised, so much so that we might say that forgetfulness is its necessary complement; an announcement of willed amnesia always follows an act of clemency in the novel. Having absolved his wife, Palliser is content to recognize the pertinent facts: "She had confessed to him, and he had forgiven her. He did not feel quite sure that he had been right, but he did feel quite sure that the thing had been done. He recognized it for a fact that, as regarded the past, no more was to be said" (618). It might be stated, in fact, that the mechanics of forgiveness in the novel are dependent on a subsequent amnesia about what had to be forgiven, as if amnesty required the retrospective erasure of the fault in question. One might note how contrary this procedure is to usual phenomenologies of reading, which insist on the temporal flow of narrative and our inability to identify a narrative with any one moment during its flow; Trollope's novel insists instead on a radical *condensation* of readerly memory, in which we are asked to identify Alice solely with the moments of her coming to a healthy forgetfulness of George and a renewed appreciation of John Grey.[9] As for the earlier Alice we, in the manner of Plantagenet Palliser, must recognize the decorum whereby no more is to be said.

The title's direct plea is echoed throughout the novel, both implicitly, in the narrative's own movements of leaving behind the damaged past, and explicitly, in ever more frequent direct addresses to the reader. So as the narratorial requests to forgive Alice multiply—"you must also forgive her before we close the book," one such request runs, "else my story will have been told amiss" (398)—the idea of forgetting becomes increasingly identical to these required absolutions. Of Alice's year of vacillation, Grey says: "Let us forget it,—or rather, let us treat it as though it were forgotten," a distinction meant to place even the forgetting of Alice's faults in the past, as if the present experience of relinquishing memory might still be too much of a remembrance; "the last twelve months," Grey announces, "shall be as though they had never been" (769). A constant, almost wearying production of scenes of announced amnesia follows: Alice's august relation Lady Midlothian proclaims that "everything is forgiven and shall be forgotten" (821), while Lady Glencora breezily states that, as far as Burgo goes, "I shan't think any more of that poor fellow now" (824). How else, then, to take the final addresses to the reader, pleading for forgiveness, except as a plea for an effacement of our recollections of Alice's misconduct? What might seem like the most sensible attitude to take toward the novel's heroine is actually grounded on a perverse, if entirely familiar, logic: forget all that you have read, because it all has to be forgotten in order for your forgiveness to be complete. Late in the nostalgic tradition initiated in the early decades of the nineteenth century, Trollope finds it necessary to demand, and not simply assume, the reader's forgetfulness of the mistakes and pains his narrative has depicted. As all Alice's friends have forgiven and forgotten her trespasses, Trollope writes, "I hope that they who have followed her story to its close will not be less generous" (830). Thus nostalgic reading: a touching up, shortening, and completing of our memories, to use Maurice Halbwachs's phrase — a refusal to remember the pain that has passed, in the name of a more generous pleasure.

This generous, amnesiac pleasure is also a culturally alluring one. When Halbwachs refers to the social obligation to shorten the past, which I have throughout this book called "nostalgia," he explains its result with a curious choice of words: a conferral of "prestige" on memory. We might think here of the undeniable prestige of the British novel of the nineteenth century, both within most scholarly accounts of the novel as well as in a wider cultural frame. How this prestige persists, when the chasm seems ever wider between the culture that produced these novels and the culture that today still voraciously consumes them or their more recent commodifications, is a question that any contemporary analyst of these narratives cannot help but ask. Their prestige is increasingly seen in an elegiac manner, as a strange fact that, as the twenty-first century begins, will not last much longer; and we might be tempted to think that the growing distance between us and the Victorians will eventually, if belatedly, make Victorian fiction stranger and less attractive. It is, however, the great talent of the nineteenth-century novel — a "nostalgic" talent — to turn distance and disconnection into the very principle of pleasure and even, to use Halbwachs's term, prestige. To use a formula that has been examined in the previous pages, the farther we get from it, the more nostalgically pleasurable it will be; the more disconnected, the more prestigious. The amnesiac self of nineteenth-century narrative is not simply a historical relic and not merely a reader-effect into which we step periodically. It might be, in fact, part of the very reason these novels have maintained, in a way the earlier British novel has not, their cultural familiarity and even eminence. The nostalgia that we learn from the nineteenth-century novel is the very nostalgia that strengthens our desire for these narratives — the continual allure of a past that we remember only as forever gone from us.

Notes

Introduction. Reading Nostalgia

1. Barthes, *Writing Degree Zero*, trans. Annette Lavers and Colin Smith (New York: Noonday, 1967), 39.

2. The names most prominently associated with this linkage of memory and the novel—from Northrop Frye to Ian Watt to Georg Lukács—will be cited in greater detail in the first chapter; it is enough here to note the extent to which certain nineteenth-century texts (Eliot's *Mill on the Floss*, Dickens's *David Copperfield*) are viewed as forerunners to such elaborately mnemonic efforts as Proust's *A la recherche du temps perdu*, as containing in embryo the modernist emphasis on detailed personal recollection, in order to understand how dominant certain modernist conceptualizations of memory have been in our own consideration of the classical novel. One excellent recent example of this tendency is the work of Paul Ricoeur, whose analysis of temporality and fictional plot rests on modernist cornerstones such as Proust, Mann's *Zauberberg*, and Woolf's *Mrs. Dalloway*; while all narratives are for Ricoeur, following a formulation of A. A. Mandilow, "tales of time," these modernist masterpieces are "tales about time"—a category implicitly denied to the classical novel of the nineteenth century. See *Time and Narrative*, trans. Kathleen McLaughlin and David Pellauer, vol. 2 (Chicago: University of Chicago Press, 1985), 101.

3. See, for instance, Richard Terdiman's influential formulation: "It is the novel, however, that most organizes itself as a projection of the memory function and its disruptions. Novels are exercises in the process of memory." *Present Past: Modernity and the Memory Crisis* (Ithaca: Cornell University Press, 1993), 25.

4. For Bergson's *mémoire pure*, see *Matière et mémoire: Essai sur la relation du corps à l'esprit* (Paris: Félix Alcan, 1911), where it denotes the state of total, unassimilated recollection, prior to any organization or winnowing into usefulness. James, in his 1890 masterwork, defines "desultory memory" as the retention of "names, dates, and addresses, anecdotes, gossip, poetry, quotations, and all sorts of miscellaneous facts"—in short, a talent for uncategorized, perhaps uncategorizable, mnemonic detail. See *The Principles of Psychology* (Cambridge: Harvard University Press, 1981), 621. Benjamin's "reminiscence" is located most explicitly in "The Storyteller," where he writes of "the perpetuating remembrance [*Eingedenken*] of the novelist" and "the short-lived reminiscences of the storyteller," where the former is "dedicated to *one* hero, *one* odyssey, *one* battle; the second, to *many* diffuse occurences." See *Illuminations*, trans. Harry Zohn (New York: Schocken, 1968), 98. Paul Valéry, in a notebook entry from 1927 entitled "Souvenir significatif," explains this distinction lucidly; most recollection, Valéry asserts, is usually a *signifying* memory, not at all accidental: "Ce qui a un sens, des valeurs. J'ai besoin d'un effort pour retrouver l'insignifiant, le brut, le réel [That which makes sense, has value. I have to make an effort to recover the insignificant, the raw, the real]." *Cahiers*, ed. Judith Robinson (Paris: Gallimard, 1973), 1241.

5. Dickens, *Our Mutual Friend*, ed. Stephen Gill (Harmondsworth: Penguin, 1971), 390.

6. Bersani, *A Future for Astyanax: Character and Desire in Literature* (Boston: Little, Brown, 1976), 55.

7. Gaskell, *Mary Barton: A Tale of Manchester Life*, ed. Stephen Gill (Harmondsworth: Penguin, 1970), 411–412.

8. Perhaps James's most sustained account of this aspect of polite discourse is from his preface to "The Altar of the Dead," in which he describes a moment of not entirely unintended transgression of the rule: "'We used sometimes to meet,'" James relates saying to a dinner companion, "'in the old days, at the dear So-and-So's, you may recall.' 'The So-and-So's?' said the awful gentleman, who appeared to recognise the name, across the table, only to be shocked at the allusion. 'Why, they're Dead, sir—dead these many years.' 'Indeed they are, sir, alas,' I could but reply with spirit; 'and it's precisely why I like so to speak of them!—Il ne manquerait plus que cela, that because they're dead I should n't!' is what I came within an ace of adding; or rather *might* have come hadn't I felt my indecency too utterly put in its place." See *Literary Criticism: French Writers, Other European Writers, Prefaces to the New York Edition* (New York: Library of America, 1984), 1247–1248.

9. White, *The Content of the Form: Narrative Discourse and Historical Representation* (Baltimore: Johns Hopkins University Press, 1987), 21.

10. Marx and Engels, *The Communist Manifesto*, ed. David McLellan (New York: Oxford University Press, 1992), 6.

11. Despite the persuasive claim of Christopher Salvesen that "the workings of memory make their first fully subjective appearance in English literature in the poetry of Wordsworth," we distort the meaning and role of that fully subjective memory if we read it as part of the mainstream of what I have called the Victorian memoryscape. See Salvesen, *The Landscape of Memory: A Study of Wordsworth's Poetry* (London: Edward Arnold, 1965), 1. If anything is most salient about Wordsworthian memory, it is its strange capacity to be at once backward-looking (to Lockean associationism) and forward-looking (to the memory-centered psychologies of the end of the nineteenth century). It is instead Victorian prose narrative that best reflects, and in fact best *produces*, the memory formations common to most of the era.

12. What is perhaps most interesting about the cultural histories of the Victorian period written in the last few decades, whether through the lenses of the literary analyst or the professional historian, is their lack of interest in memory or the discourses of memory. Whereas for earlier eras we have such crucial works as Frances Yates, *The Art of Memory* (Chicago: University of Chicago Press, 1966), and Mary Carruthers, *The Book of Memory: A Study of Memory in Medieval Culture* (Cambridge: Cambridge University Press, 1990), Victorian historians and literary critics have been silent on the subject. John Reed, in his *Victorian Conventions* (Athens: Ohio University Press, 1975), does turn some attention to memory, although significantly through such nonnovelistic figures as Tennyson, Pater, and Swinburne; Walter Houghton, *The Victorian Frame of Mind* (New Haven: Yale University Press, 1957), does contain a chapter entitled "Isolation, Loneliness, and Nostalgia," and we have the instructive recent work of Ann Colley in her *Recollection and Nostalgia in Victorian Culture* (New York: St. Martin's Press, 1998), but these are the exceptions. The Victorian novelistic evasion of memory is mirrored in the general silence on the subject of Victorian memory in current history, cultural criticism, and literary analysis. For this work I have had to turn for inspiration largely outside of the work performed on Victorian culture, most particularly to the careful historicization of modern memory-consciousness in such work as Richard Terdiman's *Present Past* and Matt Matsuda's *Memory of the Modern* (New York: Oxford University Press, 1996).

13. Histories of nineteenth-century psychology that take up these and other debates include Edward Reed, *From Soul to Mind: The Emergence of Psychology, from Erasmus Darwin to William James* (New Haven: Yale University Press, 1997); Katherine Arens, *Structures of Knowing: Psychologies of the Nineteenth Century* (Boston: Kluwer Academic, 1989); and Henri Ellenberger's magisterial work, *The Discovery of the Unconscious: The History and Evolution of Dynamic Psychiatry* (New York: Basic Books, 1970), which traces in mid- to late-nineteenth-century psychic theory the origins of a more psychodynamic, or memory-centered, discipline. One very useful overview of nineteenth-century debates is the recent collection *Embodied Selves: An Anthology of Psychological Texts, 1830–1890*, ed. Jenny Bourne Taylor and Sally Shuttleworth (Oxford: Clarendon Press, 1998), which thoroughly demonstrates the relative irrelevancy of memory to many key questions facing cognitive theorists of the time. The eventual taking-up of memory as a topic in British psychology at the end of the nineteenth century is the topic of Laura Otis's *Organic Memory: History and the Body in the Late Nineteenth and Early Twentieth Centuries* (Lincoln: University of Nebraska Press, 1994), although even here British psychology's continued denigration of personal memory, in favor of hereditary or genetic "recollection," is evident.

14. It is worth recalling that one of the first postulates of Breuer and Freud's 1895 *Studies on Hysteria* is the extension of the term "trauma" beyond the physical to any affective shock: "Our investigations reveal, for many, if not for most, hysterical symptoms, precipitating causes which can only be described as psychical traumas. Any experience which calls up distressing affects — such as those of fright, anxiety, shame or physical pain — may operate as a trauma of this kind; and whether it in fact does so depends naturally enough on the susceptibility of the person affected." *Studies on Hysteria*, trans. James Strachey (New York: Basic Books, 1957), 6. This extension of "trauma" to recollected affect is essentially a displacement onto memory of a host of concerns not unknown to nineteenth-century psychology (shock, failed perception), thus making memory the central evidentiary field for psychological research. What Breuer and Freud are implicitly

arguing against here is the neglect of memory common to many preexisting psychologies.

15. Poulet, *Studies in Human Time*, trans. Elliott Coleman (Baltimore: Johns Hopkins University Press, 1956), 23–24.

16. Thackeray, *The Memoirs of Barry Lyndon, Esq.*, ed. Andrew Sanders (New York: Oxford University Press, 1984), 102.

17. Hacking, *Rewriting the Soul: Multiple Personality and the Sciences of Memory* (Princeton: Princeton University Press, 1995), 188.

18. Koselleck, *Futures Past: On the Semantics of Historical Time*, trans. Keith Tribe (Cambridge: MIT Press, 1985), xxv.

19. M. M. Bakhtin, "Forms of Time and of the Chronotope in the Novel," in *The Dialogic Imagination*, trans. Michael Holquist (Austin: University of Texas Press, 1981), 84–85.

20. Two of the best recent examples of such historical work, where a more suspicious historicization penetrates beyond the falsely "traditional" layers of nationalist discourse and ritual, are Eric Hobsbawn and Terence Ranger, eds., *The Invention of Tradition* (Cambridge: Cambridge University Press, 1983), and Benedict Anderson, *Imagined Communities: Reflections on the Origin and Spread of Nationalism* (London: Verso, 1983). The shared methodology they employ, one that seeks to expose the recent historical formations of various national nostalgias, has been persuasive for my own work. Of particular interest is Anderson's argument that national identities depend on an experience of forgetting: "As with modern persons, so it is with nations. Awareness of being imbedded in secular, serial time, with all its implications of continuity, yet of 'forgetting' the experience of this continuity — product of the ruptures of the late eighteenth century — engenders the need for a narrative of 'identity.'" Anderson, *Imagined Communities*, 205.

21. Thackeray, *Vanity Fair: A Novel without a Hero*, ed. J. I. M. Stewart (Harmondsworth: Penguin, 1968), 711.

22. That nostalgia is an ideological formation, or what Frederic Jameson has usefully called an "ideologeme," does not preclude it from having narrative, or diachronic, properties; as Jameson reminds us, one of the defining characteristics of an ideologeme is its "fundamentally narrative character." See *The Political Unconscious: Narrative as a Socially Symbolic Act* (Ithaca: Cornell University Press, 1981), 88.

23. A disconnection that is perhaps most famously associated with the historical semantics of Reinhart Koselleck, who argues that "during the *Neuzeit* the difference between experience and expectation has increasingly expanded; more precisely, that *Neuzeit* is first understood as a *neue Zeit* from the time that expectations have distanced themselves evermore from all previous experiences." Koselleck, *Futures Past*, 276.

24. Austen, *Persuasion*, ed. R. W. Chapman (Oxford: Oxford University Press, 1982), 183.

25. A very partial list of some of the more notable examples of memory-studies might include the historiographical theories of Jacques Le Goff in *History and Memory*, trans. Steven Rendall and Elizabeth Claman (New York: Columbia University Press, 1992); revisionary histories as represented by Pierre Nora's influential *Realms of Memory: Rethinking the French Past*, trans. Arthur Goldhammer, 3 vols. (New York: Columbia University Press, 1996), David Lowenthal, *The Past Is a Foreign Country* (Cambridge: Cambridge University Press, 1985), and Terdiman's aforementioned *Present Past* as well as Matsuda's *Memory of the Modern*; the historicizing of memory, from a philosophical approach, performed by Hacking's *Rewriting the*

Soul; trauma-studies, matching psychoanalytic and historical methodologies, as represented by *Trauma: Explorations in Memory*, ed. Cathy Caruth (Baltimore: Johns Hopkins University Press, 1995); sociological considerations, as in Paul Connerton's *How Societies Remember* (Cambridge: Cambridge University Press, 1989); the cultural history of Paul Fussell's pioneering *The Great War and Modern Memory* (New York: Oxford University Press, 1975); and the psychological and neuroscientific approaches of Daniel Schacter in *Searching for Memory: The Brain, the Mind, and the Past* (New York: Basic Books, 1996). One excellent recent compendium of various vectors of memory-studies, from literary theories of autobiographical memory to neurological explanations of various mnemonic cruxes, is provided by Daniel Schacter and Elaine Scarry, eds., *Memory, Brain, and Belief* (Cambridge: Harvard University Press, 2000).

26. Halbwachs, *On Collective Memory*, trans. Lewis Coser (Chicago: University of Chicago Press, 1992), 43.

27. Ibid., 40.

28. For a definition of "ideological work" I have relied on Mary Poovey's *Uneven Developments: The Ideological Work of Gender in Mid-Victorian England* (Chicago: University of Chicago Press, 1988), 2–3.

29. From "The Meaning of Working through the Past," *Critical Models: Interventions and Catchwords*, trans. Henry Pickford (New York: Columbia University Press, 1998), 89.

30. The term is Katie Trumpener's, from *Bardic Nationalism: The Romantic Novel and the British Empire* (Princeton: Princeton University Press, 1997), 233.

31. See Althusser's "Ideology and Ideological State Apparatuses (Notes towards an Investigation)," in *Lenin and Philosophy*, trans. Ben Brewster (New York: Monthly Review Press, 1971), 160–161. For Lukács, see "Reification and the Consciousness of the Proletariat," in *History and Class Consciousness: Studies in Marxist Dialectics*, trans. Rodney Livingstone (Cambridge: MIT Press, 1971), 83–222. Adorno's famous, and often cited, claim that "all objectification is a forgetting" derives at least partially from Lukács's analysis; see Horkheimer and Adorno, *Dialectic of Enlightenment*, trans. John Cumming (New York: Continuum, 1998), 230. See also Terdiman, *Present Past*, 11–13, for a useful exposition of this theoretical point. These various analytic strands can all be traced back to several of Marx's own remarks on memory, particularly one of his more condensed descriptions of ideological erasure: "The division of profit into profit of enterprise and interest (not to speak of the intervention of commercial profit and money-dealing profit, which are founded in the circulation sphere and seem to derive entirely from this, and not from the production process at all) completes the autonomization of the form of surplus-value, the ossification of its form as against its substance, its essence. One portion of profit, in contrast to the other, separates itself completely from the capital-relation as such and presents itself as deriving not from the function of exploiting wage-labour but rather from the wage-labour of the capitalist himself. As against this, interest then seems independent both of the wage-labour of the worker and of the capitalist's own labour; it seems to derive from capital as its own independent source. . . . This is why the form 'capital interest,' as a third in the series to 'earth-rent' and 'labour-wages,' is much more consistent than 'capital-profit,' since profit still retains a memory of its origin which in interest is not simply obliterated but actually placed in a form diametrically opposed to its origin." *Capital*, trans. David Fernbach, vol. 3 (Harmondsworth: Penguin, 1981), 968. Against these more or less orthodox versions of the connection between amnesia and ideology, however, Slavoj Žižek has offered the possibility of the reverse — a process of

"over-rapid historicization" that might be even more serviceable to ideology than a forgetting of history; see *The Sublime Object of Ideology* (London: Verso, 1989), 50.

32. Perhaps the most incisive recent account of the contemporary contours of memory and amnesia, and of amnesia's feedback effect on the explosion of memory discourses and projects, is Andreas Huyssen's *Twilight Memories: Marking Time in a Culture of Amnesia* (London: Routledge, 1995).

33. Relevant here is Gillian Beer's contention that the form of Victorian fiction—as a response to the very problem of the inevitable memory-lapses involved in reading such large novels—works, through repetitions and other devices, to combat any readerly forgetting: "Many Victorian novelists set up a creative problem for themselves and their readers by combining the amplitude and arboreal form of their large narratives with an increasing insistence on the moral duty to recall and connect. . . . In Victorian multiplot novels the reader, even more than the characters, is required to recognize his or her own activity of remembering and to value it." Beer's formulation is persuasive but is largely based on texts (by Eliot and Hardy) written during or after the seismic shifts in the discourses of memory that occurred in the 1870s; furthermore, it ignores the Victorian novel's attitude toward those acts of memory that occur within it, and the problem of how that general dislike for explicit remembering can be assimilated to a supposed emphasis on readerly recollection. See Beer, "Origins and Oblivion in Victorian Narrative," in *Sex, Politics, and Science in the Nineteenth-Century Novel*, ed. Ruth Bernard Yeazell (Baltimore: Johns Hopkins University Press, 1986), 67.

1. Austen's Nostalgics

1. The epigraphs: Deirdre Le Faye, ed., *Jane Austen's Letters*, 3rd ed. (Oxford: Oxford University Press, 1995), 99; Gustave Flaubert, *Dictionnaire des Idées reçues*, vol. 17 of *Les Oeuvres de Gustave Flaubert* (Lausanne: Société Coopérative Editions Rencontre, 1965), 430. Flaubert's ironic aphorism might be translated as: *"Memory.—Complain about your own, and even boast of not having any. But howl if anyone says you lack judgment."*

Citations from Austen's novels are given parenthetically with the following abbreviations:

E: Emma, ed. R. W. Chapman (Oxford: Oxford University Press, 1982).

MP: Mansfield Park, ed. R. W. Chapman (Oxford: Oxford University Press, 1980).

MW: Minor Works, ed. R. W. Chapman (Oxford: Oxford University Press, 1980).

NA: Northanger Abbey, ed. R. W. Chapman (Oxford: Oxford University Press, 1982).

P: Persuasion, ed. R. W. Chapman (Oxford: Oxford University Press, 1982).

PP: Pride and Prejudice, ed. R. W. Chapman (Oxford: Oxford University Press, 1982).

SS: Sense and Sensibility, ed. R. W. Chapman (Oxford: Oxford University Press, 1982).

2. Several other examples could be added: in "Jack and Alice," Alice must endure being spurned by the magnificent Charles Adams but immediately forgets her hurt upon taking up a bottle of liquor; Mr. Gower, the protagonist of "Evelyn," sets out to find a picture of his sister's drowned lover but continually forgets the object of his quest; and in "Love and Friendship," the epistolary autobiographer Laura explains to her young correspondent her failure to mention her parents in the fol-

lowing manner: "To account for this seeming forgetfulness I must inform you of a trifling Circumstance concerning them which I have as yet never mentioned.— The death of my Parents a few weeks after my Departure, is the circumstance I allude to" (*MW*, 89).

3. Expectations that are provided by some of the most canonical critics of the novel. Perhaps the classic formulation is that of the young Georg Lukács: "Only in the novel and in certain epic forms resembling the novel does memory occur as a creative force affecting the object and transforming it." For Lukács, personal memory—"experiences of time which are victories over time"—is at the heart of what differentiates the novel from other genres. See Georg Lukács, *The Theory of the Novel*, trans. Anna Bostock (Cambridge: MIT Press, 1971), 124, 127. For Mikhail Bakhtin, the origins of the novel can be traced to the recollections of the writers of Socratic dialogues, a "personal memory without pre-existing chronological pattern" that contrasts with the epic's figuration of a closed-off past. Bakhtin, "Epic and Novel," in *The Dialogic Imagination: Four Essays*, trans. Caryl Emerson and Michael Holquist (Austin: University of Texas Press, 1981), 24. Northrop Frye and Ian Watt, in the Anglo-American critical tradition, have essentially concurred with these judgments, placing the novel in the context of autobiography or memoir, basing their definitions of the novel on the power and role of personal memory: see Frye, *Anatomy of Criticism: Four Essays* (Princeton: Princeton University Press, 1957); Watt, *The Rise of the Novel: Studies in Defoe, Richardson, and Fielding* (Berkeley: University of California Press, 1957). It remains to be seen how these powerful conceptualizations can be extended to fit instances of novels that perform consistent and continual dilutions of the power of personal memory—novels that are invested instead in considering the past as complete, obsolescent, unnecessary.

4. Joseph Banks, *Journal of the Right Hon. Sir Joseph Banks*, ed. Joseph Hooker (London: Macmillan, 1896), 329.

5. Some modern usage of the term "nostalgia" maintains a lineage to the eighteenth-century disease, however, predominantly in a familiar strain of argument that sees nostalgia as a form of inauthenticity or false consciousness. J. H. Plumb has lodged one of the more resonant of these claims: "The new methods, new processes, new forms of living of scientific and industrial society have no sanction in the past and no roots in it. The past becomes, therefore, a matter of curiosity, of nostalgia, a sentimentality." It needs hardly be said that for Plumb, a nostalgic society is a diseased society—demonstrating the persistence of nostalgia as an affliction, if one no longer centered on the body. Plumb, *The Death of the Past* (Boston: Houghton Mifflin, 1970), 14–15.

6. Claudia Johnson has written pertinently on the context of the word "philosophy" in Austen's time, a context in which, after Burke, the word is "associated with arrogant sophisms which, following from the oft-caricatured premise 'whatever is is wrong,' attack beliefs and customs that have been tried by time." See Johnson, *Jane Austen: Women, Politics, and the Novel* (Chicago: University of Chicago Press, 1988), 11. Elizabeth's "philosophy" is, I would argue, a perfect example of the meaning Johnson elucidates, although one without the negative connotations of Burke and his heirs, insofar as it is essentially a claim that *what has been* can be forgotten, or at least altered, through the mnemonic principle of "pleasure." Here we can glimpse the surprisingly reformist slant to Austen's new nostalgia.

7. Johnson, *Jane Austen*, xviii.

8. Marilyn Butler, *Jane Austen and the War of Ideas* (Oxford: Clarendon Press, 1987), xiv.

9. Johnson, *Jane Austen*, 167.

10. Butler, *Jane Austen*, xi.

11. Sandra Gilbert and Susan Gubar, *The Madwoman in the Attic: The Woman Writer and the Nineteenth-Century Literary Imagination* (New Haven: Yale University Press, 1979), 111.

12. Roger Sales, *Jane Austen and Representations of Regency England* (New York: Routledge, 1994), 5.

13. Henry James, "The Lesson of Balzac," in *Literary Criticism: French Writers, Other European Writers, Prefaces to the New York Edition* (New York: Library of America, 1984), 118.

14. Although she does not mention nostalgia or nostalgics, Eve Sedgwick's "Jane Austen and the Masturbating Girl," *Critical Inquiry* 17 (1991): 818–837, is perhaps the most famous example of this impulse. For Sedgwick, the target is not simply (or not only) "nostalgic" critics but "repressive" ones, and perhaps the two, in Sedgwick's view, shade into each other. Like the more explicitly antinostalgic writings of Butler and Johnson, Sedgwick's method is a dramatic historicism: an attempt to restore to cultural memory what has been repressed, diluted, or otherwise forgotten. See also Johnson's sketching of contemporary Austen nostalgia in "Austen Cults and Cultures," in *The Cambridge Companion to Jane Austen*, ed. Edward Copeland and Juliet McMaster (Cambridge: Cambridge University Press, 1997), 211–226.

15. The work of excavating its history has been initiated most notably by Michael Roth, in his work on French case histories of nostalgic sufferers, and David Lowenthal. See Roth, "Dying of the Past: Medical Studies of Nostalgia in Nineteenth-Century France," *History and Memory* 3, no. 1 (1991): 5–29; Lowenthal, *The Past Is a Foreign Country* (Cambridge: Cambridge University Press, 1985), 10–13. See also: G. S. Rousseau, "War and Peace: Some Representations of Nostalgia and Adventure in the Eighteenth Century," in *Guerres et Paix: La Grande-Bretagne au XVIIIe siècle I-II*, ed. Paul-Gabriel Bouce (Paris: Université de la Sorbonne Nouvelle, 1998), 121–140; George Rosen, "Nostalgia: A 'Forgotten' Psychological Disorder," *Clio Medica* 10, no. 1 (1975): 29–52; and Jean Starobinski, "The Idea of Nostalgia," *Diogenes* 54, no. 3 (1966): 81–103.

16. Hofer's little-known work is picked up by two thorough German histories of nostalgia: Fritz Ernst, *Vom Heimweh* (Zurich: Fretz and Wasmuth Verlag, 1949); Klaus Brunnert, "Nostalgie in der Geschichte der Medizin," *Düsseldorfer Arbeiten zur Geschichte der Medizin* 58 (1984): 1–339.

17. See Rosen, "Nostalgia," 30.

18. William Falconer, *A Dissertation on the Influence of the Passions upon Disorders of the Body* (London, 1788), 90–91.

19. D. J. Larrey, *Surgical Essays*, trans. John Revere (Baltimore: 1823), 155.

20. For Hacking the "ecological niche" is "not just social, not just medical, not just coming from the patient, not just from the doctors, but from the concatenation of an extraordinarily large number of diverse types of elements which for a moment provide a stable home for certain types of manifestation of illness." See Hacking, *Mad Travelers: Reflections on the Reality of Transient Mental Illnesses* (Charlottesville: University Press of Virginia, 1998), 13. The concept is a highly useful one, insofar as it allows us a way out of the methodological bind of reading "nostalgia" as either a comically faulty diagnosis or a mask for a deeper pathology, such as clinical depression. Hacking's study—centering on the late-nineteenth-century malady known as "fugue," or the compulsion to travel—has interesting implications for a history of its earlier opposite, homesickness.

21. See Rosen, "Nostalgia," 31–32. Although the bulk of clinical instances,

given the usual military "niche" of the disease, were male, female sufferers of the malady were known. Emily Brontë seems to have been understood as one; Elizabeth Gaskell writes that her suffering when forced to leave Haworth "became at length so much an acknowledged fact, that whichever was obliged to leave home, the sisters decided that Emily must remain there, where alone she could enjoy anything like good health." See Gaskell, *The Life of Charlotte Brontë*, ed. Alan Shelston (Harmondsworth: Penguin, 1975), 158–159. Gaskell's first use of the female nostalgic is in *Mary Barton* (1848) where Mary suffers from an evidently archaic form of nostalgia while making her inaugural trip out of Manchester, to Liverpool: "The very journey itself seemed to her a matter of wonder. She had a back seat, and looked towards the factory-chimneys, and the cloud of smoke which hovers over Manchester, with a feeling akin to the 'Heimweh.'" Gaskell, *Mary Barton: A Tale of Manchester Life*, ed. Stephen Gill (Harmondsworth: Penguin, 1970), 343. Finally, there is Balzac's Esther Gobseck, the reformed courtesan formerly known as "la Torpille," whose "patrie," outside of which she sickens, is in fact prostitution; as Balzac muses while diagnosing Esther's illness, "Il existe en nous plusieurs mémoires; le corps, l'esprit ont chacun la leur; et la nostalgie, par exemple, est une maladie de la mémoire physique [We have several kinds of memory; the body and the mind each has its own; and nostalgia, for example, is a sickness of physical memory]." Balzac, *Splendeurs et misères des courtisanes* (Paris: Gallimard, 1973), 81.

22. See, for instance, Mary Shelley's *Frankenstein*, which as late as 1818 offers us Victor Frankenstein's nostalgia—poised neatly between a medical condition and a sentimentality—for his native Geneva: "Sometimes, indeed, I felt a wish for happiness; and thought, with melancholy delight, of my beloved cousin; or longed, with a devouring *maladie du pays*, to see once more the blue lake and rapid Rhone, that had been so dear to me in early childhood." *Frankenstein; or, The Modern Prometheus*, ed. M. K. Joseph (New York: Oxford University Press, 1969), 182.

23. Falconer, *Dissertation*, 90, 92.

24. George Seymour, *Dissertatio medica inauguralis de nostalgia* (Edinburgh: 1818), 6.

25. Thomas Arnold, *Observations on the Nature, Kinds, Causes, and Prevention of Insanity, Lunacy, or Madness*, vol. 1 (Leicester: 1782), 266.

26. Arnold, however, goes on to insist that nostalgia is not an English malady: "While in England, whatever may be our partiality to our native land of plenty, opulence, and liberty, we know nothing of that passionate attachment that leads to this sort of Insanity," he states, which is found instead among the less urbanized regions, "among the inhabitants of the ice and snow of Lapland, of the bleak mountains of Switzerland, and of the remote and less civilized districts of Germany." *Observations*, 268.

27. Richard Terdiman, *Present Past: Modernity and the Memory Crisis* (Ithaca: Cornell University Press, 1993), 20.

28. Dislocation, travel, relocation: categories of *place* that until recently have been ignored in studies of Austen; one exception, to which I owe a debt, is Edward Said's argument, apropos of *Mansfield Park*, that "we have become so accustomed to thinking of the novel's plot and structure as constituted mainly by temporality that we have overlooked the function of space, geography, and location." *Culture and Imperialism* (New York: Knopf, 1993), 84. Of particular value is Franco Moretti's recent study of Austen's cultural geography in his *Atlas of the European Novel, 1800–1900* (London: Verso, 1998).

29. The gamble could be lost at a moment's notice. A persistent, if persistently debunked, anecdote of the late eighteenth century described Swiss merce-

naries in France as perpetually in danger of contracting nostalgia *en masse* were they to hear the native anthem "Ranz des Vaches"; Rousseau, in his 1768 *Dictionnaire de Musique*, relates that French army musicians were forbidden *"sous peine de mort"* to play the tune. J.-J. Rousseau, *Dictionnaire de Musique, Oeuvres Completes de J.-J. Rousseau*, vol. 14 (Paris, 1831), 79. Sauvages de la Croix's 1760 *Nosologia Methodica* seems to have been the origin of the story, but it appears in virtually every published description of nostalgia, including Falconer's *Dissertation*. Samuel Rogers, in *The Pleasures of Memory* (1792), made the anecdote a parable for any nationalist homesickness:

> The intrepid Swiss, that guards a foreign shore,
> Condemn'd to climb his mountain-cliffs no more,
> If chance he hear that song so sweetly wild,
> His heart would spring to hear it, when a child;
> That song, as simple as the joys he knew,
> When in the shepherd-dance he blithely flew;
> Melts at the long-lost scenes that round him rife,
> And sinks a martyr to repentant sighs.

See Rogers, *The Pleasures of Memory* (Oxford: Woodstock, 1989), 20–21. The story even persists into the twentieth century: it is mentioned by the American physician Charles Everett Warren in his *Medical Tractates*, vol. 4 (Boston: 1903), 13–14.

30. Francisco Boissier de Sauvages de la Croix, *Nosologia Methodica sistens Morborum Classes, Genera, et Species, Juxtà Sydenhami mentem & Botanicorum ordinem*, vol. 1 (Amsterdam, 1763), 465; Carl von Linnaeus, "Genera Morborum," in *Amœnitates Academica seu Dissertationes Variae Physicae, Medicae, Botanicae*, vol. 6 (Upsala, 1789), 464.

31. Vogel's nosology was, it seems, the most persuasive for British physicians; his classification of nostalgia as a species of "melancholia" was followed by Seymour and by the late-eighteenth-century medical theorist John Aitken. See Seymour, *Dissertatio*, 8; Aitken, *Elements of the Theory and Practice of Physic and Surgery*, vol. 2 (London: 1782), 504.

32. See Rosen, "Nostalgia," 40–41.

33. James Thatcher, a physician for the colonials, made this entry in his journal during the summer of 1780, while encamped in New Jersey: "Our troops in camp are in general healthy, but we are troubled with many perplexing instances of indisposition, occasioned by absence from home, called by Dr. Cullen *nostalgia*, or home sickness. This complaint is frequent among the militia, and recruits from New England. They become dull and melancholy, with loss of appetite, restless nights, and great weakness. In some instances they become so hypochondriacal as to be proper subjects for the hospital." Thatcher, *A Military Journal during the American Revolutionary War* (Boston: Richardson and Lord, 1823), 242.

34. One might also adduce the increasing dignity of "homesickness" in philosophical and literary registers, such as Novalis's well-known proclamation: "Die Philosophie ist eigentlich Heimweh — Trieb überall zu Hause zu seyn [Philosophy is essentially homesickness — the impulse to be at home everywhere]." Novalis, *Schriften*, ed. Paul Kluckhohn and Richard Samuel, vol. 3 (Stuttgart: W. Kohlhammer Verlag, 1960), 434.

35. S. T. Coleridge, "Home-sick," in *The Complete Poetical Works of Samuel Taylor Coleridge*, ed. Ernest Hartley Coleridge, vol. 1 (Oxford: Clarendon Press, 1912), 314. Coleridge composed the original version of the poem in a letter to Thomas Poole, dated May 6, 1799, written from Germany, and it is likely that he had in

mind and translated the more prevalent German term *heimweh*. The letter begins: "My dear Poole, my dear Poole! I am homesick. — Society is a burthen to me; and I find relief only in labour." See *The Collected Letters of Samuel Taylor Coleridge*, ed. Earl Leslie Griggs, vol. 1 (Oxford: Clarendon Press, 1956), 490.

36. In fact what one might call a "terminological nap" occurs, in which "nostalgia" disappears from active use until its reappearance, much later in the century, in its contemporary guise. Needless to say, my dating of the semantic shift is meant to account only for Britain; as Michael Roth has shown, the vibrancy of the pathological version of "nostalgia" persisted much longer in France, where it was not until the 1870s — when Charcot's "hysteria" took precedence — that the depathologization of nostalgia began in earnest. See Roth, "Dying of the Past," 21–24. Notions of fiction as allied to an almost pathological homesickness have persisted, however, particularly in Lukács's famous definition of the novel as "the literary form of the transcendent homelessness of the idea." Lukács's formulations attempt to make nostalgia constitutive of the novel, and the nostalgia he discusses is oddly close to the eighteenth-century disease; I would argue instead that if a nostalgia arose that became an important part of European fiction, it was the nostalgia that succeeded the nostalgia of eighteenth-century doctors, a nostalgia decidedly less violent and impetuous. Lukács, *Theory of the Novel*, 121.

37. Robert Hamilton, "History of a Remarkable Case of Nostalgia Affecting a Native of Wales, and Occurring in Britain," in *Medical Commentaries for the Years 1786, 1787* (Philadelphia, 1795), 215. Subsequent references are given in parentheses.

38. Insofar as it was often difficult to repatriate patients afflicted with nostalgia in distant lands, examples of the latter option of the nostalgic plot — death from homesickness — are present in the medical literature. Larrey describes the case of a soldier in the Royal Guard, a native of the north of France, who enters a wounded ward complaining of some numbness but who dies after a month of futile treatment; "he exhibited unequivocal signs of nostalgia," Larrey writes, "for during the delirium with which he was attacked, he spoke incessantly of his country." Larrey, *Surgical Essays*, 171–172. Balzac's 1840 story "Pierrette" offers a fictional instance of such a resolution; his central character dies from, among other ailments, "la nostalgie bretonne, maladie morale si connue que les colonels y ont égard pour les Bretons qui se trouvent dans leurs régiments [the Breton homesickness, a moral illness so well-known that colonels allow for it in the Bretons who serve in their regiments]." Balzac, "Pierrette," in *La Comédie humaine*, vol. 4 (Paris: Éditions Gallimard, 1976), 107.

39. What this particular alteration undoes is the ancient linkage of memory to space — architectural space, imagined interior space — that Frances Yates, in her seminal *Art of Memory* (Chicago: University of Chicago Press, 1966), traces back to the mnemonic *loci* of classical orators and rhetoricians. Perhaps part of the effect of this undoing might be described as a shift from the arts of memory described by Yates to what might be called a nostalgic art of forgetting.

40. My description of "disconnection" here owes a debt to Reinhart Koselleck's analysis of the term "Neuzeit," which — in its early-nineteenth-century formation — encapsulates a world where "the difference between past and present increased, so that lived time was experienced as a rupture, as a period of transition in which the new and the unexpected continually happened." Koselleck, *Futures Past: On the Semantics of Historical Time*, trans. Keith Tribe (Cambridge: MIT Press, 1985), 257.

41. Roland Barthes's explication of "naming" in relation to narrative is useful here: "What is a series of actions? the unfolding of a name. To *enter*? I can unfold

it into 'to appear' and 'to penetrate.' To *leave*? I can unfold it into 'to want to,' 'to stop,' 'to leave again.' To *give*?: 'to incite,' 'to return,' 'to accept.' Inversely, to establish the sequence is to find the name: the sequence is the currency, the *exchange value* of the name." *S/Z*, trans. Richard Miller (New York: Noonday, 1974), 82.

42. Cathy Caruth, *Unclaimed Experience: Trauma, Narrative, and History* (Baltimore: Johns Hopkins University Press, 1996), 6.

43. Susan Stewart, *On Longing: Narratives of the Miniature, the Gigantic, the Souvenir, the Collection* (Durham, N.C.: Duke University Press, 1993), ix.

44. Arnold, *Observations*, 266.

45. The social psychologist Michael Schudson has provided a set of terms for understanding how collective remembrance distorts the past that dovetail with those I have supplied to explain the workings of nostalgia; see Schudson, "Dynamics of Distortion in Collective Memory," *Memory Distortion: How Minds, Brains, and Societies Reconstruct the Past*, ed. Daniel Schacter (Cambridge: Harvard University Press, 1995), 346–364.

46. Austen's biographers frequently mention the apocryphal story that Austen fainted upon learning of her family's plan of moving from Steventon to Bath, which was imparted to her in December 1800. See Park Honan, *Jane Austen: Her Life* (New York: St. Martin's Press, 1987), 155. It is worthwhile noting that Reverend Austen's decision may have been forced upon him by the high taxes and low income of Steventon, as well as his increasing infirmity—the famous move to Bath, and Austen's well-known disapproval of the move, may have been of the "enforced" variety; but David Nokes in his recent biography casts needed doubt on this story, claiming that Austen's attitude toward the move might actually have been closer to that of the modern nostalgic: wistfully regretful, but by no means unwilling to move to a new locale. See Nokes, *Jane Austen: A Life* (London: Fourth Estate, 1997), 220–223.

47. Stuart Tave, *Some Words of Jane Austen* (Chicago: University of Chicago Press, 1973), 8.

48. Arnold, *Observations*, 270. Austen's juvenilia frequently skewers the personality discussed by Arnold, the personality that combines the lovesick and the homesick into a general hypermnesia; one instance is the comically downcast Eloisa Lutterell from "Lesley Castle," who complains: "You must expect from me nothing but the melancholy effusions of a broken Heart which is ever reverting to the Happiness it once enjoyed and which ill supports its present wretchedness" (*MW*, 132).

49. In suggesting that Marianne's illness parallels, and perhaps evokes, the disease of "nostalgia" as defined by eighteenth-century physicians, I am implicitly mediating between those critics who would either see in the illness a mortification of Marianne's sensibility or, as in John Wiltshire's *Jane Austen and the Body* (Cambridge: Cambridge University Press, 1992), a specific illness that carries no symbolic overtones. Marianne's illness is both a real physiological disease, as Wiltshire insists, *and* an effect of psychological factors—much as is nostalgia, which for the eighteenth century was both a mental disorder, a mortification of the inflexible memory, and a pathological disorder that, as Larrey's dissections demonstrate, was thought to alter the very tissue of the brain. Reading Marianne's disorder as bearing the signs of nostalgia permits us to mediate between the psychogenic and pathogenic accounts of her illness.

50. During the First World War novels and poetry were graded for their therapeutic efficacy by H. F. Brett-Smith, a former Oxford don employed by the British Army. In Brett-Smith's "Fever Chart," Austen's novels were selected as the most effective form of treatment, and were recommended for the severely shell-shocked

—suggesting that the therapies described by her texts could become therapies enacted upon the reader. See *Jane Austen: The Critical Heritage*, ed. B. C. Southam, vol. 2 (London: Routledge, 1987), 300–301.

51. The therapeutic effects of work upon a diseased memory were advanced by many physicians, as well as lay theorists; Dr. Johnson, in his essay "Sorrow" in *Rambler* 47, put forth the familiar theory: "The safe and general antidote against sorrow, is employment." A mind devoted to remembrance must be reoriented toward the future: "Sorrow is a kind of rust of the soul, which every new idea contributes in its passage to scour away. It is the putrefaction of stagnant life, and is remedied by exercise and motion." *The Yale Edition of the Works of Samuel Johnson*, ed. W. J. Bate and Albrecht B. Strauss, vol. 3 (New Haven: Yale University Press, 1969), 257.

52. See Mary Ann O'Farrell, *Telling Complexions: The Nineteenth-Century English Novel and the Blush* (Durham, N.C.: Duke University Press, 1997), for a revised reading of the link between teaching and shaming—precisely the sort of association, added to a rhetoric of the "therapeutic," that is visible in Marianne's convalescence at Barton Cottage.

53. My reading of these closural condensations, which I have termed "nostalgic," owes a debt to D. A. Miller's discussion of the "principles of abridgment and reorganization" that govern Elinor's narration of Willoughby's longer analeptic apology. Miller, *Narrative and Its Discontents: Problems of Closure in the Traditional Novel* (Princeton: Princeton University Press, 1981), 74.

54. Stewart, *On Longing*, 135.

55. Ibid., 145.

56. As Said reminds us, Sir Thomas's object-purge covers, or enables, a greater forgetfulness: that of the possible "clearings" and "orderings" that he might have effected in his Antigua plantations. *Culture and Imperialism*, 86–87. See, however, Katie Trumpener's compellingly revisionary reading of *Mansfield Park*, in the light of Said's work, as a text that does not naïvely "forget" imperialist contexts but that uses "ellipses and undertones to describe the indirect moral and ideological effects of empire." Trumpener, *Bardic Nationalism: The Romantic Novel and the British Empire* (Princeton: Princeton University Press, 1997), 184.

57. That the drama of travel is a key element of Austen's novels has been largely ignored by literary critics (with the exception of Said) but, oddly enough, thoroughly recognized by historians, who use Austen as an example of the growing importance of mobility to Regency culture. Linda Colley cites *Northanger Abbey* as an instance of the nascent trend of "internal tourism," while Leonore Davidoff and Catherine Hall, when discussing the early-nineteenth-century intersection of mobility and gender, turn to the tours and walks of *Pride and Prejudice*. See Colley, *Britons: Forging the Nation, 1707–1837* (New Haven: Yale University Press, 1992), 172–174; Davidoff and Hall, *Family Fortunes: Men and Women of the English Middle Class, 1780–1850* (Chicago: University of Chicago Press, 1987), 404, 531.

58. Fanny's autobiography is, in Michael McKeon's useful term, a "myth"—a story that by obtaining a certain fixity of outline "may incapacitate it for the instrumental, recollective function that it is meant to serve." McKeon, *The Origins of the English Novel, 1600–1740* (Baltimore: Johns Hopkins University Press, 1987), 31.

59. See, respectively, Tony Tanner, *Jane Austen* (Cambridge: Harvard University Press, 1986), 46; Butler, *Jane Austen*, 243; Sales, *Representations*, 113.

60. Johnson, *Jane Austen*, 116.

61. Le Faye, *Letters*, 68.

62. See Monica Cohen, *Professional Domesticity in the Victorian Novel* (Cam-

bridge: University of Cambridge Press, 1998), for an alternate account of one form of departure, the naval, as a form of domesticity—a version of "home" as continual travel.

63. Tanner, *Jane Austen*, 204. Some critics have, however, detected the importance of Anne's mobility, including Claudia Johnson, who speaks of *Persuasion*'s preference for cosmopolitanism over provincialism, and Rachel Brownstein, who notes that all of Austen's heroines begin "homeless," but that Anne, unlike her predecessors, "remains unsettled for life." See Johnson, *Jane Austen*, 158; Brownstein, *Becoming a Heroine: Reading about Women in Novels* (New York: Columbia University Press, 1982), 95.

64. The narrator's harsh comments about Mrs. Musgrove's memories have become a *cause célèbre* among Austen critics, who have usually been taken aback by the perceived tastelessness of the attack; Stuart Tave, however, defends it as "perfectly accurate." Tave, *Some Words*, 261. But it is the very accuracy of the narratorial intrusion—its unprecedented insistence upon a mnemonic "accuracy"—that is so striking, and so unusual; why the novel's energies are so mobilized by an otherwise insignificant act of remembrance is the crux of the passage.

65. Benwick's portrayal as a man who could "bring you fifty quotations in a moment" (*P*, 234) is part of a larger trend in Austen's treatment of memory: the denigration of memorization. The Bertram sisters, we learn in *Mansfield Park*, are "blessed with wonderful memories," able to recite the reigns of Roman emperors, "and all the Metals, Semi-Metals, Planets, and distinguished philosophers" (*MP*, 19), while Fanny predictably cannot retain this information. Memorization stands far from the vagueness of nostalgia, and thus is accorded little dignity. While occupying herself by recalling poetic quotations on the autumn, Anne's memorized musings are halted by hearing the conversation of Wentworth and Louisa Musgrove—the present takes immediate precedence over the merely time-consuming chatter of memorization.

66. Interestingly enough, Austen's canceled chapters of *Persuasion* present a far more "restorative" version of Anne and Wentworth's happy ending. The original version tellingly runs as follows: "They were re-united. They were restored to all that had been lost. They were carried back to the past, with only an increase of attachment & confidence, & only such a flutter of present Delight as made them little fit for the interruption of Mrs Croft, when she joined them not long afterwards" (*P*, 263). The published version stresses the present's significant improvements to the past: "There they returned again into the past, more exquisitely happy, perhaps, in their re-union, than when it had been first projected; more tender, more tried, more fixed in a knowledge of each other's character, truth, and attachment; more equal to act, more justified in acting" (*P*, 240–241). Whereas in the canceled version their "restoration" makes them unfit for social intercourse, the published version leads directly to a session of shared nostalgia, when they can "indulge in those retrospections and acknowledgments, and especially in those explanations of what had directly preceded the present moment, which were so poignant and so ceaseless in interest" (*P*, 241).

67. It is little wonder, then, that the word "nostalgia" occurs so frequently in discussions of *Persuasion*. For Tony Tanner, the novel's "dominant mood before the end is autumnal, nostalgic, a sense of the most significant period of experience being in the past, recollectable but irretrievable and unrepeatable," while Barbara Hardy claims that Anne's "memory moves away from isolated nostalgia to review the past, to understand, and to make imaginative revisions of value." See Tanner, *Jane Austen*, 214; Hardy, *A Reading of Jane Austen* (London: Peter Owen, 1975),

100. Austen's construction of modern nostalgia is so thorough, and so accomplished, that her readers and critics have rushed to supply the word that she herself does not use.

68. This account of the retreat of homesickness is true in its larger scope, although there were isolated examples of the older nostalgia's persistence. As late as 1873 one French physician, Auguste Haspel, maintained that nostalgia could still be considered a disease entity, and during the American Civil War casualties from nostalgia (572 cases with one death in 1862, 2,016 cases with twelve deaths in 1863) were noted by Union doctors. See Rosen, "Nostalgia," 46–47. Nonetheless, the great period of medical nostalgia was over by the early nineteenth century, and the term's entrance into a more literary register was well underway.

69. Stewart, *On Longing*, 23; Jameson, *Postmodernism: Or, The Cultural Logic of Late Capitalism* (Durham, N.C.: Duke University Press, 1991), 21. Jameson is perhaps our preeminent critic of nostalgia's severance from a memory that might represent a full historical consciousness; but he is aware of how dehistoricizing impulses have their own history, warning his readers that the current nostalgia he indicts is "in no way to be grasped as passionate expressions of that older longing once called nostalgia but rather quite the opposite," thus hinting at the history of the supercession of trauma (or passion, or longing) that contemporary nostalgia conceals. What Jameson exhibits here is a sense of the slight catechresis in terming a contemporary forgetfulness of history "nostalgia"—a catechresis that is nonetheless tellingly ironic, given the fact that what contemporary nostalgia most thoroughly forgets is *its own* history. Jameson, *Postmodernism*, xvii.

2. Amnesiac Bodies

1. The epigraph—I translate from the original: "Nous devons, en serrant d'aussi près que possible le contour des faits, chercher où commence et où finit, dans l'opération de la mémoire, le rôle du corps." Bergson, *Matière et mémoire: Essai sur la relation du corps à l'esprit*, 7th ed. (Paris: Librairie Félix Alcan, 1911), 71.

2. Thomas James Wise and John Alex Symington, eds., *The Brontës: Their Lives, Friendships and Correspondence*, vol. 2 (Oxford: Shakespeare Head, 1932), 258. Smith, in his recollections of Brontë written long after her death, mentions this visit. See George Smith, "Charlotte Brontë," *Cornhill* 82 (1900): 778–795. Browne would later compose a treatise, published in 1869, entitled *Phrenology: And its Application to Education, Insanity, and Prison Discipline*.

3. Brontë was not the only novelist to have been examined by a phrenologist and to have been pleased at the results. Charles Bray took the young Mary Ann Evans to London in 1844 to have a cast made of her head—a cast that was subsequently exhibited by her friends. See Gordon Haight, *George Eliot: A Biography* (Oxford: Oxford University Press, 1968), 51.

4. Quoted in Winifred Gérin, *Charlotte Brontë: The Evolution of Genius* (Oxford: Oxford University Press, 1967), 576.

5. The overarching tenets of phrenology can be isolated into three postulates: that the brain is the organ of the mind; that the brain is a collection, or "composite," of distinct "task-specific" faculties; and that the size of different parts of the skull is a true index of the power of the underlying faculties. See Anne Harrington, *Medicine, Mind, and the Double Brain: A Study in Nineteenth-Century Thought* (Princeton: Princeton University Press, 1987), 7–8.

6. For two paradigmatic instances of considering Brontë's fiction in general,

and *Villette* in particular, as exemplifying a dynamic of repression and release, see Sandra Gilbert and Susan Gubar, *The Madwoman in the Attic: The Woman Writer and the Nineteenth-Century Literary Imagination* (New Haven: Yale University Press, 1979), and Helene Moglen, *Charlotte Brontë: The Self Conceived* (New York: Norton, 1976).

7. For a comprehensive list of publications and dramatic productions dealing with phrenology from 1816 into the 1830s, see Roger Cooter, *The Cultural Meaning of Popular Science: Phrenology and the Organization of Consent in Nineteenth-Century Britain* (Cambridge: Cambridge University Press, 1984), 23.

8. "The Craniological Controversy," *Blackwood's Edinburgh Magazine* 1 (1817): 35.

9. See Sally Shuttleworth, *Charlotte Brontë and Victorian Psychology* (Cambridge: Cambridge University Press, 1996), 64. Shuttleworth's work is a crucial piece of research and theorizing, most worthwhile for its demonstration that Brontë's references to phrenology are more than epiphenomenal; I am indebted to it throughout my reading of Brontë. For earlier sketches of the topic, see Ian Jack, "Phrenology, Physiognomy, and Characterization in the Novels of Charlotte Brontë," *Brontë Society Transactions* 15 (1970): 377–391; Wilfrid Senseman, "Charlotte Brontë's Use of Physiognomy and Phrenology," *Papers of the Michigan Academy of Sciences, Arts and Letters* 37 (1952): 475–486.

10. Cooter, *Popular Science*, 120.

11. Combe's biographer Charles Gibbon admits that his candidacy was doomed to failure because of his outsider status, and surmises that Combe may have submitted his name merely to gain attention. See Gibbon, *The Life of George Combe*, vol. 1 (London: Macmillan, 1878), 318.

12. "The significance of phrenology for Brontë," Shuttleworth writes, "and for Victorian culture as a whole, lies not so much within its originality as in its function as a paradigmatic discourse of the era, condensing within one framework psychological, social, economic, and textual concerns." Shuttleworth, *Brontë*, 59. For a reading of the resemblance between the phrenological diagram and Victorian culture at large, see Cooter, *Popular Science*, 111. The diagrammatic quality of phrenology is perhaps best contextualized as an example of what Mary Poovey has termed "abstract space," a space that is "conceptualized as isotropic (as everywhere the same) and as reducible (or already reduced) to a formal (that is, empty) schema or grid." See Poovey, *Making a Social Body: British Cultural Formation, 1830–1864* (Chicago: University of Chicago Press, 1995), 29. Poovey's analysis of forms of abstraction in mid-century Britain, although not linked explicitly to Victorian theories of mind, provides valuable theoretical armature for a study of phrenological psyches.

13. O. S. Fowler, *Memory and Intellectual Improvement Applied to Self-Education and Juvenile Instruction* (New York: Fowler and Wells, 1853), 37.

14. Phrenology can therefore be usefully considered in the context of other nineteenth-century technologies or theories of vision, such as the kaleidoscopes and stereoscopes analyzed by Jonathan Crary; just as his more material instances, phrenology is a "means to recode the activity of the eye, to regiment it, to heighten its productivity and to prevent its distraction." See Crary, *Techniques of the Observer: On Vision and Modernity in the Nineteenth Century* (Cambridge: MIT Press, 1990), 24.

15. George Combe, *The Constitution of Man Considered in Relation to External Objects*, 3rd ed. (Edinburgh: John Anderson, 1835), 7. O. S. Fowler, in an 1842 pamphlet on marriage, makes the same point in more vivid, and discomfiting, lan-

guage: "*Gratify their largest organs*, and you will always hit the mark. Phrenology shows you *how* to do this, or just how to take them. Thus if Approbativeness predominates, and Causality is only so so, flatter, and if the brain is only moderate in size, put it on thick." *Fowler on Matrimony; or, Phrenology and Physiology Applied to the Selection of Companions for Life; Including Directions to the Married for Living Together Affectionately and Happily* (New York: 1842), 27.

16. Citations from Brontë's novels are given in parentheses with the following abbreviations:

JE: Jane Eyre, ed. Q. D. Leavis (Harmondsworth: Penguin, 1966).

P: The Professor, ed. Heather Glen (Harmondsworth: Penguin, 1989).

V: Villette, ed. Mark Lilly (Harmondsworth: Penguin, 1979).

17. An analogous case is to be found in the work of Balzac. In *Le Père Goriot*, for instance, the verdicts of phrenology are always validated: Rastignac's friend Bianchon, a medical student, accurately foretells Madame Michonneau's treachery by reference to her phrenological profile; similarly, Bianchon recognizes the importance of paternity to Goriot's identity by discussing his skull features. In *Goriot*, as elsewhere in the *Comédie humaine*, phrenology functions as a particularly reliable proleptic device.

18. Gall disliked the term "phrenology," which was in fact coined by a British theorist, Thomas Ignatius Maria Forster, in 1815. Although this is the term that has come down to us, references to Gall and Spurzheim's science were just as often to be found under the (often pejorative) term "craniology." See Cooter, *Popular Science*, 59.

19. George Combe, *Lectures on Moral Philosophy* (Boston: Marsh, Capen, Lyon, and Webb, 1840), 195.

20. The vagueness of phrenological aims is parodied by Flaubert in *Bouvard et Pécuchet*, when the eponymous heroes are seized with ambition during a short-lived enthusiasm for phrenology: "Une rêve magnifique les occupa: s'ils menaient à bien l'éducation de leurs élèves, ils fonderaient plus tard un établissement ayant pour but de redresser l'intelligence, dompter les caractères, ennoblir le coeur. Déjà ils parlaient des souscriptions et de la bâtisse [A magnificent dream preoccupied them: if they were successful at educating their pupils, they would later on found an establishment aimed at correcting intelligence, taming character, ennobling the heart. They were already talking about subscriptions and the building]." *Bouvard et Pécuchet* (Paris: Garnier Frères, 1965), 348.

21. "Essays on Cranioscopy, Craniology, Phrenology, &c., By Sir Toby Tickletoby, *Bart.*," *Blackwood's Edinburgh Magazine* 10 (1821): 80.

22. It is also pertinent to note here the class issues embedded in Lucy's evaluation of Rosine. Herself only marginally superior to Rosine, Lucy, when using phrenological language, adopts a lexicon associated with employers and social betters, for prospective servants were likely to be "read" phrenologically by their interviewers. Combe complains of "how many annoyances arise from the misconduct of servants and dependants in various departments of life; how many losses, and sometimes ruin, arise from dishonesty and knavery in confidential clerks, partners, and agents," and states that "one and all of the evils enumerated here might, to a great extent, be obviated by the application of Phrenology." *Constitution of Man*, 176. Combe's magisterial treatise, largely a philosophical work, includes a chapter entitled "Choice of Servants," from which this citation is taken. Lucy's use of phrenology is, therefore, expressive not only of a certain power over herself (the power of deflecting memory or desire) but also of a social power over Rosine, a social power that might otherwise seem precarious.

23. Gilbert and Gubar, *Madwoman*, 73.

24. Mulvey, "Visual Pleasure and Narrative Cinema," *Screen* 16, no. 3 (1975): 8.

25. It has been possible, however, to read even M. Paul's fortuitous, exciting, and (as I will argue) erotically tinged clinical reading of Lucy as a confirmation of our privileging of depth over surface. In this vein is Helena Michie's reading: "Although grateful for this particular reading that results in her being offered a job, Lucy finds her role of text confining, his role as reader a violation." See Michie, *The Flesh Made Word: Female Figures and Women's Bodies* (New York: Oxford University Press, 1987), 117. What needs to be demonstrated, however, is what precisely is being violated by this reading, and why Lucy proceeds to "violate" others in the same fashion habitually; as I am arguing, this notion of "violation" begs the question of whether there is a depth obscured by a surface (rather than apparent on that surface) that might be violated by a surface reading (rather than recognized, even ratified and validated, by that reading).

26. Crary, *Techniques*, 6.

27. Lavater, *Essays on Physiognomy: For the Promotion of the Knowledge and the Love of Mankind*, trans. Thomas Holcroft (London: 1793), 23.

28. Combe, *Constitution of Man*, 25.

29. Ibid., 77.

30. Even if we understand the symptom, in Slavoj Žižek's terms, as not a "content hidden by the form (the form of commodities, the form of dreams) but, on the contrary, *the 'secret' of this form itself*," as the process whereby a certain latency is transformed into a manifest form—a dream, a commodity—the notion of symptom is still one directed toward the past. Whether our question be "what is this symptom hiding?" or "how did this symptom get this way?" we inquire about the past; as such, even Žižek's key reorientation of our understanding of the symptom toward a Marxian context demonstrates the symptom's inapplicability to a study of phrenological faculties, which require a future-oriented question: what can this faculty do? See Žižek, *The Sublime Object of Ideology* (London: Verso, 1989), 11.

31. The anecdote can be found in any of the English translations of selections of Gall's work; see Gall, *On the Origin of the Moral Qualities and Intellectual Faculties of Man, and the Conditions of their Manifestation*, trans. Winslow Lewis, vol. 1 (Boston: Marsh, Capen, and Lyon, 1835), 2–3. Combe claimed that Gall's "discovery" of the schoolmate's faculty of memory occurred when Gall was nine years old; see Combe, *Lectures on Phrenology* (New York: Fowler and Wells, 1847), 23.

32. Gall's four mnemonic faculties were the following: "Sense of Things," or the memory of facts; "Recollection of Persons"; "Retaining Names and Words," or linguistic memory; and "Sense of Time," or the ability to recall "dates and epochs." See the anonymous *Manual of Phrenology: Being an Analytical Summary of the System of Doctor Gall, on the Faculties of Man and the Function of the Brain* (Philadelphia: Carey, Lea, and Blanchard, 1835), 203. Spurzheim would make these faculties, respectively, Eventuality, Form, Language, and Time. See also Edwin Clarke and L. S. Jacyna, *Nineteenth-Century Origins of Neuroscientific Concepts* (Berkeley: University of California Press, 1987), 220, for a discussion of earlier theories about the localization of memory, including Thomas Willis's 1672 postulate that the cerebral cortex provides storage space for memories; Gall was not the first to consider the location of memory to be the first challenge in any attempt to map the brain.

33. J. G. Spurzheim, *A View of the Philosophical Principles of Phrenology*, 3rd ed. (London, 1825), 208.

34. Ibid., 19–20.

35. See Combe, *Constitution of Man*, 46–49.

36. Fowler, *Memory*, 19.

37. Combe, *Constitution of Man*, 51.

38. As Anne Harrington notes, phrenological faculties were distinguished by the "*type* of information processed," that is, by categorizations of the *external* data the mind encounters; the categories of earlier psychologies, such as "memory" or "imagination" or "intelligence," were modes of the mind's *internal* operations. *Medicine, Mind, and the Double Brain*, 7.

39. Combe, *Constitution of Man*, 49.

40. Spurzheim, *Principles*, 20–21.

41. O. S. and L. N. Fowler, *The Illustrated Self-Instructor in Phrenology and Physiology* (New York: Fowler and Wells, 1855), 115–116.

42. Ibid., 116.

43. Watson, "Remarks on the Peculiarities of Memory," *Phrenological Journal* 7 (1831–32): 215–216.

44. "Psychological Inquiries," *Blackwood's Edinburgh Magazine* 77 (1855): 403. Brodie was a noted antiphrenologist, and his views accorded well with the dismissive stance *Blackwood's* had taken toward phrenology since its first issue in 1817, thus making his book an apt subject for a review.

45. Ibid., 406.

46. Ibid., 407.

47. See Lawrence Rothfield, *Vital Signs: Medical Realism in Nineteenth-Century Fiction* (Princeton: Princeton University Press, 1992).

48. Combe, *A System of Phrenology* (Boston: Marsh, Capen, and Lyon, 1835), 62–63.

49. Spurzheim, *Phrenology: In Connection with the Study of Physiognomy* (London: Treuttel, Wurtz, and Richter, 1826), 182.

50. Hegel complains that "individuality has now become the object for observation, or the object to which observation now turns"; his lengthy critique of phrenology is in essence a critique upon its emphasis on visibility, which for Hegel has become entirely too culturally dominant a mode. *Phenomenology of Spirit*, trans. A. V. Miller (New York: Oxford University Press, 1979), 185. One useful study of the widespread cultural diffusion of phrenological and physiognomical visibility, and its importance for the arts, is Mary Cowling, *The Artist as Anthropologist: The Representation of Type and Character in Victorian Art* (Cambridge: Cambridge University Press, 1989).

51. Michel Foucault, *The Birth of the Clinic*, trans. A. M. Sheridan Smith (New York: Vintage, 1975), 94. Although Foucault does not discuss the possibility that clinical gazes spread beyond the precincts of the clinic itself, such a dissemination is amply suggested by his well-known arguments for the analogous spread of disciplinary structures. Another useful description of phrenological/clinical vision is Mary Poovey's analysis of eighteenth-century anatomical representation, in which "true penetration begins with sight; its next, decisive phase is abstraction, generalization, or theory, which displaces actual bodies as surely as the knife displaces the obscuring flesh." Poovey, *Making a Social Body*, 80.

52. It is to Roger Cooter that I owe the term "surfacing": "The fact that it was only from the *surface* of the cranium that human psychology was to be read . . . could signify a total assault on traditional thought and society, in which what really matters is held to be implicit or obscure to all but the privileged." Cooter, *Popular Science*, 117. Cooter's emphasis on surfacing is a useful corrective to arguments that attempt to make body-reading sciences examples of early depth psychologies.

53. It is possible here to consider Mrs. Gaskell's famous account of the "mask game" played by Patrick Brontë and his four surviving children, in which he placed masks on each child, enabling them, therefore, to "stand and speak boldly from under the cover of the mask." See Gaskell, *The Life of Charlotte Brontë*, ed. Alan Shelston (Harmondsworth: Penguin, 1975), 94. By providing his children with a *surface*—with an exterior upon which they could displace and, to a certain extent, simplify their desires, propensities, and pains—Reverend Brontë provided them with a paradoxical security, and managed to elicit honest, dramatic, and *characteristic* responses.

54. O. S. and L. N. Fowler, *Self-Instructor*, 11.

55. Combe, *Constitution of Man*, 45.

56. Barbara Stafford, *Body Criticism: Imaging the Unseen in Enlightenment Art and Medicine* (Cambridge: MIT Press, 1991), 12.

57. Cooter, *Popular Science*, 75.

58. For discussions of the enormous influence of Étienne de Silhouette (1709–69) on eighteenth-century physiognomy and epistemology, see Graeme Tytler, *Physiognomy in the European Novel: Faces and Fortunes* (Princeton: Princeton University Press, 1982), 57, and Stafford, *Body Criticism*, 98.

59. Spurzheim discusses, with illustrations, Pope Alexander VI's head in his 1826 *Phrenology: In Connexion with the Study of Physiognomy*, stating that "this cerebral organization is despicable in the eyes of a phrenologist." Spurzheim, *Physiognomy*, 71.

60. Stafford, *Body Criticism*, 116. Roland Barthes has written of this detaching process as an almost inescapable "spitefulness of language," the ability of language to reduce the body to a disconnected series of units, a fetishized collection of discrete parts. One might say that phrenology takes this property of language and makes it into a mental theory as well as a visual practice. Barthes, *S/Z*, trans. Richard Miller (New York: Noonday, 1974), 113.

61. See Christine Alexander and Jane Sellars, *The Art of the Brontës* (Cambridge: Cambridge University Press, 1995), for reproductions of Brontë's "detached" physiognomical studies.

62. For a compelling reading of this scene as an example of Lucy's "projection" —her neurosis writing over, so to speak, the king's legible body—see Athena Vrettos, *Somatic Fictions: Imagining Illness in Victorian Culture* (Stanford: Stanford University Press, 1995), 65.

63. For this reason both phrenology and physiognomy preferred to study the face at rest, so that the transience of "expression" would disappear and be replaced by immutable and essential facial signs. Pathognomy—the study of facial expressions—was a popular contrary trend, best exemplified by Sir Charles Bell, *The Anatomy and Philosophy of Expression as Connected with the Fine Arts* (London: 1847), and Charles Darwin, *The Expression of the Emotions in Man and Animals* (London: 1872). The enterprise of physiognomy and phrenology was quite different, however, insofar as it was in search of what was static about character, as Lavater explains: "Physiognomy may be compared to the sum-total of the mind; pathognomy, to the interest, which is the product of this sum-total. The former shews what man is in general, the latter what he becomes at particular moments; or, the one what he might be, the other what he is." *Essays on Physiognomy*, 28.

64. I use an English translation to emphasize the letter's verbal and thematic continuities with *The Professor*, but the letter is in French, and runs as follows: "J'ai tout fait, j'ai cherché les occupations, je me suis interdit absolument le plaisir de parler de vous—même à Emilie mais je n'ai pas pu vaincre ni mes regrets ni mon

impatience—c'est humiliant cela—de ne pas savoir maîtriser ses propres pensées, être esclave à un regret, un souvenir, esclave à une idée dominante et fixe qui tyrannise son esprit." See Wise and Symington, *The Brontës*, vol. 3, 67–70.

65. Combe, *Constitution of Man*, 48.

66. We can take the processes of visuality in the novel—phrenology and paintings primarily—to be reflective of the novel's own processes; as Garrett Stewart reminds us in a recent study of du Maurier and Wilde, the analogical link between a novel's own representational methods, and a method depicted within the novel, is particularly strong in the Victorian period: "So strong is the Victorian novel's tendency to reflect upon the status of its own presentation and effect that the narrative embedding of other representational forms gets openly subordinated to the host text, to that system of arbitrary signification whose channels of response are known as reading rather than looking." See Stewart, "Reading Figures: The Legible Image of Victorian Textuality," in *Victorian Literature and the Victorian Visual Imagination*, ed. Carol Christ and John Jordan (Berkeley: University of California Press, 1995), 355.

67. Shuttleworth, *Brontë*, 137.

68. Crimsworth's brief but intense bout of "Hypochondria," which bears some resemblance to the hysterias Charcot, Breuer, and Freud would study decades after *The Professor*, is an odd, almost inexplicable detour in the resolutely forward-tending motion of the text. One excellent model for understanding this detour is provided by Suzanne Keen, whose "narrative annexes" are spaces in which cruxes generated by the text are solved or readjusted. The crux that is solved or readjusted by this particular "annex" might be, perhaps, the singular evasion of memory upon which the text otherwise insists so strongly. See Keen, *Victorian Renovations of the Novel: Narrative Annexes and the Boundaries of Representation* (Cambridge: Cambridge University Press, 1998).

69. Phrenological "jargon" was the most frequent butt of antiphrenological attacks. George Cruikshank attempted to deflate the weightiness of phrenological language in his *Phrenological Illustrations, or An Artist's View of the Craniological System of Doctors Gall and Spurzheim* (London: 1826), in which more familiar caricatures substitute for the obscure term—"Constructiveness," for example, becomes a spider weaving a web. By reducing the obscurity of the language, Cruikshank—as he no doubt intended—eliminates much of the allure of the phrenological enterprise. The lexicon could not, however, be reduced to such commonplaces; one of Spurzheim's initial "popularizing" maneuvers was to take Gall's straightforward organ names and, to use Roger Cooter's phrase, to "botanize" them—Gall's "Jugenliebe" or "Kinderliebe" became the infamous "Philoprogenitiveness," and Gall's "Zeugungstrieb" became "Amativeness." Obscurity—with its implied potential for mastery—played a key role in the success of phrenology in Britain. See Cooter, *Popular Science*, 78.

70. Christine Alexander, ed., *An Edition of the Early Writings of Charlotte Brontë*, vol. 2 (Oxford: Blackwell, 1987), 259.

71. Ibid., 403–404.

72. Janice Carlisle, "The Face in the Mirror: *Villette* and the Conventions of Autobiography," *ELH* 46 (1979): 265.

73. Those who do include Karen Lawrence, "The Cypher: Disclosure and Reticence in *Villette*," in *Critical Essays on Charlotte Brontë*, ed. Barbara Timm Gates (Boston: G. K. Hall, 1990), 306–319, and Shuttleworth, who finds in these scenes of phrenological assessment a sexuality "displaced onto erotic power play." *Brontë*, 170.

74. Difficult as it is at this distance to read phrenology as an erotic discourse, the Victorians themselves had no such trouble doing so. Thomas Wade's farce *The Phrenologists*, which opened at Covent Garden in 1830, is primarily interested in the prurience of phrenological gazing, as in the following scene, when Sampson, servant to the phrenologist Mr. Cranium, attempts a reading of a chambermaid:

> *Samp.* Mrs. Bracer—will you let me?—or will you not?
>
> *Mrs. Bracer.* Let you do what?
>
> *Samp.* Phrenologise you.
>
> *Mrs. Bracer.* Now, you impudent, teasing, and offensive little man!—if ever you ask me that favor again, either you or I must leave this house—or I shall break every bone in your goose's skin?
>
> *Samp. Language*, striking!—I must examine her: Mrs. Bracer, if you will only allow me the run of your head for a few minutes, I offer you, in return, the concession of my 'and and 'art.—A man can phrenologise his wife when he likes.

See Wade, *The Phrenologists: A Farce, in Two Acts* (London, 1830): 43–44.

75. See Carlisle, "Face in the Mirror," 286.

76. *Early Writings*, 294.

77. For a comprehensive account of surveillance in *Villette*, particularly in relation to the novel's erotic energies, see Joseph Boone, *Libidinal Currents: Sexuality and the Shaping of Modernism* (Chicago: University of Chicago Press, 1997).

78. This reading is admittedly a revision of Brenda Silver's useful elucidation of Brontë's "reflecting reader." See Silver, "The Reflecting Reader in *Villette*," in *The Voyage In: Fictions of Female Development*, ed. Elizabeth Abel, Marianne Hirsch, and Elizabeth Langland (Hanover, N.H.: University Press of New England, 1983), 90–111. Silver assumes that the Lucy who addresses a sympathetically inclined reader is the most secure Lucy; but as we have seen, antagonism and frustration in the novel are signs of desire, indeed a paradoxical security: the comfort of strife. It is through challenge—in particular, the harshly erotic challenge of M. Paul's gazes—that Lucy progresses. The "reflecting reader" is merely a mirror; *Villette* is concerned with a more radical otherness, the otherness of clinical gazes and attributions.

79. Anne Harrington notes that Gall's reputation, in the "long winter of phrenology's official disrepute" from 1820 to 1860, was maintained in French circles by Jean-Baptiste Bouillaud, a cardiologist and physiologist with an enthusiasm for Gall's localization theory. Bouillaud, in debates and experiments, sought to prove not only that the brain was an aggregate of specialized organs but that—as Gall had initially stated—the faculty of linguistic memory was located in the brain's frontal area. See Harrington, *Medicine, Mind, and the Double Brain*, 36.

80. Ian Hacking, *Rewriting the Soul: Multiple Personality and the Sciences of Memory* (Princeton: Princeton University Press, 1995), 203.

81. Matt Matsuda, *The Memory of the Modern* (New York: Oxford University Press, 1996), 83.

3. Associated Fictions

1. The epigraph: Carroll, *Alice in Wonderland: Alice's Adventures in Wonderland, Through the Looking-Glass, The Hunting of the Snark*, ed. Donald Gray (New York: Norton, 1971), 150.

2. Citations from Thackeray's novels are given parenthetically with the following abbreviations:

HE: *The History of Henry Esmond, Esq.*, ed. Donald Hawes (New York: Oxford University Press, 1991).

P: *The History of Pendennis, His Fortunes and Misfortunes, His Friends and His Greatest Enemy*, ed. John Sutherland (New York: Oxford University Press, 1994).

3. J. Hillis Miller offers a slightly different reading of Esmond's highly contextualized, although putatively accidental, recollection of the Jacob and Esau tile, tracing the memory to a Hogarthian visual technique of "complex resonance through uninterpreted juxtaposition." See Miller, *Fiction and Repetition: Seven English Novels* (Cambridge: Harvard University Press, 1982), 86. For my purposes, however, Esmond's "uninterpreted" memory is carried out by an associative psyche that has already classified this memory, already interpreted it so thoroughly, and so obviously, that no further textual interpretation is necessary: Esmond's mind collects two facts under the category of usurpation, presenting to us no uninterpreted "trifle" but an already organized mental juxtaposition.

4. Wordsworth, *The Prelude: A Parallel Text*, ed. J. C. Maxwell (Harmondsworth: Penguin, 1971).

5. Carlyle, "Biography," in *Critical and Miscellaneous Essays*, vol. 3 (New York: AMS Press, 1969), 49.

6. We might, with Franco Moretti's compelling analysis of the English *Bildungsroman* as a plot of "preservation" in mind, add the following: that these novels are interested in recollecting only that which can be "preserved" for future use — which, as Moretti reminds us, is indeed little enough in the English tradition, in which "the most significant experiences are not those that alter but those which confirm the choices made by childhood 'innocence.'" See Moretti, *The Way of the World: The Bildungsroman in European Culture* (London: Verso, 1987), 182.

7. It was a dominance that was reflected in the institutional world of Victorian philosophy; Bain's preeminence in the field was unmatched, and his circle included such luminaries as James Mill, G. H. Lewes, and Carlyle; even the now-unread Hamilton was elected to the chair of metaphysics and logic at the University of Edinburgh in 1836. In contrast to the phrenologists studied in the previous chapter, associationist psychologists had no difficulty in gaining access to organs of cultural influence or dissemination, be they university chairs, publications in prominent journals, or positions in hospitals and asylums.

8. Ribot, *La psychologie anglaise contemporaine: école experimentale* (Paris: Ladrange, 1870), 242. I translate from Ribot's French, which calls associationism "la phénomène vraiment fondamental" of British analytic psychology. In Ribot's view, the efforts of associationist theory were a great advance over the older "faculty" psychologies, which, as Ribot points out at length, were merely classificatory systems rather than explanatory ones.

9. Quoted in Christopher Salvesen, *The Landscape of Memory: A Study of Wordsworth's Poetry* (London: Edward Arnold, 1965), 42.

10. See J. H. Stonehouse, ed., *Reprints of the Catalogues of the Libraries of Charles Dickens and W. M. Thackeray* (London: Piccadilly Fountain Press, 1935), 103.

11. Sterne, *The Life and Opinions of Tristram Shandy*, ed. Graham Petrie (Harmondsworth: Penguin, 1967), 39.

12. David Hartley, *Observations on Man, His Frame, His Duty, and His Expectations* (London: Thomas Tegg, 1834), 237.

13. John Locke, *An Essay Concerning Human Understanding*, ed. Peter Nidditch (Oxford: Clarendon Press, 1975), 395.

14. Hamilton, however, notes that these two laws can really be reduced to one, the law of "Redintegration or Totality": "This law may be thus enounced,—Those thoughts suggest each other which had previously constituted parts of the same entire or total act of cognition." This idea, which Hamilton later calls "the unity of all our mental energies in general," perfectly expresses the nineteenth-century associationist idea of mnemonic relevance; if every association is part of one whole, there can be no desultory, surprising, unassimilated memory. See *Lectures on Metaphysics and Logic*, ed. Henry Mansel and John Veitch, vol. 1 (Boston: Gould and Lincoln, 1860), 435, 438. John Stuart Mill, in his 1865 book-length attack on Hamilton's work, criticizes this reduction of two laws into one, claiming that Hamilton is in effect making the remembered self identical to the remembering self—which may, in fact, have been Hamilton's aim: to reduce the possible multiplicity of selves that memory might create. See Mill, *An Examination of Sir William Hamilton's Philosophy, and of the Principal Philosophical Questions Discussed in his Writings*, ed. J. M. Robson (Toronto: University of Toronto Press, 1979), 251.

15. Alexander Bain, *The Senses and the Intellect*, 4th ed. (New York: Appleton, 1894), 341.

16. Ibid., 485.

17. Ibid., 477–478.

18. Dugald Stewart, *Elements of the Philosophy of the Human Mind*, ed. William Hamilton, vol. 2 (Boston: Little, Brown, 1854), 354.

19. Ibid., 355. A modern neuropsychological vocabulary would term these failures of contextualization "source amnesia," in which a fact, image, or emotion is recalled without the supplementary information as to where this memory originated; "source memory" is, as one modern theorist notes, "a dissociable component of a recollection that can occur independently of the strength of the recollection itself." See Larry Squire, "Biological Foundations of Accuracy and Inaccuracy in Memory," *Memory Distortion: How Minds, Brains, and Societies Reconstruct the Past*, ed. Daniel Schacter (Cambridge: Harvard University Press, 1995), 216. As early as Jeremy Bentham's 1827 *Rationale of Judicial Evidence*, however, this phenomenon was found to be of the utmost importance, and Bentham worries at great length about the ways in which context errors might force a witness to take an imaginative re-creation for an actual fact. See Bentham, *Rationale of Judicial Evidence, Specially Applied to English Practice* (New York: Russell and Russell, 1962), 252.

20. James Mill, *Analysis of the Phenomena of the Human Mind*, vol. 1 (London: Baldwick and Cradock, 1829), 244.

21. Ribot, in his summary of Mill's thought, expresses skepticism about the idea that "nous répétons réellement dans la pensée, quoique briévement, toute la série intermédiare [we really repeat in thought, however briefly, the entire intermediate series]." See Ribot, *Psychologie anglaise*, 58. What Ribot expresses is a classic late-nineteenth-century skepticism about whether the past and the present are as firmly linked as Mill would have them, and in this reservation of Ribot's—elsewhere an admirer of Mill's *Analysis*—we see the difference between early and late Victorian conceptions of memory.

22. Stewart, *Elements*, 349.

23. Hamilton, *Lectures on Metaphysics and Logic*, 441. However, Hamilton later adds a fascinating admission that his theory's inability to account for "the prompt, easy, and varied operation" of memory—for its more involuntary aspects—is a defect indeed, as "it is impossible, on this doctrine, to explain the rapid

and certain movement of thought, which, with a marvellous facility, passes from one order of thought to another," a frankness rare in Victorian psychological theory. See Hamilton, *Lectures on Metaphysic and Logic*, 444.

24. For examples of the critical tradition that links Wordsworthian memory and Victorian fictional autobiography, see J. Hillis Miller's work on Thackeray in *Fiction and Repetition*; Lawrence Frank's *Charles Dickens and the Romantic Self* (Lincoln: University of Nebraska Press, 1984); and Dirk den Hartog's *Dickens and Romantic Psychology* (London: Macmillan, 1987). I am arguing instead, of course, that it is precisely Wordsworthian mnemonic enigmas that the Victorian novel is in the process of abandoning.

25. Bain, *Senses and Intellect*, 474, 489–490.

26. Stewart, *Elements*, 382. Immediate mental classification was a phenomenon of great interest to theoreticians of legal evidence as well; as Bentham explains, significant evidence of a crime must be recognized as such by the witness at the time of perception; the witness who takes a bloody knife as a sign of a butcher's work will not be able to subsequently revise that memory as a sign of murder, and thus will be useless as a witness. Bentham, *Rationale*, 252.

27. Carlyle, "On History," in *Critical and Miscellaneous Essays*, vol. 2 (New York: AMS Press, 1969), 84.

28. An excursus into narrative theory might amplify this point. Dorrit Cohn has distinguished between two types of retrospective fictions: "consonant narration," in which the narrating self is immersed in the cognitive field of the experiencing self, and "dissonant narration," in which the narrating self has a cognitive privilege over its past experiences. Of course, for Victorian narratives "dissonant narration" promised the most deeply consonant stories imaginable: narratives that brought past and present into concord. See Cohn, *Transparent Minds: Narrative Modes for Presenting Consciousness in Fiction* (Princeton: Princeton University Press, 1978), 151.

29. See Hamilton, *Lectures*, 439: "It sometimes happens that thoughts seem to follow each other immediately, between which it is impossible to detect any bond of association. If this anomaly is insoluble, the whole theory of association is overthrown."

30. Charles Dickens, *The Personal History of David Copperfield*, The Oxford Illustrated Dickens (New York: Oxford University Press, 1994), 42. Subsequent references are given parenthetically.

31. Bain, *Senses and Intellect*, 572.

32. One might also say—with D. A. Miller's reading of the initial scene of Steerforth's sleeping form in mind—that the repetition occurs in order to disperse the erotic energies that are elliptically, if powerfully, shadowed forth in the initial vision; that is, the first scene's presence is allowable only if a later repetition is also present to balance, defuse, or deflect the primary scene's more destabilizing cathexes. Thus the continual pattern of Dickens's text: later versions of a memory license earlier versions; repetitions guarantee the presence of mental images in David's narrative. See Miller, *The Novel and the Police* (Berkeley: University of California Press, 1988), 198–199.

33. This claim is most insistently made in Thomas Reid's 1785 *Essays on the Intellectual Powers of Man*, where the shift from the high associationism of Locke and Hartley to a newer version begins to take place: "The identity of a person," Reid writes, "is a perfect identity . . . a person is a *monad* and is not divisible into parts." To the claim that we have no guarantee for this monadic self, Reid responds that "the proper evidence I have of all this is remembrance." No serious theorist of the

nineteenth century would disagree. See Reid, *Essays on the Intellectual Powers of Man*, ed. A. D. Woozley (London: Macmillan, 1944), 203–204.

34. Paul de Man, "Autobiography as De-Facement," in *The Rhetoric of Romanticism* (New York: Columbia University Press, 1984), 76.

35. The emphasis in this quotation, as in the others here, is mine.

36. Originating with the older French word "associe," to "associate" meant— until Locke's 1690 *Essay*—a social grouping, a joining together of various persons, an alliance or confederation. All of the *OED*'s listings for "association" in a mental sense until the late nineteenth century are derived exclusively from association theorists or writers alluding directly to association theory.

37. See Beer, *Darwin's Plots: Evolutionary Narrative in Darwin, George Eliot, and Nineteenth-Century Fiction* (London: Routledge, 1983), 5. Dickens's reliance on association theory has been noted implicitly, in Hillis Miller's discussion of associative linkages between past and present in *Copperfield*, and explicitly, in Micheal Kearns's work on associationism, education, and reformation in Dickens's mature work. See J. Hillis Miller, *Charles Dickens: The World of His Novels* (Cambridge: Harvard University Press, 1958); Kearns, "Associationism, the Heart, and the Life of the Mind in Dickens' Novels," *Dickens Studies Annual: Essays on Victorian Fiction* 15 (1986): 111–144. In addition, Fred Kaplan's *Dickens and Mesmerism: The Hidden Springs of Fiction* (Princeton: Princeton University Press, 1975) has opened up a great deal of inquiry into the link between Dickens and specifically Victorian theories of mind. However, our understanding of Dickens's associationism is still too reliant on eighteenth-century models and has yet to consider the role of memory in both the nineteenth-century version of the science and Dickens's own fiction.

38. Dickens, "The Haunted Man," in *The Christmas Books*, ed. Michael Slater, vol. 2 (Harmondsworth: Penguin, 1971), 259. See, however, Alexander Welsh, *The City of Dickens* (Oxford: Clarendon Press, 1971), for a very deft explanation of the inconsistencies—indeed the incoherence—of this motto in the tale.

39. See J. Hillis Miller, *Dickens*, 153, where David is explicitly linked to Proust's Marcel. One source of doubt about Dickens's affection for remembrance, however, is Steven Marcus's *Dickens from Pickwick to Dombey* (New York: Norton, 1965), which outlines the shift, midway in Dickens's career, from the extolling of tradition to a distaste for the past, or a realization of the way oppressions of the past have been maintained.

40. A chain that is parodied in Agnes's claim to have recorded David's romantic life, in "a little register of my violent attachments, with the date, duration, and termination of each, like the table of the reigns of the kings and queens, in the History of England" (368).

41. One might almost say that the movement of a Dickens text is to eliminate these characters, or to restore them to some more normative version of health—in short, to *forget* them. Thus Satis House is razed and sold for scrap—transformed into a sort of utility—and thus Mrs. Clennam's house collapses on itself; the traumatic cathexes of some of Dickens's characters are not allowed to outlive the novel's conclusion, and the novel itself becomes an exercise in exorcism, in a *leaving behind*.

42. The associationist idea that the first term or link in a chain of memory is always what comes to mind when one recollects, rather than any intermediate term, comes from Mill's *Analysis*; it is employed throughout *Copperfield*, most notably, perhaps, in the novel's one case of pathological amnesia. Emily, after fleeing Steerforth and finding refuge in Italy, goes through a period when her memory of Italian disappears; it is recovered when a child cries, "Fisherman's daughter, here's a

shell!" (728). An inadvertent allusion to her earliest memories, her life at Yarmouth, facilitates the resumption of all her later memories, including the Italian language.

43. Bain, *Senses and Intellect*, 476.

44. Summing up, fixing in place: my descriptions of memory here bear a certain relation (and a certain debt) to recent accounts of Dickens's method of epitomizing and containing the flux of experience. See Garrett Stewart, *Death Sentences: Styles of Dying in British Fiction* (Cambridge: Harvard University Press, 1984), and Audrey Jaffe, *Vanishing Points: Dickens, Narrative, and the Subject of Omniscience* (Berkeley: University of California Press, 1991).

45. See Miller, *Dickens*, 152–158.

46. The Freudian account of déjà vu is relevant here. Freud defines it as "the recollection of an unconscious fantasy"—that is, the incorporation into conscious meaning of a previously unconscious, or as yet uncontextualized, desire. See Freud, *The Psychopathology of Everyday Life*, trans. James Strachey (New York: Norton, 1989), 339. The Dickensian version of déjà vu is somewhat similar: it proclaims "I have already seen what I am now seeing, except that now I have a context for it, can understand it, can incorporate it into my life-narrative."

47. A comment of Moretti's on *Copperfield* is appropriate here: "Upon his first encounter with every other character (an encounter which as a rule takes place in childhood), he unfailingly reacts in such a way that the 'experience' of the adult reader proves to be absolutely superfluous, and it has to give way to the child's naive perception." See Moretti, *Way of the World*, 183.

48. G. K. Chesterton, *The Victorian Age in Literature* (New York: Holt, 1913), 126.

49. A tradition reinvigorated by Myron Taube, "Thackeray and the Reminiscential Vision," *Nineteenth-Century Fiction* 18, no. 3 (1963): 247–260; for a fuller expression, see Juliet McMaster, *Thackeray: The Major Novels* (Toronto: University of Toronto Press, 1971). A reading of Thackeray's use of remembrance that is more oriented toward the mnemonic ethics I call nostalgia is provided by George Levine, who asserts that, by employing Pendennis as narrator in a variety of novels, "Thackeray, unlike Flaubert, found strategies by which to sustain nostalgia (not merely bitterness) for the childish dreams he could no longer allow himself." See *The Realistic Imagination* (Chicago: University of Chicago Press, 1981), 138. My understanding of Thackeray's reminiscential tones has profited from Levine's example.

50. Bain, *Senses and Intellect*, 572–573.

51. Stewart, *Elements*, 396–397.

52. Reid, *Essays*, 196.

53. Although Thackeray did, because of his wife Isabella's mental illness, take a great deal of interest in psychological accounts of insanity; his library included such works as J. G. Millingen, *Mind and Matter Illustrated by Considerations of Hereditary Insanity* and Forbes Winslow, *On Obscure Diseases of the Brain*. See Stonehouse, *Reprints*, 148, 156.

54. That Thackeray should have invented the term "Oxbridge" (as well as "Camford") for this novel is no irrelevant fact: it demonstrates his insistence on generalizing experience, combining formerly discreet entities into larger, more vague cultural facts; it perfectly expresses his ruling epistemology, that seemingly different paths often, one might say, "come to the same thing." No matter the name, no matter who had the experience, no matter when it was had, it is the same experience. This journalistic talent of generalizing and naming large cultural tendencies is perhaps best expressed by Thackeray's introduction into demotic usage of the term "bohemia," as well as his contributions to a symbology of "bachelor-

hood"; on this, see Eve Sedgwick, *Epistemology of the Closet* (Berkeley: University of California Press, 1990), 188–195.

55. Miller, *Novel and the Police*, 145. For a recent development of the study of nineteenth-century urban boredom, see Laurie Langbauer, *Novels of Everyday Life: The Series in English Fiction, 1850–1930* (Ithaca: Cornell University Press, 1999), 128–162.

56. See John Sutherland, *Thackeray at Work* (London: Athlone Press, 1974), for a convincing account of the "pruning" that Thackeray performed on *Pendennis*, particularly in the sections that deal with Pen's writing and revision of *Walter Lorraine*, in which a charged diction is excised in favor of a more mundane lexicon.

57. Thackeray's most perceptive critics have noted the lack of a traditional *Bildung* in Pen's story; Catherine Peters contrasts Pen to David Copperfield and Maggie Tulliver, claiming that "Pendennis springs fully armed from his creator's head as a lovesick adolescent," shortcircuiting the growth of childhood; Juliet McMaster notes, in a phrase whose significance to associative memory should be clear, that Thackeray's narrator is constructed in order "to foresee the end in the beginning." Peters, *Thackeray's Universe: Shifting Worlds of Imagination and Reality* (New York: Oxford University Press, 1987), 141; McMaster, *Thackeray*, 58. See also Jerome Buckley's argument: "Insofar as he 'develops' at all during a prolonged and protected adolescence, Pen moves from a naive provinciality to a bland worldliness, a Thackerayan acceptance of human nature and society." Buckley, *Season of Youth: The Bildungsroman from Dickens to Golding* (Cambridge: Harvard University Press, 1974), 29.

58. As is evident in the text's continual production of anachronisms. From the very first serial numbers, readers have noticed Thackeray's none-too-veiled insertions of political and social material from the late 1840s into his narrative: references to the anti-Jesuit hysteria of 1849 and the then-fashionable parodies of philanthropists occur in the context of Pen's Oxbridge career, which is set in the early 1830s. The narrator claims that "we only commit anachronisms when we choose, and when by a daring violation of those natural laws some great ethical truth is to be advanced" (*P*, 668)—the truth being the lack of truly significant historical change, the way, for Thackeray, history reveals persistence rather than alteration: the persistence of unalterable *categories* of experience.

59. See Barbara Hardy, *The Exposure of Luxury: Radical Themes in Thackeray* (London: Peter Owen, 1972), 143.

60. J. Hillis Miller and Elaine Scarry, to mention two of the most notable recent readers of *Esmond*, both note this strange voice-from-the-hereafter mechanism of Esmond's memories and offer readings of it. See Miller, *Fiction and Repetition*, 94–95; Scarry, "Untransmissable History in Thackeray's *Henry Esmond*," in *Resisting Representation* (New York: Oxford University Press, 1994), 115.

61. See Scarry, however, for a significant account of how the supposedly veridical nature of Esmond's recollections is constantly being undermined and of how the recollective faculty itself is far from being unproblematically celebrated in Thackeray's novel.

62. Miller, *Fiction and Repetition*, 87.

63. See Lukács, *The Historical Novel*, trans. Hannah Mitchell and Stanley Mitchell (London: Merlin Press, 1962), 202–203.

64. Garrett Stewart offers a compelling account of this common notion in relation to *David Copperfield* and the idea of drowning, employing the idea of the near-death life-review as a path into "the whole story's sense of itself as explicitly

written epitaph for lives flashed past and gone under." See Stewart, *Death Sentences*, 73.

65. For Thackeray, writing and researching *Esmond* was a confirmation of his lack of memory, as he admitted in a letter to his mother: "I wish I had 6 months more to put into the novel: now it's nearly done it's scarce more than a sketch and it might have been made a durable history: complete in it's [*sic*] parts and whole. But at the end of 6 months it would want another 6: it takes as much trouble as Macaulays History and he has the vast advantage of remembering everything he had read, whilst everything but impressions I mean facts dates & so forth slip out of my head in wh. there's some great faculty lacking depend upon it." See *The Letters and Private Papers of William Makepeace Thackeray*, ed. Gordon Ray, vol. 3 (Cambridge: Harvard University Press, 1946), 38.

66. Dickens, *Great Expectations*, ed. Angus Calder (Harmondsworth: Penguin, 1985), 477–478.

67. Ibid., 478.

68. Cathy Caruth, *Unclaimed Experience: Trauma, Narrative, and History* (Baltimore: Johns Hopkins University Press, 1996), 4, 61.

69. Benjamin, "On Some Motifs in Baudelaire," *Illuminations*, trans. Harry Zohn (New York: Schocken, 1968), 160–165. For Benjamin a late-nineteenth-century psychological emphasis on traumatic memory and a late-nineteenth-century fictional emphasis on involuntary memory (Proust) is explicitly linked; the "traumatophilic" and the novelistic start to merge.

4. The Birth of Amnesia

1. The epigraph: Arthur Conan Doyle, *The Hound of the Baskervilles*, ed. W. W. Robson (Oxford: Oxford University Press, 1993), 158–159.

2. Norman Page, ed., *Wilkie Collins: The Critical Heritage* (London: Routledge and Kegan Paul, 1974), 84.

3. Ibid., 174–175.

4. Catherine Peters, *The King of Inventors: A Life of Wilkie Collins* (London: Secker and Warburg, 1991), 303. Peters also mentions an analogous instance: Scott's inability to recall the composition of *The Bride of Lammermoor* because of illness.

5. Citations from Collins's novels are given parenthetically with the following abbreviations:

A: *Armadale*, ed. Catherine Peters (Oxford: Oxford University Press, 1989).
DS: *The Dead Secret*, ed. Ira Nadel (Oxford: Oxford University Press, 1997).
M: *The Moonstone*, ed. J. I. M. Stewart (Harmondsworth: Penguin, 1966).
WW: *The Woman in White*, ed. Harvey Peter Sucksmith (Oxford: Oxford University Press, 1973).

6. Sue Lonoff offers some further evidence of Collins's careful dilution of his physiological reading, including his avoidance of the term "somnambulism." Lonoff adds that Collins's interest in psychology, and the psychologically aberrant, was censured by critics in a way that Dickens's similar depictions never were—a fact that can best be explained, perhaps, by Collins's careful annotation of his sources, by his more patent mixture of the novelistic and the scientific. *Wilkie Collins and His Victorian Readers: A Study in the Rhetoric of Authorship* (New York: AMS Press, 1982), 159–60.

7. Page, *Critical Heritage*, 115.

8. One important exception is Jenny Bourne Taylor, who asserts that "sensa-

tion fiction itself was positioned through reference to particular psychological paradigms." *In the Secret Theatre of Home: Wilkie Collins, Sensation, Narrative, and Nineteenth-Century Psychology* (London: Routledge, 1988), 10. But D. A. Miller's comments on the tendency of Collins's critics to ignore the physicality of "sensation" in his fiction, and thus by extension to ignore the historical meanings of "sensation," are relevant here: "the sensation novel is relegated to the margins of the canon of approved genres, and on the infrequent occasions when it is seriously discussed, 'sensation'—the modern nervousness that is as fundamental to this genre as its name—is the first thing to be dropped from the discussion." *The Novel and the Police* (Berkeley: University of California Press, 1988), 147.

9. Ian Hacking, *Rewriting the Soul: Multiple Personality and the Sciences of Memory* (Princeton: Princeton University Press, 1995), 189.

10. Ibid., 206. See also Michael Roth, "Remembering Forgetting: *Maladies de la mémoire* in Nineteenth-Century France," *Representations* 26 (1989): 52.

11. William Carpenter, *Principles of Human Physiology* (Philadelphia: Henry Lea, 1842), 582. Carpenter is here approvingly quoting a fellow physiologist, Sir H. Holland, but the point is his own: that the instances of forgetfulness or "dislocations of memory" are so confusingly varied that no category can be built around them; what they evince for Carpenter is, in the end, a bewildering mess of accidental, and not yet truly significant, phenomena.

12. See Edwin Clarke and L. S. Jacyna, *Nineteenth-Century Origins of Neuroscientific Concepts* (Berkeley: University of California Press, 1987), 30–31. See also the recent work of Peter Melville Logan, who claims that by "1840 the concept of the brain as the sole, centralized source of authority in the nervous system was dead"—which is accurate, although it predates the shift in studies of memory, from the cerebrum to the nervous system, by at least thirty years. *Nerves and Narratives: A Cultural History of Hysteria in Nineteenth-Century British Prose* (Berkeley: University of California Press, 1997), 167.

13. Alexander Bain, *The Senses and the Intellect*, 4th ed. (New York: Appleton, 1894), 8.

14. Relevant here is Michael Kearns's discussion of the difficulty, for Victorian psychologists, of "representing a connection between physiological and mental phenomena," a difficulty that, for Kearns, is most glaringly illustrated by Bain's text. *Metaphors of Mind in Fiction and Psychology* (Lexington: University Press of Kentucky, 1987), 106.

15. Bain, *Senses and Intellect*, 101.

16. Ibid., 105.

17. G. H. Lewes, *The Physiology of Common Life*, vol. 2 (London: Blackwood, 1860), 107.

18. Kearns, *Metaphors of Mind*, 108.

19. Hacking, *Rewriting*, 198–199. Roth's "Remembering Forgetting" offers perhaps the most intriguing recent reading of Ribot's volume; for Roth its project is largely ethical, insofar as it attempts to define—through its examinations of amnesia and hypermnesia—how much memory is "right" for individual health. See also Laura Otis, *Organic Memory: History and the Body in the Late Nineteenth and Early Twentieth Centuries* (Lincoln: University of Nebraska Press, 1994), 14–17, for a summary of Ribot's impact on late-nineteenth-century psychologists and physiologists.

20. Théodule Ribot, *Les maladies de la mémoire* (Paris: Germer Baillière, 1881), 51.

21. Ibid., 1.

22. Henry Maudsley, *Body and Mind: An Inquiry into Their Connection and*

Mutual Influence, Specially in Reference to Mental Disorders (New York: Appleton, 1886), 25.

23. William Carpenter, *Principles of Mental Physiology, with Their Applications to the Training and Discipline of the Mind, and the Study of its Morbid Conditions* (London: Henry King, 1874), 441.

24. The *Times*'s reviewer mocked the epidemic of forgetting that the plot demands: "We have said that the object of this method of storytelling is to make play with our ignorance. Sometimes, however, the author cannot even in this way get ignorance enough, and he has to invent more of it. For example, the principal complication of the story depends upon the loss of a date. Recover that date, and, everything else being cleared up, the story must come to an untimely end. The date might be very easily recovered if the author chose — but he doesn't choose, and he insists, against all probabilities, upon everybody forgetting it." See Page, *Critical Heritage*, 100.

25. The veracity of the various memoranda a Collins text amasses has been often brought into question, most forcefully by Richard Barickman, Susan McDonald, and Myra Stark, who claim that "records are not to be trusted": "Because of their importance, records are the likely targets of fraud — and, in Collins' vision, particularly sexual fraud." *Corrupt Relations: Dickens, Thackeray, Trollope, Collins, and The Victorian Sexual System* (New York: Columbia University Press, 1982), 145. There is something to be said for this vision of fraudulent, masculine texts; but ultimately the frauds perpetrated through textual forgery or alteration are solved only through their replacement by other texts (Marian's diary; everyday, bureaucratic paperwork such as a carriage order-list or a lawyer's copy of a marriage registry). Textual evidence — calendars, pocketbooks, letters — are, after all, far more reliable than the fungible memories of the novel's population, who cannot (in the particularly telling instance of the Limmeridge townsfolk) be counted on to remember the difference between Anne Catherick's and Laura Fairlie's appearances or voices.

26. See Kate Flint, *The Woman Reader, 1837–1914* (New York: Oxford University Press, 1993), 282–293, for a catalogue of some of the techniques through which sensation novelists, particularly female sensation novelists, sought to rebut these charges — particularly through an often dense literary allusiveness.

27. Page, *Critical Heritage*, 84.

28. Ibid., 159.

29. For one possible connection between "forgettable" plots and "forgotten" characters, see Tamar Heller, *Dead Secrets: Wilkie Collins and the Female Gothic* (New Haven: Yale University Press, 1992), 84.

30. Patrick Brantlinger, "What Is 'Sensational' about the Sensation Novel?" *Nineteenth-Century Fiction* 37, no. 1 (1982), 18. Brantlinger's usage is, to my knowledge, one of the very few times "amnesia" has been brought into relation to Collins's work. See also Tamar Heller's claim that erasure functions as a self-protective device designed to shield Collins from his more radical critiques of society; see Heller, *Dead Secrets*, 143.

31. See Miller, *Novel and Police*, 53–55.

32. Taylor, *Secret Theatre*, 130.

33. The way in which this scene, with its allegedly real-life counterpart in Collins's experience, has the capacity to summarize sensation fiction's usual practices has made it the site of several intriguing readings. Two particularly interesting examples are D. A. Miller's account of this sensation, in *Novel and the Police*, as a sort of contagion — in which a feminine figure, crucially a no longer confined figure, transfers a feminized affect to Hartright, and by extension to the reader —

and Ann Cvetkovich's surmise that the physical nature of the shock Hartright experiences is merely an alibi for his encounter with a socially unacknowledged, perhaps unacknowledgable, but not, finally, all that mysterious sexual fantasy. *Mixed Feelings: Feminism, Mass Culture, and Victorian Sentimentalism* (New Brunswick, N.J.: Rutgers University Press, 1992), 79. Of additional interest is Alison Winter's contextualization of this "shock" within the framework of mid-Victorian mesmerism, which for her represents a common "framework for understanding the psychological and physiological phenomena that accompanied reading in general, and certainly the sort of intense reading activity that surrounded *The Woman in White*." *Mesmerized: Powers of Mind in Victorian Britain* (Chicago: University of Chicago Press, 1998), 327.

34. Although the gender of the physiologized individual is certainly not an irrelevant factor; as Kate Flint reminds us, mid-Victorian discussions of literary sensation concentrated on the female reader, since for mainstream physiology "anyone of a 'feminine nature' (most probably, though not exclusively, also biologically female) would by her very physiology be especially liable to the perturbing effects of literature calculated to shock and surprise." *Woman Reader*, 55.

35. Taylor, *Secret Theatre*, 182. There have been, however, some interesting and worthwhile recent attempts to take sensation seriously, particularly Jonathan Loesberg's compelling claim that the sensation response is systematically dissociated from "thematic readability" in Collins in order to cast as illicit the very response it evokes. "The Ideology of Narrative Form in Sensation Fiction," *Representations* 13 (1986): 118.

36. See Logan, *Nerves and Narratives*, for a perceptive discussion of Marshall Hall's "reflex arc" and the significance for later nineteenth-century narrative of unwilled action.

37. J. D. Morrell, *Elements of Psychology*, vol. 1 (London: William Pickering, 1853), 171.

38. See Clarke and Jacyna, *Nineteenth-Century Origins*, 140–146.

39. Carpenter, *Human Physiology*, 582–583.

40. Carpenter, *Mental Physiology*, 466.

41. Ibid., 459–465. See also Hacking's *Rewriting*, which offers a compelling history of "double consciousness" and its eventual transformation into more modern psychological categories.

42. See S. T. Coleridge, *Biographia Literaria*, ed. James Engell and W. Jackson Bate (Princeton: Princeton University Press, 1983), 112.

43. Hacking, *Rewriting*, 155.

44. Ribot, *Maladies de la mémoire*, 76. It is nonetheless curious that double consciousness recurs as late as the early work of Breuer and Freud, where it is claimed to be "present to a rudimentary degree in every hysteria." See *Studies on Hysteria*, trans. James Strachey (New York: Basic Books, 1957), 12.

45. Ribot came close to Jennings's analysis in his famous Law of Regression, in which the destruction of mnemonic data "descend progressivement de l'instable au stable [descends progressively from the unstable to the stable]." See *Maladies de le mémoire*, 95. According to this law, the "stable" *categories* of Mr. Candy's consciousness, such as having plans, would last longer than the "unstable" *content* of those categories (i.e., what those plans were).

46. See Clarke and Jacyna, *Nineteenth-Century Origins*, 124–156.

5. The Unremembered Past

1. The epigraph — I translate from the original: "Le passé *oublie* qu'il est passé; et à ce prix, joue dans le présent." *Cahiers*, ed. Judith Robinson (Paris: Gallimard, 1973), 1244.

2. See *The George Eliot Letters*, vol. 4, ed. Gordon Haight (New Haven: Yale University Press, 1954), 42.

3. See Gordon Haight, *George Eliot* (Oxford: Oxford University Press, 1968), 362. Later critics have picked up on the note of pain in *Romola* — Dianne Sadoff has written of the novel as "nothing short of traumatic for its author" — but usually in the service of denying the novel's value, rather than as an example of an interesting cultural predilection, whereby a detailed historical or mnemonic recovery is always *painful*. See Sadoff, *Monsters of Affection: Dickens, Eliot and Brontë on Fatherhood* (Baltimore: Johns Hopkins University Press, 1982), 90.

4. See Haight, *Letters*, vol. 3, 474.

5. One excellent account of the British historical novel in the nineteenth century, and its relative failure, is John Maynard's discussion of the intense antiquarian detail of such texts as Bulwer-Lytton's *The Last Days of Pompeii* and the inability of such detail to reconcile antiquities with a sense of felt individual experience; see "Broad Canvas, Narrow Perspective: The Problem of the English Historical Novel in the Nineteenth Century," in *The Worlds of Victorian Fiction*, ed. Jerome Buckley (Cambridge: Harvard University Press, 1975), 237–265. See also Nicholas Rance, *The Historical Novel and Popular Politics in Nineteenth-Century England* (Totowa, N.J.: Barnes and Noble, 1975), and Andrew Sanders, *The Victorian Historical Novel, 1840–1880* (London: Macmillan, 1978).

6. Eliot, *Romola*, ed. Andrew Sanders (Harmondsworth: Penguin, 1980), 378. All subsequent references to the novel are given in parentheses.

7. Baldassare is not the only example, simply the most vivid in his thematic connections; one could cite as well the amnesiac Dr. Manette from Dickens's 1859 *A Tale of Two Cities* as a further instance of the collision of personal amnesia with historical reconstruction. What is surprising about Victorian historical fiction — built as it is on the labor of so much detailed recovery of the past — is how familiar its personal mnemonic values are: like the social novel or the fictional autobiography, obsessive rememberers, such as *Felix Holt*'s Mrs. Transome, are still the figures the novel works hardest to eliminate.

8. It is important to note here the difference between *Romola* and Eliot's other major novels, where memory, particularly a memory linked to piety, is a chief concern. Philip Fisher's formulation is telling: "The disconnection of memory as the price of entrance into the world of Florence is a major problem of the novel." See Fisher, *Making up Society: The Novels of George Eliot* (Pittsburgh: University of Pittsburgh Press, 1981), 12. It is a disconnection, as Fisher stresses, from Eliot's own personal experiences, and a disconnection as well from the idea of memory as a sanctifying, purifying force; in *Romola* Eliot is paradoxically much closer to the trajectory of Victorian nostalgic processes than elsewhere in her work. Sally Shuttleworth's claim is worth citing in this connection: "Memory does not function for Romola, as for George Eliot's earlier characters, as a positive force which might link past to present, and hold forth images of future growth. It is related solely to death." Shuttleworth, *George Eliot and Nineteenth-Century Science: The Make-Believe of a Beginning* (Cambridge: Cambridge University Press, 1984), 110. By "memory," I take Shuttleworth to mean the specificities of dense, particularized recall that nostalgia works against.

9. The "presentness" of Eliot's novel is also argued for by Alison Booth, who positions *Romola* within a cultural landscape much more contemporary to Eliot than Renaissance Florence: the careers and ambitions of Victorian reforming women such as Barbara Bodichon, Florence Nightingale, and Anna Jameson. See "The Silence of Great Men: Statuesque Femininity and the Ending of *Romola*," in *Famous Last Words: Changes in Gender and Narrative Closure*, ed. Alison Booth (Charlottesville: University Press of Virginia, 1993), 110–134; *Greatness Engendered: George Eliot and Virginia Woolf* (Ithaca: Cornell University Press, 1992). It is perhaps symptomatic of the "presentness" of *Romola* that some of the best and most sympathetic work on the novel has been oriented more toward mid-Victorian realities than Eliot's studiously achieved reproduction of Renaissance life.

10. Time and again Eliot's labor comes in for such easy criticism, although Maynard, possibly alone among critics of *Romola*, praises not just the effort but the effect of such thorough research: "If we compare George Eliot's reconstruction of Florence, even admitting its occasional touch of the lamp, to the historical world we are given by Bulwer or even Dickens or Scott we must recognize an important improvement not just in antiquarian accuracy but in social conception." See "Broad Canvas," 252.

11. See James, "The Novels of George Eliot," in *Literary Criticism: French Writers, Other European Writers, Prefaces to the New York Edition* (New York: Library of America, 1984), 1006.

12. See Orel, *The Historical Novel from Scott to Sabatini* (London: St. Martin's Press, 1995), for a full account of Macaulay's impact on historical novelists from the 1850s onward. Some of the finest work on the historiography of *Romola* and its sources has been done by Nancy Paxton, who has read the novel through the lens of Comte and Spencer; see particularly *George Eliot and Herbert Spencer: Feminism, Evolutionism, and the Reconstruction of Gender* (Princeton: Princeton University Press, 1991).

13. See Haight, *George Eliot*, 350.

14. The notebook, entitled "Florentine Notes" in Eliot's hand, is currently in the British Library (Ms. 40768). It most probably was used during Eliot's study, in May 1861, at the Maglibecchian Library in Florence, where she and Lewes spent several days consulting original manuscripts and illustrated volumes.

15. See Haight, *Letters*, vol. 4, 45.

16. See Lukács, *The Historical Novel*, trans. Hannah Mitchell and Stanley Mitchell (London: Merlin Press, 1962), 189. As is well known, Lukács does not devote much space to the British historical novel after Scott and entirely ignores *Romola*; but the venom Lukács expends upon Flaubert can be easily extended to Eliot's novel, as the two novels provide us with the nineteenth century's greatest examples of laboriously constructed narratives about historical periods and places that are difficult to assimilate to contemporary topics or concerns (ancient Carthage, fifteenth-century Florence)—they are the preeminent instances of authorial research and authorial mnemonics.

17. See Mary Wilson Carpenter's "The Trouble with Romola," which discusses these small-scale amnesias and invokes the late-nineteenth-century medical notion of "hypermnesia" (first explicitly discussed by Ribot) in an analysis of Eliot's faulty antiquarians. Carpenter adduces the novel's instances of hypermnesia or amnesia as signs of authorial trauma, however, whereas I read these instances as more than motifs—as in fact enabling structures of historical fiction—whose sources lie not in

any postulated authorial trauma but rather in the cultural conditions of the novel's production, in the negative valences Victorian fiction habitually, even symptomatically, attached to capacious and particular retrospects. Carpenter, "The Trouble with Romola," in *Victorian Sages and Cultural Discourse: Renegotiating Gender and Power*, ed. Thaïs Morgan (New Brunswick, N.J.: Rutgers University Press, 1990), 105–128.

18. See *George Eliot: The Critical Heritage*, ed. David Carroll (London: Routledge, 1971), 220, 235. Not all critics were so dismissive of Baldassare, however; R. H. Hutton's laudatory review in the *Spectator*, for which Eliot thanked him, states that there "are few passages of subtler literary grandeur in English romance than that which paints the electrifying effect of a thrill of vindictive passion on Baldassare's paralyzed memory." See Carroll, 200. In any case, Eliot's experiments with mental pathology were not limited to *Romola*—we have, shortly before her Florentine researches begin, *Silas Marner* (1861) and Silas's cataleptic fits; there is also the more extreme example of *The Lifted Veil* (1859), and Latimer's quasi-mesmeric visions of the future. Various forms of aberrational psychology were not as foreign to Eliot as Baldassare's critics would have it.

19. Those commentators who have understood the importance of the disappearance of Bardo's library—rather than the importance of Tito's deceitful sale of it—have been those who have stressed the gendered dilemma in Romola's duty to protect Bardo's collection of male texts. As Margaret Homans puts it, "it is in this contradiction between a woman's obligation to act as conduit for male words and the pain such a role brings her, the contradiction found in the other novels but framed most acutely here, that Eliot both accomodates and criticizes women's place in androcentric literature." See Homans, *Bearing the Word: Language and Female Experience in Nineteenth-Century Women's Writing* (Chicago: University of Chicago Press, 1986), 196.

20. Fleishman, *The English Historical Novel: Walter Scott to Virginia Woolf* (Baltimore: Johns Hopkins University Press, 1971), 8. An analogous investigation of the object-world of historical fiction can be found in Lukács, where the "archaeological faithfulness towards things and customs of no concern to us" in the post-1848 historical novel comes under scrutiny. See Lukács, 195.

21. Scott, *Waverley; or, 'Tis Sixty Years Since*, ed. Claire Lamont (New York: Oxford University Press, 1986), 294.

22. Ibid., 338.

23. As Philip Fisher has pointed out, Eliot does not permit us to build up a series of reading-memories of the ring; it is "purely symbolic; it is not a lived, used token like Bob Jakin's knife or the mill itself. In our reading experience, the ring never existed until the moment it is removed. . . . A wedding ring is abstract." See Fisher, *Making up Society*, 136. Thus Eliot prevents the ring, like so many other objects in the text, from constituting a memory in itself for her readers. It enters the text only when it becomes an object of present controversy, while its past remains merely hypothetical or implied.

24. Propp, *Morphology of the Folktale*, trans. Laurence Scott (Austin: University of Texas, 1968), 45–50.

25. Or the conversion can take more fantastic forms; Eliot describes the "votive waxen images" of the Church of the Nunziata as "a perfect resurrection-swarm of remote mortals and fragments of mortals, reflecting, in their varying degrees of freshness, the sombre dinginess and sprinkled brightness of the crowd below" (200). Here the religious objects under consideration threaten to fantastically *come*

alive and mingle with the living—a perfect, if phantasmatically distorted, version of the threat every object in the text presents.

26. Haight, *Letters*, vol. 3, 457.

27. Some such idea is lurking in the many accounts, from those of Lewes to current criticism, which call Eliot's novel an attempt to make history "come alive." Eliot, writes Andrew Sanders, "is not concerned to show how the past has moulded the present, but that history can be alive to us, and in us"—less a positivist or Hegelian history, as Sanders argues, than one based on Scott or Riehl. See Sanders, *Victorian Historical Novel*, 174. But ultimately, as I have argued, the question is less a historiographical one and more, as *Romola* itself always insists, one of *personal* memory and how it might "recognize" the past in the present (and limit itself to the past that can be so "recognized").

28. There is a pertinent resemblance between the "recognitions" offered by *Romola*, particularly its activations of the past in the present, and Bergson's arguments more than three decades later in *Matière et mémoire* about the essential oneness of perception and memory. While any too strict correspondences between Eliot's novel and Bergson's theories should be canvassed skeptically, there remains an important common ground: an interest in mnemonic processes that are rooted in perceptual acts rather than any more purely imagistic "unconscious."

29. See Neil Hertz's suggestive "George Eliot's Life-in-Debt," *Diacritics* 25, no. 4 (1995): 59–70, in which a sophisticated account of the temporality of debt (as well as other figures for gestation, such as seeds, germs, and dying) provides a look inside a version of textual memory that insists on the eventual reappearance of mnemonic material: as a debt will come due or a seed promises a sprout, so memories in Eliot imply an eventual return to active perception.

30. Eliot, *Felix Holt, the Radical*, ed. Peter Coveney (Harmondsworth: Penguin, 1972), 468.

31. Thus the interesting choice of 1492 as opening date of the novel's action; although the reference to Columbus is obvious and not unmentioned within the text, the date actually signifies the *end* of something: the end of Florence's political dominance and unrivaled cultural authority heralded by the death of Lorenzo the Magnificent, which is the first historical "event" recorded by the novel. This preference for historical moments that express decline, loss, or finality—the end of Florentine stability, the end of effective Jacobite rebellion (Scott, Thackeray), the decadence of ancient civilization (Flaubert)—furnishes us with a clue to the influence nostalgic disconnection had on historical fiction and remains one of the more salient features of the genre, particularly in the way this historical disconnection is matched with various forms of personal, mnemonic disconnection (amnesia, nostalgia).

32. Bailin, *The Sickroom in Victorian Fiction: The Art of Being Ill* (Cambridge: Cambridge University Press, 1994), 126.

33. Lukács, *Historical Novel*, 195.

34. See George Levine, "*Romola* as Fable," *Critical Essays on George Eliot*, ed. Barbara Hardy (London: Routledge and Kegan Paul, 1970), 78–97; Margaret Homans, *Bearing the Word*; Gillian Beer, *George Eliot* (Bloomington: Indiana University Press, 1986); Susan Winnett, "Coming Unstrung: Women, Men, Narrative, and Principles of Pleasure," *PMLA* 105, no. 3 (1990): 505–518.

35. John Kucich offers an interesting and in some senses complimentary reading of Romola's time in the plague village, stressing the "libidinal necessity" of freeing herself from the past. See Kucich, *Repression in Victorian Fiction: Charlotte Brontë, George Eliot, and Charles Dickens* (Berkeley: University of California Press,

1987), 175. His reminder that the excision of memory is libidinally productive as well as more generally psychically beneficial is useful here, although one might add a twist: the more sinister libidinal energy of Tito is similarly matched to an avoidance of, or failure to achieve, remembrance.

36. Nora, "General Introduction: Between Memory and History," in *Realms of Memory: Rethinking the French Past*, trans. Arthur Goldhammer, vol. 1 (New York: Columbia University Press, 1996), 3.

37. See Kerwin Lee Klein, "On the Emergence of *Memory* in Historical Discourse," *Representations* 69 (2000): 127–150, for a thorough account of the various contestations to Nora's dichotomy as well as reasons for its continued presence in a variety of disciplines.

38. The assertion is made in a May 1861 letter to Blackwood: "As I often tell her most of the scenes and characters of her books are quite as historical to her direct personal experience, as the 15th century of Florence; and she knows infinitely more about Savonarola than she knew of Silas, besides having deep personal sympathies with the old reforming priest which she had not with the miser." Haight, *Letters*, vol. 3, 420.

39. Eliot, *The Impressions of Theophrastus Such*, ed. Nancy Henry (Iowa City: University of Iowa Press, 1994), 18.

Conclusion. Nostalgic Reading

1. The epigraph: Halbwachs, *On Collective Memory*, trans. Lewis Coser (Chicago: University of Chicago Press, 1992), 51.

2. Jameson, *The Political Unconscious: Narrative as a Socially Symbolic Act* (Ithaca: Cornell University Press, 1981), 56.

3. See Gillian Beer's "Origin and Oblivion in Victorian Narrative," in *Sex, Politics, and Science in the Nineteenth-Century Novel*, ed. Ruth Bernard Yeazell (Baltimore: Johns Hopkins University Press, 1986), 63–87, for one nuanced confrontation of this problem—how such a copious form as the Victorian novel could thrive, given the facts of readerly forgetfulness—that runs the risk of making New Critical habits of reading (connection, organization, attention) the *telos* of these narratives.

4. A useful examination of this issue can be found in Regenia Gagnier, *Subjectivities: A History of Self-Representation in Britain, 1832–1920* (New York: Oxford University Press, 1991), 99–137. Gagnier connects the failure of Victorian narrative's reformist aims to the necessarily constricted structure of sympathetic identification; for Gagnier, sympathetic identification limits a reader to what is already familiar and known, whereas my analysis of nostalgia depicts a reader limited, eventually, to only what is already gone and disconnected, already solved.

5. For Jameson's "process of production," see *Political Unconscious*, 56–58. Iser's study of the individual reader is best located in *The Act of Reading: A Theory of Aesthetic Response* (Baltimore: Johns Hopkins University Press, 1978); for Jauss and the "horizon of expectation," see *Toward an Aesthetic of Reception*, trans. Timothy Bahti (Minneapolis: University of Minnesota Press, 1982). Paul Ricoeur has put forth a claim for a theory of "affect" or *aiesthesis* that would bridge the gap between Iser's individual reader and Jauss's public, collective readership: "On the one hand, it is through the individual process of reading that the text reveals its 'structure of appeal'; on the other hand, it is inasmuch as readers participate in the sedimented expectations of the general reading public that they are constituted as competent readers. . . . Literary history, renovated by the aesthetic of reception, may thus claim to include the phenomenology of the act of reading." See Ricoeur, *Time and*

Narrative, trans. Kathleen Blamey and David Pellauer, vol. 3 (Chicago: University of Chicago Press, 1988), 167.

6. Theories of affect to which I owe a debt include Iser's merging of "meaning" with an affective "happening": "The constitution of meaning, therefore, gains its full significance when something happens to the reader. The constituting of meaning and the constituting of the reading subject are therefore interacting operations that are both structured by the aspects of the text." *Act of Reading*, 152. See also Jameson's instructive definition of the novel "as process rather than as form," as "the transformation of the reader's subjective attitudes which is at one and the same time the production of a new kind of objectivity." *Political Unconscious*, 151–152.

7. The "forgive and forget" cliché to which Trollope's title alludes was noticed immediately, and savagely, by Henry James in his September 1865 review in the *Nation*: "Can we forgive Miss Vavasor? Of course we can, and forget her, too, for that matter." See *Literary Criticism: Essays on Literature, American Writers, English Writers* (New York: Library of America, 1984), 1318.

8. Trollope, *Can You Forgive Her?* ed. Stephen Wall (Harmondsworth: Penguin, 1972), 66. Subsequent references are given parenthetically.

9. I am thinking here of Iser's strong claim that "the aesthetic object cannot be identified with any of its manifestations during the time-flow of the reading," a claim that helps illustrate Iser's concept of the "wandering viewpoint," the continually retrospective and prospective phenomenology of reading. *The Act of Reading*, 109. Much of nostalgic reading, one might say, is an attempt to fix this wandering viewpoint to the place of closure, to prevent the retrospections that reading narrative, for Iser, necessarily involves.

Bibliography

Adorno, Theodor. *Critical Models: Interventions and Catchwords*. Trans. Henry Pickford. New York: Columbia University Press, 1998.

Aitken, John. *Elements of the Theory and Practice of Physic and Surgery*. 2 vols. London, 1782.

Alexander, Christine, ed. *An Edition of the Early Writings of Charlotte Brontë*. 2 vols. Oxford: Blackwell, 1987.

Alexander, Christine, and Jane Sellars. *The Art of the Brontës*. Cambridge: Cambridge University Press, 1995.

Althusser, Louis. *Lenin and Philosophy*. Trans. Ben Brewster. New York: Monthly Review Press, 1971.

Anderson, Benedict. *Imagined Communities: Reflections on the Origin and Spread of Nationalism*. London: Verso, 1983.

Arens, Katherine. *Structures of Knowing: Psychologies of the Nineteenth Century*. Boston: Kluwer Academic, 1989.

Arnold, Thomas. *Observations on the Nature, Kinds, Causes, and Prevention of Insanity, Lunacy, or Madness*. 2 vols. Leicester: 1782.

Austen, Jane. *Emma*. 1816. Ed. R. W. Chapman. Oxford: Oxford University Press, 1982.

——. *Mansfield Park*. 1814. Ed. R. W. Chapman. Oxford: Oxford University Press, 1980.

——. *Minor Works*. Ed. R. W. Chapman. Oxford: Oxford University Press, 1980.

——. *Northanger Abbey and Persuasion*. 1818. Ed. R. W. Chapman. Oxford: Oxford University Press, 1982.

——. *Pride and Prejudice*. 1813. Ed. R. W. Chapman. Oxford: Oxford University Press, 1982.

——. *Sense and Sensibility*. 1811. Ed. R. W. Chapman. Oxford: Oxford University Press, 1982.

Bailin, Miriam. *The Sickroom in Victorian Fiction: The Art of Being Ill*. Cambridge: Cambridge University Press, 1994.

Bain, Alexander. *The Senses and the Intellect*. 1855. New York: D. Appleton, 1894. 4th ed.

Bakhtin, M. M. *The Dialogic Imagination: Four Essays*. Trans. Caryl Emerson and Michael Holquist. Austin: University of Texas Press, 1981.

Balzac, Honoré de. *Le Père Goriot*. 1835. Paris: Garnier-Flammarion, 1966.

——. "Pierrette." *La Comédie humaine*. Vol. 4. Paris: Gallimard, 1976. 29–163. 12 vols.

——. *Splendeurs et misères des courtisanes*. 1838–1847. Paris: Gallimard, 1973.

Banks, Joseph. *Journal of the Right Hon. Sir Joseph Banks*. Ed. Joseph Hooker. London: Macmillan, 1896.

Barickman, Richard, Susan McDonald, and Myra Stark. *Corrupt Relations: Dickens, Thackeray, Trollope, Collins, and the Victorian Sexual System*. New York: Columbia University Press, 1982.

Barthes, Roland. *S/Z*. Trans. Richard Miller. New York: Noonday, 1974.

——. *Writing Degree Zero*. Trans. Annette Lavers and Colin Smith. New York: Noonday, 1967. Trans. of *Le Degré Zero de L'Écriture*. Paris: 1953.

Bate, W. J., and Albrecht B. Strauss, eds. *The Yale Edition of the Works of Samuel Johnson*. 16 vols. New Haven: Yale University Press, 1969.

Beer, Gillian. *Darwin's Plots: Evolutionary Narrative in Darwin, George Eliot and Nineteenth-Century Fiction*. London: Routledge, 1983.

——. *George Eliot*. Bloomington: Indiana University Press, 1986.

——. "Origins and Oblivion in Victorian Narrative." In *Sex, Politics, and Science in the Nineteenth Century Novel*, ed. Ruth Bernard Yeazell. Baltimore: Johns Hopkins University Press, 1986. 63–87.

Bell, Charles. *The Anatomy and Philosophy of Expression as Connected with the Fine Arts*. 4th ed. London: 1847.

Benjamin, Walter. *Illuminations*. Trans. Harry Zohn. New York: Schocken, 1968.

Bentham, Jeremy. *Rationale of Judicial Evidence, Specially Applied to English Practice*. 1827. New York: Russell and Russell, 1962.

Bergson, Henri. *Matière et mémoire: essai sur la relation du corps à l'esprit*. 7th ed. Paris: Librairie Félix Alcan, 1911.

Bersani, Leo. *A Future for Astyanax: Character and Desire in Literature*. Boston: Little, Brown, 1976.

Boone, Joseph. *Libidinal Currents: Sexuality and the Shaping of Modern Literature*. Chicago: University of Chicago Press, 1987.

Booth, Alison. *Greatness Engendered: George Eliot and Virginia Woolf*. Ithaca: Cornell University Press, 1992.

——. "The Silence of Great Men: Statuesque Femininity and the Ending of *Romola*." In *Famous Last Words: Changes in Gender and Narrative Closure*, ed. Alison Booth. Charlottesville: University Press of Virginia, 1993. 110–134.

Brantlinger, Patrick. "What Is 'Sensational' about the Sensation Novel?" *Nineteenth-Century Fiction* 37 (1982): 1–28.

Breuer, Josef, and Sigmund Freud. *Studies on Hysteria*. Trans. James Strachey. New York: Basic Books, 1957.

Brodie, Benjamin. *Psychological Inquiries: In a Series of Essays, Intended to Illustrate the Mutual Relations of the Physical Organization and the Mental Faculties.* London: Longman, Brown, Green, and Longmans, 1854.

Brontë, Charlotte. *Jane Eyre.* 1847. Ed. Q. D. Leavis. Harmondsworth: Penguin, 1966.

——. *The Professor.* 1857. Ed. Heather Glen. Harmondsworth: Penguin, 1989.

——. *Villette.* 1853. Ed. Mark Lilly. Harmondsworth: Penguin, 1979.

Brownstein, Rachel. *Becoming a Heroine: Reading about Women in Novels.* New York: Columbia University Press, 1982.

Brunnert, Klaus. "Nostalgie in der Geschichte der Medizin." *Düsseldorfer Arbeiten zur Geschichte der Medizin* 58 (1984): 1–339.

Buckley, Jerome. *Season of Youth: The Bildungsroman from Dickens to Golding.* Cambridge: Harvard University Press, 1974.

Butler, Marilyn. *Jane Austen and the War of Ideas.* 1975. Oxford: Clarendon, 1987.

Carlisle, Janice. "The Face in the Mirror: *Villette* and the Conventions of Autobiography." *ELH* 46 (1979): 262–289.

Carlyle, Thomas. *Critical and Miscellaneous Essays.* 4 vols. New York: AMS Press, 1969.

Carpenter, Mary Wilson. "The Trouble with Romola." In *Victorian Sages and Cultural Discourse: Renegotiating Gender and Power,* ed. Thaïs Morgan. New Brunswick, N.J.: Rutgers University Press, 1990. 105–128.

Carpenter, William. *Principles of Human Physiology.* 1842. Philadelphia: Henry Lea, 1868.

——. *Principles of Mental Physiology, with Their Applications to the Training and Discipline of the Mind, and the Study of its Morbid Conditions.* London: Henry King, 1874.

Carroll, David, ed. *George Eliot: The Critical Heritage.* London: Routledge, 1971.

Carroll, Lewis. *Alice in Wonderland: Alice's Adventures in Wonderland, Through the Looking-Glass, the Hunting of the Snark.* Ed. Donald Gray. New York: Norton, 1971.

Carruthers, Mary. *The Book of Memory: A Study of Memory in Medieval Culture.* Cambridge: Cambridge University Press, 1990.

Caruth, Cathy. *Unclaimed Experience: Trauma, Narrative, and History.* Baltimore: Johns Hopkins University Press, 1996.

——, ed. *Trauma: Explorations in Memory.* Baltimore: Johns Hopkins University Press, 1995.

Chesterton, G. K. *The Victorian Age in Literature.* New York: Holt, 1913.

Clarke, Edwin, and L. S. Jacyna. *Nineteenth-Century Origins of Neuroscientific Concepts.* Berkeley: University of California Press, 1987.

Cohen, Monica. *Professional Domesticity in the Victorian Novel.* Cambridge: Cambridge University Press, 1998.

Cohn, Dorrit. *Transparent Minds: Narrative Modes for Presenting Consciousness in Fiction.* Princeton: Princeton University Press, 1978.

Coleridge, Samuel Taylor. *Biographia Literaria.* 1817. Ed. James Engell and W. Jackson Bate. Princeton: Princeton University Press, 1983.

——. *The Complete Poetical Works of Samuel Taylor Coleridge.* Ed. Ernest Hartley Coleridge. 2 vols. Oxford: Clarendon, 1912.

Colley, Ann. *Recollection and Nostalgia in Victorian Culture.* New York: St. Martin's Press, 1998.

Colley, Linda. *Britons: Forging the Nation, 1707–1837.* New Haven: Yale University Press, 1992.

Collins, Wilkie. *Armadale.* 1866. Ed. Catherine Peters. New York: Oxford University Press, 1989.

——. *The Dead Secret*. 1857. Ed. Ira Nadel. New York: Oxford University Press, 1997.

——. *The Moonstone*. 1868. Ed. J. I. M. Stewart. Harmondsworth: Penguin, 1966.

——. *The Woman in White*. 1860. Ed. Harvey Peter Sucksmith. New York: Oxford University Press, 1973.

Combe, George. *The Constitution of Man Considered in Relation to External Objects*. 3rd ed. Edinburgh: John Anderson Jun., 1835.

——. *Lectures on Moral Philosophy*. Boston: Marsh, Capen, Lyon, and Webb, 1840.

——. *Lectures on Phrenology*. New York: Fowler and Wells, 1847.

——. *A System of Phrenology*. Boston: Marsh, Capen, and Lyon, 1835.

Connerton, Paul. *How Societies Remember*. Cambridge: Cambridge University Press, 1989.

Cooter, Roger. *The Cultural Meaning of Popular Science: Phrenology and the Organization of Consent in Nineteenth-Century Britain*. Cambridge: Cambridge University Press, 1984.

Cowling, Mary. *The Artist as Anthropologist: The Representation of Type and Character in Victorian Art*. Cambridge: Cambridge University Press, 1989.

"The Craniological Controversy." *Blackwood's Edinburgh Magazine* 1 (1817): 35–38.

Crary, Jonathan. *Techniques of the Observer: On Vision and Modernity in the Nineteenth Century*. Cambridge: MIT Press, 1990.

Cruikshank, George. *Phrenological Illustrations, or an Artist's View of the Craniological System of Doctors Gall and Spurzheim*. 1826. London: 1873.

Cvetkovich, Ann. *Mixed Feelings: Feminism, Mass Culture, and Victorian Sentimentalism*. New Brunswick: Rutgers University Press, 1992.

Darwin, Charles. *The Expression of the Emotions in Man and Animals*. London: 1872.

Davidoff, Leonore, and Catherine Hall. *Family Fortunes: Men and Women of the English Middle Class, 1780–1850*. Chicago: University of Chicago Press, 1987.

de Man, Paul. *The Rhetoric of Romanticism*. New York: Columbia University Press, 1984.

den Hartog, Dirk. *Dickens and Romantic Psychology: The Self in Time in Nineteenth-Century Literature*. London: Macmillan, 1987.

Dickens, Charles. *Great Expectations*. 1861. Ed. Angus Calder. Harmondsworth: Penguin, 1985.

——. "The Haunted Man." In *The Christmas Books*. Vol. 2. Ed. Michael Slater. Harmondsworth: Penguin, 1971. 245–253.

——. *Little Dorrit*. 1857. Ed. John Holloway. Harmondsworth: Penguin, 1967.

——. *Our Mutual Friend*. 1865. Ed. Stephen Gill. Harmondsworth: Penguin, 1971.

——. *The Personal History of David Copperfield*. 1850. The Oxford Illustrated Dickens. New York: Oxford University Press, 1994.

——. *A Tale of Two Cities*. 1859. Ed. Andrew Sanders. New York: Oxford University Press, 1988.

Doyle, Arthur Conan. *The Hound of the Baskervilles*. 1902. Ed. W. W. Robson. New York: Oxford University Press, 1993.

Eliot, George. *Felix Holt, the Radical*. 1866. Ed. Peter Coveney. Harmondsworth: Penguin, 1972.

——. *Impressions of Theophrastus Such*. Ed. Nancy Henry. Iowa City: University of Iowa Press, 1994.

——. *The Lifted Veil*. 1859. London: Virago, 1985.

——. "Quarry for *Romola*." Ms. 40768. British Library, London.

——. *Romola*. 1863. Ed. Andrew Sanders. Harmondsworth: Penguin, 1980.

———. *Silas Marner: The Weaver of Raveloe*. 1861. Ed. Q. D. Leavis. Harmondsworth: Penguin, 1967.

Ellenberger, Henri. *The Discovery of the Unconscious: The History and Evolution of Dynamic Psychiatry*. New York: Basic Books, 1970.

Elliotson, John. *Human Physiology*. London: Longman, Orme, Brown, Green, and Longmans, 1840.

Ernst, Fritz. *Vom Heimweh*. Zurich: Fretz & Wasmuth Verlag, 1949.

"Essays on Cranioscopy, Craniology, Phrenology, &c., By Sir Toby Tickletoby, Bart." *Blackwood's Edinburgh Magazine* 10 (1821): 73–82.

Falconer, William. *A Dissertation on the Influence of the Passions upon Disorders of the Body*. London: 1788.

Fisher, Philip. *Making up Society: The Novels of George Eliot*. Pittsburgh: University of Pittsburgh Press, 1981.

Flaubert, Gustave. *Bouvard et Pécuchet*. Paris: Garnier Frères, 1965.

———. *Dictionnaire des Idées reçues*. In *Les Oeuvres de Gustave Flaubert*. Vol. 17. Lausanne: Société Coopérative Editions Rencontre, 1965. 374–448.

Fleishman, Avrom. *The English Historical Novel: Walter Scott to Virginia Woolf*. Baltimore: Johns Hopkins University Press, 1971.

Flint, Kate. *The Woman Reader, 1837–1914*. New York: Oxford University Press, 1993.

Foucault, Michel. *The Birth of the Clinic*. Trans. A. M. Sheridan Smith. New York: Vintage, 1975.

Fowler, O. S. *Education and Self-Improvement, Founded on Physiology and Phrenology; or, What Constitutes Good Heads and Bodies, and How to Make Them Good, by Enlarging Deficiencies and Diminishing Excesses*. New York: 1844.

———. *Fowler on Matrimony: or, Phrenology and Physiology Applied to the Selection of Companions for Life; Including Directions to the Married for Living Together Affectionately and Happily*. New York, 1842.

———. *Memory and Intellectual Improvement Applied to Self-Education and Juvenile Instruction*. New York: Fowler and Wells, 1853.

Fowler, O. S., and L. N. Fowler. *The Illustrated Self-Instructor in Phrenology and Physiology*. New York: Fowler and Wells, 1855.

Frank, Lawrence. *Charles Dickens and the Romantic Self*. Lincoln: University of Nebraska Press, 1984.

Freud, Sigmund. *The Psychopathology of Everyday Life*. 1901. Trans. James Strachey. New York: Norton, 1989.

Frye, Northrop. *Anatomy of Criticism: Four Essays*. Princeton: Princeton University Press, 1957.

Fussell, Paul. *The Great War and Modern Memory*. New York: Oxford University Press, 1975.

Gagnier, Regenia. *Subjectivities: A History of Self-Representation in Britain, 1832–1900*. New York: Oxford University Press, 1991.

Gall, F. J. *On the Origin of the Moral Qualities and Intellectual Faculties of Man, and the Conditions of their Manifestation*. Trans. Winslow Lewis. 2 vols. Boston: Marsh, Capen, and Lyon, 1835.

Gaskell, Elizabeth. *The Life of Charlotte Brontë*. 1857. Ed. Alan Shelston. Harmondsworth: Penguin, 1975.

———. *Mary Barton: A Tale of Manchester Life*. 1848. Ed. Stephen Gill. Harmondsworth: Penguin, 1970.

Gérin, Winifred. *Charlotte Brontë: The Evolution of Genius*. Oxford: Clarendon Press, 1967.

Gibbon, Charles. *The Life of George Combe.* 2 vols. London: Macmillan, 1878.

Gilbert, Sandra M., and Susan Gubar. *The Madwoman in the Attic: The Woman Writer and the Nineteenth-Century Literary Imagination.* New Haven: Yale University Press, 1979.

Goethe, Johann Wolfgang von. *The Sorrows of Young Werther.* Trans. Elizabeth Mayer and Louise Bogan. New York: Vintage, 1971.

Griggs, Earl Leslie, ed. *Collected Letters of Samuel Taylor Coleridge.* 6 vols. Oxford: Clarendon, 1956.

Hacking, Ian. *Mad Travelers: Reflections on the Reality of Transient Mental Illnesses.* Charlottesville: University Press of Virginia, 1998.

———. *Rewriting the Soul: Multiple Personality and the Sciences of Memory.* Princeton: Princeton University Press, 1995.

Haight, Gordon. *George Eliot: A Biography.* Oxford: Oxford University Press, 1968.

———, ed. *The George Eliot Letters.* 6 vols. New Haven: Yale University Press, 1954.

Halbwachs, Maurice. *On Collective Memory.* Trans. Lewis Coser. Chicago: University of Chicago Press, 1992.

Hamilton, Robert. "History of a Remarkable Case of Nostalgia Affecting a Native of Wales, and Occurring in Britain." In *Medical Commentaries for the Years 1786, 1787.* Philadelphia: 1795.

Hamilton, William. *Lectures on Metaphysics and Logic.* 2 vols. Ed. Henry Mansel and John Veitch. Boston: Gould and Lincoln, 1860.

Hardy, Barbara. *The Exposure of Luxury: Radical Themes in Thackeray.* London: Peter Owen, 1972.

———. *A Reading of Jane Austen.* London: Peter Owen, 1975.

Harrington, Anne. *Medicine, Mind, and the Double Brain: A Study in Nineteenth-Century Thought.* Princeton: Princeton University Press, 1987.

Hartley, David. *Observations on Man, His Frame, His Duty, and His Expectations.* 1748. London: Thomas Tegg, 1834.

Hegel, G. W. F. *Phenomenology of Spirit.* Trans. A. V. Miller. New York: Oxford University Press, 1979.

Heller, Tamar. *Dead Secrets: Wilkie Collins and the Female Gothic.* New Haven: Yale University Press, 1992.

Hertz, Neil. "George Eliot's Life-in-Debt." *Diacritics* 25, no. 4 (1995): 59–70.

Hobsbawm, Eric, and Terence Ranger, eds. *The Invention of Tradition.* Cambridge: Cambridge University Press, 1983.

Homans, Margaret. *Bearing the Word: Language and Female Experience in Nineteenth-Century Women's Writing.* Chicago: University of Chicago Press, 1986.

Honan, Park. *Jane Austen: Her Life.* New York: St. Martin's Press, 1987.

Horkheimer, Max, and Theodor Adorno. *Dialectic of Enlightenment.* Trans. John Cumming. New York: Continuum, 1998.

Houghton, Walter. *The Victorian Frame of Mind, 1830–1870.* New Haven: Yale University Press, 1957.

Huyssen, Andreas. *Twilight Memories: Marking Time in a Culture of Amnesia.* London: Routledge, 1995.

Iser, Wolfgang. *The Act of Reading: A Theory of Aesthetic Response.* Baltimore: Johns Hopkins University Press, 1978.

Jack, Ian. "Phrenology, Physiognomy, and Characterisation in the Novels of Charlotte Brontë." *Brontë Society Transactions* 15 (1970): 377–391.

Jaffe, Audrey. *Vanishing Points: Dickens, Narrative, and the Subject of Omniscience.* Berkeley: University of California Press, 1991.

James, Henry. *Literary Criticism: French Writers, Other European Writers, Prefaces to the New York Edition*. New York: Library of America, 1984.

——. *Literary Criticism: Essays on Literature, American Writers, English Writers*. New York: Library of America, 1984.

James, William. *The Principles of Psychology*. 1890. Cambridge: Harvard University Press, 1981.

Jameson, Frederic. *The Political Unconscious: Narrative as a Socially Symbolic Act*. Ithaca: Cornell University Press, 1981.

——. *Postmodernism: Or, The Cultural Logic of Late Capitalism*. Durham, N.C.: Duke University Press, 1991.

Jauss, Hans Robert. *Toward an Aesthetic of Reception*. Trans. Timothy Bahti. Minneapolis: University of Minnesota Press, 1982.

Johnson, Claudia. "Austen Cults and Cultures." In *The Cambridge Companion to Jane Austen*, ed. Edward Copeland and Juliet McMaster. Cambridge: Cambridge University Press, 1997. 211–226.

——. *Jane Austen: Women, Politics, and the Novel*. Chicago: University of Chicago Press, 1988.

Kaplan, Fred. *Dickens and Mesmerism: The Hidden Springs of Fiction*. Princeton: Princeton University Press, 1975.

Kearns, Michael. "Associationism, the Heart, and the Life of the Mind in Dickens' Novels." *Dickens Studies Annual: Essays on Victorian Fiction* 15 (1986): 111–144.

——. *Metaphors of Mind in Fiction and Psychology*. Lexington: University Press of Kentucky, 1987.

Keen, Suzanne. *Victorian Renovations of the Novel: Narrative Annexes and the Boundaries of Representation*. Cambridge: Cambridge University Press, 1998.

Klein, Kerwin Lee. "On the Emergence of *Memory* in Historical Discourse." *Representations* 69 (2000): 127–150.

Koselleck, Reinhart. *Futures Past: On the Semantics of Historical Time*. Trans. Keith Tribe. Cambridge: MIT Press, 1985.

Kucich, John. *Repression in Victorian Fiction: Charlotte Brontë, George Eliot, and Charles Dickens*. Berkeley: University of California Press, 1987.

Langbauer, Laurie. *Novels of Everyday Life: The Series in English Fiction, 1850–1930*. Ithaca: Cornell University Press, 1999.

Larrey, D. J. *Surgical Essays*. Trans. John Revere. Baltimore: 1823. Trans. of *Recueil de Mémoires de Chirurgie*. Paris: 1821.

Lavater, J. C. *Essays on Physiognomy: For the Promotion of the Knowledge and the Love of Mankind; Written in the German Language by J. C. Lavater, Abridged from Mr. Holcroft's Translation*. Trans. Thomas Holcroft. London: [1793].

Lawrence, Karen. "The Cypher: Disclosure and Reticence in *Villette*." *Critical Essays on Charlotte Brontë*. Ed. Barbara Timm Gates. Boston: G. K. Hall, 1990. 306–319.

Le Faye, Deirdre, ed. *Jane Austen's Letters*. 3rd ed. Oxford: Oxford University Press, 1995.

Le Goff, Jacques. *History and Memory*. Trans. Steven Rendall and Elizabeth Claman. New York: Columbia University Press, 1992.

Levine, George. *The Realistic Imagination*. Chicago: University of Chicago Press, 1981.

——. "*Romola* as Fable." *Critical Essays on George Eliot*. Ed. Barbara Hardy. London: Routledge and Kegan Paul, 1970. 78–97.

Lewes, G. H. *The Physiology of Common Life*. 2 vols. London: Blackwood, 1860.

Linnaeus, Carl von. "Genera Morborum." In *Amoenitates Academica seu Dissertationes Variae Physicae, Medicae, Botanicae*. Vol. 6. Upsala: 1789. 452–486.

Locke, John. *An Essay Concerning Human Understanding*. 1690. Ed. Peter Nidditch. Oxford: Clarendon Press, 1975.

Loesberg, Jonathan. "The Ideology of Narrative Form in Sensation Fiction." *Representations* 13 (1986): 115–138.

Logan, Peter Melville. *Nerves and Narratives: A Cultural History of Hysteria in Nineteenth-Century British Prose*. Berkeley: University of California Press, 1997.

Lonoff, Sue. *Wilkie Collins and His Victorian Readers: A Study in the Rhetoric of Authorship*. New York: AMS Press, 1982.

Lowenthal, David. *The Past Is a Foreign Country*. Cambridge: Cambridge University Press, 1985.

Lukács, Georg. *The Historical Novel*. Trans. Hannah Mitchell and Stanley Mitchell. London: Merlin Press, 1962.

——. *History and Class Consciousness: Studies in Marxist Dialectics*. Trans. Rodney Livingstone. Cambridge: MIT Press, 1971.

——. *The Theory of the Novel*. Trans. Anna Bostock. Cambridge: MIT Press, 1971.

Manual of Phrenology: Being an Analytical Summary of the System of Doctor Gall, on the Faculties of Man and the Function of the Brain. Philadelphia: Carey, Lea, and Blanchard, 1835.

Marcus, Steven. *Dickens from Pickwick to Dombey*. New York: Norton, 1965.

Marx, Karl. *Capital*. Trans. David Fernbach. 3 vols. Harmondsworth: Penguin, 1981.

Marx, Karl, and Friedrich Engels. *The Communist Manifesto*. Ed. David McLellan. New York: Oxford University Press, 1992.

Matsuda, Matt. *The Memory of the Modern*. New York: Oxford University Press, 1996.

Maudsley, Henry. *Body and Mind: An Inquiry into Their Connection and Mutual Influence, Specially in Reference to Mental Disorders*. 1873. New York: Appleton, 1886.

——. *The Pathology of Mind*. 1879. New York: Appleton, 1880.

Maynard, John. "Broad Canvas, Narrow Perspective: The Problem of the English Historical Novel in the Nineteenth Century." In *The Worlds of Victorian Fiction*, ed. Jerome Buckley. Harvard English Studies 6. Cambridge: Harvard University Press, 1975. 237–265.

McKeon, Michael. *The Origins of the English Novel, 1600–1740*. Baltimore: Johns Hopkins University Press, 1987.

McMaster, Juliet. *Thackeray: The Major Novels*. Toronto: University of Toronto Press, 1971.

Michie, Helena. *The Flesh Made Word: Female Figures and Women's Bodies*. New York: Oxford University Press, 1987.

Mill, James. *Analysis of the Phenomena of the Human Mind*. 2 vols. London: Baldwick and Cradock, 1829.

Mill, John Stuart. *An Examination of Sir William Hamilton's Philosophy, and of the Principal Philosophical Questions Discussed in his Writings*. 1865. Ed. J. M. Robson. Toronto: University of Toronto Press, 1979.

Miller, D. A. *Narrative and its Discontents: Problems of Closure in the Traditional Novel*. Princeton: Princeton University Press, 1981.

——. *The Novel and the Police*. Berkeley: University of California Press, 1988.

Miller, J. Hillis. *Charles Dickens: The World of His Novels*. Cambridge: Harvard University Press, 1958.

———. *Fiction and Repetition: Seven English Novels*. Cambridge: Harvard University Press, 1982.

Moglen, Helene. *Charlotte Brontë: The Self Conceived*. New York: Norton, 1976.

Morell, J. D. *Elements of Psychology*. Vol. 1. London: William Pickering, 1853.

Moretti, Franco. *The Atlas of the European Novel, 1800–1900*. London: Verso, 1998.

———. *The Way of the World: The Bildungsroman in European Culture*. London: Verso, 1987.

Mulvey, Laura. "Visual Pleasure and Narrative Cinema." *Screen* 16, no. 3 (1975): 6–18.

Nokes, David. *Jane Austen: A Life*. London: Fourth Estate, 1997.

Nora, Pierre. *Realms of Memory: Rethinking the French Past*. 3 vols. Trans. Arthur Goldhammer. New York: Columbia University Press, 1996.

Novalis. *Schriften*. Ed. Paul Kluckhohn and Richard Samuel. Stuttgart: W. Kohlhammer Verlag, 1960.

O'Farrell, Mary Ann. *Telling Complexions: The Nineteenth-Century English Novel and the Blush*. Durham: Duke University Press, 1997.

Orel, Harold. *The Historical Novel from Scott to Sabatini: Changing Attitudes toward a Literary Genre, 1814–1920*. London: St. Martin's Press, 1995.

Otis, Laura. *Organic Memory: History and the Body in the Late Nineteenth and Early Twentieth Centuries*. Lincoln: University of Nebraska Press, 1994.

Page, Norman, ed. *Wilkie Collins: The Critical Heritage*. London: Routledge and Kegan Paul, 1974.

Paxton, Nancy. *George Eliot and Herbert Spencer: Feminism, Evolutionism, and the Reconstruction of Gender*. Princeton: Princeton University Press, 1991.

Peters, Catherine. *The King of Inventors: A Life of Wilkie Collins*. London: Secker and Warburg, 1991.

———. *Thackeray's Universe: Shifting Worlds of Imagination and Reality*. New York: Oxford University Press, 1987.

Plumb, J. H. *The Death of the Past*. Boston: Houghton Mifflin, 1970.

Poovey, Mary. *Making a Social Body: British Cultural Formation, 1830–1864*. Chicago: University of Chicago Press, 1995.

———. *Uneven Developments: The Ideological Work of Gender in Mid-Victorian England*. Chicago: University of Chicago Press, 1988.

Poulet, Georges. *Studies in Human Time*. Trans. Elliott Coleman. Baltimore: Johns Hopkins University Press, 1956. Trans. of *Études sur le temps humain*. Paris, 1953.

Propp, Vladimir. *Morphology of the Folktale*. Trans. Laurence Scott. Austin: University of Texas Press, 1968.

"Psychological Inquiries." *Blackwood's Edinburgh Magazine* 77 (1855): 402–420.

Rance, Nicholas. *The Historical Novel and Popular Politics in Nineteenth-Century England*. Totowa, N.J.: Barnes and Noble, 1975.

Ray, Gordon, ed. *The Letters and Private Papers of William Makepeace Thackeray*. 4 vols. Cambridge: Harvard University Press, 1946.

Reed, Edward. *From Soul to Mind: The Emergence of Psychology, from Erasmus Darwin to William James*. New Haven: Yale University Press, 1997.

Reed, John. *Victorian Conventions*. Athens: Ohio University Press, 1975.

Reid, Thomas. *Essays on the Intellectual Powers of Man*. 1785. Ed. A. D. Woozley. London: Macmillan, 1944.

Ribot, Théodule. *Les maladies de la mémoire*. Paris: Germer Baillière, 1881.

———. *La psychologie anglaise contemporaine: école expérimentale*. Paris: Ladrange, 1870.

Ricoeur, Paul. *Time and Narrative*. Trans. Kathleen Blamey and David Pellauer. 3 vols. Chicago: University of Chicago Press, 1984–1988.

Rogers, Samuel. *The Pleasures of Memory*. 1792. Oxford: Woodstock, 1989.

Rosen, George. "Nostalgia: A 'Forgotten' Psychological Disorder." *Clio Medica* 10, no. 1 (1975): 29–52.

Roth, Michael. "Dying of the Past: Medical Studies of Nostalgia in Nineteenth-Century France." *History and Memory* 3, no. 1 (1991): 5–29.

——. "Remembering Forgetting: *Maladies de la mémoire* in Nineteenth-Century France." *Representations* 26 (1989): 49–68.

Rothfield, Lawrence. *Vital Signs: Medical Realism in Nineteenth-Century Fiction*. Princeton: Princeton University Press, 1992.

Rousseau, G. S. "War and Peace: Some Representations of Nostalgia and Adventure in the Eighteenth Century." In *Guerres et Paix: La Grande-Bretagne au XVIIIe siècle I-II*, ed. Paul-Gabriel Bouce. Paris: Université de la Sorbonne Nouvelle, 1998. 121–140.

Rousseau, Jean-Jacques. *Dictionnaire de Musique. Oeuvres Completes de J.-J. Rousseau*. Vol. 14. Paris: 1831.

Sadoff, Dianne. *Monsters of Affection: Dickens, Eliot and Brontë on Fatherhood*. Baltimore: Johns Hopkins University Press, 1982.

Said, Edward. *Culture and Imperialism*. New York: Knopf, 1993.

Sales, Roger. *Jane Austen and Representations of Regency England*. New York: Routledge, 1994.

Salvesen, Christopher. *The Landscape of Memory: A Study of Wordsworth's Poetry*. London: Edward Arnold, 1965.

Sanders, Andrew. *The Victorian Historical Novel, 1840–1880*. London: Macmillan, 1978.

Sauvages de la Croix, Francisco Boissier de. *Nosologia Methodica sistens Morborum Classes, Genera et Species, Juxtà Sydenhami mentem & Botanicorum ordinem*. 2 vols. Amsterdam: 1763.

Scarry, Elaine. *Resisting Representation*. New York: Oxford University Press, 1994.

Schacter, Daniel. *Searching for Memory: The Brain, the Mind, and the Past*. New York: Basic Books, 1996.

——, and Elaine Scarry, eds. *Memory, Brain, and Belief*. Cambridge: Harvard University Press, 2000.

Schudson, Michael. "Dynamics of Distortion in Collective Memory." In *Memory Distortion: How Minds, Brains, and Societies Reconstruct the Past*, ed. Daniel Schacter. Cambridge: Harvard University Press, 1995. 346–364.

Scott, Walter. *Waverley; or, 'Tis Sixty Years Since*. 1814. Ed. Claire Lamont. New York: Oxford University Press, 1986.

Sedgwick, Eve Kosofsky. *Epistemology of the Closet*. Berkeley: University of California Press, 1990.

——. "Jane Austen and the Masturbating Girl." *Critical Inquiry* 17 (1991): 818–837.

Senseman, Wilfrid. "Charlotte Brontë's Use of Physiognomy and Phrenology." *Papers of the Michigan Academy of Sciences, Arts and Letters* 37 (1952): 475–486.

Seymour, George. *Dissertatio medica inauguralis de nostalgia*. Edinburgh: 1818.

Shelley, Mary. *Frankenstein: or, The Modern Prometheus*. 1818. Ed. M. K. Joseph. New York: Oxford University Press, 1969.

Shuttleworth, Sally. *Charlotte Brontë and Victorian Psychology*. Cambridge: Cambridge University Press, 1996.

——. *George Eliot and Nineteenth-Century Science: The Make-Believe of a Beginning*. Cambridge: Cambridge University Press, 1984.

Silver, Brenda. "The Reflecting Reader in *Villette.*" In *The Voyage In: Fictions of Female Development*. Eds. Elizabeth Abel, Marianne Hirsch, and Elizabeth Langland. Hanover, N.H.: University Press of New England, 1983. 90–111.

Smith, George. "Charlotte Brontë." *Cornhill* 82 (1900): 778–795.

Southam, B. C., ed. *Jane Austen: The Critical Heritage, 1870–1940*. 2 vols. London: Routledge, 1987.

Spurzheim, Johann Gaspar. *Phrenology: In Connexion with the Study of Physiognomy*. London: Treuttel, Wurtz, and Richter, 1826.

———. *A View of the Philosophical Principles of Phrenology*. 3rd ed. London: [1825?].

Squire, Larry. "Biological Foundations of Accuracy and Inaccuracy in Memory." In *Memory Distortion: How Minds, Brains, and Societies Reconstruct the Past*, ed. Daniel Schacter. Cambridge: Harvard University Press, 1995. 197–225.

Stafford, Barbara. *Body Criticism: Imaging the Unseen in Enlightenment Art and Medicine*. Cambridge: MIT Press, 1991.

Starobinski, Jean. "The Idea of Nostalgia." *Diogenes* 54, no. 3 (1966): 81–103.

Sterne, Laurence. *The Life and Opinions of Tristram Shandy*. Ed. Graham Petrie. Harmondsworth: Penguin, 1967.

Stewart, Dugald. *Elements of the Philosophy of the Human Mind*. 1792. Ed. William Hamilton. 2 vols. Boston: Little, Brown, 1854.

Stewart, Garrett. *Death Sentences: Styles of Dying in British Fiction*. Cambridge: Harvard University Press, 1984.

———. "Reading Figures: The Legible Image of Victorian Textuality." *Victorian Literature and the Victorian Visual Imagination*. Eds. Carol Christ and John Jordan. Berkeley: University of California Press, 1995. 345–367.

Stewart, Susan. *On Longing: Narratives of the Miniature, the Gigantic, the Souvenir, the Collection*. Durham, N.C.: Duke University Press, 1993.

Stonehouse, J. H., ed. *Reprints of the Catalogues of the Libraries of Charles Dickens and W. M. Thackeray*. London: Piccadilly Fountain Press, 1935.

Sutherland, J. A. *Thackeray at Work*. London: Athlone Press, 1974.

Tanner, Tony. *Jane Austen*. Cambridge: Harvard University Press, 1986.

Taube, Myron. "Thackeray and the Reminiscential Vision." *Nineteenth-Century Fiction* 18, no. 3 (1963): 247–260.

Tave, Stuart. *Some Words of Jane Austen*. Chicago: University of Chicago Press, 1973.

Taylor, Jenny Bourne. *In the Secret Theatre of Home: Wilkie Collins, Sensation Narrative, and Nineteenth-Century Psychology*. London: Routledge, 1988.

———, and Sally Shuttleworth, eds. *Embodied Selves: An Anthology of Psychological Texts, 1830–1890*. Oxford: Clarendon Press, 1998.

Terdiman, Richard. *Present Past: Modernity and the Memory Crisis*. Ithaca: Cornell University Press, 1993.

Thackeray, William Makepeace. *The History of Henry Esmond, Esq.* 1852. Ed. Donald Hawes. New York: Oxford University Press, 1991.

———. *The History of Pendennis: His Fortunes and Misfortunes, His Friends and His Greatest Enemy*. 1850. Ed. John Sutherland. New York: Oxford University Press, 1994.

———. *The Memoirs of Barry Lyndon, Esq.* 1844. Ed. Andrew Sanders. New York: Oxford University Press, 1984.

———. *Vanity Fair: A Novel without a Hero*. 1848. Ed. J. I. M. Stewart. Harmondsworth: Penguin, 1968.

Thatcher, James. *A Military Journal during the American Revolutionary War*. Boston: Richardson and Lord, 1823.

Trollope, Anthony. *Can You Forgive Her?* 1864–65. Ed. Stephen Wall. Harmondsworth: Penguin, 1972.

Trumpener, Katie. *Bardic Nationalism: The Romantic Novel and the British Empire*. Princeton: Princeton University Press, 1997.

Tytler, Graeme. *Physiognomy in the European Novel: Faces and Fortunes*. Princeton: Princeton University Press, 1982.

Valéry, Paul. *Cahiers*. Ed. Judith Robinson. Paris: Gallimard, 1973.

Vrettos, Athena. *Somatic Fictions: Imagining Illness in Victorian Culture*. Stanford: Stanford University Press, 1995.

Wade, Thomas. *The Phrenologists: A Farce, In Two Acts*. London, 1830.

Warren, Charles Everett. *Medical Tractates*. 4 vols. Boston, 1903.

Watson, Hewett. "Remarks on the Peculiarities of Memory." *Phrenological Journal* 7 (1831/32): 212–224.

Watt, Ian. *The Rise of the Novel: Studies in Defoe, Richardson and Fielding*. Berkeley: University of California Press, 1957.

Welsh, Alexander. *The City of Dickens*. Oxford: Clarendon Press, 1971.

White, Hayden. *The Content of the Form: Narrative Discourse and Historical Representation*. Baltimore: Johns Hopkins University Press, 1987.

Wiltshire, John. *Jane Austen and the Body*. Cambridge: Cambridge University Press, 1992.

Winnett, Susan. "Coming Unstrung: Women, Men, Narrative, and Principles of Pleasure." *PMLA* 105, no. 3 (1990): 505–518.

Winter, Alison. *Mesmerized: Powers of Mind in Victorian Britain*. Chicago: University of Chicago Press, 1998.

Wise, Thomas James, and John Alex Symington, eds. *The Brontës: Their Lives, Friendships and Correspondence*. 4 vols. Oxford: Shakespeare Head, 1932.

Wordsworth, William. *The Prelude: A Parallel Text*. Ed. J. C. Maxwell. Harmondsworth: Penguin, 1971.

Yates, Frances. *The Art of Memory*. Chicago: University of Chicago Press, 1966.

Žižek, Slavoj. *The Sublime Object of Ideology*. London: Verso, 1989.

Index

Adorno, Theodor, 16
Ainsworth, W. H.
  Mervyn Clitheroe, 127
Althusser, Louis, 17
amnesia, 7, 11, 17, 168–171, 177–179,
  181, 185–186, 199–205, 207–209,
  212–214, 216, 224, 227, 231, 234,
  241
  birth of, 171–172, 177–178, 236–237
  case studies of, 197–203
  and sensation, 191–196
amnesiac self, 6–7, 11, 15, 17, 21, 78, 102,
  166, 168, 170, 172–173, 179, 181,
  187, 190, 202, 237, 242
Arnold, Thomas, 31, 40, 43, 46, 53
associationism, 8–10, 16, 90, 127–139,
  150–151, 244 n.11
  dominance over Victorian psychology, 128–129, 139, 265 n.7
  eighteenth-century version of,
  129–130, 132
  principle of concordance in, 134,
  136–137, 144–145, 157, 158, 165, 224

principle of integrity in, 134, 137,
  144–145, 158, 165, 224
principle of relevance in, 134–136,
  141, 144–145, 158, 165, 224
repetitiveness of memory in, 150–151
Victorian revision of, 130–134
Austen, Jane, 3, 8, 14–15, 19–29, 31–33,
  35–75, 95, 147, 168, 170–171, 174,
  178, 186–188, 192, 204–205, 207,
  209, 211, 213, 222, 225, 228,
  230–232, 234, 236, 238, 240, 254
  n.46, 254 n.50
  "The Adventures of Mr Harley," 22
  Emma, 32, 40–43
  "Evelyn," 248 n.2
  "Henry and Eliza," 21
  "Jack and Alice," 248 n.2
  "Lesley Castle," 254 n.48
  "Love and Friendship," 248 n.2
  Mansfield Park, 13, 16, 20, 22, 31,
  35–39, 53–64, 69–70, 73, 173, 207,
  211, 217, 225
  Northanger Abbey, 21

Kingsley, Charles
  Alton Locke, 127
Kipling, Rudyard, 27
Koselleck, Reinhart, 11, 246 n.23, 253
    n.40

Lacan, Jacques, 85
Larrey, D. J., 30, 36, 253 n.38, 254 n.49
Lavater, J. C., 86, 98
Leighton, Frederic, 206
Levine, George, 230
Lewes, G. H., 127, 176, 207, 222, 233
  Physiology of Common Life, 176
  Ranthorpe, 127
life-review, 12–13, 37–39, 163, 232
Linnaeus, Carl von, 23, 32, 97
Locke, John, 11, 129–130, 132–133, 139,
    244 n.11
Logan, Peter Melville, 272 n.12
Lukács, Georg, 17, 161, 212, 230, 243
    n.2, 249 n.3, 253 n.36, 276 n.16

Macaulay, Thomas Babington, 211
Mann, Thomas, 243 n.2
Marx, Karl, 7, 10, 17, 247 n.31
Matsuda, Matt, 124
Maudsley, Henry, 178
memorials, 15, 218–219
memory
  absence of in Victorian psychology,
      9–10, 172
  associationist, 128–134
  contemporary studies of, 14, 74
  everyday or pure, 4, 6–7, 244 n.4
  history and, 209–210, 214, 232–235
  modernist conceptions of, 11, 22,
      124, 243 n.2
  representation of by the novel, 4, 8
Meredith, George
  Evan Harrington, 127
mesmerism, 139
Mill, James, 128, 130–134, 137, 139, 145,
    152, 156, 165, 175
Mill, John Stuart, 128–129, 266 n.14
Miller, D. A., 153, 255 n.53, 267 n.32, 272
    n.8, 273 n.33
Miller, J. Hillis, 143, 159, 265 n.3
mnemotechnics, 211–212, 256 n.65
mobility, 7, 12, 30–32, 44, 45, 59,
    64–66, 70–73, 255 n.57, 256 n.63

Morell, J. D., 193
Moretti, Franco, 265 n.6, 269 n.47
Mulvey, Laura, 85

Newman, John Henry
  Loss and Gain, 127
Nietzsche, Friedrich, 177
Nora, Pierre, 233–235
nostalgia
  and belief, 17
  communal purpose of, 15, 35, 40–43,
      51–52, 61, 67, 207, 229, 232
  definition of, 4–7, 10–11, 74, 232,
      238
  depathologization of, 24, 33, 47,
      49–50, 73, 102, 240, 253 n.36, 257
      n.68
  dilutions of, 14, 52, 230
  disconnections of, 12, 14–15, 26, 35,
      37–39, 43, 49, 52, 58, 61, 66–67,
      72, 215, 224, 229, 232, 237, 242
  and forgetting, 5–7, 16–17, 23
  and historical memory, 209, 211–213,
      233–235
  naming and, 14, 35, 39, 43, 48–49,
      52, 67, 207, 228–229, 232
  origin as eighteenth-century
      clinical disease, 8, 23–24, 28–35,
      253 n.38
  pleasure and, 5, 14, 26, 35–36, 43, 45,
      49, 52, 61, 66–67, 207
  reading and, 18–19, 237–242
  repathologizing of, 170, 173, 204,
      236–237
  as response to social disruption, 8,
      12–13
  temporal orientation of, 35–37, 43,
      45, 61, 253 n.39
Novalis, 65, 252 n.34

object-reappearance, 13, 49, 51, 55–58,
    140, 218–222
Oliphant, Margaret, 172, 196

Pater, Walter
  Marius the Epicurean, 207
pathognomy, 262 n.63
Pavlov, I. P., 204
phrenology, 9–10, 73, 139, 236, 257 n.5,
    259 n.18

absence of faculty of memory in, 78,
  86, 88–94, 260 n.32
cerebral localization and, 88,
  123–124
decontextualizing in, 98–99, 101,
  104–105
detaching in, 99–100, 107, 115, 117
erotics of, 112–116, 122–123, 264
  n.74
fixing character in, 101, 110–111, 120
future-oriented emphasis of, 83–84,
  86–87
mastery promised by, 82, 103,
  108–112, 259 n.22, 263 n.69
prevalence in Victorian culture,
  80–81
surfacing in, 95–96, 101, 261 n.52
taxonomizing in, 96–98, 101, 104,
  110–111, 113, 118, 121
physiognomy, 9, 83, 86, 262 n.63
physiology, 169–179, 192–195,
  200–204
Plumb, J. H., 249 n.5
Poovey, Mary, 258 n.12, 261 n.51
Poulet, Georges, 9
Propp, Vladimir, 220
Proust, Marcel, 3–4, 11, 124, 140, 243
  n.2
psychology, history of, 8–9

Reade, Charles, 167
recognition, 209, 220–231, 278 n.28
Reid, Thomas, 90, 151
Ribot, Théodule, 128–130, 177–178,
  184, 197, 199–200, 266 n.21
  Les maladies de la mémoire, 177
  La psychologie anglaise contemporaine,
  128
Ricoeur, Paul, 243 n.2, 279 n.5
Rogers, Samuel, 33, 252 n.29
Roth, Michael, 272 n.19
Rothfield, Lawrence, 93
Rousseau, Jean-Jacques, 9, 11, 252 n.29

Sales, Roger, 27
Sauvages de la Croix, Francisco
  Boissier de, 32, 172
Scott, Walter, 129, 222, 278 n.31
  Waverley, 217–218
Sedgwick, Eve Kosofsky, 250 n.14

sensation novel, 3, 8, 167–171, 177, 185,
  196, 208
Seymour, George, 31
Shelley, Mary
  Frankenstein, 251 n.22
Shuttleworth, Sally, 80, 106, 258 n.9,
  258 n.12, 275 n.8
Silver, Brenda, 264 n.78
Smith, George, 76
souvenirs, 13, 55–58, 69, 217–218, 222
Spurzheim, Johann Gaspar, 80, 88–91,
  93–94, 98, 104, 123–124
Stafford, Barbara, 97, 100
Stendhal, 153
Sterne, Laurence, 129–130, 132, 134, 163
  Tristram Shandy, 129, 132, 134
Stewart, Dugald, 90, 129–135, 150, 153
Stewart, Garrett, 263 n.66
Stewart, Susan, 40, 55–56, 74

Tanner, Tony, 65
taxonomy, 15–16
Taylor, Jenny Bourne, 192–193,
  271 n.8
Terdiman, Richard, 31, 243 n.3
Thackeray, William Makepeace, 8, 16,
  125–134, 136, 140, 147–166, 168,
  171, 175, 207, 269 n.54, 271 n.65,
  278 n.31
  History of Henry Esmond, 125–134,
  147, 157–165, 207
  Memoirs of Barry Lyndon, 10
  Pendennis, 127–128, 134, 148–157,
  159, 162–166, 180
  Vanity Fair, 12–13, 159
  The Virginians, 207
Thatcher, James, 252 n.33
trauma, 9–11, 15, 22–23, 36, 74–75, 101,
  140, 165–166, 170, 197–198, 237
Trilling, Lionel, 27
Trollope, Anthony, 153, 211, 239–242
  Can You Forgive Her?, 239–242

Valéry, Paul, 206, 244 n.4
Vogel, Rudolf, 32, 252 n.31

Wade, Thomas
  The Phrenologists, 264 n.74
Watson, Hewett, 91–92
Watt, Ian, 243 n.2, 249 n.3

White, Hayden, 7
Wiltshire, John, 254 n.49
Winnett, Susan, 230
Winter, Alison, 274 n.33
Woolf, Virginia, 3, 7, 124
  Mrs. Dalloway, 7, 243 n.2
Wordsworth, William, 8, 117, 119, 122,

126–128, 131, 134, 140, 160, 163,
  244 n.11, 267 n.24
  The Prelude, 126, 131

Yates, Frances, 253 n.39

Žižek, Slavoj, 247 n.31, 260 n.30

* <u>Benani's</u> idea is that allegory is absent, visible—

1) what makes allegories <u>deceptive</u>: even, unreadable is what I am interested — The surprising phenomenon of us being able to read allegories.

↓ different frames of perception / representation.

↓

2) it's an embedded question in, for example, the different versions of allegory — Protestant, self-reflective in Bunyan's work.

↓

~~scripture~~ allows us to see how allegory transformed from * a personification into an impersonation in the novel —

↑ into a performance of itself rather than just itself.

~~[As A figure of contradiction]~~

⇒ Reading it this way is to read against Benani — and our understanding of allegory. ALLEGORY
of course allegory has always been read as a difficult figure — not least by its critics & practitioners

But more than just set the complexity of allegory itself. The dissertation traces how this particular unreadability works in the novel itself.

↓ [allegory + judgment]

[Moral Performances.] → Smith / Hume.
⤷ Diderot etc —   (christian)
              ↑   at the very intersection of character — (literary)
              ↓   materials
[As descriptive Agents] = "actor" — "character"

In two   1. [Protestant allegory] (Bunyan)
                        ↓
although these are   2. Character readers of
all very   ↙ ↓ ↓
intertwined things
                        3. Material. (craft)
                        4. literary (C. Richardson)
                        5. Ethical (Trelang) — M

9 780195 173093